"The Common (Non)Sense Revolution: The Decline of Progress and Democracy in Ontario"

by

Byron Montgomery

For my parents ...

You know how I feel about you even if I don't say it.

A Mad River Publishing book
Mad River Publishing
Box 36, Creemore, ON
L0M 1G0

Montgomery, Byron.
    The Common (Non)Sense Revolution:
    The Decline of Progress and Democracy in Ontario
    ISBN 0-9730682-0-5

Printed and bound in Canada.

Contents

Acknowledgements

Just as I was finishing the writing of this book, a good friend of mine was killed in a car accident. R. Greig Fowler was a man of great integrity and intelligence, who spent most of his life as an educator, passing along knowledge and encouragement to thousands of students. He was also a Liberal from his youth in the Maritimes and he knew all the tricks of politics. But even at that, his principles and enthusiasm kept him from crossing over into the *dark side* of politics. He never believed that the end justified the means, and that striving for justice and equality was the true endeavour. To him, there was no higher ambition than to serve the people. Though I only knew Greig for five or six years, he was an example to all who knew him. I am better for having known him, but I regret that he never got a chance to read this work, as he had expressed his desire to do so, many times. Greig, this is in lieu of your autographed copy.

I would also like to thank my father, John, and my friend, Viola Poletes, for their work as editors. Both made many valuable comments, and my father did a great job of questioning my rants and making me tone them down a bit, though not as much as he suggested.

And two people who have done a tremendous job of working on public policy for the Simcoe-Grey Provincial Liberal Association, Craig Laing and Harold Marshall, must be acknowledged. Both men are canny and thoughtful in their consideration of where government is going. As well, they are examples for all of why people need to participate in the political process. Though both come from very different backgrounds, listening to them makes it clear that the "big picture" is shared by many. Our discussions have stimulated my thinking on many issues, most of which are right here for all to read.

I must also thank those who have explored these waters before me. A number of works have been done on the Harris Tories, though most were completed in their early days. I found the work of John Ibbitson particularly useful, as his thoroughness and insights have added to my own. I must also thank the powers-that-be at *The Toronto Star* for coming up with a valuable on-line search engine that permits their archives to be investigated. It is it's superior nature, compared to its competitors, that led me to so many more *Star* articles.

Preface

Politics during the last few years have been very frightening and concerning. I have watched as the neo-conservative wave has swept over government after government, particularly after the fall of the Soviet Union. It was as though the collapse of Russian communism signalled some sort of victory for the West. However, instead of democracy becoming dominant, capitalism seems to have been the real winner. At the same time, global free trade has become the catch phrase for business, and it seems determined to throw out the one principle that restrains capitalism – that of competition. As time passes, business buys business and a competitive marketplace is restructured into oligopolies, where just a few, mega-multinational corporations run an ever-less competitive market.

One of the reasons to have government is so that it protects citizens from danger – be it military, health, or unfair practices. As corporations have expanded their size, they have also expanded their influence. Instead of government protecting its citizens, more often than not, it is now acting to assist these corporations. Politicians are selling out to commercial interests at the expense of government doing what it is supposed to do – protect it citizens. Ontario during the Harris years is an example of just how this is happening, and why it must be stopped.

* * * * *

I should note that there were a number of topics that I have left out of this work – like casino contracts or the Transportation ministry selling personal information to businesses – or have mentioned only in a minimal way – like Queen's Park riots and compensation for the Dionne sisters. These issues varied in importance and media attention, but could easily have led to the book getting out of hand in size (which some might argue it already has).

As well, I should add that any mistakes, should they have crept in, are mine alone.

Introduction

Since the Second World War, the governments of Ontario have shown a remarkable ability to balance progressive change with competent, conservative management. In fact, it was the hallmark of the Tory regimes from 1943 to 1985 that they were able give people the social and economic reform with stable fiscal policies they wanted. Well, for most of that time, at least. Increasingly toward the end of this era, they let the balance slip away and, with it, their grasp on power.

Then, the Liberals took over. They showed great potential regarding this balance, starting with a burst of reform that seemed to impress people. However, they quickly got caught up in other matters – national issues, the constitution, scandal, arrogance – and allowed themselves to get off the progressive track. They believed they were the product of destiny, but were instead a hiccup in history.

Replaced by the NDP, this new government had very little chance for success. They hadn't expected to win and had a caucus that displayed a spectrum that ranged from brilliant to buffoon, got caught in a horrible recession, and were unprepared for the rigours of balancing progress and management. In the end, their progressive changes cost too much of the money they didn't have to spend. And when they stopped spending it, it cost them most of their friends, too.

The Mike Harris Conservatives came to power in 1995 promising fiscal responsibility and the ideas of *The Common Sense Revolution*. As the only party of the three which was offering simple, decisive principles, they found significant favour and a wide scope of approval to go ahead. But the public failed to grasp the consequences of these promises. Instead of moves to advance society, they got regressive change. In the guise of financial competence, they got a devious, short-sighted shell game that leaves the provincial treasury without enough money to survive an economic downturn. In fact, the Harris Tories derailed Ontario's trip along the track of progressive reform and a strengthening democracy.

As Ontario moves into the 21st century, it is clear that its citizens face a choice in the type of politics they really want: a system which grows out of the trends from World War II up to 1995; or, the kind of politics it has seen since. That choice may be as stark as between democracy and a corporate *Big Brother* which simply uses politicians as its puppets. Unfortunately, we seem headed down the road to the latter rather than the former.

The point of writing this book is as an examination of public-policy and how ideology can drive it beyond all reason, a look at history to see how success and failure has come to Ontario's political parties, and ... as a warning to all people who believe in democracy. The Second World War was supposed to be the event that cemented democratic values across the world. Where it did, however, the cement never really dried. We thought it had, but it is just a hard crust that continues to set underneath. And with politicians like Mike Harris and his brethren, who like to poke holes in the crust and pour water inside, democracy is in real danger of being watered down to the point where, one day, it will no longer be able to hold itself together.

And while politics is being sold to the highest bidder, we, the voters, are apathetic. We have taken our democratic system of government for granted. Comfortable in our apparent wealth, we haven't been careful about keeping our politicians in line. In a quest for efficiency, we have allowed governments to continually shrink democratic representation and the accountability that comes with it. We now accept what government does, even if we don't like it, because it's the best we can expect from those we see as crooks and incompetents. Our opinion of those we elect to oversee our affairs is now so poor we hold them to almost no level of accountability. We think they're doing a bad job, but we re-elect them anyway. Either that or we're not paying any attention, don't know what they're doing and don't care.

As our disinterest in politics has grown, we have become inattentive and alienated, and politicians have used this to become less accountable and more open to the seductions of big money. Commercial interests, as the only source for truly big money, are increasingly taking control of the agenda of government and exploiting it for their own benefit. Public services are being undermined, making private delivery seem all the more attractive. Some are being sold off to make business interests rich and give government ministers directorships to which to retire.

Having grown up in Ontario, I saw it as a province that was both progressive and conservative. It was a place where government worked on a balance between the two: advancement in matters of public concern, like health, welfare, and education, while under the restraint of careful and competent financial management. For most of the last half of the 20th century, that fine balance remained intact, for the most part.

In fact, I see the Ontario of this period as an almost perfect example of the relationship between progress and democracy (with the definite exception of it being a one-party state, most of that time). The progressive nature of its society solidified its democratic nature. As reform expanded needed public services, like universally accessible health care and a public education system, people gained a greater connection with their government and society, as they had more invested in it. In my mind, there is no question that some mistakes were made that started to undermine the connection, but mostly ones that could have been corrected.

However, as progressive change became more ingrained, reactionary forces eventually began to fight back, using the overspending of the time as the basis for arguing that all government was gorged and decadent. Over time, their attack on this progressive movement undermined the values that were the underpinnings of the democratic nature of government, and society for that matter. In effect, the credo became *government is bad*. If it was run or regulated by government, it must be overblown, wasteful, and ineffective. As this message was forced on the population through a never-ending barrage, *government is bad* began to limit and reduce progress and turn back the tide of change.

One of the mistakes of the past was the undermining of truly democratic debate. The Legislature's rules have become increasingly restrictive, with debate of the issues increasingly cut off. The number of elected representatives has been reduced while appointed ones have grown out of control. Higher election spending limits have made all political parties increasingly partners, or servants, with those who were willing and able to *pay the piper*. And as the old saying goes ... he who pays the piper calls the tune.

But the true devastation to Ontario politics only came with the election of the Mike Harris Conservatives. Elected as the *party of ideas*, the public did not recognize the regressive nature of their thinking. Harris and his band of angry, white, middle-aged men and women took advantage of the negative attitude of the electorate at the time and they swept to power with their reactionary ideas. Instantly, 50 years of progressive advances began to be destroyed. The balance between progress and steady management was rejected. But these Tories are so bad, even their managerial competence is in question. Democracy itself is being endangered as people are told it is better for them if they fend for themselves.

* * * * *

When I talk about progress, I mean an improvement of the social and economic conditions under which people live. When people want *progressive change*, it means they want government to enact further measures to guarantee this kind of advancement. Why by government? Because Canadians have a state founded by political ideologues of many stripes, all of whom shared a belief that government was the instrument of "peace" and "order", and it should seek "good government" by doing what was in the public interest. No other mechanism exists to assure that people are protected in a civil society. We look to our governments to guarantee this. It is probably even more true for citizens of Ontario, people who have always prided themselves on being the heart of Canada.

What is *progress*? It is easy to just give a dictionary definition: an advance; growth; development; improvement; a moving forward; going ahead. And being *progressive* is being: interested in or using new ideas, etc. in order to advance to something better[1]. In the political sense of Ontario, it might be put as using government to make social and economic changes in order to improve peoples' lives. Of course, Mike Harris and his minions would undoubtedly argue that, using this definition, his government is progressive. For my purposes, I will narrow it somewhat. To me, progressive government uses its authority – authority derived from its citizens – to protect and expand their rights, wages, working conditions, health, education, and welfare in order to create a more equal, more just, and flourishing society.

By this definition, Ontario governments have been progressive for most of the last sixty years. The successive administrations of Drew, Frost, Robarts, and Davis as well as those of Peterson and Rae, demonstrated the use of government leadership and influence to establish social programmes and regulations to protect the needy, redistribute wealth to those who do not have it, and help each Ontarian to maximize their personal growth, as well as using public services to assist business and industry to create jobs and wealth for people. Most of the time, they did so without setting members of society against each other for personal or political gain.

By this definition, the Harris government is anything but progressive. The rights of many have been abused and/or abridged so that others may benefit. Overall wages have changed little, except that those at the very top are earning more, while those at the bottom are making far less. Working conditions have been diminished to benefit owners. Health care and education have been undermined due to chronic administrative malfeasance. And peoples' welfare has been under near constant attack. As a woman said at a dinner I recently attended, she no longer feels the sense of safety and security she had before *The Common Sense Revolution.*

Ontarians demand that progress be balanced with fiscal prudence and time – 'good government', if you will. The management of our shared economy and society demands a careful, moderate hand. Spending willy-nilly, no matter the subject, is unacceptable. Government raising reasonable taxes is appropriate, as long as the money is spent wisely, and on progressive things. And the speed of progress must be tempered with the ability of people to keep up with it. At times, society will accept more rapid change. Most of the time, people want it no faster than a rate that allows them to catch their breaths. It is my belief that Harris came to power as much as by promising to end the *excesses* of the Rae NDP as the CSR. In effect, progress would be restored in this way, or that's the way many people took it.

And it is in this that we can define the balance between progress and management. Ultimately, progressive change is the goal, but only on a slow, steady pace that moderates financial cost and does not force people to suddenly accept different personal beliefs. If a crowd of people are asked to run a kilometre, some will arrive at their destination quickly while others will take some time, or fail to arrive at all. So it is that progressive change demands that the fast runners slow down to permit the others to keep up, and those that can't are assisted to the finish line. People, and budgets, need time to adjust.

In Ontario, progressive change with conservative management has actually helped to reinforce and strengthen the democratic nature of our society. As people have more invested in something, be it society or stocks and bonds, they tend to pay more attention to it. As citizens have more at stake – public health, public education, etc. – it is more important for them to participate in these things to see that their interests are protected. In many ways, democracy is fundamentally a result of popular self-interest.

And it is with the Harris government that we most clearly see this breaking down. The Harrisites have dropped traditional Canadian conservatism – slow, measured change with an eye to helping your neighbour – in favour of the neo-conservative mantra – that individuals can look out for themselves and government is not generally needed. In essence, *government is bad* and you'd do better to be responsible only for yourself. However, this goes intrinsically against democratic values and institutions. As citizens have less invested in their society, they have less reason to participate because their self-interest is no longer at stake. In fact, self-interest demands they look after themselves alone. As a result, the bonds that draw us together weaken, and we become alienated from our friends and neighbours because we cannot see beyond the ends of our own noses. The adoption of a neo-conservative philosophy guarantees the inevitable displacement of a democratic society with one that is unjust and ensures the rise to power of the wealthy and influential at the expense of everyone else, the massive majority. If we follow this path, we will inevitably reap a 21st century corporate feudalism, where most people are once again the serfs of those ennobled by economic success.

If this is really so, how is it that people accepted a political party which goes against their basic wishes of 50 years? Well, why do people choose one particular party at election times? Is it that they recognize that one offers this balance between progressive reform and cautious administration? Not consciously, I suspect. However, the party that offers progressive ideas, that offers advances, is usually the victor ... even over one that offers the greatest promise of management skill. In effect, the progressive *party of ideas* wins. In the case of the Harrisites, they offered Ontario voters a party of negative ideas at a time when Ontarians were feeling oppressed and vengeful. *The Common Sense Revolution* fit perfectly.

The CSR was a manifesto of unusual clarity and consistency that perfectly fit the mood of a plurality of Ontarians. Times had been hard for many for five long years, yet they saw others benefit, or at least not suffer as badly as they, and it didn't seem fair. They had wanted progressive change, yet had seen this desire stymied by government after government. The Davis Tories had given them some, but less than they wanted. The Peterson Liberals had revelled in it initially, then were made all the more conspicuous by slowing it to a snail's pace. The Rae New Democrats had promised it, then not delivered. Harris promised a *revolution* of change, with specifics. He also committed to making those suffer who hadn't had to bear their share of the pain. At another time, the CSR would have been interesting but would have been rejected as regressive. In 1995, negativity and progress demanded regress.

* * * * *

It is only fair that I am clear about my own biases. As someone who was a critic of the Tories prior to their 1995 election, and has been actively working to get them out of office since – I am presently a provincial Liberal riding president – I am far from neutral in my opinions.

Nevertheless, I have a Master's degree in Political Science and a good understanding of the ramifications of public policy decisions. As a former university lecturer, college instructor, and political consultant, I see government and politics as they are perceived by people – a dirty business most would just as soon ignore.

As a teaching assistant at The University of Western Ontario some years ago, I had a very intelligent student who had definite beliefs and was not hesitant about expressing them. In a class of hopeful kids who tended toward being a little more left-wing, her Thatcherite views usually set eyes to rolling. Finally, after some exasperation had built up amongst her classmates, I felt it was time to burst her balloon. I challenged her to justify one of her opinions. She had all the "common sense" arguments, but not a shred of evidence to bolster her standpoint. Though our class together ended shortly afterward, I noted her final essay was much improved on justification, though I still differed on her conclusions. Not that I let that affect her mark! But it was a good lesson for me, too. If you're going to have opinions, you'd better be able to justify them.

Another student, in that same class, reinforced a lesson, which I already knew. Zoning by-laws were about to be changed that would deny more than a certain number of unrelated people being able to live in a residence. This was an attack on the city's university and college students, and their reputations for partying in rented houses. It would have ended this student's fraternity. He raised the concern during the class' current events discussion, and made the arguments against the by-law – it was unfair, they paid property taxes, they didn't have wild parties – though it wasn't entirely clear what he was suggesting as a solution. When I said to him he should be making his arguments before the city council, because they were the ones making the decision, he demurred. What good would a student's argument be? I responded that if you truly believe in something, but do nothing to defend it, then you get what you deserve. He went to council and made his argument and, though he lost, he did tell me he felt better for trying. (If memory serves, his argument eventually carried the day, as the by-law was struck down in court as being unconstitutional.)

Part 1

Setting the Mood

For anyone who believes that our democratic processes are under attack, it's not hard to blame Mike Harris and his band of trolls as the perpetrators of the assault. To my mind, there's no doubt they are seriously undermining our system of government and our society. But I don't think they started it. Their government is the catalyst that has accelerated the process by many times. In fact, the practice of subverting our system began over 30 years ago, partly from within Ontario, partly from ideas that originated in other parts of the world.

As government, both national and provincial, began to expand to meet the demands of the 1950s, '60s, and '70s, politicians saw a clear need to seek efficiencies. Given the massive expansion of responsibilities, however, these were often more a matter of suggestion than reality. Yet in one area, they were not. The province had to deal with thousands of municipal government bodies and it found it difficult to do so on an effective basis. As a result, it began to legislatively cut down on them. One school board representing a single, one-room school became one that looked after 100, multi-room schools. Hamlets of 50 people and towns of 50,000 were amalgamated, creating municipalities that were made up of urban retail cores, industry, housing subdivisions, farms, and natural areas. And while this rationalization may have made some sense, it was also the beginning of the diminution of local representation that has continued. In fact, it has become so prevalent that referring to it as 'local' is now just plain wrong.

Another result was the creation of what academics refer to as special purpose bodies or ABCs – agencies, boards, and commissions. Efficiency demanded planning, so planning boards were created to consider land-use, transportation, the environment, and other matters on shared concerns across municipalities, regions, counties, watersheds, or the entire province. But these bodies demanded thousands of people to man them, and so it was that the heart of the modern system of patronage in Ontario was created. Who better to carry out *government will* but those who are the friends of the government? Of course, that meant that thousands of unelected people were now making virtually unaccountable decisions.

Then, while democracy was being restrained and contracted at the local level, philosophy was also becoming a consideration in politics. While

Canada had seen an almost unbroken line of expansionist governments, the same was not true in all other western democracies. In fact, two of the oldest and largest had experienced near-cataclysmic events that caused them to move toward increasingly reactionary politics. In Britain, after a post-war boom, there was increasing discontent, as much of the country's resources had been used up and economic expectations could not be met. Socially, the *avant garde* of a wanton modern age mixed uneasily with the conservative precepts still alive from Victorian England. The combination was garish freedom followed by the self-righteous backlash of Margaret Thatcher.

In the United States, Watergate and defeat in the Vietnam war left Americans unsure of themselves for the first time since Civil War. How could God's Country be defeated and be corrupt at its very core? It didn't take many years for self-doubting introspection to be replaced by the collective mindset of retributive puritanism. And who better to lead this nation than Ronald Reagan, a third-rate actor that came with the fanaticism of late-life conversion or, at least, came with fanatics.

For the conservative conservatives in Canada, these two were the demigods of right-wing political theory. After Thatcher and Reagan were elected, the entire Western World came to be inundated with the alleged benefits of supply-side economics and how cutting taxes for the wealthy would "trickle down" to the middle-class and the poor. The fact that it didn't work did not seem to bother its proponents. After all, they were the ones who wanted to get rich!

Here in Canada, we got that message over and over again from the Brian Mulroney government ... even though it was an intellectually impotent government completely unable to do anything other than triple 117 years' worth of national debt in less than nine years. They were hardly those to listen to when it came to fiscal responsibility and wisdom. The complete smashing of the Progressive Conservative party in the 1993 election, down to 2 seats out of 295, seemed to indicate that the public understood that, to some extent at least. However, the conduct of their successors, the Jean Chretien Liberals, has hardly inspired confidence. Though they have transformed massive deficits into large surpluses (until now), their tax cuts were also slanted to benefit the wealthy over the middle-class and poor. As well, their embracing of worldwide free trade, as Mulroney's Conservatives had done (and despite running against it in 1988 and 1993), also shows that they care less for their own citizens' democratic rights and more about corporate acquisition and wealth.

However, of all jurisdictions, it is Ontario that most clearly demonstrates the decline in democracy and in the social and economic progress of most of the 20th century. It is here where a history of steady progress has been tossed aside in favour of radical lurches that cut rights, ignore citizen concerns, and slice apart *government for the people*, redesigning it as *government for the well-off*. In fact, six years of Mike Harris government has gone a long way to break down over 50 years of advancement, both economic and social, and set this province on a path to end representative government, democratic rule and, ironically, individual rights.

1. The "Dynasty"

But as I said, the assaults on progress and democracy did not begin in 1995, but more around 1965. John Robarts and Bill Davis are considered two of the most progressive premiers to have ever led Ontario, yet, in Davis' last term in power (1981-1985), his government seemed to lose its balance between being progressive and managerial. What little it did came from being reactive, rather than active.

The Tories ruled Ontario with a velvet glove from August 1943 right up to June 1985, which hardly makes it seem the most democratic of systems. But this had mostly to do with a horrid Liberal premier, Mitch Hepburn, who turned his party from being the government of 66 seats into the third party of 16 seats. The Tories seemed to grasp the whole mindset of the post-war, where people wanted a balance that favoured progressive growth and development, but not at a speed that overran more traditional concerns (the oft-mentioned small town Ontario values), like family and individuality and respect. People wanted the past and the future, but with a clear desire that progress would be slightly favoured.

The Tory dynasty was one built on two factors: understanding the need to balance progressive change with solid management; and, strong, careful leaders. But it wasn't a foundation that they understood instantly. It was one that grew over a few years, and was cemented by "The Great Tranquillizer", Leslie Frost.

Mitchell Hepburn was the first Liberal leader in many years when he came to power in 1934. It was the darkest days of the Great Depression, and people were looking for change and, perhaps moreso, hope. Hepburn was a fiery orator and populist, who stirred the imaginations of many, taking over 50% of the popular vote in both the 1934 and 1937 elections, a feat unrivalled since. However, he was also a man who was at least as conservative as his Tory predecessor, George Henry, and he had a dark, nasty streak that occasionally needed to be exercised. This led to much violence as unions tried to gain acceptance and his government actively supported business against them. It also gave him an unforgiving personality. His eventual demise would grow from his petty hatred of Mackenzie King.

But what Hepburn represented most was a small business, small farm attitude – one that went back into the previous century, in many ways. It denied any kind of collectivist nature, and vehemently attacked the notion of social reform. During a world war that was leading many people to reject the *tried-and-true* in favour of real change, Hepburn was a man out of his time.

By 1942, he was also a broken man, having seen his desires for a strengthened Ontario and decentralized Canada blocked and fading. But he had broken his party as well, and the quest for progressive change was initially lain at the feet of the Conservative party ... but just barely.

The (for its time) radical Cooperative Commonwealth Federation came within four seats and four percent of the Tories in the 1943 election. The public mood for change was clear, and Tory leader George Drew recognized it well enough to know that he had to include some elements of it in his party's platform – cooperation with the federal government on veterans' benefits and social assistance, a stop to the attacks on labour, and a greater provincial investment in health, education, and housing. Yet, as a conservative, he knew to mix this with a good dose of traditional Ontario values – protection of agriculture, the exploitation of natural resources, and the renewed dominance of Protestantism. It was the beginning of the formula that would keep them in power for 42 years.

But if Hepburn had been a man out of his time, then Drew was a man out of place in politics. He disliked campaigning and eschewed the whole social nature of it, even inside his party. He was a former colonel of the artillery who had fought in the Great War, and he preferred the authoritarian ways of the military and felt a great loyalty to the ways of the British Empire. Given there was another world war on, he had little use for those who opposed conscription, and that included Quebec as a whole. He also disliked the creeping power of the national government, as the war seemed to give it more and more of an ascendancy to act with authority once exclusively provincial in nature. On the other hand, he had Ontarians do all they could for the national war effort, and he planned for how the province's natural materials and new manufacturing base would be needed to rebuild England after the conflict had ended.

The Tories kept their promises of change. Plans for the use of natural resources and agriculture were established. A Labour Relations Board was created to improve workers bargaining rights and benefits, including an eight-hour workday and paid vacation. Hundreds of millions of dollars were spent to convert the electrical system to 60 cycles, a move which would permit the industrial growth to come, and Drew saw to it that 10,000 skilled tradespeople were brought in from England to man these new factories. Money was poured into construction to build new housing and new highways, mostly under the auspices of a new planning and development department. The organization of schools was streamlined and expanded, and their funding increased. And this helped educate more doctors, dentists, and nurses, to improve heath care.

However, Drew also hurt his cause. He repealed funding for Catholic schools and brought in strictly Christian religious instruction for young children. These actions offended many, though mostly amongst the province's minorities who generally supported the Liberals anyway. He also allowed his asocial political nature to keep him from strengthening his position inside the Conservative party.

As little changes usually bring a demand for greater changes, pressure grew to keep expanding and modernizing government. Yet there was little of the discontent that had fuelled the CCF support in 1943 and 1944. It was more of great hope for the future ... and Drew was no man to bring them that. Like Hepburn, his time had passed as well.

This did not affect his party, however. They had cruised to a massive majority in 1945 and continued to be popular. With the war over, Drew was right that Ontario was going to be an important cog in the wheel of rebuilding and development. Growth and employment were burgeoning. The government busied itself assisting industry to change over to a civilian economy and plan out the public reforms necessary to accommodate this, both economic and social. There can be no question, however, that George Drew himself favoured economic reform over social change.

The man himself, however, lacked charisma and was stubborn in his own assuredness. Though his party took an only slightly reduced majority in the 1948 election, he lost his own seat on a seemingly minor issue. Proclaiming a law to allow liquor sales in cocktail bars and hotels, he offended those in his own riding, one that was particularly against such un-

Christian imbibing. He could have chosen to run in a by-election but, instead, sought out and won the federal, now renamed, Progressive Conservative party leadership. With him out, his party chose Leslie Frost, the provincial Treasurer, as his replacement.[2]

It is an interesting, but moot, point to wonder what would have happened to the Tories had Drew been re-elected. Though most observers cite him as the beginning of the Conservative party's dynasty – the one who instituted the principle of strong development with a social orientation sufficient to undercut the Liberals and CCF/NDP – it actually seems more likely that this recipe for success was set in concrete under Frost.

Frost was a man of small town Ontario, who held mostly to small town values. Nevertheless, he governed Ontario at a time of unparalleled growth and development. With hundreds of thousands of people moving to the province every year, both from overseas and other provinces, and so many people needing so many different things from government all at the same time, perhaps it was virtually required that government become all things to all people. Though it was the manufacturing base that had turned Ontario into such a super-charged economic engine, it was all the growth in population that forced social change. And it was Frost who recognized this.

It was Mr. Frost who perfected the Tory policy mix of evolving social commitments and strongly directed economic development. It won him – and successive Tory premiers – the allegiance of a broad voter coalition in the middle of the political spectrum. (*The Globe and Mail,* "Pragmatism plus reform is secret to Tory dynasty", 3 May 1985, p. 11.)

Frost took after Drew, but moreso. More money went into highways, schools, and hospitals. He was behind Ontario's first Human Rights' Code. Discrimination was banned in employment and housing. His government set up the Ontario Water Resources Commission to build water treatment facilities and see that standards were adhered to.

As a slight aside, Leslie Frost also instituted a unique, and never-again repeated, method of dealing with scandal and dubious Cabinet ministers. In modern days, governments often try to protect a minister who runs into trouble, usually suffering a good deal of negative publicity in the process. Not Frost. He would quickly fire the offender, then have them run in a by-election. If they won, it was a signal the voters didn't think their transgression was all that great and was forgiven. If not, the people had spoken. In 1958, when the Northern Ontario Natural Gas Company gave three Cabinet ministers an advance opportunity to buy stock before it went to the public, the Premier simply fired the lot and called a general election a short time later. The losses were minimal, and the Tories received a renewed majority.

And in the name of progress, his government established Metropolitan Toronto. What came to be called Metro Toronto was actually 13 different municipalities in 1950. There was the core city with most of the business, both administrative and industrial, and the towns that surrounded it, primarily residential "bedroom" communities. Because development and planning was sloppy and mismatched, these already-existing municipalities ended up "running into each other", such that factories were abutting houses and many streets ended at municipal boundaries. Though some had agreements in place to share services, for the most part, growth was disorganized and wasteful.

In the past, city leaders had opposed any suggestions that these suburbs required assistance from Toronto, especially given that the city had a nicely bundled tax base it didn't want to share. However, by 1950, the chaos of development was becoming such a concern that even civic "fathers" were worried that business expansion would collapse under the weight of it. As a result, various proposals were put forward to the Ontario Municipal Board for annexations and/or amalgamations involving these communities.

It was at this time the Frost government decided to intervene. In 1953, it put all 13 municipalities together as a metropolitan government, modelled very much like a typical Ontario county. Each lower-tier entity would continue to exist, but an upper-tier would be created to look after matters that were of concern region-wide. As well, each lower-tier municipality would send a designated member of their council to sit on the Metro council, with the exception of Toronto, which apparently merited 12 all of its own. Under the early leadership of chairman Frederick Gardiner, Metro Toronto soon displaced the city as the leading municipal authority in the area.[3] This would eventually come to have a profound effect on municipal government in the province, and the way the provincial government treated Toronto.

And there had been those within Tory circles who didn't approve of this *solution* but they found they were opposed by the Premier, and that was sufficient to quiet them. Many of these were the same who did not like the way Frost dominated his party, but his personal popularity with the electorate seemed to assure victory ... and the coattails of triumph were better than outright defeat. Frost certainly had a kind of charisma that may be difficult to understand in our 21st century world. He would stop people in the street and greet them personally, unafraid of facing criticism, but usually finding friends. So it was a great surprise for many when he decided to retire in the summer of 1961, at the height of his popularity. He, thus, set another precedent for his party – the leader should go while things are good, before the *fruit starts rotting on the vine*. He handed his successor the glow of popularity and a formula for keeping it that way.

John Robarts was Frost's education minister from 1959 to 1961. Though he wasn't the favourite going into the leadership convention, many identified him as an ideal successor. He was seen as a reformer having shepherded through changes on curriculum, having seen that grants were increased to again allow a cut in property taxes, and he increased financial support for universities and vocational schools. At the same time, he had been a corporate lawyer with an honours degree in business administration, and clearly knew his way around management issues. When the vote came, at worst, he was everyone's second choice and won a sixth ballot victory.

For the next ten years, he was to be *chairman of the board* of Ontario. Unlike Frost, he didn't try to come across as a friendly, small town lawyer, though he was gregarious and friendly. His method was to run the province as a large corporation, streamlining the ministries and other bodies, though that didn't mean government would get smaller. Clearly, he hoped to operate *Ontario, Inc.* as efficiently as possible, while maintaining the social responsibility demanded by the public.

The Robarts' government continued to put large amounts of money into economic and social development. Pensions were made portable between jobs, a minimum wage was instituted, another new school curriculum was created, grants were given to start the building of subways in Toronto, and funding to separate schools was increased. In his last term, his government brought forward free legal aid, created GO Transit and started many public housing programmes through the new Ontario Housing Corporation.

Education seemed to be a favourite area for reform. Trent, Windsor, and York universities were built. The community college system was established. And there was a massive expansion in the number of elementary and secondary students across the province. School enrolment grew from just over 880,000 public school students to over a million. However, while new schools were rapidly being built, this expansion was in concert with a consolidation of other schools and boards of education. In 1965 alone, 480 elementary and 69 secondary schools were closed and replaced by fewer others that were larger and more regional. Between 1964 and 1967, more than 2,000 schools, mostly small and rural, were shut down. As well, 3,676 school boards were eliminated by amalgamation, as many county-based ones were created. By 1967, there were just 192 left.

As with Frost, municipal consolidation became a theme of the Robarts' regime. In the light of what seemed an ever-more-successful Metro Toronto, studies were established regarding the possibility of *regionalising* the counties in southern Ontario that were under extreme development pressures. The government appointed a royal commission into Toronto in 1963 to assess the success of the metro experiment. The Goldenberg Report stated it was, though the members also decided that having 13 municipalities existing under the Metro tent was inefficient. Instead of going with the city's recommendation to allow it to take over the whole area, the commission actually proposed the amalgamation of the 12 suburban entities into five, with greater representation on Metro council. The province agreed.

While Leslie Frost had kept his own counsel, for the most part, Robarts was different and almost literally established a provincial *board of directors* made out of his friends from his hometown. To many, they were known as the "London mafia". Unfortunately, they were not elected and this irked many in government who felt they were denied their rightful influence. As well, Robarts was also not shy about expanding the size of his office. When he came to power, the premier's office cost about $75,000 to operate. When he left, it was up by just over five times.

When William Grenville Davis succeeded Robarts in 1971, he continued on in Robarts' tradition of progress, on the surface, at least. As Robarts' Minister of Education, he had been behind most of the changes in the late 1960s and it garnered him many laurels, at first. Time would alter the opinions of many on these reforms.

That didn't mean he walked into the leadership unchallenged. Seven men ran to succeed Robarts, presumably expecting it was the ticket to a long premiership. Most of the focus shone on Davis as favourite, and Allan Lawrence, Northern Affairs' minister and a man described as a maverick. He was favoured by a growing number of party members who didn't necessarily like all the changes being made.

The convention was a massive affair at Toronto's Maple Leaf Gardens. And this size wasn't helped by a failure of voting machines and the first ballot having to be re-done by paper ballot, at a loss of about four-and-a-half hours. Though Davis led throughout, had it not been that Darcy McKeough, another Robarts' minister, threw his support behind him, he would undoubtedly have been defeated by Lawrence. As it was, he was victorious on the fourth ballot, 812 to 768. Though the media hadn't really seen this battle coming, after-the-fact analysis appeared to indicate Davis' popularity amongst the rank-and-file had been damaged by his cutting school boards. It had effectively eliminated hundreds, if not thousands, of positions for many, most of whom were Tories. (I think it's fair to say that, at this time and presently, most local politicians have sympathy with the Conservatives.) What should have been an easy victory became a very close one.

The character that became "Brampton Billy" was a cross between the styles of Frost and Robarts. He continued the expansion of management-oriented government, but also came across to people as the small town lawyer who was your friend. In fact, he established what would be dubbed the "Big Blue Machine", a group of advisors he recruited from his own leadership team, and that of his major opponent, Lawrence. They used modern polling, focus groups, and unsentimental decision-making to run the next election and, thereafter, the party. The 1971 majority gave the Tories the image of a political party that would continue its success forever. However, Davis wasn't everyone's friend. I think it's fair to say he may have offended more in his own party than those outside it, but more of that later.

While Davis' first term gave him a majority, he was unable, in the next two, to grab the full loyalty of Ontario's voters. In 1975 and 1977, he couldn't gain more than a minority government. There never seemed one reason for this. There was concern over the economy, yet growth did not stop. It had just levelled off. And while inflation was high, it was caused as much by high wage increases that undoubtedly didn't irk those who received them.

In his first term, his government was plagued by scandals. Attorney-General Dalton Bales was faced with insider information charges, having bought land that eventually was slated for development by the provincial government. It was the 'eventually' that saved him, perhaps along with being a long-time friend of the Premier's, and he sold the land before it could be developed and donated his profits to charity. The much-vaunted Darcy McKeough, Treasurer at the time, was forced to resign over having approved a land deal in 1969 as Municipal Affairs' minister, even though his brother was the secretary of the development company involved and McKeough himself had money in the company. This transgression seemed much worse, and Davis never tried to save him. McKeough would be out of Cabinet for a year-and-a-half and, though he would regain the stature of being Treasurer, his authority would never be quite the same. Another problem came with the contract that went to build the new Ontario Hydro headquarters in Toronto. It was granted to a personal friend of Davis'. Then there was a Workman's Compensation Board contract that went to a company that had donated $50,000 to the Tories. While cleared of wrongdoing in these last two matters, all the scandals resulted in tighter conflict-of-interest rules and, in 1975, contributed to the *Election Finances Reform Act*, which finally set out limits on donations and election spending.

Many have suggested these hurt Davis and kept him from his majorities. I doubt it. Davis' predecessors had faced many scandals, some worse, and never paid much of a price. Historically, governments have seldom suffered greatly for infamous behaviour, except when it seems government-wide or the episode is particularly heinous. Perhaps this is because scandal does not resonate with voters the way that something does when it touches them personally.

One of the issues of the time that touched many was the creation of regional government in much of Ontario, particularly in the urban areas of the south. Politicians, particularly provincial ones, looked on Metro Toronto as a tremendously successful *reform*. It had apparently put order in the growth around Toronto and turned the area into a mecca of business and development. Given that the same growth pressures were now being felt in other areas, it was decided that studies should be done to explore the notion that a similar solution might work there.

In late 1968, the province published "Design for Development, Phase Two". Though some local government reform studies had already been completed, this document was the provincial vision for any municipal changes and, in practice, this meant a modified version of Metro Toronto was about to be applied throughout Ontario. Ten regional governments were created, mostly in the south, between 1969 and 1974. But that wasn't enough.

Even before the last region came into existence, the provincial government announced the County Restructuring Program, a sort of regional system for counties, with more money and powers for those that went along. Many counties felt pressured to acquiesce, and a number set up such studies. It has been my impression for many years that those that did go along were simply trying to buy time in hopes the whole initiative would go away.

And it did.

Even as the Tories were announcing their county proposal, the move to regionalise had run out of steam. Though the regional governments were still in their infancies, there was already a groundswell of discontent about them, and the Tory government began to back off. They had other problems to deal with, too.

With the exception of stopping the Spadina expressway from cutting a swath right through Toronto and making city residents see Davis as a progressive, concerned about community and its quality of life, his first term had actually been pretty miserable. The province's burgeoning growth had quieted greatly by the time he came to office, and government coffers were not filling as easily. The oil shocks of 1973 then set the economy into a pattern of high inflation with stagnating development. *Stagflation* became the main concern of the country, particularly on the federal scene, but it hurt Ontario's manufacturing core. The imposition of regional government damaged them in a variety of areas. And then there were the scandals. All told, the Davis Tories had a lot of the soil shaken from their progressive roots.

They knew they were going to be in tough in the next election, so it was to their progressivism they returned. Rent controls would be the main plank for the 1975 election, even if it was borne of desperation and stolen from the NDP. The Tories had done well in-and-around Toronto, and they needed to hold this if they had any chance at re-election, so they promised those renting apartments that annual rent hikes, which had been shooting up to 20-30% would be limited to 6%. This limit would not apply to buildings put up after 1975.

Other promises for the election was a temporary cut in the sales tax from 7% to 5% to get people spending. They also increased the cut-off for provincial income taxes, which dropped 450,000 people from the rolls. Eighty-three million dollars was promised for $1,500 grants to first-time home buyers or builders. A $15 million programme was established to help seniors with their drug prescription needs.

The Tories ran hard, Davis in particular. Yet, if it had not been for a poor campaign by the Liberals, and its leader Bob Nixon in particular, they would have been defeated. Nixon's difficulty was a condescending and nasty attitude that he directed at the Conservatives every day of the campaign. During a leaders' debate, he became downright insulting, something that turned off many voters. The Tories dropped from 78 to 51 seats, but held on with a bare minority. But the Liberals couldn't turn a big increase in popular vote into seats, and actually dropped to third place. Stephen Lewis, NDP leader, slipped into the Official Opposition leader's seat by nearly routing the Conservatives in Toronto.

Victory didn't stop the Tories scrambling, however. Davis was determined to restore his majority. They kept most of their election promises, as well as coming out with plans on how to deal with 50% projected growth over 25 years with development outside Toronto while saving agricultural and recreational land, and measures to fight inflation. *Progressive, yet conservatively enacted.* And realizing that the public was not enamoured of an earlier move to cut the drinking age to 18 from 21, they pushed it back to 19. Though it wasn't much, many saw it as a fair compromise. They also dropped property tax reform which would have made an increasingly irrational system more equitable, but would also have raised taxes for many people. *Conservative, not letting progress go too far.* The Tories moved up in the polls, especially once Liberal leader Bob Nixon quit and was succeeded by psychiatrist Stuart Smith. It didn't take long for Davis' personal popularity to more than double that of Lewis and quintuple Smith's.

It led the Tories to the wrong conclusion. Thinking they could cake-walk back into a majority, they called another election in 1977, three months shy of two years into their term. Promises included 100,000 new jobs, 900,000 new houses over a decade, lower property taxes for seniors, two trees planted for every tree taken by the timber industry, and a balanced budget by 1981. Unfortunately for the Conservatives, the truth was that they had taken too little time to show voters they had changed substantially from their first term, and questions still existed in people's minds. They gained seven seats, but still fell five short of a majority.

Much of the next term was spent on national issues which overwhelmed provincial ones. The oil pricing wars usually pitted central Canada against Alberta, though Davis was normally careful to let Pierre Trudeau carry the water for the industrial heart of the country, and take the blame. And though he campaigned for Joe Clark in 1979, he immediately regretted it, as the federal Tory leader took Alberta's side against Ontario. Davis wasn't asked to help Clark in 1980 until defeat was already certain.

As well, with the separatist *Parti Québecois* in power, the Constitution came to take a central role in practically everything, as decisions all across the country, but especially Ontario, became the *indépendentistes'* examples of how the Anglos discriminated against the French. Bill Davis advanced bilingual provincial services in areas where there were significant numbers of those for whom French was their first language. This included French language instruction. His thanks came in the form of the PQ complaining that these students didn't get their own high schools.

Anyway, the Davis government continued on, making small changes here and there. Much of the initiative one might have expected was restrained by the minority status of the government. The Tories saw themselves as guides of "the good ship Ontario", navigating a straight course that only needed minor tending. Over time, if a storm appeared, they would weather it out by making increasingly minor course changes, perhaps emboldened by the fact that no storm had managed to swamp them in almost 40 years.

In fact, in the last five years he was premier, many of Bill Davis' concerns may have been more national in consideration, as Canada was in the debate over constitutional patriation, and Ontario took on a primary place in that controversy. Many of the more conservative in society saw Ontario's acceptance of unilateral patriation, and amendments to the *British North America Act* before it came back, as a sell-out. It was crawling into bed with the Trudeau Liberals, and that was a position that alienated many elements inside the Tory party. Unfortunately for them, most of Ontario's citizens were under the covers with Davis and Trudeau. And while this was an issue in the 1981 election, it was one that only helped the provincial party with voters.

The true centrepiece, though, of the 1981 Tory election strategy was the BILD (Board of Industrial Leadership and Development) programme. It was a $1.5 billion plan for economic stimulation and job creation. In fact, BILD was a massive slate of promises that went far beyond what one would expect for an election. It promised a six-pronged initiative in community improvement, energy, skills training, resource development, technology, and transportation. The scheme involved subsidies for municipal transit to go electric and for improved rail service, support to upgrade shipyards and harbours and to set up a ferry between Oshawa and New York state, money for farmers, food processors, and cooperatives to expand, more funding for the development of wood lots, nurseries, and plant research, incentives for oil and gas exploration in northern Ontario, setting up an electronics' testing facility, an IDEA corporation to coordinate research and development into new technologies, a possible new automotive research centre, a Centre for Toxicology, new money for skills development and community counselling centres, a fund for small communities to provide water and sewerage to industry, a new tourist incentive programme, new convention centres in Toronto, Ottawa, and

Hamilton, along with a host of other notions. All-in-all, these promises were to create 100,000 jobs over five years.

Without being unfair, I think it is safe to say the Tories delivered on few of these commitments. Not only were they an odd hodgepodge of seemingly disconnected themes, but they did not seem intended for average people, just specific interests across a rainbow of communities. Though BILD gave the veiled impression of past Tory progressivism, in fact it was more a sign of the stench of intellectual gangrene in the party.

Regardless, it got them through the campaign. The Liberals, acting very conservative, had offered a few promises of economic tinkering, but nothing visionary. Their platform was so limited that the *Globe and Mail* endorsed the party, and leader Dr. Stuart Smith. In many ways, it was a kiss of death. Supporters of the party hardly wanted approval from the staid, musty *Globe*. And it was a half-hearted recommendation at that. The affirming editorial ended with "The Liberals ... *are* the alternative for those voters who wish to give the Tories a time in opposition to restore their faltering Conservatism ...". Hardly a rousing endorsement.

It also didn't help that the Tories were able to paint Smith as "Dr. No", as his tendency to harp on things negative gave them the opening to be positive and hopeful. After the economic decline of 1979-1981, coming on the heels of the stagflation of much of the 1970s, hearing little but the doom-and-gloom of things did not engender anything but further apprehension. For the Tories who were offering positive reform and investment, the Liberal position just reinforced the public comfort level with Bill Davis.

The NDP, after the hope of the years under Stephen Lewis, had been reduced to a smaller, weaker, and also more conservative party under the uninspiring Mike Cassidy. Where Davis touted the benefits of public transit, Cassidy denounced provincial intervention as an attack on the free market. In a world where the alleged socialists defend capitalism and the conservatives actively intervene in the economy, the New Democrats had little hope of holding their supporters.

For some (the editorial board of the G&M perhaps), the results of the election were a surprise. Not only had the Davis Tories been re-elected, but they had increased both their seat total and percentage – from 58 to 70 and 39.7% to 44.4%. The change in support apparently came directly from the NDP who lost 12 seats and almost 7% of the vote. The PC majority seemed to solidify the Tories as Ontario's *natural governing party*. In reality, it simply masked the growing problems it had.

One of the things that was hidden in the Tory success was that it was a party strained between left- and right-wing elements in its membership. Since the progressive branch tended to dominate the leadership, they controlled the agenda. As a result, the right wing was stuck with little say in decision-making. Almost shut-out of the senior levels of Cabinet, the party, and many of the best patronage jobs, for most of 30-plus years, the undercurrent of dissatisfaction could do nothing but fester. And there were other reasons for the internal splits to increase. The constitutional question had driven a wedge between the Left who liked Trudeau and the Right who despised him. When Davis chose to support unilateral patriation, there were many who called themselves Tory who were shocked and outraged. Many felt that government had to stop growing in size and scope, as its influence was beginning to be too pervasive, touching people's everyday lives instead of simply watching from a distance. And it had to stop spending beyond its means. The point of government was to collect a minimum of taxes to do a minimum of jobs. Expanding into ever-more areas meant ever-higher taxes, and that was just plain wrong. Policies like rent control made them queasy, as it was such an unnatural intervention in the economy. And the whole ideological bent of the party – toward progressive change – was beginning to wear more than thin on those long-time stalwarts who wanted far less public intrusion into the free market. Yet as long as Davis and his types controlled the party apparatus, that wasn't about to change.

During the 1981 election, Treasurer Frank Miller, a right-wing exception in Cabinet, made his opinion known.

> *His "Tory blue" instincts have been offended by the amount of government intervention in the private sector, (Miller) said, but he has learned that in Ontario the political world is more red than blue.* (The Globe and Mail, "Cost of Conservative promises put at $348.6 million", 17 March 1981, p. 4)

It was a view that was likely far more widespread in the party than Davis and most of his reformist Cabinet knew, or chose to accept.

But if democracy was questionable inside the Tory party, it was also under attack in the broader system. One sign of this was seen in the Legislature and its rules. The longer the Tories held power, the more frustrated the Opposition parties became. More and more often, they began to use the rules of the Legislature against the government, holding up some bills for weeks with filibusters of different kinds. It was in the early '80s that the

PCs apparently became less than enthralled, and began moving to change these rules, to make filibusters more difficult to start or to keep going once they had begun. Their argument was that the democratic will was being foiled and that, in the name of more efficient government, these types of demonstrations had to be cut down on. Again, however, once a government begins to change rules to stifle debate, it just becomes easier to do over and over. The Liberals would add more restrictions, because of NDP delays, then the NDP would change the rules before even experiencing a filibuster, anticipating that the Liberals would use their own tactics against them. Of course, these were just the beginning compared to what the Harrisites would do later.

The bigger problem for the Conservatives was that their party was losing its edge – its ability to be both progressive and conservative was evaporating. As the economy became less vigorous yet social demands increased, the Tories were left with a decision – would they go ahead with progressive policies they wanted to follow, would they delay them for better economic times expected in two or three years, or would they shelve them entirely? They never did answer the question for themselves.

As well, Davis and most of his ministers had been in place since the late 1960s or early 1970s and, like cars that don't get their gas tanks refilled, they were running on the fumes of ideas. Perhaps they still knew how to make the promises, as the 1981 election showed, but keeping them was something else.

The final term of the Tory dynasty was one marred by inaction. A number of issues in the frying pan had begun to sizzle, yet the government had taken little action. One of the biggest was extra-billing. The federal government passed the *Canada Health Act*, which demanded that provinces not allow doctors to charge patients more than established fees. As punishment for those that did, beginning in June 1984, it withheld $1 for every $1 extra-billed. That meant Ontario was going to lose over $50 million per year in federal transfers. Probably because most in Cabinet didn't mind extra-billing, the government seemed unable to decide what to do and, thus, did nothing. It allowed the Liberals and NDP to make real points by attacking their failure to ban this publicly perceived extortion, especially given than Davis himself had changed his view, from finding extra-billing "unacceptable" to saying he wasn't about to force doctors into OHIP.[4]

If there was one issue that dominated Davis' final term, it was labour and wages. Practically every group of workers wanted more money and/or security, given inflation that was moving into the high teens, and the economy, which dropped into recession in 1982, was losing jobs and not creating them. While it was one problem for business to constantly be under stress to up salaries at the cost of higher priced goods, government had to consider what would happen to taxes if they gave into the demands. From public sector unions to doctors, threats and walk-outs seemed unending. The best the Tories could do was to invoke serious restraint – limit wage hikes, transfers to municipalities, as well as on fees charged by government. The easy money which had flowed through most of the dynasty politics was gone, and to spend on big ticket items was difficult, to say the least.

Having said that, though, the Premier didn't wait many months after re-election and shocked everyone, including his caucus, when he announced the government's $650 million purchase of 25% of Suncor, a consortium involved in finally exploiting the Alberta tar sands. Perhaps one might suggest it was the fad of the day – Canadianizing the domestic oil industry – but it is likely Davis saw this along the lines of Frost's switch-over of the electrical system. It would guarantee competitiveness for industry in Ontario with a secure source and, eventually, lower prices. The move caused a sensation, as many nationalists saw it as a brilliant purchase reinforcing the federal government's National Energy Programme, while Westerners saw it as another attack on their getting their due – world price for oil and the benefits, thereof. The image of Albertans in Arabian garb was widespread. Right-wing conservatives simply lamented it as unnecessary spending at a time of growing deficits and debt.

* * * * *

The hallmark of the Frost, Robarts, and Davis Tories was an ability to manage the affairs of the province in an adept and competent fashion, while bringing people the social and economic reform they desired. In many ways, though, the challenge was somewhat different for each of them. Frost led a society that wanted change but also held more conservative attitudes, as well, thus perhaps restraining demand for that progress. With a fast-growing economy, paying for it could not have been a great problem, once the decision was made to spend. Robarts also governed during tremendous growth in the 1960s, yet he faced a society that was becoming more liberal, and the demands for progressive change must have been louder. Davis, however, probably had the hardest time. For him, growth had levelled off, the economy stagnated, inflation was high, and then he faced the first bad recession since the 1930s. On the other hand, the "Me Generation" was impatient for positive reform and increasingly threw off concerns of the past. Yet all were able to balance these two elements for thirty-plus years.

But that's not to say that Ontario Tories always favoured reforms in the balance with cautious management. Leslie Frost had to pay for change, yet opted to create a regressive sales tax for the province. In fact, on several occasions, they were quite conservative in their desire to change. Occasionally, they were dragged along, other times they opted for efficiency over progress. One example of each that crosses leaders' administrations was the move to public health care, and the regionalisation of local government.

While the Tories seemed particularly attracted to education reform over the years, they came across as less sanguine about adopting public health care. While the federal Liberal government was proposing a national health system based on free, universal access for citizens, the Ontario Tories were opposing the idea (as did a vast majority of Ontario doctors). Instead, they countered with a more conservative option that would have only gone part way toward this ideal. However, they were outgunned and, eventually, capitulated to the logic of the situation, and the money offered by the feds. However, in a few short years, the Tories would become hard-core proponents of this system, for the most part (at least until the rise of Mike Harris).

The idea of public health insurance for Canadians was first enunciated by the federal government at the 1945-1946 Dominion-Provincial Conference on Reconstruction. While the Mackenzie King Liberals were enthusiastically pushing the implementation of such a policy proposal, most of the provinces were more interested in winning a struggle with Ottawa over who would get money. And so, the Green Book proposals, as they were called, were mothballed.

It would be almost another eight years before the hierarchy of the Ontario government was again faced with the consideration of public health insurance. Many developments had entirely changed the environment from 1945. Saskatchewan, British Columbia, Alberta and Newfoundland had all implemented some type of hospital insurance. In May 1948, Prime Minister King announced the national health grants' programme (the non-health insurance part of the Green Book proposals), which all provinces utilized. A year later, the Canadian Medical Association, representing doctors nationwide, withdrew their endorsement of the earlier proposals and took up the idea of an extension of voluntary plans, with government paying the premiums for those who couldn't afford to themselves. This would, shortly after, become the position of the Canadian Hospital Association and the insurance industry. Most importantly, with Louis St. Laurent's ascendancy to power, the Liberal party's platform changed to one which forced the provinces to take the lead in any public health insurance scheme, making any federal support conditional on a nationwide effort.

Over late 1953 and '54, Ontario Premier Leslie Frost set several of his senior bureaucrats at creating a report to analyse the possibilities of health and medical insurance for Ontario. The Taylor Report was submitted to Frost on 31 August 1954 and stated, basically, that health insurance was a desirable step for Ontario.

And so, from 1955 to 1957, the Ontario and Canadian governments argued back and forth about a programme for Ontario. Frost demanded federal assistance and only wanted hospital insurance, while Ottawa wanted at least six provinces and Ontario to guarantee 85% popular enrollment in a universally available plan before they would begin funding. Agreement finally did come and was written up in the *Hospital Insurance and Diagnostic Services Act* by the federal government and by Ontario in the *Hospital Services Act*. Implemented on 1 January 1959, the provincial legislation created the Ontario Hospital Services Plan (OHSP) under control of a commission (OHSC), headed by the Minister of Health. The OHSC was operated through the rump of the Ontario Hospital Association, with many Blue Cross employees transferring to the civil service. The plan began with 91% of the population enrolled, and within two years was up to 94%.

The next major move to public health insurance in Ontario didn't occur until January 1966, with the establishment of the Ontario Medical Services Insurance Plan. OMSIP, also under a commission, took on the task of insuring low-income and high-risk groups who were then covered under private insurance. Immediately, this took in nearly 600,000 people and brought those with some type of medical (not hospital) insurance to 95.2% of the population.

In 1968, the *Medical Care Act*, passed by the federal government in 1966, came into effect. It made the administration of programmes almost totally provincial while bringing those provinces that joined it under one uniform scheme, not several. They had to agree to specific requirements to get federal funding.

Ontario joined Medicare one year later. This brought the OHSP and the

OMSIP together as the Ontario Health Services Insurance Plan. The commissions were replaced by incorporating the plan into the Ministry of Health and having it run by a general manager. As well, the rest of the medical insurance business came under provincial control but, instead of operating it directly, it was subcontracted out to Physician's Services, Inc., Blue Cross, and thirty-nine other private, non-profit health insurance agencies to handle claims and payments to doctors. However, after three years of seeing this decentralized system become more and more disorganized and heterogeneous, the Ontario government decided to take on the business of claims and doctors' payments directly. And OHSIP became OHIP.

In 1977, five-and-a-half years of negotiations between the federal and provincial governments resulted in Parliament passing the *Federal-Provincial Fiscal Arrangements and Established Programmes Financing Act* (EPF). EPF did not change OHIP per se, but altered the way in which it was financed. The cost-sharing arrangements of the past were replaced by a cash transfer coupled with surrendered federal tax room. The change consisted of one corporate and 13.5 personal income tax points, equalized to the national average, as well as cash contributions of 50% of federal contributions from 1975-1976 adjusted by the rate of growth of the GNP. This made the Ontario government quite happy, especially because the federal tax share increased over time. (Needless to say, the federal government was not happy about this, as it was an unintended part of the change.)

But there was one particularly controversial aspect that continued. Many doctors, still not at peace with the changes, continued to charge patients over-and-above the rate dictated through OHIP. The Trudeau government passed the *Canada Health Act* with an eye to forcing provincial governments to stop the practice or face financial penalty. The Tories began to take a great deal of abuse from people, yet refused to take away this last vestige of private health. It took the rise to power of the Liberals in 1985 for extra-billing to be banned, and for the end to health premiums.

In 1996, the federal and provincial governments negotiated a new financing agreement. The Canada Health and Social Transfer (CHST) provides the provinces and territories with cash transfers and the continuation of transferred tax points for the support of health care, post-secondary education, social assistance and social services. However, where EPF was based on conditional transfers, that is specific amounts for specific services, the CHST is a lump sum which the provinces can spend according to their priorities. This concession to the provinces came at the price of their acceptance of cuts to transfers overall. Unfortunately, many have taken advantage to misuse the money for things that were not people's priorities.

OHIP was anything but a great leap into progressive change for the Ontario Tories. Their natural alliances with doctors and insurance companies had them drag their feet, practically at every turn. Had it not been for the pushing of the federal government and, moreso, the public, a universally-accessible public health plan might never have come to Ontario. Premier John Robarts called it a "Machiavellian scheme" and only joined up once he saw how much money Ontario was losing out on. And it took the Peterson Liberals to end extra-billing, after the pro-doctor Tories vacillated. Perhaps this is a sign of why Canadians, as a whole, tend to identify medicare as one of our country's proudest achievements rather that one that is provincial.

As well, the dynastic Conservatives were, on occasion, led astray by a desire to *corporatise* elements of the public sector. A phenomenon that is much more in the European or American experience is urban sprawl. Yet it is something that has plagued southern Ontario, as a result of the massive growth in and around Toronto from the 1950s on. But it is also an area where the Ontario Tories ignored progressivism and democracy and fully endorsed management principles as their response. It would be a habit that they haven't lost to this day.

In the early 1960s, the pressures of rapid urban growth led the Ontario Legislature to establish the Select Committee on the Municipal Act and Related Acts, chaired by Hollis Beckett. The last volume, released in 1965, recommended "that larger units of local government, designated as 'regional' be established with ... the county ... as the basic unit. A year later, as part of the "Design for Development", Premier John Robarts outlined the province's intention to create a series of local government reviews in areas which the province saw as potential regions. Details were later announced by the Minister of Municipal Affairs, Darcy McKeough. The intent was to establish "mini-metro", two-tier governments, based on the model of Metropolitan Toronto. Despite the fact that some of the reviews recommended one-tier government, the Ontario Government imposed a two-tier system on ten regions. The regions were given all, or most, of the responsibility for welfare, roads, water, sewage disposal, planning, and capital borrowing. All municipalities in a region were included in the regional government, even if they had been previously separated from the county system.

The change to regional government was not welcomed by many residents and municipal politicians, who felt adversely affected by the amalgamation of dozens of small municipalities to create larger, bottom-tier units. For example, the City of Cambridge, in the Regional Municipality at Waterloo, was created out of the City of Galt, the Towns of Hespeler and Preston, as well as significant portions of Waterloo and North Dumfries townships.

Realising that regional government had not been popular, but still believing in its merits, the province undertook a new policy of reforming county government. John White, the Treasurer and Minister of Economics and Intergovernmental Affairs, announced the province's intentions while addressing the annual meeting of the Association of Counties and Regions of Ontario on 29 October 1973. He proposed the County Restructuring Studies Program: provincial assistance and fifty percent (up to $50000) of the costs for any county not reorganised by regionalisation which wanted to conduct a review of local government effectiveness. The guidelines for the studies were similar to those in the regional reviews, and several conditions were attached if counties were to have additional funds and powers. These conditions made it quickly apparent that the province wanted counties to willingly restructure themselves as regions by another name.

Twelve counties took advantage of the provincial offer, but the only study which actually resulted in county restructuring was not one of these. By 1970, local government politicians in Oxford County felt seriously threatened by the neighbouring regional government studies taking place nearby in Waterloo, Brant, Haldimand, and Norfolk Counties. There was talk coming from these areas that parts of Oxford County might well be added into any future regional government. So the county council created a committee to examine a potential restructuring of their own in January 1970 and, as a result, the Restructured County of Oxford came into being on 1 January 1975. The Oxford innovation was not repeated by any other county, probably because the policy of regionalisation had been abandoned by the time restructuring studies were completed. (Montgomery, p. 8-9.)

Regional government was established in Ottawa-Carleton in 1969, Niagara in 1970, York in 1971, Sudbury and Waterloo in 1973, and Durham, Haldimand-Norfolk, Halton, Hamilton-Wentworth, and Peel in 1974. The Muskoka area was redesigned as a District Municipality on 1 January 1971, with somewhat different rules.

I suspect that John Robarts perceived regionalisation *as* progressive change. After all, being more managerially efficient is progressive. Having hundreds of communities, all with their own administrations and equipment, was duplicative and wasteful. Creating larger, more corporate, municipal entities not only meant administrative savings, but these savings could be ploughed back into *soft services*, like welfare and planning, that municipalities hadn't really dealt with before.

In fact, the creation of these regional governments was one of the first moves made by the province that fundamentally went against democratic values. If democratic government is supposed to be by the people, and for the people, then this centralization of power, and its incumbent reduction of local representation, went against the whole spirit of democracy. I live in a municipality that was amalgamated, not in this regionalisation but later. An issue arose that is most instructive of the change that occurs as municipal government, or government in general, moves away from the people.

In 1999, a year prior to municipal elections, the council of the Township of Clearview decided that the former Village of Creemore required a sewer system. (This was actually a discussion that went back three decades, but the councils of the village had the same foresight as Richard Nixon in taping his Oval Office conversations.) The decision was not wrong, in my view, but was handled terribly. Instead of asking the people what they thought, the councillors told them it was going ahead regardless. It was only after extreme local rancour that they held public meetings, and those were only to give out the most meagre details and not really to listen to people's concerns. (It is my belief that, while some opposed the sewers, most others simply opposed their *imposition*.) In the end, they went ahead, Creemore got its sewers, and because the province reneged on a commitment of 75% funding, giving only 25%, local home owners got the bill for roughly $10,000-$20,000 each, to be paid over the next few years.

The point is, when it was just Creemore, the 1,400 residents could make up their own minds and could demand accountability at election time. Once Clearview was created in 1992, the former village had only one ward-based representative on a council of nine. In other words, they had little recourse either prior to, or at, the election.

Losing one's hometown is often traumatic and creates a groundswell of irritation that I believe has always been downplayed by government officials. On several occasions, I put this theory to Ron Farrow, then a special advisor to the Minister of Municipal Affairs and co-author of the study that recommended regional government for what was Waterloo County. Now Ron is a good guy, but I always felt he was so steadfast in his belief that regionalisation was positive that he rejected my theory out of hand, as he rejected the suggestion that regional government did not save money. It is a view I think permeates the Ministry of Municipal Affairs, as it has done for at least 40 years. We never did discuss what regional government has done to democracy.

Yet even for someone who thinks that the Tories, particularly under Davis, were somewhat less progressive than they seemed, public perception is ultimately more important. The Progressive Conservatives had been behind most major innovations and had supported the creation of innumerable jobs. Voters saw them as the force of change and treated them accordingly. It was only when this was doubted that they were punished. Particularly in 1975, this came very close to ending the dynasty, but the Tories held on. And wishing to re-establish their majority government, they purposely moved back into making progressive promises and keeping just enough of them to regain their place as the political party of public choice.

2. Empire falls, but progress returns

Bill Davis' last big decision as premier was the extension of public funding to Catholic separate schools and private schools on 12 June 1984. It was an announcement that caught most within his own party by surprise, because he made it alone and only warned his caucus a few hours before it came out in the Legislature, much as he had done with the Suncor purchase. While he seemed to understand he was "testing the core" of the Progressive Conservative party, he also said it was the right thing to do, fulfilling "those contracts and obligations which were struck to create a united Canada in 1867". In a party that had prided itself as the heart of Protestant Ontario, for many in caucus and even more regular members, it was a hard pill to swallow.

Yet, strangely, Davis did not choose to stick around to see to the policy's implementation. A year before, he had contemplated a move to federal politics, but had rejected it. This gave many of his supporters hope that he would run for another term. The polls seemed to indicate an easy majority victory. It was not to be.

On Thanksgiving Day, he announced his intention to retire, and set off a run for the leadership laurels. This left the party with a serious decision to make. Over the 42 years and three leadership contests of the dynasty, the contenders for succession had been fairly moderate-progressive people, and the membership had mirrored this, at least at the conventions. However, by 1984, times had changed. The economy had shuddered through the last few years, and the demands of restraint had led the members, perhaps, to take on a more prudent view.

If it's fair to say that leaders generally arise from the ranks of Cabinet, and are often the best of these, then Bill Davis had too many good ministers. Larry Grossman and Dennis Timbrell both ran for the leadership, and both came from the progressive wing of the party. Frank Miller and Roy McMurtry ran from the right wing. But McMurtry's views were much more moderate, and he was perceived as such. This gave Miller a great advantage, especially in the light of the funding of separate schools. Many in his party saw him as the only chance to undo this decision, though he denied he would.

Miller was the favourite, though I am dubious he was Davis' choice. While he claimed his right-wing views had been tempered by experience and a recognition of the reality of Ontario politics, that was more of a statement to stifle his critics. As Treasurer he had overseen deficit budgeting, but had made few bones that he didn't like doing it, which may have explained his eventual shuffle to the Industry portfolio. It didn't pay in Bill Davis' Cabinet to be too overt in your conservative views. Gord Walker, an invidious London Tory of Republican proportion, had written a book in 1983 proclaiming his opinions for all to read. It got him stripped of his Cabinet portfolio and destroyed his career. He and Miller were very good friends.

Larry Grossman was probably seen as Miller's biggest threat. He had succeeded him as Treasurer and had done what Miller seemingly couldn't, cut the budget. Yet everyone knew him to be a Red Tory with a social conscience. It gave him the same appeal as Robarts or Davis. And it didn't hurt his father had been a Tory MPP and he had many contacts among older Conservative members. On the other hand, it didn't help he was from Toronto proper, he came across as being smart and sophisticated ... and he was Jewish. He wasn't going to fool any Average Joe into thinking they could go out with him for a drink. Not like Miller. It also didn't help that he came with a warning – the Tories had weakened over the Davis term, as they were no longer representative of the diversifying population. His advice was *change or lose*. Grossman was seen by many as the Establishment candidate, and the successor wanted by the Davis loyalists.

Dennis Timbrell was a one-time history teacher who pushed his experience in matters urban and rural. He could give the party the balance it needed for the future. A Cabinet minister since 1973, he had never held a portfolio dealing with rural Ontario until asking for Agriculture in 1982, presumably to widen his base for just such a leadership run. But that didn't change how he came across to people. Davis had once said "bland works" and Timbrell was nothing if not bland. Presumably, branding oneself as bland was akin to saying "inoffensive". For Timbrell, "boring" seemed more apt. He even appeared careful to be characterless. Regardless, he and Grossman were deemed to be in a dogfight for second.

Roland Roy McMurtry may have been the best political choice of the lot as leader, but he had the least support. Well-liked by ordinary Tories, he had been Attorney-General exclusively during his decade in Cabinet. It meant he had a very narrow base from which to draw support. As well, he had entered the race late – a no-no for serious contenders. While he was the least left-wing of the contestants except for Miller, his views were generally the same as Grossman's and Timbrell's on social issues. He wanted social justice and said the party had to help the disadvantaged. This hurt him with the more extreme conservatives. Yet his economic views did not make him a choice acceptable to the party hierarchy either.

While Catholic school funding caused some upset in the province, most of the rancour came from inside the Tory party. The PCs seemed unable to even write up the necessary legislation to enact the decision, as month after month passed with no movement on the issue. Once Davis decided to go, and the leadership campaign was in full swing, implementation for a September 1985 start would have to wait until after a new leader was chosen. Or perhaps not.

There were many who believed that, if Miller was successful, separate school funding could be delayed, diminished, or shelved entirely. It was a sign, perhaps, that the party's more right-wing members were no longer willing to be quiet and let the more progressive elements run the show. In fact, it may explain a lot about the grassroots of the party, which was clearly more incensed by the decision than were its elites.

The delegates selected for the convention were older, wealthier, better-educated, and more likely to be Protestant than Catholic, according to profiling done by the Miller campaign. They were people with interests that fit much better with Miller than his opponents. However, given that the four were all seen as credible candidates, no one could be cast aside as a possible winner, except for McMurtry, who most everyone believed would drop off the ballot first.

And they were right, and McMurtry did just that. But he did better than expected, scoring 300 out of 1,691 votes. Timbrell had actually out-done Grossman, 421 to 378, but both trailed Miller at 591. For many, this last total was surprisingly poor. Perhaps it emboldened the others. McMurtry threw his support behind Grossman, in what was clearly a previously-agreed-to act. That pushed Grossman past Timbrell on the next ballot, 514-508. Many who had supported Timbrell had done so believing only he would defeat Miller head-to-head, as the latter had gained a mere 68 votes. With him out, that wouldn't happen. And though he crossed to support Grossman after a recount, he couldn't bring his supporters with him. Only 278 went with the Treasurer, while 210 went to the former Treasurer, and Miller barely scraped through with a third-ballot victory of 77 votes.

As with all leadership conventions, it takes time to heal the rifts, after-the-fact. Miller said all the right things, and it seemed the party would soon be ready to fight a united election campaign. But that ignored the people behind Miller. They were a little less willing to compromise.

Almost immediately, his transition team broke with one of the Tory's traditions. Normally, the changeover from one leader to his successor was done quietly and with any style variations made in a slow, friendly fashion, professional to professional. But many of Miller's people were anything but professional. Given that most of the right-wingers in the party had been left out of senior positions in the past, they lacked the experience necessary to make them proficient political managers. As well, most had been alienated from the leadership for some time, as they saw it as too leftist and too willing to run up debt. So in their rush to make changes, they neglected to ask for advice, sure that the powers-that-be would try to deter them from their new course.

Miller inherited a party that was at about 50% in the polls and far more organizationally strong than that of its opponents. The Liberals were licking their wounds from the disastrous federal campaign of 1984 and the loss of ten sitting MPPs[5], and the NDP had still to expand its support beyond the urban areas. He could have pushed an election off for about a year, but claimed, after the fact, he was pressured to go before the Tories faced the full force of the separate school funding controversy. It may well have been the reality that he and others recognized the Tories might well split down the middle, no matter what action they took. Go ahead with full funding and you alienate your own supporters. Back off on funding, and you alienate most senior party officials, Cabinet members, and the party elite as a whole, not to mention most Catholic voters. If this was the case, an election prior to the school year beginning in September was vital. And it was called on 25 March, for a 37-day campaign.

It is my belief that most Ontario voters either saw the funding as a good idea, or were Tories so annoyed by it they chose to stay at home for the election of 1985. As well, for many, they recognized that this was a government that was now moribund, and had lost its progressive nature, and Frank Miller certainly wasn't the type of leader to bring it back. Quite the reverse.

I also think that the Tories deluded themselves into thinking their support was strong. Ontarians have had a habit of *parking* their support with the party they perceive as centrist between elections. In the 1990s and today, that is the Liberal party. In the early 1980s, it was the Tories. As people would say of the David Peterson Liberals in 1990, their support was a mile wide and an inch deep. So it was for the Miller Conservatives in 1985.

As provincial Treasurer, Miller's strength was the economy, and polls showed he had a great deal of credibility on that subject. The result was an election campaign centred on him and economic growth. However, they also had a number of other policies on many other issues, from health to the environment. The strategists just chose not to use them. It gave people the impression the Tories had lost their balance, all management and no progress.

On the other hand, the Liberals had a newly coiffed and apparently forward-thinking leader. Fresh from a makeover by image consultants – out with the longish mousy brown hair and glasses and in with stylish light grey hair, contact lenses, and some exercise – David Peterson appeared to be a man of the 1980s ... maybe 1990s. Not only did he exude the Yuppie temperament of the day, but he came with a number of policies that gave the Liberals a real edge in seeming progressive. Liberals would end extra-billing. Liberals would allow beer to be sold in corner stores. Liberals would extend rent controls to newer buildings. The Liberals would legislate the workplace principle of equal pay for work of equal value. The Liberals would extend full funding to Catholic schools, though not private ones.

So, on election day, the people voted Liberal ... not in scads but by a plurality, 38% to the Tories' 37% to the New Democrat's 24%. However, a vagary of the first-past-the-post system – in this case, an over-representation of rural voters – gave a minority government to the PCs, though they had lost ten incumbents, eight of whom were Cabinet ministers. There was some talk of the Liberals supporting the PCs initially, but that disappeared right away. Instead, by mid-May, Peterson was offering the *silver-spoon socialist* leader of the NDP, Bob Rae, a written deal to get his party's support for a Liberal government. On 18 June, the government of Frank Miller lost two motions of confidence, and the Tory dynasty was at an end.

The portent of this fall from grace may have come in January when then-leadership hopeful Larry Grossman came forward with a study suggesting that the Conservative party had a core vote of just 33%, and that the party had lost its understanding of people after the massive demographic changes of the Davis years. This view seems to have been very accurate, given the party membership's choice of Miller, as he was easily the most right-wing of the four leadership candidates. In fact, the right-wingers in the Progressive Conservative party had become dominant and, despite their defeat, would become even stronger over time. But first, the party had to endure the splinters of opposition seats for the first time in over four decades.

For two years the Liberal government lived up to its very progressive promise ... but it had no choice. I'm not suggesting the Liberal caucus didn't want to go ahead – it did – but the price of power had been to sign an accord with the NDP which actually laid out what was expected of the government.

An Agenda for Reform – Proposals for Minority Parliament

On May 2, 1985, the people of Ontario created an opportunity for change after 42 years of Conservative government. We are determined to accept responsibility for bringing about that change.

During the election campaign, both the Liberal and New Democratic parties advanced significant public policy and legislative reform proposals. These proposals contained many elements in common, which are outlined in the attached documents.

In the interests of making minority government work, we are committed to a program of public policy reforms which will improve the quality of life for everyone in this province. We are also committed to legislative reforms designed to improve public access to and information about the legislative process in Ontario.

It will take time to achieve these objectives. We have agreed on the need for a period of stability during which this program can proceed.

Should the lieutenant-governor invite the leader of the Liberal party to form a government, this agreement will be for two years from the day that the leader of the Liberal party assumes the office of premier.

It is understood that the traditions, practices and precedents of the Ontario Legislature are that individual bills are not considered matters of confidence unless so designated by the government.

We undertake the following:

1. *The leader of the Liberal party will not request a dissolution of the Legislature during the term of this agreement, except following defeat on a specifically framed motion of non-confidence.*
2. *The New Democratic Party will neither move nor vote non-confidence during the term of this agreement.*
3. *While individual bills, including budget bills will not be treated or designated as matters of confidence, the overall budgetary policy of the government, including the votes on supply, will be treated as a matter of confidence.*

(Signed David Peterson and Bob Rae)

Attached Document 1: Legislative Reform

- *Legislation on freedom of information and protection of privacy.*
- *Reform of the House by strengthening and broadening the role of committees and individual members and increasing pubic involvement in the legislative process. Select committees will be established to investigate the commercialization of health and social services in Ontario and to study and report on bilateral environmental issues affecting Ontario.*
- *Changes to broaden the powers of the pubic accounts committee and the provincial auditor to cover current and proposed expenditures and to reiterate the authority of the committee to direct investigations of all aspects of public spending.*
- *Establishment of a standing committee on energy to oversee Ontario Hydro and other energy matters.*
- *Establishment of a select committee on procedures for appointments in the public sector to recommend changes in the system of*

recruitment and selection of pubic appointees.
- *Election financing reform to cover spending limits and rebates, at both the central and local campaign level.*
- *Redefinition and broadening of the rights of pubic service workers to participation in political activity.*
- *Electronic Hansard (television in the Legislature.)*

Attached Document 2: Proposals for action in first session from common campaign proposals, to be implemented within a framework of fiscal responsibility.

- *Begin implementation of separate school funding:*
    - *Release present draft legislation immediately;*
    - *Introduce legislation upon a Liberal government meeting the Legislature and refer to committee for public hearings.*
- *Introduce programs to create employment and training opportunities for young people.*
- *Ban extra-billing by medical doctors.*
- *Proclaim the sections of the Environmental Protection Act dealing with spills.*
- *Reform Ontario's tenant protection laws, including:*
    - *Establishment of a rent registry;*
    - *Establishment of a 4-per-cent rent review guideline;*
    - *Inclusion of the provisions of Bill 198 as a permanent part of the Residential Tenancies Act;*
    - *Extension of rent review to cover post-1976 buildings;*
    - *An end to the $750-a-month exemption from rent review;*
- *Introduction of a rent review procedure to deal with costs no longer borne by landlords;*
- *Introduction of enabling legislation to permit demolition control by municipalities.*
- *Introduce legislation for equal pay for work of equal value in both the public and the private sector.*
- *Include a first-contract law in Ontario labour legislation.*
- *Introduce reforms to the Occupational Health and Safely Act including toxic substances designation and regulations to give workers the right to know about workplace hazards.*
- *Continue the pre-budget freeze on the ad valorem gasoline tax and establish an inquiry into gas price differentials between Northern and Southern Ontario.*
- *Wind up the royal commission on the northern environment and obtain release of all working papers and reports.*
- *Provide full coverage of medically necessary travel under the Ontario Health Insurance Plan (OHIP) for residents of Northern Ontario.*

Attached Document 3: Program for action from common campaign proposals, to be implemented within a framework of fiscal responsibility.

- *Affirmative action and employment equity for women, minorities and the handicapped and expansion of the role and budget of Human Rights Commission to deal with workplace and housing discrimination.*
- *Establishment of an Ontario housing program to fund immediately 10,000 co-op and non-profit housing units, in addition to those provided for under federal funding arrangements.*
- *New enforceable mechanisms for the control of pollution to enable Ontario to deal effectively with acid rain and to establish the principle that the polluter pays.*
- *Reform of services for the elderly to provide alternatives to institutional care and a reform of the present nursing home licensing and inspection system.*
- *Reform of job security legislation, including notice and justification of lay-offs and plant shutdowns and improved severance legislation.*
- *Farm financing reform, including low-interest loans for farmers.*
- *Workers' compensation reform.*
- *Private pension reform based on the recommendations of the Ontario select committee on pensions.*
- *Reform of day-care policy and funding to recognize child care as a basic public service and not a form of welfare.*
- *An independent audit of Ontario's forest resources, and additional programs to provide for on-going regeneration of Ontario's forests.*

First, the Liberals completed Bill Davis' promise of funding for Catholic schools, though they dropped anything for private schools. Extra-billing was banned, though it caused a serious doctors' strike (which, amusingly, lowered the death rate and improved the Liberals' standing in the polls). Pay equity was legislated, as were more expansive labour laws. Fines and enforcement of environmental regulations were increased. More money went into public housing, help for farmers, and northern development. Appointments based strictly on partisan loyalty were ended.

But as all political leaders desire a majority, so did David Peterson and, once time was up and the terms of the agreement with the NDP had been more-or-less completed, he quickly called an election in August 1987. The voters saw the Liberals as their new progressive party, but also one that was likely to be managerially competent, as the Tories had been.

In most ways, the campaign was anticlimax from start to finish. The momentum the Liberals had built up in their two years of progressive reforms and strengthening economy was nearly unstoppable. And they didn't rest on their laurels. Further promises were made: $1.5 billion over five years for elementary education, with $170 million of that to cut the student-teacher ratio in Grades 1 and 2 by hiring 4,000 new teachers; the creation of an Ontario Home Ownership Savings Plan to give families of under $40,000 income the opportunity to save up to $10,000 over ten years for a mortgage; $150 million to help financially-troubled polluters clean up; $140 million over five years to build Highway 416 to run from Ottawa to Highway 401 through Kemptville; $26 million to set up a province-wide recycling programme in concert with municipalities (and contingent on municipal funds, too); and, $10 million to redevelop the Hamilton waterfront.

The NDP, after being the apparent silent partner of the accord, probably expected some credit for their prodding of the Liberals, and kept their promises smaller than in past, though they still added up to more than the Liberal ones. They committed to $1 billion to set up and operate an Ontario Pension Plan, $870 million for new day-care spaces, $660 million for a variety of environmental programmes, $500 million for a fund to help in Northern Ontario, and $325 million for new non-profit and co-op housing. All these spending promises were over a period of three years. The exception was a home ownership plan of their own, which was to cost more than a billion dollars over ten years.

The Tories, running a poor third in the polls and clearly desperate, seemingly chose to out-promise both the other parties, while also appealing to the Red Tories of Bill Davis and the more right-wing element of Frank Miller. On the progressive side, they pledged to return the provincial share of education taxes from 49% to 60%, relieving municipal property taxpayers of some of their load. The party costed this out as $1.3 billion over five years. Unfortunately for them, the media pointed out an error in their accounting which really made the cost $3.9 billion. A promise was made to help farmers, as well, at a cost of between $750 million and $2 billion over five years, depending on how many farmers participated. The Tories also promised to cut the sales tax to 6% from 7%, but also reduce personal income tax, which was more appealing to the true Blue conservatives. These two combined vows would cost the provincial treasury $9 billion over five years in lost revenue. The sum total of all their promises – up to a massive $20 billion – didn't make them look particularly progressive, as the tax cuts would benefit the wealthy more, nor did it make them look fiscally responsible, as it was $20 billion in promises. The media and other parties made such a fuss over it that, by campaign's end, leader Larry Grossman was said to have been "in a battered emotional condition ... lashing out at the media, and even his own former premier Bill Davis".[6] He had, in fact, said Peterson was too much like Davis, and the time for his kind of competent, "fuzzy" leadership was past.

As well, free trade had become a significant issue. The federal Tories had decided Canada's salvation lie in a pact with the United States to eliminate tariffs on goods travelling between the countries and, with 87% of Ontarians polled defining it as an important issue, it did take on a life during the provincial campaign. Only the NDP came out as unequivocally against it, not surprising given their allegiance to the unions, while the Tories came out with the opposite position, also not a revelation given their connections to the business community. And the last non-bombshell was that the Liberals placed themselves in-between, with conditions for acceptance, but acceptance only if they were met. Though it had the aura of significance, the truth was the issue was only peripherally provincial in jurisdiction, and even an opposing jurisdiction couldn't have stopped it. The real tug-of-war over free trade would wait a year for the next national campaign.

The election result's die had been cast in 1985. The Tories were no longer seen as able to balance societal advancement and consistent management, and the Liberals were. And what must have been an appallingly painful lesson for the NDP, supporting another party as government and even forcing them to implement some of your ideas only leads to that other party getting the credit. David Peterson and his Liberal party were seen as the new *progressive conservatives*, and the electorate swept them to power with 47% of the vote and 95 of 130 seats. The New Democrats lost four seats, but gained 1.8% of the popular vote and claimed Official Opposition status. The Tories were massacred, going from 50 seats to 16, 37% to 24.5%. Even Larry Grossman lost his seat. For many, one dynasty had now been replaced with another. It was a view that would permeate the Liberal hierarchy and lead to their speedy downfall and humiliation.

Had the newly-minted majority continued with consistent reform, they might well have survived and flourished. Almost instantly, however, an arrogance and desire to exploit their newfound power set in. When Grossman had said David Peterson was too much like Bill Davis, he was wrong on more grounds than one. Davis had always been careful to come across to the public as a laid-back, modest man. Thus the moniker "Brampton Billy" was applauded, not discouraged. Peterson may have been every bit as able and bright as Davis, but humble he wasn't. He was very much the upwardly-mobile Yuppie of the late '80s.

3. The 1990 surprise!

The Liberals could not, or would not, live up to their progressive image. Instead of continuing the fine balance of progress slightly over management, they arrogantly and lazily fell back on the latter, doing little beyond administering and tinkering with what they had done between 1985 and 1987. So convinced were the party leaders that they had some sort of divine right to a dynasty of their own, they failed to recognize that the public very much wanted more profound progressive change. When the Liberals failed to supply it, they quickly lost their chance.

The 1990 election came as a surprise to most people, and an outright shock to a few. The Peterson government hadn't quite completed its third year as a majority when the Premier went to the Lieutenant-Governor to ask for dissolution of the Legislature. In hindsight, the obvious reason was that they saw the economy bottoming out and didn't want to have to go to the voters in the middle of a recession. In fact, the economy was already in recession, but the numbers to confirm two quarters of negative growth wouldn't be processed for a few months yet. However, in the summer of 1990, this reason wasn't quite so evident.

As well, Peterson claimed he needed a strong hand to deal with the constitutional changes that were supposedly coming. I have no doubt he fancied himself as John Robarts or Bill Davis on the national stage. When Brian Mulroney chose to rewrite history and re-open the whole debate over Quebec's place in Canada, Peterson jumped in to stand tall with Ontario's traditional place as protector of the national interest over the parochial demands of other provinces. However, the public was not with Mulroney, for many different reasons, and when Peterson allied himself to Mulroney's position, he badly damaged himself and his provincial party.

The election was a calculated risk, going so early with a majority, but it seemed a reasonable bet. The party had been sitting at 50% in the polls for some time. They had balanced the 1989-1990 budget, the first balanced budget in the province in many years. The post-accord promises they had made they had followed through on, at least to some extent.

But what the Liberal strategists failed to see was that the party was carrying tremendous baggage, as well. Perhaps the greatest was unfulfilled expectations. People had turned their backs on the Tories in 1985 when they had shown they were unable to renew their ideas. They had become simply managers. Nothing more. But the Liberals had made promises and, in 1987, even more promises. Massive reform was coming, brought to you by the Ontario Liberal Party. And it did come, but not at the speed or to the degree promised. Yes, the government made moves on cleaning up pollution, improving health care, and cutting class size in elementary schools. And while prosecuting polluters made good headlines, it didn't pick up garbage on the side of the road. And while doing away with OHIP premiums was what people wanted, it forced the creation of a payroll tax that hurt small businesses. And while getting more teachers in classrooms was good, it was a slow process.

There were also other problems. There was the Patti Starr affair, perhaps the one scandal that did have some effect on a government. Starr was a former Tory supporter who worked on the 1984 federal campaign of David Peterson's bother, Jim, then switched provincially. Amongst other things, Starr also acted as a party fundraiser, receiving "explicit direction from the premier's office advising her which candidates, MPPs and ministers required assistance"[7]. Perhaps as a result, in June 1987, Premier Peterson appointed her to head Ontario Place, the government-owned, pseudo-science centre in Toronto.

However, in the course of investigating a number of unfounded allegations made by one of its columnists against Chaviva Hosek, the Housing minister, other *Globe and Mail* reporters stumbled upon illegal political contributions by the Toronto branch of the National Council of Jewish Women of Canada (NCJWC), a registered charity, all in contravention of the *Income Tax Act* which bans donations from charities. The president of the Toronto NCJWC was Patti Starr.

The NCJWC had developed a 160-unit complex for seniors and the disabled, which was built by Tridel Corporation, a large developer in southern Ontario. In 1985, the group received a quarter-million dollar sales tax rebate for the housing project, the money of which was supposed to go to reducing rents for those with low incomes. Instead, $85,000 of it went to political donations, with the cheques signed by Starr.

Though not all the money went to provincial Liberals – one donation went to federal Tory Employment minister Barbara McDougall – most of it was tied to Liberals. One-thousand dollars of the money went to Elvio Del Zotto, the president of Tridel and the Ontario wing of the federal Liberal party.[8] Many allegations were made and a number of illegal contributions were found. Two, in particular, did damage.

Citizenship minister Lily Oddie Munro was found to have made personal use of three campaign contributions, two of which came from Starr through the NCJWC. As well, she admitted Starr had paid her mother $5,000 to do some campaign mailing. It also came out that Gordon Ashworth, Peterson's executive assistant, had taken a refrigerator and the free painting of his house from Tridel, as arranged by Starr. He resigned.

In the end, several Cabinet ministers, including Hosek and Munro, were shuffled into the backbenches because of their connection to the incidents, and Patti Starr went to jail for a short time. It blackened the shiny armour of the clean and progressive, *white knight* Liberals, who just in 1986 had strengthened the *Election Finances Reform Act* to limit contributions and spending because of the "distorting influence (donated money has) on the electoral process"[9]

And, of course, there was the Meech Lake constitutional accord. It didn't matter that Bob Rae and Mike Harris had supported it, too. It was a backroom deal that ignored the public. The Liberals had led people to believe they were different ... above that sort of old boys' game. Starr and Meech proved that wasn't true.

It's not that the Liberals didn't make any commitments in the 1990 election. They offered their record to the public. They had promised to balance the budget, one that had increasingly fallen into deficit under the Tories, and they had delivered with Ontario's first balanced budget in 20 years in 1989-1990. They had promised to strengthen the economy, and create more tax fairness, especially for the poor. They claimed the province had the strongest economy in Canada, that they had instituted 28 tax decreases and had reduced or eliminated income taxes for 625,000 people, especially for middle-income families and seniors. They had promised to reduce unemployment, and Ontario now had the lowest unemployment in the country, having created 700,000 jobs in 5 years. They had promised to increase support to small business. They established the New Ventures programme, which had helped create 45,000 jobs, generating $1.5 billion in economic activity. They promised fair treatment for working women, and came through with pay equity legislation to establish the principle of equal pay for work of equal value. They promised to take action to stop acid rain, and had enacted the toughest legislation in North America, and been the first to ban CFCs. They had promised to get tough with industrial polluters, and were now prosecuting four times as many polluters as had the Tories, with tougher fines. They had promised to set up an effective waste recycling programme. Ontario now had two million blue boxes in use, recycling 800 tonnes per day. They had promised to reduce toxic chemical discharge into waterways. They now claimed to have strict pollution controls on industry, with funding for beach clean-ups having doubled. They promised to work on improving children's basic education skills, and claimed to have instituted curriculum changes to renew the emphasis on reading, writing, and mathematics. They had promised to cut class sizes in primary grades, and had done so. They had promised more classroom computers, and had increased funding so there were now 112,000 available for children's use. They had promised to establish and fund an optional junior kindergarten programme, and had instituted such a programme. They had promised to eliminate individual OHIP premiums, and had done so, saving families up to $700 per year. They had promised an increased provincial commitment to high quality health care, and had expanded emergency, cardiac, cancer, AIDS treatment, and kidney dialysis programmes. They had promised action to promote drug-free communities. As a result, they had brought in tougher law enforcement, stronger anti-drug messages, and more community involvement. They had promised to make drug education mandatory in schools, and had done so. They had promised to recognize and support the changing role of policing, and had brought in a new Police Services Act, and improved police training. They had promised to increase opportunities for all Ontarians, including the disabled, to participate in society, and had said they would put $400 million into social assistance in the next year to turn "welfare cheques into pay cheques". They promised to work toward affordable housing for everyone. They had set up the largest non-profit housing programme in Canada, and increased tenant protection. They had promised to increase commitment to child care, and had quadrupled funding with 44,000 new licensed spaces, and 24,000 subsidized spaces for low-income families. They had promised to work toward greater independence for seniors and the disabled, and had improved services, like visiting homemakers, Meals-on-Wheels, and Alzheimer's day programmes.

As to new commitments, the Peterson Liberals promised that, if the GST was implemented by the federal government, they would cut the sales tax to 7% from 8%. They would more than double funding to the Ontario Training Fund in order to emphasize long-lasting portable skills to assure a well-educated, highly-trained workforce. They would help workers understand and deal with technological change, and provide counselling, support, and training for laid-off workers. They would provide assistance for 12,000 new apprentices over five years. They promised to nearly double Go Transit, building on a $5 billion commitment to improve GTA transportation, provide a province-wide free breakfast programme for children who might not otherwise get to eat, supply new funds to recruit and retain nurses, continue to invest in community-based, long-term care and support services for seniors and the disabled, and expand northern health travel grants to aid northern Ontarians who had to travel to receive specialized medical services. They promised to introduce a Drinking Water Protection Act to ensure safe and plentiful drinking water, and a Ground Protection Strategy to protect supplies, and provide information and training to help farmers reduce the risk of fertilizer polluting water. They promised to tighten emission controls for car and trucks and industrial polluters. They said they would order a reduction in packaging and the flow of such into landfill. They committed to a Rural Ventures programme to help develop innovative agricultural practices, and more funding for expanded drug treatment. On safety matters, they promised a new marine RIDE programme to cut boating deaths, and 90-day on-the-spot license suspensions for those who refused a Breathalyzer test.

It is clear the Liberals were committing to continue a strategy of progressive change. The problem was, it was too late. The public had already stopped seeing the Peterson government as progressive. In a way, their election promises confirmed this. Many of the promises they claimed as kept were works-in-progress and, thus, were things that people didn't see as promises kept. Many others from this record were ones from the period between 1985 and 1987, when the NDP was a prodder of change. Indeed, the Liberal election strategy may have legitimized the possibility of a New Democratic government.

But who to choose from? The Tories were still bedraggled, with an unknown leader and no real policy ideas beyond tax cuts. The NDP, on the other hand, had been behind many of the new ideas of the Liberal minority. As well, the New Democrats offered *An Agenda for People*, a manifesto of many ideas that resonated quietly with the public. As a result, they were victorious, though it was a somewhat flukey, and ultimately hollow, success.

The NDP ran a thoughtful campaign but one that in other circumstances would have been unlikely to win them an election. They did, however, present their *Agenda for People*, a short 11-page platform for reform. It was not to become the tag-line document that the CSR would be for the Tories in 1995, perhaps because it was only presented part-way into the election campaign. Nevertheless, it contained the core of NDP beliefs and desires. The centrepiece was to be change to the tax system. While personal income tax and sales tax were to be frozen, a minimum corporate tax averaging 8% of profits was to be instituted. Rae maintained that it was "obscene" that up to 40,000 profitable corporations in the province were paying no tax while their employees were. As well, anyone living below the poverty line, then considered as being less than 53% of the federal income tax rate, was going to be exempt from the provincial income tax. A succession tax would be applied on estates over $1 million. Properties that were "flipped" within two years of purchase, to gain speculators quick profits, would also be taxed at 75% of the capital gain, 50% within three years, and 25% within four.

And though clearly connected to finances, the agenda included other commitments. An NDP government would increase grants for education to 60% of the cost, up from 33-40%, and thus relieve property taxpayers, particularly seniors and those with low incomes. They would borrow on long-term bonds in order to offer interest rate relief to farmers, small businesses, and new homeowners. With a minimum wage of $5 per hour meaning someone would have to work 94 hours per week for an income above the poverty line, the NDP would increase it to 60% of the average industrial wage, to a minimum of $7.20 per hour in their first term. Financing would be provided for 10,000 new child care spaces. The budget would be doubled for home care workers and homemakers' services. Pay equity legislation would be enhanced to apply to all women, and not just those in occupations where there were men with comparable jobs, such as with child care workers. There would also be legislation to promote the hiring of women and minorities, natives and the disabled. Pension funds would become the property of workers, not employers, and would be indexed for inflation. Stricter rent controls would be applied, with annual increases being based solely on inflation and ignoring building owners' capital or financing costs. An Environmental Bill of Rights would be passed to allow individuals to take legal action against polluters. A plan would be put into place so there would be no discharge of chemicals into the air or water by the year 2000. Garbage reduction would become a priority, with the reinstatement of a refillable pop container programme, and a new tax on non-recyclable packaging. GO Transit would be expanded, with this paid for by long-term government loans with low interest rates. An economic development fund of $400 million would be established to help northern Ontario over two years. And $25 million would go into training for native teachers and health care workers to improve literacy and health on reserves. Nuclear power development would be frozen, with an eye to phasing it out eventually.

But the promise that may have stuck out most, for most people, was to scrap no-fault auto insurance and bring in a government-run, non-profit plan that would save consumers a significant portion on rates. As well, those injured in accidents would regain their right to sue, lost when the Liberals established a "no-fault" system. It went back to the previous election, and caught the eye of both the public and the media.

Costs for the commitments in *An Agenda for People* were estimated at $4.2 billion more per year, while the new tax measures would bring in just $2.4 billion. The Liberals and Tories criticized the New Democrats for planning to put the province into deficit. However, Rae argued that the extra spending would help stimulate the economy and this would take care of any short-term deficit.

Many commentators believe, to this day, that this so-called socialist manifesto did not appeal to voters. These people will tell you the NDP won simply as a rejection of the arrogant Liberals and the tired Tories. I disagree. Polling during and after the election showed, in fact, widespread support for the ideas in the *Agenda*. The great irony is that the New Democrats delivered on virtually none of them, perhaps because the recession threw them off this plan, perhaps due to their lack of experience in governing. Whatever the reason, *An Agenda for People* would become an albatross around their collective neck before long, especially with their alleged friends.

But that didn't change the fact that the ball was still in the Liberal's court. It is a cliché that political parties don't win elections, they lose them. Yet it is quite true, most of the time. As I said earlier, the Liberals quickly found their support was indeed 'a mile wide and an inch deep'. From Day One, protesters and critics dogged the Premier, and it was quickly evident the campaign strategy was also an inch deep. Instead of keeping to the plan, the leader began to respond to critics by changing the message he was supposed to be getting across, or he made his point then vanished. For the *man of the people* who normally waded into crowds with a smile and sleeves rolled up, his discomfort was apparent for all to see. His increasingly nasty retorts also made his words seem somewhat hollow.

The moment of truth came on Wednesday, 22 August, in Cornwall, when he suddenly announced a plan to cut the sales tax from 8% to 7%[10]. Given that it was his government that had increased it from 7% to 8% just two years earlier, this action had all the earmarks of desperation. Then, in the final days, Peterson set about attacking his former NDP allies as dangerous socialists who would destroy the province. Given their alliance between 1985 and 1987, this appeared patently untrue and not a little ridiculous.

In his book, <u>From Protest to Power</u>, former premier Bob Rae expressed his opinion that politics is about impression. That was why David Peterson won in 1985 and was defeated in 1990.

People liked David because he seemed young and bright and modern in 1985. They disliked him because he seemed too smooth and too arrogant and too far removed from their pain in 1990. He unwittingly gave the impression of taking the public for granted. (Rae, p. 141.)

For the most part, I agree with this analysis. The David Peterson of 1985 came across as progressive-minded and prepared to push Ontario in that direction, and that's what most people wanted. However, within five years, they understood him differently ... as an arrogant man who had allowed power to corrupt his ideals, assuming he really had them to begin with. The Liberals were managers and reformers, but they were not nearly as good at it as they thought they were. As for Peterson giving 'the impression of taking the public for granted', it looked that way because he did take them for granted. By 1990, the public no longer saw him as trustworthy, and Liberal ideas were no longer seen as commitments but just as things to say to get them elected. It would be a tag that would continue to bedevil his successors.

I had the advantage of living in London for most of the Peterson years, and in his home riding for a year or so of that. Having unofficially run the election office of one of the federal candidates in 1988 during evenings, I met many of the senior Liberals in the city. In my mind, there is no doubt that London Liberals were an incestuous lot, figuratively-speaking. The local party leadership tended to gravitate between federal and provincial, as well as toward the city riding where they thought they had the best opportunity to win. The office I worked in was their choice in 1988.

When the provincial election was called, I had been busily working on a case study of Sarnia annexation, as well as editing one on municipal development funds. This left my time under some strain. So, when I was called and asked to assist in Peterson's riding, I got the impression there might be concern about it. However, I declined. I would have said no, regardless. Peterson had alienated even me. When I was asked if I could help, I responded with, "Why? Is he going to lose?" I'm sure it wasn't funny to the woman who asked me to assist, but I smiled. You see, almost everyone in London knew Peterson was politically finished in his own riding. It is not that locals felt the Liberal party would lose the election, but most of us felt he was going down to defeat in his own riding. Not only was he facing a New Democrat who had done surprisingly well as a federal candidate in the 1988 election, but his arrogant attitude seemed all too acute to locals who felt he had done nothing for them.

More than one person related a symptom of this self-importance. In 1985 and before, Peterson had run with regular election signs, displaying candidate, party, and riding name. In 1987, his photo had been added. By 1990, the photos had been replaced by sketches – his face, profile, and one of him jogging. It is seldom a good idea to put photographs on election signs. It gives voters the impression the candidate thinks an awful lot of themself. The drawings just went that much further. It may seem a minor point, but it was an example of peoples' underlying suspicion of the man. I heard Liberals claim they weren't going to vote for him just because of the signs.

Being in London at the time of the election might have given us locals a better view of what was to come, but even we didn't see the possibilities. Yes, Peterson was going to lose his riding and it was going to New Democrat Marion Boyd. Had we applied this thinking across the province, we might have realized what was happening. It just didn't seem realistic to think the Liberals would fall from half to a third of the vote. A minority? Sure, and well-deserved. That was the price to be paid for being sloppy and haughty and not keeping enough of your promises. But defeat?

It was only a week prior to election day that polls came to be interpreted as showing a possible NDP victory. An Angus Reid-Southam News survey showed NDP support at 38%, the Liberals at 34%, and the Tories at 24%. But it was Metro Toronto that told the tale. In 1987, the Liberals had taken 24 of 30 seats but, now, the NDP was showing a 40% to 30% lead. If this held up, the Peterson government would drop sufficient seats to actually lose the election. There was no talk of a majority for the NDP though.

That came only with the shocking results of election night. At first, it was hard to believe the Rae New Democrats had managed to win 74 seats. It was such a sea change for Ontario voters. However, in the light of a little analysis, the result made some sense. Unlike in the past, the majority came from an unprecedented three-way split in the vote. In some cases, the split was even four ways.[11] The NDP got 37.6%, the Liberals 32.4%, and the Progressive Conservatives 25.5%. But the New Democrats were able to wring out a number of small victories which led to the greater success. They won 15 ridings by less than 1,000 votes. Twenty-four of the new NDP caucus were elected with less than 40% of the vote in their ridings, with half of those under 35%.

As pollsters have since said, had election day come a week, or even a few days, later, it is likely the Liberals would have regained a minority, as the NDP was sinking fast in the polls in the final week of the campaign. They had actually moved beyond 50% at one point, but then began to drop as the Liberal attacks became more vicious and foreboding. In the end, while the NDP had a plurality, a significant majority opposed them in almost every riding. So while many citizens wanted to see the progressive nature of government continue, they weren't necessarily thrilled by the banner-carriers.

The thing about the NDP is that, while many applied the socialist label to them, they weren't all that socialist. In fact, mostly, they were just *Liberals in a hurry*. With the exception of public auto insurance, they never talked about nationalizing businesses or spiking taxes for the very rich. They were more socially-oriented and more concerned about the apparent unfairnesses in society, and they felt that no time could be lost in redressing these injustices. Bob Rae has admitted they had never expected to win the election. As a result, while their desires were to move fast, they didn't have the experience or competence to do so.

Unfortunately for them, it's not clear whether they didn't recognize these disabilities or felt they had to go along regardless. There is no question that Rae had little talent from which to work to create his Cabinet. Most of his available members were people that, in a normal election, would never have been considered as electable. In his book, he refers to 12 of his choices with respect to reverence. The others he doesn't mention at all. One, for example, who made Cabinet as Tourism minister was Peter North, a fellow who had made his living doing small, handy-man jobs in and around St. Thomas. He had no political experience and had clearly run for office as much on the chance of improving his family's standard of living as helping people.[12] Why Rae put him in Cabinet only he and his advisors know.

As one wag said when the NDP was elected, they would either be one of the best governments Ontario had ever seen, or one of its worst. What I meant was ... they would either be one of the most socially progressive governments and would advance the lot of the poor far beyond where it then stood, or they would be bumpkins unable to handle governing and would spend money like water. Unfortunately, I was right. While trying to advance the plight of the poor, the disabled, women, and immigrants, they just couldn't get a handle on how to manage things ... not until it was too late, anyway.

But they came to power on the contents of *An Agenda for People*. These commitments did not seem to be any more or less grand than those of the Liberal party but, for once, their promises also did not seem out of line in an economic sense. The *Agenda* was costed out at $4.2 billion more per year against the provincial treasury, but it was to generate an extra $2.5 billion per year in revenue. The party estimated a resultant deficit of $900 million (presumably based on the Liberals projected surplus of $800 million).

In his memoir, Rae states categorically that his party knew the Liberal budget numbers were wrong going into the election, yet they clearly used them as the basis for their own cost calculations. This may have been a ploy to fool people. They would not have been the first political party to come to office, then fall back on the tired cliché that the government was lying and things were worse than they thought. But to use the government's numbers and fool even yourself seems a dubious strategy.

Of course, things might have been much different had this country not hit its worst recession since the 1930s. For the first time, government revenues actually dropped. Meanwhile, and perhaps not understanding the depth of what was happening, the NDP spent their first year in office on a bender of spending, jumping it 13% in their first budget, no doubt trying to help as many groups as possible. What they didn't care about until later was that the business and investment communities felt this was inappropriate. As a result, the province's credit rating dropped, making things even worse, and Ontario businesses refused to invest further in Ontario to any great extent. Almost instantly, the New Democrats were in so far over their heads, there was nothing to do but drown.

Bob Rae entitled one of the chapters of his book, "Anyone can sail in good weather". Of course, this is in reference to the economic storm that eventually capsized the NDP's ship. And, of course, it isn't true. Not just anyone can sail, no matter the weather. Perhaps I'm taking it too literally, but this might have been part of their problem. To me it seemed the New Democrats could never get a handle on how to govern. Only they know how well they sail.

Though they would come to blame the Liberals for horrific spending, the facts were a little more plain than the New Democrats like to admit. Yes, they saw they were sinking into a bad recession and, as a result, felt it necessary to increase welfare benefits in April 1991 to help those who would suffer the most, even though the Liberals had increased them in 1989. But it was the overall spending jump of 13% that sealed their fate, almost before they had settled into office, because it set patterns of thinking that would be difficult to break. For one, the size of the deficit didn't matter. Though this did not appear to be Rae or Finance minister Floyd Laughren's view, they went along with the rest of Cabinet, for the most part.[13] Amongst the public, for another, was the view that the NDP had no grasp on fiscal reality.

On the non-financial side, it didn't take long for government members to stream off in all directions, most with their own area of interest that they were determined to promote. Some were social activists pushing assistance for battered women, immigrants who needed help adjusting to life here, accessibility and employment concerns for the disabled, and financial and job assistance for the poor. And there were union activists who wanted stronger rules to protect labourers, to help workers organize, to protect them from unsafe and unfair working conditions. And there were those who had no fixed gaze, and just wanted to *do good*. The difficulty quickly became that many just went ahead, with no plan, and without being in concert with each other or the government as a whole. Within months, the NDP was disorganized and, with caucus members acting as advocates for many groups and organizations, the members of these got their hopes up far beyond what the NDP could deliver. It was all with the best of intentions, however. In other words, they were quickly on the road to political Hell.

An example I can give came from the constituency office of the woman who defeated David Peterson. In a very short time, Marion Boyd, who had become a Cabinet minister, got a tremendous reputation around London for the good works coming out of her office. It seemed that dozens of local social groups were meeting with her and discussing all the possibilities for changes that needed to be made. And most kept saying these good words, even as the term moved along and they were finding their early grants of money dried up. But this wasn't the situation for ordinary citizens.

About a year into the NDP's term, I was seeking information on a subject. I cannot today recall what it was or what I wanted it for. Then living in London South, the riding held by the milquetoast New Democrat David Winninger, I contacted his office, but was told my request was beyond their abilities. However, I should try Boyd's office, as they had a much larger office with staff more able to get what I needed. I tried calling for several days, always got voice-mail, but never got a return call. Finally, I drove to her office. I found it was access-controlled, and I buzzed. The hollow voice that replied said I'd have to call for an appointment. They were too busy with people that really needed help. Somewhat angered by this, I walked around back and found an open door. I went inside. A surprised staff member explained much more pleasantly that this was their day of the week which was exclusively dedicated to helping immigrants. I left without help, and was later told by a disaffected local NDPer that Boyd's office was seldom, if ever, open to *ordinary* people, as everyday of the week was dedicated to a specific group of one sort or another.

And that was a trouble the NDP had. They so wanted to help the disadvantaged that they forgot they were supposed to represent everyone. They were so busy dealing with the *few* that they forgot they were supposed to represent the *many*. Issues that were of concern to most Ontarians were not ignored, but did not appear to get the attention another party would have given them. This was particularly true of the ballooning deficits, and the impact it had on peoples' confidence in the economy. Though the government spending helped many, for many more it just scared them not to spend at all.

The imposition of the *Social Contract* in 1993 was the final nail in the coffin of the Rae government, hammered in by its supposed friends. It was the government's attempt to get a handle on the rising deficit, once they realized how much it was affecting the public attitude. Ministry of Finance estimates were that the fiscal 1993-94 deficit might grow to as much as $17 billion and this was simply unacceptable to the Premier. He was determined to keep it under $10 billion.

At a Cabinet retreat in West Lake, south of Belleville, Rae laid out the plan for his colleagues.

> *The provincial debt had grown from $48 billion to $68 billion since the NDP took office; within three years, the debt would top $120 billion if nothing was done. Speaking without notes, Rae described the government strategy as a fiscal "three-legged stool". The first leg was tax increases; the second, expenditure reductions through program streamlining and downsizing; and the third, savings from a 5 per cent reduction in public-sector wages. The government would net $2 billion from each leg, for a total saving of $6 billion, which would keep the deficit for 1993-94 below the key figure of $10 billion.* (Monahan, p. 175.)

Ignoring that $6 billion in savings might not be enough, the main concern seemed to be about from where the $2 billion cut in wages was going to come. The reality was that this could be done by axing the jobs of about 40,000 civil servants. Rae had something else in mind.

In his memoir, he is clear that the Social Contract was about an attempt to be fair ... to save the jobs of civil servants by spreading the pain of cuts across the whole public sector.

My objective was more focused: to get public-sector management and their unions to address the need for savings, and to achieve these savings without big reductions in service to the public or unemployment among public sector workers. (Rae, p. 238)

He proposed that these wage cuts would be strictly voluntary. They would be negotiated with the unions in exchange for job security and more say in decision-making. They would not be across-the-board either, but would hopefully apply as a larger cut for the better paid, with a total exemption for the poorest workers.

With only one dissenter, the Cabinet moved ahead and informed the caucus. Those in disagreement were still small in number, so the offer was made to the unions. In order to make up savings of 5%, workers would have to take unpaid days off, but with no loss of jobs. Rae thoroughly expected the unions to understand and accept. At an earlier meeting between himself and union heads, the concept of a "social accord" between government and the unions had been presented by a couple of the labour leaders. It would cement an understanding between the two in regards to how the unions would help fight the deficit. However, there was no mention of this notion including wage cuts. Rae referred to it as a "Social Contract". His version did include cuts.

The initial union reaction was one of horror and disillusionment. How could a social democratic government want to ignore collective agreements and attack the wages of *the working man*, given that these NDP MPPs were supposed to be its inherent supporters? It was unthinkable. Nevertheless, the government moved ahead, and appointed Deputy Health Minister Michael Decter to negotiate. It had been considered quite a coup when the Rae government was able to attract the former Manitoba bureaucrat to Ontario, as he was seen as very competent and quite sympathetic to NDP dogma. In my mind, he never lived up to this latter billing and, in fact, has always appeared as the purveyor of more conservative philosophies, especially when employed by the Harris Tories.

For the most part, the negotiations that began on 5 April went badly. At first, everything was unofficial and no one could agree on anything. This led the government to take a provocative step. It publicly announced its proposal: all public sector employees making over $25,000 per year would have to take one day off out of every four weeks worked – a 5% cut. Pension contributions would be lowered, as existing surpluses meant the extra was not needed to keep amounts up to full. Telling the union representatives the other $4 billion the government needed would come through the restructuring of ministries and programmes, and a tax hike, did not make the proposal a sweeter pill to swallow. The unions quickly rejected it.

The difficulty seemed to be centred around any wage cuts. Yes, the unions were willing to accept a freeze, but no rollback. However, a freeze was not going to save the government any money and was, effectively, useless. From the NDP's point of view, the alternative to which they kept returning was 40,000 lay-offs. But the unions didn't see why their members should be penalized when the government's tax increase could simply be larger and more targeted at the wealthy. As a result of the failure, the government felt it was forced to up the ante.

Once negotiations moved to an official basis, the NDP government effectively opened up the contracts for amending. Their proposals would have forced public sector employers to exact additional measures if savings' targets were not met. These included more unpaid days off, lay-offs, or other undefined courses of action. Effectively, everything was on the table and the unions were forced to negotiate.

However, in the end, the government out-smarted itself. Decter told the media that an agreement was imminent when there were still individual unions that wanted nothing to do with agreement as long as the sanctity of collective agreements was under threat. Presumably, this was to pressure the hold-outs to give in. However, as a result, union negotiators became even more vexed and angry. On top of this, the union leaders no longer trusted Decter, as his aggressive actions seemed to be at odds with his soothing words.

Ultimately, the unions walked out, breaking off talks for good. The government, desperately needing to save money and have those savings start immediately, imposed their solution, the Social Contract. Most of the public sector union leaders and their members, and some in the private sector as well, never forgave them.

Were these reasonable positions for the sides to take? To an observer such as myself, it was almost immediately evident what would happen. There is no question that Rae was offering the unions something that was more-than-fair. A guarantee not to lose your job in the middle of the worst recession since the Great Depression, especially given the lack of government revenues, was generous. And he truly believed they would accept it. Initially, he had no doubt at all, presumably because he thought they would want to save the jobs of their members.

However, most union leaders believe you should *dance with da one dat brung ya*. The unions supported the NDP through generations, then, once it formed the government, they get asked to pay the price for a bad economy. Or that's how they saw it. And the union leaders believed they were owed something. They felt their groups were an important spoke in the wheel that had driven over the Peterson Liberals. They had made financial contributions. Their members had gone door-to-door for NDP candidates. They had taken out advertising attacking the Liberals. They had organized rallies and funding for the NDP. New Democrats were supposed to be their friends and allies. Sticking the unions with the government's economic problems made them no better than the Liberals or Tories.

There was an underlying vision, as well, that many in the union movement had. The shared view was that it had been proven for 20 years that deficit budgeting caused little economic harm, so why now lay this on them as the reason for hitting union members? Going further in debt meant nothing except to Bay Street and the business elite. If the Rae government wanted more money, it should get the cash from them, not hard-working supporters. In fact, the NDP's actions simply proved they had become *the government* and all parties-in-power fell to the influence of business. In other words, once they told the unions their members would have to sacrifice, they no longer had any special protection. Those who the NDP felt had been their allies now mostly fell to the side, leaving them with little support.

Bob Rae and his government would have been much better off – politically – to have just cut jobs for some and saved the wages and benefits of the rest. Some would have suffered extreme pain but the rest would have felt next-to-none. Instead, the Social Contract meant pain for all. In politics, that's death.

As well, they were perceived to have dared attack their friends. Though it would have isolated them even more from the general public than it did, not *attacking* the unions might have saved the New Democrats from the crushing defeat of 1995. Never wound your core constituency. Politicians have too few friends to hurt the ones they do have.

Of course, Rae never saw it coming, never believed he was unfairly assaulting his friends. But once it was clear that the best he could hope for was wage cuts agreed to by screaming and kicking union leaders, he should have also realised that they might not agree at all. In that case, the cuts would have to be forced and hatred would be engendered. Instead, he seems to have taken the attitude that he was simply forcing them to be fair through "shared restraint". Problem is ... what's fair to one may not be fair to another. After all, the first leg of the fiscal stool was tax hikes, yet they were not aimed primarily at the rich and corporations. Many union members would have to pay them, as well.

The Social Contract cost the NDP more than money and votes, it cost them organization. Come the 1995 election, they had thousands less people to walk the streets and knock on doors. That meant fewer voters contacted, and fewer votes received. Not imposing this wouldn't have saved them from defeat, but it might have saved them a few MPPs. They lost eight ridings by 1,638 votes or less.

From this point, May 1993, to the end of their term, the NDP limped along, virtually without allies. They tried to make good, but it was far too late. The truth is it was very much a death watch. It just took two years for them to pass on.

4. The Tories lurch Right

To understand how we got where we are, it is necessary to take a closer look at the Progressive Conservative Party of Ontario. Under Bill Davis, it came to be known as the Big Blue Machine, so named because of its ability to win at election time. In the 'machine' sense, much of its ability to get candidates and workers and money came from its ability to hand out patronage. For those who actually wanted to get involved in politics, the Davis Conservatives were probably the most adept and willful in their use of blatant patronage. (This is not to compare Ontario with the Maritimes, where road crews were hired depending on the party in power.) If you worked to get them elected, there was an excellent chance you would be appointed to something. In her book, Hard Right Turn, Brooke Jeffrey points out that agencies, boards, and commissions flourished under the Davis Tories (though she seems to indicate this was a good thing – it wasn't), and this was because, to some extent, they needed these to pay off their friends for their support. Even at the municipal level, the provincial government began imposing these unelected special purpose bodies. It became so rampant, in fact, that Mike Harris would later decry it, simply due to cost and duplication (though he is undoubtedly the worst premier since Davis to use patronage as a sword).

When a longtime political leader retires, it is often the time for his longtime helpers to go, too. This is what happened with Bill Davis. When he left politics, much of the senior backroom of the Tories went as well, or was pushed, leaving the Big Blue Machine sputtering on far less than eight cylinders. In fact, between Davis' announcement he was going and the party falling from power, most of the machine had either retired or left to go to Ottawa with the new Mulroney government. By the time Larry Grossman would succeed Frank Miller, the provincial PCs had a crumbling organization, was deeply in debt, and saw little chance of climbing out of this hole anytime in the near future. After 1987, a huge election defeat, and Grossman deciding to quit, they really had nothing at all, save for a few of the right-wingers who still clung to the party, perhaps because they had nowhere else to go.

Many see the swing to the *right* as having come with Mike Harris' leadership, or even Frank Miller's. But the truth is that the move in that direction really was coming throughout the last couple of terms of Bill Davis. He didn't start it, but his reaction to it gave it a beachhead from which to grow.

The economic situation of the late 1970s and early 1980s was a bad one for Ontario, for the most part. Recession and high-spending damaged the Tory tradition of progress and conservative management. Be it because they had no new ideas, or because they were held back by the economy, or both, the Davis government truly stopped being progressive. Yet they continued to spend beyond their means, denying the long-held public impression of administrative competence. I truly believe that the Tories would have been hard-pressed to win a majority in 1985 even with Davis as leader[14], and that might still have led to the Liberal-NDP accord.

What this did, though, was give a boost to the right-wingers in the Tory caucus and party who were getting positive signals from the United States and United Kingdom. Reaganomics and Thatcherism seemed to be working or, at least, sold themselves as successful methods of running government. For the first time in decades, *real* conservatives were inspired. But for their creativity to ever flower it would mean actually taking power. This was satisfied when Frank Miller became leader. The fact it didn't last should have been a hint that the public was not as enamoured.

And this *purer* conservatism could have been stopped almost immediately when Larry Grossman became leader. The problem was that he and his advisors took the wrong lesson from the end of the Tory dynasty. Instead of returning to the *progressive conservative* vision of Frost, Robarts, and early Davis – a view that Grossman had always indicated he shared – he retained the more conservative outlook and expanded on it, now proclaiming it boldly, not as Miller would have done, quietly and in a restrained fashion. He rejected the leadership style of Bill Davis publicly, saying it was fine for the time he had been premier, but was no good for the late '80s and early '90s. "That competent, confident style of management is not what's needed", he told reporters during the 1987 election. Instead, he offered himself to voters as a "real and significant change, in both style and policy content, from my predecessors". It was exactly the wrong message at the wrong time.

The only explanation for Grossman's failure to follow the formula laid out by Drew and Frost and followed by Tory leaders up to Miller was that the party was no longer run by people willing to accept that message. Though it had cost them the previous election and ended the dynasty, the right-wing had assumed control of the party. For Grossman to have won the leadership, he had to go along to get along, to some extent. It won him the battle and lost him the war.

With his departure, the Conservative caucus then decided not to choose a new leader right away. Though party president Tom Long was vociferous in his opposition, arguing the party constitution would not allow a delay, the caucus ignored him. Many knew of Long's desire to lead, and many of them shared the want, just not for him. They felt they needed time to get ready. A convention was put off indefinitely.

Andy Brandt, a class of '81 MPP from Sarnia, was selected as the interim leader and, basically, did nothing. It was the safest strategy to keep the rump members together, as they still had elements of Red, moderate, patrician, and right-wing Tory clinging to the party. But it was at this time, 1989, the new party hierarchy of Tom Long and Tony Clement decided to shed the elitist image of the traditional political leadership convention and adopt an alleged one-member/one-vote system. In the past, each riding would elect a certain number of delegates to attend the convention, and these few would actually choose the leader. It might be suggested this had made it easier for the party aristocracy to maintain control, as delegates are usually those who can afford the expense and time to travel to, and spend a weekend at, the convention, and they may be more representative of the inner circle than those ordinary members in their ridings. As well, once they are at the convention, the party leadership has an easier time buttonholing them for their support.

With one-member/one-vote, or actually an American electoral college system, the party would change this. All paid-up members would vote in their ridings, and these vote results would be forwarded to the convention to be totalled. Much of the time and expense was eliminated in this way, and the process certainly appeared somewhat more democratic.[15]

For some in the old guard, this was akin to blasphemy but any argument against it seemed nonsensical. For ordinary members who couldn't afford to attend conventions, this method allowed for their real participation. To stand up and defend the *status quo* was the same as saying 'we don't want the ordinary members to vote because they're too dumb to know who's the best leader'. Most didn't think they were dumb.

The May 1990 leadership was fought between only two people, Dianne Cunningham of London, and Mike Harris of North Bay. While it had been speculated that there were many possible successors, only these two came forward, perhaps because leadership of the Tories in those days appeared more like a booby prize than a gold ring.

Both were former school board chairs and trustees from their respective areas. Cunningham was elected to the Legislature in a by-election in 1988, while Harris had been an MPP for nine years. This should have made him the obvious choice, as he had also been a Cabinet minister in the short-lived Miller government. However, that's not how it appeared.

His near-decade in office had proven Harris was not particularly wise nor charismatic, as he had not gained much of a following, save those who recognized he was a fellow right-winger and someone who bled Tory blue. By early 1989, he had a team out *twisting arms*. Cunningham, on the other hand, definitely came across as a Red Tory in the mould of Bill Davis, with a more progressive bent. She was seen as smart and hard-working, and she had taken a very Liberal seat. Also, she gave the Tories a chance to bring in a segment of the population that the party was having increasing trouble attracting – women. However, she was also seen as the choice of the old Establishment.

Living in London at the time of the leadership contest, a friend of mine and I had several conversations regarding who we thought would win. Though it didn't seem terribly important, we were both political science graduates and enjoyed discussing the minutiae of all politics. He was convinced that

Cunningham would win, as she was clearly brighter and more alive than the unpolished, dull Harris. He thought she might even be able to bring the Tories back to respectability because she seemed so much like a female Davis. To the extent that the media paid any attention, they agreed with him.

I picked Harris to win, not because I didn't agree with my friend on his opinion of Cunningham but because I did. As I explained to him, this wasn't anyone's father's Tory party. To me, they seemed like a group of grumpy men who wanted to roll the clock back to a 1950s' vision of *Leave it to Beaver* that never really existed. Simply put, they weren't about to support a woman. The one-member/one-vote process would exaggerate their control. When Harris won, I did not revel in being right. I simply thought the Tories had chosen to remain in the wilderness for another six or eight years.

But who was Mike Harris? No one really seemed to know, beyond being the Tory MPP for Nipissing. In North Bay, perhaps for the first time in his life, he was Michael D. Harris, no longer just Deane Harris' kid. Throughout the 1960s, his father was working to build up a successful resort on Lake Nipissing, as well as speculating in some other less prosperous ventures. However, he was well-known and liked.

Meanwhile, his second child Michael was whiling away his days, not doing an awful lot. His friends from that time all recognize him as an average student who preferred playing sports to doing homework. In 1963, he attended Waterloo Lutheran University in Waterloo for a year before dropping out. At 22, he married Mary Alyce Coward, and they moved to Quebec so he could qualify to be a ski instructor. He moved out on her less than a year later, and returned home to go to teacher's college. Its apparent attraction came from free tuition, free books, no dress code, and 400 of the 500 students there being women.[16] The next summer, he informed Mary that their marriage was over ... by mail. After two years as a popular, but usually unprepared, elementary teacher, he quit to work at a ski hill his father had purchased. He apparently disliked that senior teachers get promotions before junior ones.[17] In 1974, he married Janet Harrison. They had met while water-skiing. That would last until 1999, when they separated shortly after the election. When the ski hill failed, he qualified as a golf pro and went to work as a golf course and pro shop manager for a developer acquaintance. At the time, he had a significant social life with friends.

Then, in late 1974, he ran for the Nipissing school board and won. It isn't clear why he suddenly seemed to become interested in politics, though he did have a propensity for letters-to-the-editor of the local newspaper. Even his parents hadn't thought he was into politics. Within two years, he had become board chairman. Within five, he was president of the Northern Ontario Trustees' Association.

In the late 1970s, the local Tories were looking for a new candidate. Two minority governments in a row meant they were searching for new blood. Nipissing was considered a Liberal stronghold, but times seemed to be changing. Mike Bolan, the incumbent, had won in 1977 with just over 1,600 votes, which was a healthy margin for a northern riding but hardly an overwhelmingly one. Alan Pope, a Tory Cabinet minister and Bill Davis' northern kingpin, thought of a friend he had made while at Waterloo Lutheran University. He travelled to North Bay and approached Harris about the nomination. As John Ibbitson notes in his book, <u>Promised Land</u>, it was Harris' ticket out of "provincial, restricted" North Bay.[18] In fact, Pope was instrumental in getting him the nomination and organizing the riding to run an effective campaign. Given the coattails of a majority Tory victory and Harris being well-known from the school board, he won. His *reward* was a spot deep in the back of the Tory benches – a conservative Conservative surrounded by more left-leaning, more qualified, more senior colleagues.

Harris' rookie term must have been a disappointment. Initially given little to do, in 1983, he was made parliamentary secretary to the new Minister of the Environment, Andy Brandt. This may have annoyed him more than it pleased him given that Brandt was also in his first term, as was Susan Fish, who also made Cabinet. And Harris' attitude had never been to sit back and wait his turn. Any disappointment was likely more due to his unrealistic expectations.

With Bill Davis' retirement, Harris supported Frank Miller, someone more ideologically in tune with him. This time, he got his reward. Miller made him Minister of Natural Resources. It lasted four months until the election, then he was shifted to Energy. That lasted about two weeks longer, until the Liberals and NDP united to force the Tories out of government.

In Opposition for the first time, Harris toiled away in greater obscurity. With Miller defeated and having resigned as leader, there was another leadership campaign. Two of the year's earlier combatants returned, Larry Grossman and Dennis Timbrell. Grossman again had the remnants of the Big Blue Machine with him, while Timbrell shed his prosaic image to attack his Toronto colleague because he was the establishment man. In just a few short months, being linked to Bill Davis' crew was akin to having a creeping rash. They were joined by Alan Pope, the former Cabinet minister from Cochrane, who argued the party needed to listen to its grass roots in order to renew itself. Never seen as a contender, mostly because the other pair had organizations in place from the last leadership, his campaign was also plagued by gaffes. However, he was perceived as the potential kingmaker.

He chose not to be. Though he did better than expected, his 271 votes could not get him out of third and he freed his delegates. Timbrell had come in second with 661, 91 behind Grossman, and he needed just over two of every three of Pope's delegates. He came up just short, losing 848-829. Though all three called for unity after-the-fact, the two close fights so soon together had pushed a wedge between the supporters of Grossman and Timbrell.

During the battle, Mike Harris remained aloof. He must not have liked the choices. This was in spite of his friend Pope being in the race. His failure to support the man who had helped him get elected caused a split in their friendship that was permanently splintered when Harris stood behind Andy Brandt for interim leader, two years later. In retrospect, it seems likely that Harris didn't want Pope as leader because it might have delayed Harris' ascendancy. As early as 1981 when he was first elected, he had expressed his desire to someday be leader. If Pope had succeeded, he would have been the northern/rural/populist candidate, something that Harris wanted to be. Not supporting Pope was in his self-interest. They became so alienated from each other that Pope would openly campaign against Harris for the 1990 leadership and, then, resign when he was selected.

In the interim, Red Tory Larry Grossman took over leadership, and again Harris faced the prospect of being at odds with the leadership of his own party and not getting any real power. Though he was made Tory House Leader, this job is hardly one of the high profile ones. So when Brandt became interim leader after the 1987 slaughter, there can be little doubt Harris felt a little more positive about his personal future, even if his party had been cut to just 16 seats.

There was great speculation as to who would lead the Tories once a full leadership campaign was called. When this hadn't happened in two years – a time when the party found itself so far in debt it couldn't afford to hold a leadership convention – many observers believed Brandt would back away from his commitment not to seek the position himself. The neo-cons who had assumed some party positions, such as Tom Long and Tony Clement, felt there were those who wanted Brandt to stay on and, if a leadership could be put off until an election was called, he would gain it by default. They worked hard to see that didn't happen. Whether he was a man of his word, or he just saw no future in being an Ontario Tory leader, Brandt stayed out of the campaign and left it to Harris or Cunningham.

The votes were tallied before an unimpressive crowd at the CNE Coliseum. Harris won by a small margin – about a 55/45 split – and the Tories were never the same. If there had been progressive elements in the party, they were excised now, either by choice or the antediluvian leadership of the defeated and demoralized party. But the victory seemed a hollow one to the media and other commentators. The Tories were in the low 20% range in the polls, and looked to be going nowhere. It didn't help that after all the debate over one-member/one-vote, not even 16,000 people voted in the party leadership, just about half its actual membership.

In short order, the Conservatives faced another election and they were again humbled. Mike Harris may have become leader, but it was now of a party of 20 of 130 seats in the Legislature, down from 70 of 125 just nine years before. And the party's debt had ballooned to $5.4 million, even before the election. There appeared nowhere else for them to go but even further into obsolescence.

And his actions during the 1990 campaign hardly seemed to inspire confidence of an early Tory turnaround. On the first full day of campaigning, Harris told the editorial board of the *St. Thomas Times Journal* that "atheist children have to recognize that this is a society that has some principles that we operate by – that if you do something contrary to laws, many of which are based on the principles that have been handed down to us by religions, that you'll be punished for that." This was his justification for saying that religious classes should be returned to school, as though 'atheist children' especially lacked moral guidance.

On a radio show in Belleville the next day, he suggested the federal government should surrender its responsibility for languages to the provinces so Ontario and Quebec could declare themselves unilingual. "Quebec will say we'll be French first, but we'll provide services to the English minority." "Ontario is 95-5(%), I think English should be the main language in Ontario." Apparently he hadn't noticed Bill 101 in Quebec and that the province *had* declared itself unilingually French 13 years earlier.

When he stopped to ask a young man in Cornwall how he was doing, and the fellow started to complain that youth in the city were being harassed by police, Harris wished him a good day and said he hoped he'd vote Conservative. He told people in Brockville they should be applauded for going to church on Sundays but, in more urban areas, spoke in favour of Sunday shopping. So when his party was again battered at the polls, it came as no great surprise.

But writing off a party with a history of the Tories, one that still had a sizable membership, and not recognizing the turbulent times that would be the 1990s, was a huge mistake. Perhaps it was one borne of looking too much at a party leader, and not enough at looking who's behind that leader.

In the late '80s, with the Tories in turmoil, one would have expected that few would be drawn to a party on its way down. A federal Tory government made it enticing for the *best and brightest* to leave for Ottawa. The tsunami-like change that had occurred made provincial electoral fortunes look bad for years to come, so most of the veteran Tory politicians who had sat as Cabinet ministers under Davis chose to leave public life between the 1987 and 1990 elections. And the party's financial insolvency led to drastic changes, such as the closing of the party headquarters and the loss of all nine paid political staff in 1990. In effect, there was a vacuum at many levels.

However, some are not attracted by success as much as by potential. And while this financial vacuum may have seemed daunting, to those who saw the intellectual and organizational vacuum, their attraction to the party would be so because of a strong ideological streak that had left them on the outside looking in during the days of success. This was their chance to have their say. In some ways, it might be suggested a *takeover* of the Progressive Conservative party occurred. And because the only people left to run the party's affairs were volunteers, they tended to be the most driven – the true believers. Not only had the *raison d'être* for the Tories been shifted to the Right, but these right-wingers began to make up almost all of its organization, as well.

One must remember, these were not the *old* Tories. These were right-wingers who, not only didn't like social democratic, or even Liberal, principles, eschewed the whole concept of being progressive and conservative. The dislike the *new* Tories had for their predecessors was plainly evident. Harris pointed it out himself at a surprising time, during the 1990 election. He said that the cynicism of voters was at least partly due to past Tory governments who had betrayed the public trust. "I acknowledge that our own party has been part of the problem in the past. Let's face it, PC governments of the past practised the same old and tired style of government for many years." He said these governments had a tightly-controlled and too political system of appointments to agencies, boards, and commissions. Given what would come under his regime, this was an ironic statement indeed.

As well, given the policy lockstep of the provincial Davis PCs with the federal Trudeau Liberals during the 1970s and early '80s, it would likely be fair to take Harris' view of that federal government and apply it to the Davis regime.

> *... He was irritated by his policies of "big spending and interfering with business". "(Trudeau) was destroying my country ... I just thought that was terrible. I got so mad at him that he motivated me into party politics."* (Toronto Star, "Trudeau was start of Harris' odyssey", 1 May 1995, p. A15)

If Trudeau's policies vexed Harris, can there be any question that Davis' did as well? Nevertheless, he managed to swallow any concern he had over government 'interfering with business' and become a provincial Tory candidate. Nevertheless, there can be no question that those who came to be his trusted advisors also shared these views.

Unlike Harris, his new advisors were, by and large, well-educated or had more relevant experience. The key three were probably Tom Long, David Lindsay, and Leslie Noble. The best known nowadays is Tom Long, his *fame* connected to his painfully insipid Canadian Alliance leadership attempt in 2000. Elected provincial party president in 1987 while still in his 20s, Long's ambition was not only to turn the party to the Right, but to be its leader. After several years of pushing the Tory youth into ever-more radical stances that suited his personal neo-conservative ideals, he was able to step into the power vacuum that was created by the 1985 and '87 defeats. With the support of the youth wing, he was chosen as president. His big – and pretty much only – success in that position was in bringing about the one-member/one-vote constitutional amendment.

The problem was that his personal aspirations got in the way when he too-openly campaigned for the leadership, even though it wasn't then available. He was supposed to be the party president promoting the party. Instead, he seemed to be using party funds to travel about the province and promote himself. Many, especially long-time riding people, found this naked ambition about as objectionable as they would have public nudity in any form. It was uncommonly galling from a *neophyte*. And it didn't help that he only turned 30-years-of-age while in office. As a result, Long gave up the presidency in 1990 and receded into the private sector as a corporate recruiter.

David Lindsay had been an assistant of Dennis Timbrell's when he was House Leader in 1985, but had jumped ship to join Harris when he took over the post. At the time, he was in his mid-20s and would have been Number Two to Bill King, a former reporter in North Bay who had come with Harris to Queen's Park in 1981 as his assistant, but he would soon supplant him as Harris' most important advisor.

Leslie Noble had also been involved in student politics, though she was somewhat younger than her right-wing peers. When Larry Grossman sought the leadership, both times, she actively worked for him, though he was more of a leftie than she must have cared for. Regardless, he seemed to be the one who was most likely to bring these young turks into positions of authority. Then, with Grossman gone and another leadership in the offing, she went looking for another candidate to support. Like many of the other youth activists, she found Mike Harris an interesting choice. Introduced by Ernie Eves, she warmed to the North Bay MPP as "an acute mind hidden by a simple exterior".[19] Indeed, his *good ol' boy* guise was very real and it gave people a comfort level with the man. This made him a saleable commodity. And, unlike Grossman, he wasn't left-wing. He was a conservative's conservative, and that made even more attractive to the neo-con.

His 1990 leadership campaign brought her together with Alister Campbell and Mitch Patten. Patten and Noble had also been involved in conservative politics at university. Campbell, an associate of Tom Long, had been involved in the Tory campus club at the University of Toronto with Tony Clement, who at 29 replaced Long as party president (and despite his neo-con views had to stay neutral for the campaign). The obvious split between Harris the Conservative and Cunningham the *Progressive* Conservative was clear enough that the young ideologues were attracted to the man probably without much forethought. He was the only possibility they had to see the Tories entrench their newfound Rightist tendencies. Should Cunningham win, it was quite likely she'd be leader for two or three elections, meaning they'd lose their chance for the better part of a decade.

Harris' victory brought the party completely under the control of the right-wing, and with so many of his advisors now being these young Tories, they, in many ways, controlled the future direction of the party. They were a cohesive group of like-minded individuals with a free-hand to design an entire political party. Virtually without exception, they were of one mind and vision, and this meant everything could be planned without significant debate. And a lack of questioning means there's no hint of grey in decisions – they're black and white. This was certainly not something not to be found in the Liberals or NDP ... especially the former.

And there was another advantage or two. Harris had been selected by the membership, or 55% of those who voted anyway. While Bill Davis or Frank Miller might have been beholden to a colleague for twisting a few arms, or for throwing his or her support behind them at a leadership convention, Harris had no such debts to pay. As well, with the 1990 election having been fought on nothing much but *tax-fighting*, the party's policies could be re-written from scratch, as there really weren't any but the one.[20]

Of course, this rebuilding had to be done on a shoe-string budget. Yet the Tories did have one thing going for them. Even during these lean years, they had managed to hold about 25% of Ontario's voters, and a 30,000-name database for stable, if minimal, funding. It was a solid base and if anything can be suggested by the succession of more right-wing leadership and right-wing policies, it was that most of this 25% was right-wing as well, and could be expected to stay loyal.

Given these *whiz kids* and their propensity to love things *business*, they began with the typical management option of the 1990s: strategic planning. Today, this tool has been largely rejected as time-consuming and of limited value. However, for a political party on the precipice of irrelevance, it was a focal point for regaining direction and recruiting like-minded souls. It was the sort of *visioning* exercise for which David Lindsay would become well-known.

As Christina Blizzard describes it in her book, Hard Turn ...

They needed to identify opportunities, strengths, and weaknesses. They had to do some mission planning. So the Tories invited the party youth, campus clubs, women's groups, riding associations, fundraising people, and even staff at Queen's Park to participate in these strategic planning sessions. Just as the management of Harvey's might sit down to figure out just how they can make the best darned hamburgers in town, or the folks at Tim Horton's might strategize on donuts, Ontario's Tories sat down to figure out what it was they were trying to deliver. And once they'd figured out where it was they wanted to be, they looked for ways to get there. (Blizzard, pg. 10-11)

The "product" for delivery became *The Common Sense Revolution*. But not yet. On October 1992, at the party's AGM in Windsor, they distributed a booklet entitled *Mission '97*. Though the next election would occur in 1994 or 1995, this was supposed to be a plan for taking power and running government, so it was aimed at the mid-term. Conceptually and practically, it may have been presumptuous, but it was also enlightened planning. But it wasn't the CSR. It wasn't policy and it wasn't platform. It was *vision* – principles by which to operate.

"We will build a safe and prosperous Ontario by: - adhering to the shared values based on individual rights and responsibilities, fairness and equality of opportunity'.'(sic) *And it went on: "(by) Governing with responsive, competent and principled leadership (by) Implementing consistent, innovative and responsible policies."* (Blizzard, pg. 11)

These were high-sounding words that would herald the coming of the CSR. 'Individual rights and responsibilities' could be interpreted as *look out for yourself*. 'Fairness and equality of opportunity' sounds impressive, but fairness is not defined by equality, just *equal opportunity* ... to succeed *or* fail. Not weasel words, but a sign of the party's increasingly solid ideology.

The booklet also asked the members for advice on policy and election tips, and for their notions on the what their party should do centrally and locally. And it quite realistically asked what they needed to do to get elected, since bringing forward any agenda required being the government. But those behind this process, like Lindsay, were convinced that focusing on *being the government* was "crucial to restoring the heart and soul of the party"[21].

Along with this, many of the financial and corporate elite of the province were invited to meet with Harris in hopes of bringing them into the fold, not to mention picking their pockets for donations. Not only was this a recruiting exercise, but it was also a way of teaching Harris how corporate finance and management worked. And I suspect the Bay Street crowd saw it as a two-way street. For the cost of a little time, a few ideas, and a taxpayer-underwritten donation, they might well gain some significant influence over the man who might be premier, some day.

Yet, at that time, it was even more important to *sell* Harris to his own members. Yes, they had chosen him as leader, but they also had to want to donate their time and money to the party's cause. They could vote Tory, but 25% of the electorate was never going to win an election, especially when you were starting in a debt hole. They needed new recruits to build a strengthened organization, and only the average member could bring that about.

So Harris was sent all over the province to meet the members, and not just to large gatherings. The apocryphal story suggests the typical meeting was in someone's livingroom, drinking coffee with a half-dozen of the faithful, and maybe a couple of people they hoped to convert. He would give them his ideas and ask for theirs. But there were also larger meetings, though few got beyond half-filled church basements. Nevertheless, there can be little doubt that this impressed those involved. How often does one get the leader of a political party with the history of the Ontario Tories to sit in their small town hall just like a neighbour, or in their neighbour's house like a friend?

Regardless, the money situation continued to be a problem. By the end of the party's fiscal year, 1991-1992, they were still $5.3 million in debt, but they were able to bring in enough to pay their day-to-day costs and not add to it. The strategy of *pressing the flesh* began to have a real effect, as the debt was cut to $2.9 million by the end of 1993, while expanding their operations. But that success meant it was time to make use of all this development and unveil "the product".

As early as 1991, the Tories had begun putting out policy pamphlets called *New Directions*, a series outlining Tory ideas on cutting taxes and the public service, balancing the budget, and returning to a back-to-basics curriculum for schools. The first of these appeared in January of that year. Premier Bob Rae had gone on television to explain to people the difficult economic situation they were facing and his government's resulting actions. The Liberals were given six minutes, the Tories four, in rebuttal. Instead of refuting the New Democrats, Harris used this as an opportunity to ask people for their views and hock *New Directions*. About 20,000 requests came in for it. It set a pattern where people would be asked for their response to these policy pamphlets, which were the forerunners of the much-expanded CSR.

The presentation of *The Common Sense Revolution* barely made a ripple in the popular media. However, it was now out there for the party members and its friends to see. But I do not see as true, as many in the media have said, that it was the whiz kids who were responsible for *The Common*

Sense Revolution. Yes, they wrote the document and supplied it style and sales' technique and even some details but, perhaps surprisingly, they were not the people behind its substance. In fact, much of what is found in the CSR comes from the musings of Mike Harris in the period from his leadership victory up to when the CSR was written.

In his leadership campaign, he touted the benefits of government by "common sense", no doubt using the phrase favoured by his father and Leslie Frost. He said rent controls don't work and should be eliminated. He said that user fees should be applied to wealthier Ontarians to pay for health care. He said that property tax breaks should be scrapped for all those except the most needy. He said the federal and provincial governments should each levy a 7% tax on everything, including food. It would be cheaper than the provincial sales tax and the federal GST.

In the 1990 election, he promised to cut government spending by $2.2 billion, partly through "administrative efficiencies". He said a government of his would eliminate 4,500 civil service jobs, stop public sector wage hikes, and cut extras such as travel expenses, consultants, and advertising. And, of course, a government of his would cut taxes. The CSR reflected most of these ideas, but it was harder and larger, probably because the economy was in far worse shape four years on, and conservatives surrounded by neo-cons likely had their right-wing attitudes strengthened and stiffened.

Yet as the core of the CSR would come from Harris' thoughts, so would the hard-edged vindictiveness and ignorance it also represented. One example is the Hulgaard episode. It would show Mike Harris' personal view of those on welfare as lazy, and his contempt for the whole concept of social assistance.

In August 1993, when the Conservatives were desperately trying to get someone to notice them, the Tory leader joined a press conference held by a woman named Helle Hulgaard. She had just quit as a $41,353 per year social worker with the Metro Toronto Housing Authority, claiming she was better off on welfare. Why work hard to barely make ends meet for her kids when the state would pay her the same – take-home – to stay home and look after her children? She said this was her personal protest against high taxes, the Social Contract, and the idea welfare would pay her as much. Harris touted her action as proof that hundreds of thousands of workers had quit their jobs to improve their standard of living by going on the overly generous welfare system. He said, it "takes the heart out of good people who want to work and pay their way". In effect, the province was twisting the work ethic of ordinary Ontarians and promoting sloth.

They were both very wrong. As it turned out, social assistance officials and an independent accounting firm immediately pointed out the woman would end up receiving under $20,000 on welfare, or at least $5,000 income less per year compared to her previous take-home pay and expenses. However, it was too late for Harris, whose foot was already solidly ensconced in his mouth. "Many people might call Helle Hulgaard lazy. She's able-bodied and intelligent. She should be working." "Helle wants to work. But who can blame her for seizing the chance to make the same or more money while caring for her children at home?"

Hulgaard had made mistakes in calculating a welfare cheque that gave her the erroneous impression she would be better off. But even after this was pointed out, she said the loss in income was not great and would be made up for by the extra time she would be able to spend with her children. Her ex-husband, apparently behind on child support because of a failing business, said he was embarrassed for his kids.

And the Tories, even as they admitted they had just assumed her calculations were accurate, would not concede the point entirely. "Harris spokesperson Peter Varley said the figures were close enough to make the point that the tax burden is too great and the current welfare policies undermine the work ethic and destroy incentive."[22] He added that the woman's numbers had not been checked because she really quit her job on principle, rather than for the money.

However, it must be said that it wasn't a little ironic that, on the same day the media reported this story, they also had one on welfare fraud. A couple from Mississauga were charged with fraudulently receiving more than $16,000 in social assistance benefits over the previous year. It seems to me that even though the news stories clearly repudiated Harris' view of the Hulgaard affair, the mere suggestion that she would be better off stuck with a lot of people. Many voters were left believing the false claim or were simply so disgusted someone quit their job to go on welfare, the "generosity" of welfare benefits had to be at fault.

What it says about Harris is fairly clear. First, his opinion of people on welfare was that they were freeloaders trying to cheat honest citizens out of their tax money, and that the present and previous governments were complicit in making them that way. Second, he was so willing to stir up publicity that he and his people either failed to do their research or they lied. While the former seems more likely than the latter -- why lie when you're very likely to be caught at it? – it is a dubious distinction. Evidently, making their point was more important to the Harrisites than accuracy. It was certainly a sign of things to come.

But even this kind of embarrassing mistake didn't seem to damage the Tories' self-assurance. Of course, the core of the party was now made up of people who were anything but lacking in self-confidence, so this trip-up must have seemed a tiny bump in the road. And the road did seem to be smoothing out somewhat. There were signs that good things were beginning to happen. The party's debt was disappearing rapidly as donations increased. Marginally, the party was creeping up in the polls, and that was despite sharing the party's name with the marginalised federal Progressive Conservatives.

As a result of these changes, their confidence, and their desire to show a party ready to govern rather than just fight an election, they were emboldened to set up a transition committee for the possibility of victory and the need to quickly implement their agenda. The two given the job were David Lindsay and Bill Farlinger. Farlinger is Bill King's uncle, as well as having been a Bay Street executive and Tory bagman. He was one of the first recruits of the new-thinking party who actually had a *legitimate* pedigree.

As well, Long had returned from his self-imposed exile. Apparently, Harris intrigued him as another "outsider" and yet shared his right-wing views. Though he was not a member of the inner circle, he began to participate in strategy and policy sessions that were set up at the Bradgate Arms Hotel. This *Bradgate Group* was made up with the core of Lindsay, Noble, Long, Campbell, and Patten. It, and they, would take on mythic status for the creation of the CSR. It was also this group that would choose to unofficially jettison *Progressive Conservative* as the party's moniker.

As Tom Long later identified, "The PC brand was damaged goods ... in fact, the label was virtually radioactive"[23], due to its connection with the Mulroney Tories. The concern was simply that the loathing of the now-dispatched federal party was holding back its provincial cousin. The answer to this must have been simple. Given that the party's focus had been on Mike Harris since his assumption of the leadership, and he now out-distanced the party in polls, not to mention the leaders of the NDP and the Liberals, they would simply drop the name and refer to themselves as the *Mike Harris Team*. It was a tactic that would remain effective through their re-election campaign in 1999.

And while he and Noble *et. al.* didn't always get along, Long brought "keen analysis" to the work[24], apparently so much so that he and Noble were appointed campaign co-chairs in January 1994. Given Long's propensity for *divide and conquer*, it must have been hoped he would use this against the opposition parties and not his own.

But the CSR would be their *pièce de résistance*. Not only did it take the musings of Mike Harris and turn them into a consistent platform but it was so simple and straightforward that it could be (mis)understood by just about everyone. Perhaps this was partly because of its oxymoronic title – common sense is hardly revolutionary. Yet it seemed to say that government had lost the ability to recognise and use *common sense* it its decisions and, in the sweeping change of a *revolution*, this ability would not only come back to government but it would become its base. All decisions made by the government would be common-*sensical* ... for the first time in years. Of course, its only connection to real common sense was that it delivered simplistic solutions to problems that usually defied simplicity. However, *The Simple-Minded Revolution* wouldn't have been quite so catchy.

Part 1 Endnotes

1. Avis, Walter S. *et.al.* Gage Canadian Dictionary. (Toronto: Gage Publishing Limited, 1983), p. 899.
2. Tom Kennedy was interim leader from October 1948 to April 1949.
3. Magnusson, Warren and Sancton, Andrew (eds.). City Politics in Canada. (Toronto: University of Toronto Press, 1973), p. 109.
4. Hoy, Claire. Bill Davis: A Biography. (Toronto: Methuen, 1985), p. 154.
5. Four ran federally, one defected to the Tories, and five were retiring.
6. Toronto Star. "Tories fell apart when Grossman lurched to right", 11 September 1987, p. A11.
7. Gagnon, Georgette and Rath, Dan. Not Without Cause: David Peterson's Fall From Grace. (Toronto: HarperCollins, 1991), p. 62.
8. Del Zotto was also connected to Starr through another company which had signed a contract to do work for the Metro Toronto Housing Authority, when Patti Starr was a member of its board.
9. Toronto Star. "Why money and politics are an explosive mix", 17 Sep 1989, p. B5.
10. This was predicated on the federal Goods and Services Tax being enacted.
11. In 1990, a new party had fielded a large number of candidates. The Confederation of Regions didn't do all that well and took mostly Conservative votes, but it clearly took some who had supported the Liberals in 1987. It didn't need to exist in 1995 because the Harris Tories covered most of its concerns.
12. He was eventually tossed from Cabinet for allegedly offering a government job to a former bartender who claimed they had an affair. Though the allegation was never proven, he never returned to Cabinet. However, a staff member I knew claimed North was "chasing skirts" around Queen's Park almost from his first day there and that was the reason he never got back. In August 1993, he quit the caucus and tried to join the Tories. Even they wouldn't have him. In a major surprise, though, he was re-elected as an Independent in 1995. In 1999, the Tories gave him a patronage appointment to open up his riding, but they lost it to the Liberals.
13. Rae says that "every estimate I received from the experts in Finance was wrong on revenues ... (Deficit estimates were wrong) not because of 'socialist overspending,' or because of bureaucratic incompetence or malevolence, as the myths would have it, but simply because the recession was worse, revenues were collapsing, and the impacts on people and their families were much greater than anyone had thought".

Rae, Bob. From Protest to Power: Personal Reflections on a Life in Politics. (Toronto: Penguin Books Canada Limited, 1997), p.228.

It was to protect the poorest of the public that the NDP chose to increase welfare benefit rates, part of the extra spending. However, in doing so, they locked themselves in when the numbers on welfare began to explode upward. Nevertheless, when the deficit was shooting up, there was little indication that most of the Cabinet or caucus thought it was a big problem.

14. The polls put the Davis-led Tories in the high 40s or low 50s in percent approval, but the party's fundamentals were weak.

15. Actually, the system seriously over-represents ridings with small memberships. No matter how many people vote in a riding, the percentage is converted to a score out of 100, and each riding's vote applies equally. For example, if Candidate A gets 1,000 votes in a riding with 2,000 ballots cast, (s)he gets 50 for that riding. However, if Candidate B gets 100 of 200 in another riding, (s)he also gets 50. In other words, the winner could end up getting far less than 50% of the vote and could even win with a smaller total vote than an opponent.

16. Ibbitson, John. Promised Land: Inside the Mike Harris Revolution. (Scarborough: Prentice Hall Canada Inc., 1997), p. 8.

17. Ibbitson, ibid.

18. Ibbitson, ibid., p. 11.

19. Ibbitson, ibid., p. 41.

20. Ibbitson, ibid., p. 50.

21. Blizzard, Christina. Right Turn: How the Tories Took Ontario. (Toronto: Dundurn Press, 1995), p. 12.

22. Toronto Star. "Mom quits $41,500 job to go on welfare", 25 August 1993, p. A24.

23. Ibbitson, op.cit., p. 57.

24. Ibbitson, ibid.

Part 2

Tax cuts good, welfare bums bad!

The election of 1995

Unlike most political parties, which start planning for re-election 24-30 months into office, the NDP only began to contemplate their campaign a few months before they called it. Bob Rae wanted to write up a detailed platform which included how they planned to counter federal transfer cuts while cutting their own deficit. Pretty much everyone else in the New Democratic braintrust wanted to avoid going on the record about anything.

Meanwhile, the Liberals didn't think they had to run to get elected. All they had to do was sit tight, carry on a minimalist, traditional campaign, and they would again be in power. Of course, this was also partially forced on them, as they hadn't been able to raise huge amounts of money after the 1990 debacle, and they were only able to pay off their debt months before the election.[1] What they did do was write a platform that failed to set out any kind of cogent vision, and was long and overly complicated.

The Tories had been naively playing "soldier", and plotting to be "general" and save their land from the God-(Ayn Rand)-less hordes ... at least at first. Then, they went out-and-about and they found that a lot of people were genuinely struggling, anxious, and cynical, and their *angry, middle-aged man* routine actually had an audience. Despite past electoral defeats and years of being told to wear the dunce cap and sit in the corner, they were cocky and confident. Maybe they weren't playing after all. Maybe *destiny* was on their side.

1. The Common Sense Revolution

Nineteen-ninety-five saw the election that took Ontario onto a path it had never before seen. The NDP was not going to win, and everyone knew it. (I suspect even those who refuse to admit it.) The question wasn't even who would beat them. Most everyone assumed it would be the Liberals. The question was ... how much would they win by, and could the NDP hold Official Party status. Few gave the Tories any chance of forming the government, and rightly so. They appeared like neanderthals far out of their time. They only seemed like this, though, because most observers failed to recognize two things: the surly attitude of voters had not been appeased by kicking David Peterson out in 1990, and then decimating the federal Mulroney/Campbell Tories in 1993; and, a party that presents far-reaching ideas to the voters is automatically more desirable than ones that don't, even if the ideas seem to go against the voters' best interests.

The Tories, however, had nothing to lose. They had been beaten into a shadow of their former successful selves and could afford to take risks. In fact, the biggest lesson they took was from the federal Liberals, who, in the fall of 1993, set out their *Red Book* of promises. It wasn't perhaps visionary but it was far-reaching in that it rejected the Mulroney Goods and Services Tax, and promised to return Canada to the days of socially progressive government. (The fact that they didn't live up to this is a whole other book.)

The Tories saw their success with it and figured they could take a chance by creating a "Blue Book" of sorts, one that set out an entirely different agenda for Ontario. While federal Liberals may have claimed to be for progressivism, the people now behind the PCs were right-wing conservatives to the bone. Their vision, *The Common Sense Revolution*, was one of less government, lower taxes, and individual responsibility. It may not have been the utopia Ontario voters were looking for but, superficially, it was idealistic and it showed the Tories as the *party of ideas*. The voters bought it, and them. If they had moved left-of-centre to choose the NDP in 1990, then they were prepared to move right-of-centre to reject them and balance the books, so to speak.

The whole idea of putting out a platform booklet was not new, but putting it out a year before an election was unique. Now, it's clear the Tories had no way of knowing when the NDP was going to call the election. The writ didn't have to be issued until September 1995 and no one was quite certain how long New Democratic leader Bob Rae would wait. Given his party was 30-odd percent behind in the polls in spring 1994, it wasn't likely to be soon. It seems reasonable to think the Tories knew they had some time to trumpet their plan, perhaps until the fall of 1994, but they were probably only hoping to get the full year. It would have been foolish to expect otherwise.

But they didn't get much cooperation. The media barely noticed the launch of *The Common Sense Revolution* (CSR) on 3 May 1994. The *Globe and Mail*, Bay Street's national newspaper, gave it about 250 words on Page A4, hitting the major points but with no analysis, and no mention of the CSR tag. *The Toronto Star*, the largest circulation daily in Canada, gave it a similar number of words, but in somewhat more detail, along with some mention of the Tory strategy. They were going to use a "pyramid scheme". For those interested, they were asked to contact ten of their friends and relatives to promote the plan. Then, each of those ten would be asked to contact ten more, and so on. Harris then hoped to get some coverage of his two-week "road trip" to promote the CSR around the province. There is no question he got some coverage, though it was partly lost in Finance minister Floyd Laughren's 1994 budget.

One cannot underestimate the importance of *The Common Sense Revolution*. It is truly the cornerstone of everything the Harris Tories have done. Though most of its provisions had been passed into law by the spring of 1998 and pretty much implemented by 2000, it was, and is, the fundamental basis from which to understand this government and its actions. It is their bible, manual, and playbook. Nothing they do strays far from its tenets, even if they have carried through on its specifics. In the early days, it was also their day-planner. It is for this reason I will quote it extensively.

The Tories wanted it to be a call-to-arms for the people. They seemed to be the only politicians who recognized that the voters were feeling angry and ignored, and they wanted something they could put in front of them that played to this, as well as something that called on the public to sweep away those politicians who were ignoring their wishes. *If you put us in power, we will do what you want. We will listen to your concerns and desires.* And that's how the CSR document began, after a claim of economic validity, with a message directly from Mike Harris.

The Chief Economist at Midland Walwyn, one of Canada's most respected securities firms, concludes... "This plan will work. The Mike

*Harris plan to cut provincial income tax rates by 30% and non-priority
services spending by 20% will give Ontario a balanced budget within
four years, and create more than 725,000 new jobs. "*
    - Mark Mullins, Ph. D. (Economics)

*The people of Ontario have a message for their politicians:
government isn't working anymore. The system is broken. You sent
that message when you handed the provincial government its dramatic
defeat in 1990. You sent it in the* (Charlottetown constitutional)
*referendum campaign in 1992. You sent it in the federal election. And
yet, no one seems to be listening.*

*Over the last few years, I have been out talking with the people of
Ontario. In Town Hall meetings, in living rooms and around kitchen
tables.*

*I have heard your message. You are looking for a Common Sense
Revolution in the way our province is run. Well, I'm prepared to
actually do something about it.*

*It's time for government to make the same types of changes all of us
have had to make in our own families and in our jobs. If we are to fix
the problems in this province then government has to be prepared to
make some tough decisions.*

*I'm not talking about tinkering, about incremental changes, or about
short term solutions. After all, the changes we have all experienced in
our personal lives have been much more fundamental than that.*

*It's time for us to take a fresh look at government. To re-invent the way
it works, to make it work for people. While many goals remain
important to us – creating jobs, providing safe communities, protecting
health care – we are governed by a system that was designed to meet
the needs of the 1950's* (sic)*, not the challenges of the 1990's* (sic) *or
beyond.*

*It's time to ask ourselves how government spending can double in the
last ten years, while we seem to be getting less and less value for our
tax money.... To ask ourselves why we spend more money on education
than ever before, but our children aren't able to get the kind of
education they need to secure a good and prosperous future....*

Time to ask ourselves how we can spend more and more money fighting crime, while our streets end up becoming more dangerous.

The words reflected the concerns that people had. 'How government spending can double in the last ten years, while we seem to be getting less and less value for our tax money'. The comment that politics is about perception is right on here. Government spending had increased a lot, by about 60%, at a time when inflation ran about 38.4%, yet government, especially on the environment, had started to be far more active in protective measures which people wanted. Nevertheless, average people were getting beat up financially. While this was due to recession, it mirrored the questioning people had ... that government couldn't help them when times got tough.

'Why we spend more money on education than ever before, but our children aren't able to get the kind of education they need to secure a good and prosperous future'. The perception was that schools had been failing kids for years. Even when they didn't pass a grade, they were pushed on regardless, so as not to damage their psyches. Many were graduating without being able to read and write properly, or at all.

'How we can spend more and more money fighting crime, while our streets end up becoming more dangerous'. Crime was rife. If you weren't a victim, then you knew a victim. And criminals were coddled by a system that didn't demand true punishment and, thus, penance, for their offences. *Give us a chance and we'll fix this!* Perception was more important than truth. Crimes rates were dropping, not rising ... but people seemed unable to distinguish between reality and the fiction of American TV dramas and sensationalised local newscasts.

And so the statement that change will be revolutionary, not incremental, doesn't seem to come across as frightening. It appears to be a promise forcefully made. And when such a promise is made, not to carry it out demands expeditious retribution. Consider George Bush and "read my lips". He broke this promise not to increase taxes within months and was turfed from office at the next opportunity. The Harris Tories were making such a pledge and taking on the potential of such punishment if they failed to live up to their words.

But that was only the beginning of the promise.

I have been troubled by these realities for some time. I fear that Janet and I cannot hope for a better future for our children. I want to do something about it. So, today I'm putting forth a plan to help build a better future.

There are more than half a million people unemployed in this province. The bottom line is that Ontario needs jobs.

This plan will create more than 725,000 new jobs over the next five years.

Ontario is among the highest-taxed jurisdictions in North America. There have been 65 tax increases in the past decade, including 11 hikes to your income tax.

This plan will cut your provincial income tax rate by 30%. Government spending has more than doubled in the past ten years, pushing both the tax burden and the provincial deficit higher. This plan will reduce non-priority government spending by 20%.

Too many services essential to the public are now being cut, or are under such financial pressure that the quality of service is in danger.

This plan guarantees full funding for health care, law enforcement, and education spending in the classroom. A decade of tax-and-spend economics has pushed our annual deficit over the $10 billion mark, mortgaging our children's future.

This plan will fully balance the budget in four years. This is not a wish list or a bunch of empty political promises.

This is a solid plan based on four years of study, analysis, consultation with workers, employers, party members and ordinary Ontarians through extensive public hearings.

To be sure of our conclusions, we subjected this plan to an independent analysis by one of Canada's leading economic experts.

In short, our plan will work, and bring hope, opportunity and jobs back to Ontario.

For people who had, for the most part, been battered by four years of declining economic fortunes, belt-tightening, and a lack of hope, this hit all the major concerns – more than enough jobs for the unemployed and, by intimation, more job security for those still with a job, a tax cut which will

give people back some much-needed cash, along with a balanced budget
that forces government to become more efficient. And the plan is backed
by the chief economist of a major investment firm, lending it legitimacy.

However, already, claims are being made in the document that stretch the
truth. 'Ontario is among the highest-taxed jurisdictions in North America'.
Yes, and no. Yes, most American states had lower taxes, but they don't
have public health care as we do. Include that cost, and most Americans
pay more than we do. And no. Ontario taxes were some of the lowest in
Canada in 1995. While the statement might be technically true, it was
morally and realistically false. This playing with the truth was a habit to
which the Tories would become addicted.

But the CSR offered more than just fiscal responsibility. Ontarians had
long believed that they lived in the most dynamic and forward-thinking
province in Canada. The CSR wanted to confirm this, as well, while
pointing out what had gone awry.

*There is nothing wrong with Ontario that a new vision, a new direction
and turn-around management can't fix.*

*We can build a safe and prosperous province, but first we need a major
change in the way government works.*

It will not be easy, but it CAN be done, and it WILL be worth it.

*In order to create the jobs we so badly need, and to renew our
economy, we will have to set priorities and stick to them. Tinkering
with the system will not be enough. It is time for fundamental change,
and change is never easy.*

*The political system itself stands in the way of making many of the
changes we need right now.*

*Our political system has become a captive to big special interests. It is
full of people who are afraid to face the difficult issues, or even talk
about them. It is full of people doing all too well as a result of the
status quo.*

We need a revolution in this province....a Common Sense Revolution.

*It will be a revolution of practical ideas for making government work
better for the people it serves, and a revolution against the last ten*

years of government thinking when it comes to job creation.

Ontario needs jobs today, and jobs tomorrow.

This plan will show you how this can be done....how Ontario can once again become an economic powerhouse, full of hope, opportunity and real jobs.

If you believe, as I do, that we need lower taxes, less government and 725,000 new jobs in Ontario, I am asking you to join me in my fight for a Common Sense Revolution.

- Mike Harris

Note the comment that 'our political system has become a captive to big special interests. It is full of people who are afraid to face the difficult issues, or even talk about them. It is full of people doing all too well as a result of the status quo.' This was a direct reference to the NDP and the seeming deference it had to interest groups, apparently at the expense of ordinary people. Employment equity (more money) was available for women and minorities. Multi-million-dollar programmes had been established to help a few hundred disabled or immigrants. And while the unions screamed about the Social Contract, the fact was they were being insulated from the job losses everyone else had to face. And while many people might, or should, have been offended by being lumped into these, they weren't.

So the promise of the *common sense* of pragmatism returning to government couldn't help but be enticing. As for the *revolutionary* application of it, many might consider this less an overthrowing of government than perhaps changing the manner in which politicians had governed in recent years.

It should be noted that, along with the economic affirmation, it was Harris who fronted this. It wasn't his plan, *per se*, but it was his to put forward and 'If you believe, as I do, that we need lower taxes, less government and 725,000 new jobs in Ontario, I am asking you to join me in my fight for a Common Sense Revolution'. But it was his plan in as much as he was its head salesman, and like anyone good in sales, he had to believe in enough of it to make you believe in it, too.

But this was just the beginning. The document then laid out the five key components of the job creation plan. Many commentators, including the

Tories, would come to confuse these five as *The Common Sense Revolution* itself, but that was not the intention. There was much more to the CSR than these *bare bones* promises.

1. CUT PROVINCIAL INCOME TAXES.

Our tax rates, which are currently among the highest in North America, will be cut by 30% over three years, with half that cut coming in the first year. This plan will give Ontario the lowest provincial income tax rate in Canada. For an average, middle-class Ontario household, this will mean tax cuts of more than $4,000 in the first three years alone.

2. CUT GOVERNMENT SPENDING.

Total spending will be reduced by 20% in three years, without touching a penny of Health Care funding. Other priority areas of law enforcement and classroom funding for education will also be exempt.

3. CUT GOVERNMENT BARRIERS TO JOB CREATION, INVESTMENT AND ECONOMIC GROWTH.

This will send a signal around the world that Ontario is open for business again. Immediate action will be taken to:
- *Abolish the job-killing payroll health tax for small businesses*
- *Eliminate all red tape and reduce the regulatory burden*
- *Freeze Ontario Hydro rates for the next five years*
- *Cut WCB premiums for all employers by 5%*
- *Repeal the NDP's job-killing labour legislation – Bill 40*
- *End inter-provincial trade barriers through bilateral negotiations*
- *Encourage the private sector to provide child care for working parents.*

4. CUT THE SIZE OF GOVERNMENT.

We will provide the people of Ontario with BETTER for LESS. There isn't a household in this province that hasn't had to make the family budget stretch further, and there isn't a company in Ontario that hasn't found creative ways to cut costs and improve products or services at the same time. It's time we demanded the same from the people we elect and the bureaucrats that we hire. Performance standards will be set for all government services. The best people, in or out of the public service, will be hired to provide those services.

5. BALANCE THE BUDGET.

*This plan will fully balance the Ontario budget in four years. An
independent econometric model shows that, by the fifth year, Ontario
will be in a position to cut taxes even more AND start paying down the
provincial debt.*

Already, the plan began to make its points over-and-over. 'Our tax rates,
which are currently among the highest in North America ...' '... Job-killing
... tax ...' '... BETTER for LESS ...' If the Tories knew how to do one
thing, it was pound their points home with people. Even if they strained
credulity, a point made often enough does tend to sink in and gain
credibility that way.

And despite the earlier comment that these changes wouldn't be easy to
make, the CSR does an elegant job of playing down the *pain* that would
come with *gain*. Tax cuts mean a cut in revenue. Where will that money
be made up or, if not, how will the cuts be made to make up the
difference? Government will be cut by getting rid of staff, but what of
these new unemployed? But, of course, details were promised later on in
the plan, where we will be told that they will be taken care of through
private sector expansion.

LOWERING YOUR TAXES

*Ontario is among the highest taxed jurisdictions in North America.
Our taxes have been raised 65 times since 1985, and that includes 11
hikes to personal income taxes.*

*This excessive burden drives away new investment and jobs, and makes
it incredibly difficult for us to compete, not only in the global
marketplace but against other provinces.*

*Consumer spending accounts for 60% of our economy's activity.
Reducing taxes stimulates consumer spending and investment, a direct
boost to job creation. In fact, taxes MUST be cut if we want to create
jobs.*

*And that will only be the start, only the tip of the iceberg. With more
dollars in your pocket, with more of your friends and neighbours at
work and paying their way and with government operating more
efficiently – we are convinced that Ontario will experience much
stronger and more broadly based growth. This plan is really a vote of*

confidence in you and in our province. There is no telling what we can accomplish if initiative and hard work are rewarded once again!

"Having reviewed the Mike Harris plan, I am convinced that the tax incentives for people and business will help create an economic climate of dynamic growth and new jobs in Ontario."
- Bill Young, CEO, Consumers Distributing.

It is perhaps fortunate that the CSR and the election came and went just prior to Consumers Distributing going bankrupt but, they say, timing is everything.

Though there are still no real details, this is where the Tories unveil the rationale behind much of the scheme. 'Reducing taxes stimulates consumer spending and investment, a direct boost to job creation.' It was stated as a fact and, apparently, justified by the economic testimonials of Mullins and Young.

As well, the comment is made that 'there is no telling what we can accomplish if initiative and hard work are rewarded once again!', as though these had somehow become lost virtues, presumably under the NDP and Liberal governments.

INCOME TAX

We will cut your provincial income tax rates by 30% in three years. Half of the cuts would come up front – in year one.

These cuts will return billions of dollars to taxpayers in the first three years alone.

For a middle-class family of four making a total income of $50,000, this will mean more than $4,000 in tax savings in the next three years alone. And these savings will continue, year after year.

... These are the actual amounts of money that would be saved....the amount that would go into YOUR pocket, NOT the government's.

These tax cuts will give Ontario the lowest income tax rate in Canada. It will re-set our income tax level back to rates not seen since 1976.

These tax cuts will be the first step in redistributing wealth and decision-making power away from the politicians and the bureaucrats, and returning it to the people themselves. That's what The Common Sense Revolution is all about.

So, the CSR was guaranteeing that money would go back to the people for them to choose how to spend. This was a theme the Tories would carry on for most of their first term in office, as was that of the next section. The redistribution of wealth and decision-making would leave those in government and return it to people. Given that the redistribution of wealth had, since the late 1960s, been from rich to poor, presumably its change from government to 'the people' was a signal that this was going to change. If people were going to be able to keep more of their own money, then it is reasonable to say 'rich to poor' was going to end, at least to some degree, and the rich would be allowed to keep more of their own money.

ONLY ONE TAXPAYER

Historically, municipalities have responded to provincial funding limits by simply increasing local property taxes. There may be numerous levels of government in this province, but there is only one level of taxpayer – you.

We will work closely with municipalities to ensure that any actions we take will not result in increases in local property taxes.

We want to ensure that municipalities and regional governments do everything possible to deliver services more efficiently. You'll find more information on our policies for local government in the "Less Government" section.

In fact, the notion of there being 'only one taxpayer' would usually be used against the federal government when the provincial Tory one demanded they cut taxes, too. Of course, when they actually did cut federal taxes, it would cause the province a little difficulty. But more about that later.

The Tories also pledged a "Fair Share" health tax to offset the elimination of the 'job-killing' employer payroll tax. Lest they be seen to be giving too much money back to the rich, this tax would apply to those making $50,000 a year or more. At $50,000, the amount would be $100 and would rise as incomes rose. But the Tories were careful to state that "an average middle-class family will still save more than $4,000 over three years". In fact, the Fair Share health tax was supposed to make up for more inequities of the past though it was, in fact, financed primarily on the backs of the middle-class, not the wealthy.

For some time now, there has been growing debate over the most effective way to ensure more responsible use of our universal health care system. In the last decade, user fees and co-payments have kept rising and many health care services have been "de-listed" and are no longer covered by OHIP.

We looked at those kinds of options, but decided the most effective and fair method was to give the public and health professionals alike a true and full accounting of the costs of health care, and ask individuals to pay a fair share of those costs, based on income. We believe the new Fair Share Health Care levy, based on the ability to pay, meets the test of fairness and the requirements of the Canada Health Act while protecting the fundamental integrity of our health care system.

Under this plan, there will be NO new user fees.

In fact, this Fair Share levy, 'based on the ability to pay' and meeting 'the test of fairness and the requirements of the Canada Health Act' gave people the notion that the Tories were indeed not playing to the rich, and that they believed in universal public health care. And as the NDP had been accused, not unfairly, of instituting a plethora of fees for government services, this stress on 'NO new user fees' must have been re-assuring.

As important as these earlier parts were, in addition to the tax cuts, there can be little question that the core of the CSR was the cuts to government spending. If there was one area of which the NDP had been publicly seen as losing control, it was spending. Fair or not, that was the perception. And the Tories were clear that the Liberals had been out-of-control spenders as well. They had just been fortunate enough to have a good economy to cover it up through tax hikes. The CSR was clear on the point that the Harris Tories would be different.

LESS GOVERNMENT SPENDING

Over a three year period beginning immediately after the election, total spending, except for health care, will be cut by 20% – twenty cents on the dollar. Law enforcement and classroom funding for education will also be exempt.

On our current estimates for 1996 revenues and expenses, spending will be reduced by $3.605 billion in the first year. At the end of three years, this plan will have reduced annual government spending by $6 billion.

Ontario government spending has more than doubled over the last ten years. Between 1985 and today, the budget increased from $26 billion to $53 billion. Year after year, in good times and in bad, spending has continued to rise, adding to existing programs and creating many, many new ones.

To be fair, Ontario has grown and inflation has driven costs higher. However, even after these factors are taken fully into account, the Ontario government still spends far more than it needs to.

As a result of this uncontrolled spending, Ontario is broke! As the money has run out, our political system, unaccustomed to setting priorities, has come under increasing pressure. Without a clear sense of priorities, the lack of new revenues has meant that the quality of EVERYTHING the government does has suffered.

That includes the priority services such as health care, education and law enforcement that all of us want to see maintained.

But, it goes deeper than that. As government's appetite for cash has grown, it has turned to us, the taxpayers, to bail it out.

The first place the government has looked to satisfy its appetite for money has been your pay cheques, leaving each of us with fewer dollars to spend on the things we need for ourselves and for our families.

This has to stop. We need to get our priorities straight.

That's what The Common Sense Revolution is all about.

We want to provide efficient government service. That means setting priorities, cutting out fat and waste, and putting people first.

The key here was that 'EVERYTHING the government does has suffered' due to its inability to come up with 'a clear sense of priorities'. Had they priorities, they would have known to protect 'health care, education and law enforcement'. The CSR was saying the Tories had these priorities and the CSR was an outline of them. In other words, the cutting would take place in other areas that were not real priorities. Had they actually outlined what they were thinking of chopping, it might have expanded priorities for the public a great deal.

There was the promise not to cut health care. "It's far too important. And frankly, as we all get older, we are going to need it more and more." But at the same time, it did wedge the issue slightly. "As government, we will be aggressive about rooting out waste, abuse, health card fraud, mismanagement and duplication. Every dollar we save by cutting overhead or by bringing in the best new management techniques and thinking will be reinvested in health care to improve services to patients." So what they were really saying was there would be cuts based on inefficiencies, but the money saved would be returned to the system. This did not guarantee the *status quo*, just that the same amount of money would be spent. However, it might fairly be said that a person not reading this clearly might not have come away with this impression.

In law enforcement, the CSR stated, "The people of Ontario are rightly concerned about community safety in our province, particularly the increasing incidence of violent crime. That is why funding for law enforcement and justice will be guaranteed." However, details of how they would "make our communities safer and our justice system more efficient at less cost" was left to their policy paper, *New Directions III: A Blueprint for Justice and Community Safety*, which was not included for public perusal. And, "again, any savings we find in our justice system through greater efficiencies will be reinvested to ensure public safety in our streets and in our homes".

The CSR also guaranteed "classroom funding". This would become a particularly divisive phrase over the next years. While it was not defined, *non-classroom funding* seemed to be. "Too much money is now being spent on consultants, bureaucracy and administration. Not enough is being invested in students directly." They neglected to mention the status of clean classrooms and text books.

But it wasn't just money. The Tories wanted to make sure people understood they wanted to "ensure that this essential service is protected and, indeed, that excellence in education and training is enhanced. Education reform is essential if Ontario's next generation is to find high-paying, productive jobs in increasingly competitive world markets." However, they also left their proposals for another policy document, *New Directions II: A Blueprint for Learning*.

The CSR then returned to its economic base. How would they "find the savings"? "Consensus among Ontarians is that there is plenty of fat to be cut, and many ways that government can reduce its spending without affecting services." They identified nine areas to cut, far less in order of the amount to be saved than the symbolic effect they would provide. As a result, the first proved they were willing to accept the 'pain' themselves.

You have told us that we have too many politicians. Under this plan, we will reduce the number of MPPs from 130 to 99, simply by using the same boundaries we use to elect federal MPs. We will enter into discussions with the federal government to ensure the new boundaries are fair.

Not only does each politician draw a salary and an expense allowance, but we must also pay for their office staff at Queen's Park and in their riding. Cutting the number of MPPs by 24% will set an example of cost-cutting to be followed by all levels of government and all departments and ministries.

As well, we will end the sweet deals politicians have created for themselves. Under this plan, MPPs' pensions will be abolished and replaced with an RRSP contribution program similar to those used by other professionals in Ontario. The tax-free benefits paid to politicians will also be abolished. They will be paid a straight salary, just like ordinary Ontarians.

These measures will save Ontario taxpayers another $1.1 million. With fewer MPPs, we can also cut the cost of running elections by working co-operatively with Elections Canada to do the job. We estimate that this could save Ontario taxpayers an additional $10 million.

Given a $53 billion budget, this 0.0002% saving was pretty small. Yet it showed that they were willing to accept that times had changed and they had to absorb some of the cutting that other regular people had already suffered. The big point here was less the cuts to numbers than the elimination of the *gold-plated pensions* that many people perceived they received. An RRSP was what anyone could get themselves. The Tories were going to treat politicians like they were ordinary people. They weren't greedy and wouldn't get *drunk on power* and take advantage for their own personal gain.

More savings could be found in restructuring what they portrayed as a burgeoning civil service.

The provincial bureaucracy has grown by leaps and bounds over the past ten years. Not surprisingly, the government has tried to hide the exact number by talking about "person years" and by putting a vast number of bureaucrats on contract.

We are convinced that top quality public services can be provided at less cost, with fewer people. We will trim the cost of the direct provincial government workforce by 15% – the equivalent of some 13,000 employees, returning the system to the approximate size it was in 1985. Some parts of our current system may no longer be needed at all.

This will save Ontario taxpayers $650 million over two years.

Where possible we'll make our reductions through attrition and retirement packages. Where necessary, this process could mean cutting some positions. We are confident that the tremendous growth in the private sector will provide ample job opportunities for those who may be displaced.

Savings would be had by eliminating unnecessary staff, but they failed to deal with who would be declared as such. And they would get a golden parachute, not through pricey buy-outs but through 'the tremendous growth in the private sector'. But, of course, there was no growth in the private sector at this time, quite the opposite. And as their actions would show, the Tories had no intention of waiting for employees to leave through attrition and retirement. They had every intention of the swinging the axe firmly and fast as soon as they took power.

However, far greater savings would be had through welfare reform. This took up several pages of the CSR. Yet it went much further than savings. Welfare was the Tory bogeyman and had to be attacked.

We want to open up new opportunities and restore hope for people by breaking the cycle of dependency. That will be the goal of our welfare reform. The best social assistance program ever created is a real job, and this plan will generate hundreds of thousands of those. In the meantime, we must move to control costs and help people return to the workforce.

The facts are staggering. In the recession of 1982, just a dozen years ago, total welfare costs in Ontario were $930 million. Coming out of the current recession, we have four times as many people in the welfare system, and our costs are more than 6 times higher - an astonishing $6.3 billion a year.

We believe that government can play a key role in providing opportunity to those who want to get off welfare and back into productive lives. That's why our plan includes a commitment to invest $500 million in new and innovative programs to help those most in need and those who genuinely want a hand up, not a hand-out.

'A hand up, not a hand-out' was a key phrase, one which would be used by virtually every Tory candidate, over-and-over again, throughout the election campaign and afterward. The point was very simple. It wasn't supposed to just appeal to middle-class citizens but to the people actually receiving welfare benefits. 'The best social assistance program ever created is a real job, and this plan will generate hundreds of thousands of those.' And, in one way, this was a tacit admission that people on welfare really did want jobs and to pay their own way. Either that or public relations' wording to con gullible voters.

If the 'astonishing' $6.3 billion a year cost of welfare was supposed to scare or disgust people, I'm sure it did, especially given the comparison to $930 million from 1982. However, this six-times-more in cost relative to four-times as many people made it sound as though benefits had risen 50%. At best, this can be described as disingenuous. In fact, given the 56.9% rate of inflation over 13 years, benefits were far lower in real terms, barely $10 a week more on a per person basis.

But the CSR went much further, both with the carrot and the stick. While criticizing "a (welfare) system that justifies the existence of the bureaucrats who run it, but fails to work for the people who need it", the CSR touted plans for change. It contained five parts: "workfare" and "learnfare"; children in need; seniors and the disabled; welfare fraud and overpayments; and, welfare benefits.

Workfare and Learnfare, or so they were titled, were not specifically defined, and the latter would never come to pass. However, the CSR did say that people ...

... want to replace welfare with a work, education and training social policy that rewards individual initiative and demands responsible behaviour from recipients of public assistance, even as it expands opportunities to achieve self-sufficiency. ... We should prepare welfare recipients to return to the workforce by requiring all able bodied recipients – with the exception of single parents with young children – either to work or be retrained in return for their benefits.

However, the Tories did recognize "there are no short term cost savings in this, but we believe that for every life we get back on track we are avoiding further costly programs down the road." The platform also saw that charitable groups and other community organizations would be needed to make this come to pass, as well as the government to set up a Youth Jobs Corps, "which will provide younger people with the opportunity to learn new skills while doing useful work for their community". Of course, the Tories didn't set this up.

Our obligation to those in need is even greater in the case of our children. Children living in poverty suffer from significantly higher infant mortality rates, lower life expectancies and tend to receive poor nutrition and education. As well, there are nearly 200,000 welfare families headed by single parents. Children in those families face even greater challenges.

For this, the CSR also proposed solutions. Because "studies have found that children who go to school hungry tend to do poorly in class, are more disruptive and suffer more health problems", it offered a community nutrition program for school-aged children. "With leadership from the Premier, and with private sector and volunteer support, a breakfast or nutrition program can be implemented at little or no cost to taxpayers." In other words, the Tories never intended a government of theirs to institute and run such a programme. It would be entirely voluntary.

A "Learning and Earning and Parenting" programme was offered for up to 23,000 young, single parents on welfare if they stayed in school and completed their educations. For their children to get into child care, and for bonuses in their welfare cheques, they would also have to meet undefined attendance standards. There would be Homework Assistance Centres, based on a project in the North Bay area, which would be community-based centres staffed by volunteers to serve as tutors and role models. "Such centres will help motivate students, improve their school work, increase their appreciation for learning and enhance future employment opportunity." Such centres never came to pass.

As well, a Tory government would change the enforcement of child support, mostly to get government out of it.

While inroads have been made in collecting child support over the past few years, there are still hundreds of millions of dollars owed to parents and their children. However, the current mandatory program of deducting child support from parents' pay cheques has created an overburdened bureaucracy that fails to help all neglected parents and children.

There are thousands of children paying the emotional price for their parents' separation because of tensions and disputes between the separated parties. A program of mandatory mediation will help resolve many of those problems and reduce the need for courts or government to intervene.

Government should concentrate its efforts on tracking down "deadbeat" parents and enforcing payment orders. Parents who have reached amicable separation settlements and who have no dispute over support payments should be able to opt out of the government-mandated program. In the case of disputes, an immediate return to the mandatory deduction system will occur.

While this might have seemed like three throw-away paragraphs, they were far from it. The Tory attempt to clean-up this system would cause them a great deal of trouble.

And while the CSR promised to "establish a new and separate income supplement program" to remove 170,000 seniors and the disabled from the welfare system, people who "should never have been there in the first place", it was only to be directed at those "specifically ... unable to work." But it was clear that "aid for seniors and the disabled will NOT be cut". However, the definition of those who are 'disabled' did change and, in fact, cut the numbers receiving some kind of assistance.

Yet the CSR also took a dim view of welfare fraud and overpayments. It would be an important component of many of the changes the Tories would make once in power.

Every penny that is paid to the wrong person through mistake or fraud is food taken from the needy. Fraud and overpayments must be stopped.

The government has already admitted to the existence of massive overpayments in welfare benefits. One estimate runs as high as $247 million since 1990.

The government seems unable to tell how much fraud there is in the welfare system. Until recently, it denied there was a problem at all. Estimates of welfare fraud have ranged from a few million to hundreds of millions of dollars.

A province-wide computer system coupled with a strictly enforced program of photo-identification for all welfare recipients will be at the centre of this effort.

Improved management techniques, stricter eligibility requirements and fraud reduction will save Ontario taxpayers more than $500 million over two years.

Yet the CSR was not very specific about how to solve these problems beyond 'a strictly enforced program of photo-identification' and 'improved management techniques' and 'stricter eligibility requirements'. And the claim of $247 million in fraud over five years worked out to less than 1% of the money paid to welfare recipients. Regardless, 'every penny that is paid to the wrong person through mistake or fraud is food taken from the needy', and that is clearly true ... assuming the Tories had planned to recover such funds and reimburse the poor with them.

But the document went much further.

Ontario pays the highest welfare benefits not only in Canada, but anywhere in North America. This is one of the reasons our welfare caseload has swollen to record levels. The simple fact of the matter is that we can't afford it.

Our plan will set welfare benefits at 10% ABOVE the national average of all other provinces. This initiative is fair to all involved.

It will save Ontario taxpayers $1 billion.

Under the plan, a family of four currently on welfare would receive less than it gets today. However, we will allow anyone on welfare to earn back the difference between the current rate and the new, lower rate without penalty and without losing their eligibility.

Under the current rules, a welfare recipient who earns extra money is penalized. This discourages initiative and encourages welfare dependence.

Although the amount of money involved may not be large, the possibility of part-time work opens the door for welfare recipients to learn new skills, work towards full-time employment and increase their self-esteem.

We will devote $100 million to a joint program between the public, private and volunteer sectors to ensure those opportunities are there. Any welfare recipient who is willing to work will be able to maintain their income at the current level.

For most, this 'fairness' was eminently appealing. It offered benefits above the average, yet their reduction meant these recipients had to pay the price most regular people were already paying with the poor economy. And given the inability of the government to stop the deficit's rise, the 'common sense' simplicity of 'we can't afford it' was undeniable.

That having been said, however, there were *outs* built into this section. 'Our plan will set welfare benefits at 10% ABOVE the national average of all other provinces.' '... All *other* provinces.' They weren't planning to include Ontario in the average, a move which would significantly lower the average.

'Any welfare recipient who is willing to work will be able to maintain their income at the current level' ... assuming there are jobs available. Given that Ontario had been in and out of recession for five years, this seemed a big assumption.

After this significant section of the CSR, it resumed its "find the savings" portion with promises on reforming education. This was an area of greater natural concern for people and the Tories had to be extremely careful. Simply proposing financial cuts to education would have been received with tremendous trepidation, perhaps outright rejection.

For years now, we have been spending more and more on education, but getting less and less in the classroom. International comparisons have shown us all too clearly where Canada stands against its global competitors in this field. ... Interprovincial comparisons are worse. Ontario spends $14 billion a year on primary and secondary education – more per-pupil than any other province – and still gets a failing grade.

We believe Ontario's education system is in need of system-wide reform, based on the principles of providing opportunity to students, excellence in curriculum and teachers, and accountability to parents and taxpayers. Our education reform plan is spelled out in our policy paper, "New Directions II: A Blueprint for Learning". Here, we will concentrate on how these reforms can reduce the burden on taxpayers.

The education system needed to be made better for students, but the CSR focused on the money that could be saved through reform. Again, for details on the rest, there was another policy paper that was not readily available.

The CSR had five areas of proposed change, the first being on "setting priorities".

A large part of the problem is how little of our education investment actually reaches the classroom. Under this plan, we will move to a system of "classroom-based budgeting".

A greater share of our education spending must go to children in the classroom, not to "edu-crats", consultants and managers. More than 45% of the education personnel we are paying for don't teach. The system pays hundreds of millions of dollars to duplicate work done in other Boards and by the Ministry.

Fundamental review is also required of the duplication of services and staffing among School Boards themselves.

Cuts in these areas will save Ontario taxpayers at least $400 million.

There are currently 171 school boards in the province. There are boards representing English public schools, French public schools, English separate schools and French separate schools. Most of them run their own transportation services, do their own planning and make their own purchases. Bureaucratic barriers stand in the way of more cost-efficient methods of operation.

When the province of New Brunswick reduced the number of school boards from 42 to 18, the change saved five million dollars in the first year.

Of course, constitutional guarantees of separate school education must be respected, while at the same time, providing the best possible education in the most effective manner.

With a core curriculum set province-wide, and with standardized testing at all levels, we know that we can spend more efficiently, while improving the quality of education we offer to students.

Central to this reform will be increased autonomy and decision-making for each school, and a significantly increased role for parents and community leaders.

A core curriculum and standardized testing appealed to many, especially those who felt that kids were not getting as good an education as they had when they were young. A bit of work and discipline might well get the "lost ones" back on track.

Savings would come from eliminating duplication and the wasteful practices of school board administrators. And since practically no one likes school board administrators, this promise couldn't have helped but be a popular commitment ... as, of course, would be the one regarding school board trustees.

Somehow, the system has lost the idea that people run for school boards as a part-time commitment to make education better for our children. Too many of today's trustees have become full-time politicians with a full-time salary, paid with our tax dollars. Across Ontario, hospitals and universities with huge budgets and charitable organizations with large client bases are managed by volunteer boards. We are convinced that top people will also help manage our schools without being paid high salaries. We believe that our children's education should be overseen by citizens, not politicians. So, we will enter into discussions with trustees and parents, to establish new job descriptions and methods for remuneration.

Again, this change would effect the administration of school boards primarily, avoiding any classroom disturbance. But asking for volunteers to look after the system was indeed revolutionary. Clearly, 'citizens' had shown sufficient disinterest to let 'politicians' take over the school boards. The Tories were unclear on why they would suddenly become interested. And they really didn't want to get into the vast staffs of hospitals and universities and the costs associated with them.

However, while the avoidance of classroom cuts might have been sacrosanct, eliminating entire classrooms was not.

The role of the primary school system has been expanded over the last few years to include much younger children. Government has continued this trend by making Junior Kindergarten mandatory for all primary schools as of the new school year in September.

There is growing uncertainty among educators and parents about the wisdom of busing three- and four-year old children and putting them in formal classroom settings. Until a complete review has been made of the impact of Junior Kindergarten, we will allow school boards to opt out of the program.

In fact, there was no such 'growing uncertainty'. There was, however, great concern that the government had opened itself up to seriously increased education funding demands with mandatory JK, and the Tories were not about to ally themselves with that..

As well, the sanctity of classroom funding did not apply to post-secondary institutions. Though it was to be applied in a different way, the result was the same. The amount colleges and universities had to fund themselves would not drop, the revenue stream would just be altered somewhat.

Our universities and community colleges have suffered from government's failure to set priorities. A lack of sufficient funding has resulted in lower quality service to students.

Providing proper funding will mean charging students a fairer share of the costs of the education they receive.

In 1992, a university student's tuition fee represented only 19% of the total cost of his or her education for the year. In the 1950's (sic), by contrast, tuition fees represented 35% of the total operation costs of a university program. We propose to partially de-regulate tuition over a two year period, enabling schools to charge appropriately for their services. This will enable Ontario taxpayers to save $400 million while maintaining funding for our post-secondary system at current levels.

Access to higher education is central to our long-term economic potential as a province. We will implement a new income-contingent loan program, similar to others being introduced around the world. Our plan, to be called the Equal Opportunity Education Fund, will mean that no student with appropriate qualifications will be denied access to funding. Student loans will be repaid in the years after graduation, as a percentage of income on each student's provincial income tax form. Because repayments under this program are geared to future income, students will never be required to repay more than they can afford.

Estimates differ on the total cost of establishing such a plan. However, experts agree that such programs, with strong private sector involvement, can become self-financing in the medium to long term with considerable future savings to taxpayers.

We will work with all concerned parties to ensure that this program will provide equality of access to our essential post-secondary education system.

Now the Tories must have understood that this would cause some middle-class parents to be concerned. Partial deregulation of tuition guaranteed that student debt would rise. However, for anyone without children headed off to a post-secondary education, or for youthful Ontarians who were bypassing this option, it must have seemed quite fair to put more of the financial load onto the people who would benefit from such an education. As well, with a system of loan repayment contingent on future earnings, on the surface, it did seem that these students would not be unfairly punished.

And the final proposal of the CSR on education reform was to change the number of years that high school students spent at that level.

Ontario is the only province that still has a five-year secondary school program. Reducing this to four years would save an estimated $350 million a year.

This program would have to be phased in, to allow time for curriculum schedules to be changed and to make sure current secondary school students are not affected. Any reductions in the number of teachers required could be managed through attrition.

Increasing the number of school days in a year from 185 to 190 would bring Ontario into line with Alberta and British Columbia, and approximate the instructional levels in Great Britain. The quality of our secondary education would be protected.

This was a major change, and the Tories must have expected it would raise some eyebrows. However, they made little effort to hide that this was for the purpose of saving money. In fact, they under-estimated the savings. The 'reductions in the number of teachers' would also reduce wages being paid, and this would be a significant saving, too. But for one of the few times in the CSR they were quite clear. They were going to get rid of teachers.

The CSR proposed a further five ways of saving money. Generally, they appeared smaller and of less importance to most who would read the document. They had little resonance with the average person. Generally, this was probably correct ... at least with all but one.

The jobsOntario programme of the NDP was to disappear. It had placed far fewer people in jobs than had been hoped, and most of its budget had been lost to bureaucracy, according to the Tories. Government grants and subsidies to business were to be cut, as were those to arts and cultural programmes. The former was corporate welfare, just as unacceptable as individual welfare. The latter was unnecessary, especially in bad times. If people want art and culture, the private sector will step in to offer it. Also, the capital budgets for transportation were to be reduced. This would affect highway construction, GO Transit, municipal roads and transit, and some airports. Legal aid was to be changed to reduce its fees and use by "repeat offenders", so costs would be cut to 1989 levels. Total savings from these changes would be almost $1 billion.

The other reform was to save $250 million and still would not affect many people. However, for those it would touch, it would be a profound change. Funding to build government-owned and operated public housing would end and be replaced with a shelter subsidy. "By spending money on people instead of bricks and mortar, we will be in a position to eliminate the two-year waiting list for affordable housing." This signalled a fundamental change in housing for the poor. Of course, the housing subsidy would come to naught, which made for a much larger savings in the end.

The third major point of the CSR was "dismantling active barriers to job creation, economic growth, savings and investment". The argument was very simple.

The Ontario Government has been driving jobs out of the province through 10 years of ideologically-driven legislation and over-regulation. No-one knows for sure how many jobs these policies have cost us, but estimates range up to the hundreds of thousands.

We do know that many businesses looked at Ontario as a prospective location for expansion or new investment, compared us to other provinces and U.S. states, and then gave us a pass. It doesn't have to be like this.

New Brunswick would have had a much tougher time wooing

employers, large and small, ten years ago. The decision there to make some of the same kind of economic reforms we are proposing here has revitalized the economy of that province and made it more competitive. The same thing has happened under a Labour government in New Zealand.

We don't have time in Ontario for a sterile political debate using the outdated labels of "left" and "right". In our opinion, it is time to stop the arguing and take the common sense, practical steps we know will work here in Ontario.

That's what the Common Sense Revolution is all about!

The types of reforms the Tories were intimating were much more radical than these few lines suggest. Though New Brunswick had established a more business-friendly environment, its changes were not anything in magnitude compared to New Zealand. This country had bankrupted itself, then savaged public services to save themselves. However, *salvation* didn't mean they hadn't continued to run deficits to pay for their tax cuts for the rich.

A number of "key steps" were listed to deal with this 'over-regulation'. The Tories proposed cutting payroll taxes, eliminating "red tape", reforming Ontario Hydro, cutting Workers' Compensation Board premiums, labour law reform, abolition of inter-provincial trade barriers, and giving people a freer choice in child-care. In fact, much of this had little to do with ideological legislation or over-regulation.

As it had already stated, the CSR proposed eliminating the Employer Health Tax on small businesses. It added detail, in that it would apply to companies with payrolls less than $400,000, supposedly to save them an estimated $400 million. This was considered most important as it was "small business" that created 80% of the new jobs in Ontario and they had to be competitive.

As to "eliminating red tape", the CSR made a couple of dubious claims, that the province "passes up to a thousand new regulations" each year and that "employers have to devote the equivalent of a month's work every year completing forms and complying with regulations". It stated the Tory promise to "appoint an arms-length commission on red tape to review all current regulations affecting business" and, within a year of taking office, to eliminate "any regulation which can't be justified".

They also committed to a five-year freeze on Ontario Hydro rates. This would "give consumers, employers and industries guaranteed stability in planning their budgets ... to bring Hydro back to its proper role, providing reliable and affordable electrical power to Ontario." It also suggested that "some moves (might be made) towards privatization of non-nuclear assets".

And in another move to counter 'ideologically-driven legislation', the CSR pledged to cut Workers Compensation Board Premiums by 5%, for a saving of $98.5 million for Ontario employers. They planned a total restructuring in order "to restore business confidence, protect workers and bring fiscal sanity to the Board's operations". They also promised to eliminate the unfunded liability of the WCB by 2014, "as demanded by the Employers' Council of Ontario".

The Tories said they would repeal the NDP's labour legislation, Bill 40, because it was a "proven job killer". This statute had made it easier for workplaces to be unionized. In order to "restore the balance between labour and management", the Tory paper intoned, "we will also shift power from labour bosses to union members, restore individual choice and democratize internal union decision-making by introducing secret balloting for certification and strike votes."

The CSR blamed the federal government for not ending the "job-killing inter-provincial trade barriers", though it didn't give any examples and failed to point out only the provinces could end these barriers. The document stated they cost each Ontario family as much as $1,000 a year in lost income and the CSR pledged the Tories to immediately "initiate bilateral trade negotiations with any interested province" in order to "break the current log-jam by offering to work with any other government that is willing to co-operate in driving down costs", such as "shar(ing) the costs of administration for transportation".

The Tories also looked down on "the NDP's efforts to nationalize all child care operations". By this, they meant that the Rae government had proposed forcing minimum standards for child-care that would have effectively meant only those who were certified could operate such centres. The Conservatives took much the opposite view. "... We will open more options for parents to choose the kind of care they want for their children. This will encourage more centres to open, allowing more single parents to find the daycare spaces they need while working." This would include private ones with lesser standards or even home baby-sitting by anyone.

DOING BETTER FOR LESS

The people of Ontario have been sending a clear message to government for many years now, "We are not getting value for our money".

The fourth part of the Common Sense Revolution will mean a sweeping change in the attitudes of those inside government and the expectations of all of us who consume its goods and services.

The fact is that each of us invests more in government that we do in anything else ... our homes, our children's education or planning for our retirement. We depend on the government to provide us with some of the things we need most in life, such as health care, community safety and education. And yet, we don't demand the same quality of service from government that we expect at the corner store.

In too many cases, wasteful spending has become entrenched in the system. We will weed it out.

All too often, public servants are ignored or even punished for trying to improve the system. We will reward them.

For too long, government has grown larger and still failed to meet the needs of the people. We will put people first.

Many of the things that government does can be done cheaper, faster and better if the private sector is involved. In England, property tax collection and some welfare payments are being administered by private sector firms. The result .... lower costs, higher collections, less fraud AND more money for genuinely needy recipients. In Michigan, just over the border, every government function is being opened to private sector scrutiny.

Bids are welcome from anyone who thinks they can do the same service better and cheaper.

The Common Sense Revolution will have a significant impact on the way in which government and its employees do business on a day-to-day basis, because it will demand that government does business LIKE a business. In other words, in an efficient and productive manner that focuses on results and puts the customer first.

In many ways, this section is the key part of the neo-conservative manifesto. It states pretty much the ideological belief that will govern the entire Harris *revolution*. 'In too many cases, wasteful spending has become entrenched in the system'. 'For too long, government has grown larger and still failed to meet the needs of the people'. 'Many of the things that government does can be done cheaper, faster and better if the private sector is involved'. 'The Common Sense Revolution will ... demand that government does business LIKE a business'. In other words, *business is good, government is bad*. If government can be made to be business-like, it too can be good. So ... how to do this? The CSR's prescription is "spending smarter", "less government", and "asset sales".

SPENDING SMARTER

We will reduce the costs of government administration. The same kind of innovations being employed in the private sector are likely to produce even greater savings when applied to government's bloated bureaucracy.

We will look at creative ideas for increasing the private sector's role. We will create an expenditure review committee called the "Fat-Finding" Commission with a mandate to find waste that can be cut, and ways of simplifying the government structure.

We estimate that this new initiative will save Ontario taxpayers $500 million over two years.

The budgetary system within the government bureaucracy must also be changed. Right now, the system actually encourages the waste of public funds. For example, a department must spend all of the money allocated it in a fiscal year in order to get full funding for the next year. This encourages wasteful spending, particularly towards the end of each fiscal year. Instead, departments should be encouraged to save money and be rewarded for efficiency, not waste.

Another way we will prevent wasteful spending is to legislate mandatory "sunset clauses". A sunset clause is a requirement that when a new government program is created, a set date for termination of that program is included. As the date approaches, the program is reviewed and either terminated, changed, or continued.

There are other initiatives we will take to encourage smarter spending. Performance bonuses for all public servants will be based on both results and savings to the taxpayer, and senior civil servant salaries and benefits would be disclosed to encourage greater accountability and restraint.

We will start pilot projects measuring taxpayer satisfaction with a number of direct services (e.g length of line-ups at driver's licence offices) and explore ways to directly link a part of public servants' pay to this measure. If leading, forward-thinking businesses can make this shift, then government can do it too. This change will be genuinely exciting and genuinely revolutionary. We'll have attractive, fast-tracked career paths in the Ontario government for smart, efficient, change-oriented women and men – people genuinely committed to "public service".

We know there are many more sound ideas for making government more efficient. The Ontario Public Service Employees Union has developed several common sense proposals for ending waste and duplication. We will work with government employees, listening to their ideas and eliciting their help in taking action.

LESS GOVERNMENT

Canadians are probably the most over-governed people in the world. We do not need every layer – federal, provincial, quasi-governmental bodies, regional, municipal and school board -- that we have now. We must rationalize the regional and municipal levels to avoid the overlap and duplication that now exists.

The example being set by a Harris government, of a 24% reduction in the number of MPPs and a 20% cut in non-priority spending, will set the benchmark for municipal politicians and trustees. We will sit down with municipalities to discuss ways of reducing government entanglement and bureaucracy with an eye to eliminating waste and duplication as well as unfair downloading by the province.

Different solutions may well apply in different regions across this province. But by the end of our first term, taxpayers deserve a restructuring of these cumbersome bureaucracies. This will save Ontario taxpayers $250 million.

Resolving the issue of efficient local government will take a great deal of hard work. It is rare that politicians and bureaucrats voluntarily surrender power. But it must happen. It's time to stop government growth once and for all.

ASSET SALES

We will sell off some assets, such as the LCBO and surplus government land, to the private sector. We will actively explore the sale of other assets, including TV Ontario. History has shown that the private sector can use such assets more efficiently and provide better service to the public.

We believe the value of such assets is greater when being used to pay down the massive provincial debt than sitting on the government books.

Marketable provincial assets will be transferred to an arms-length corporation charged with their sale. Strict criteria will be established for selecting which assets we sell, and rigid guidelines will be established for protecting the public interest.

When a deal for a sale is made, it will be independently reviewed. A rigorous conflict of interest policy will be enforced and the entire process will be open to scrutiny by the Legislature and the public.

The money we make from such asset sales will not go into the government accounts. Every penny will go directly to pay down the $80 billion provincial debt.

So the Tories were promising to liposuction the 'bloated bureaucracy' to remove unneeded 'fat', make the civil service more accountable to the government and the public, reduce the amount of government overlap or entanglement, and sell off parts of government where the private sector could give better service to the public. While specifics were minimal, it was clear that this was both a statement of the beliefs of the Harrisites and a commentary on the ill-will that many ordinary citizens felt toward a civil service that they perceived as privileged. Finally, someone was going to whip them into shape, just as private employers had been doing to most of their workers.

The final section of the CSR dealt with a balanced budget. This was as much a promise for the rank-and-file Tory member who supported Mike Harris as it was for the public. When Bill Davis' government had been running up deficit after deficit, no one seemed to care. And when the Liberals did finally balance it, many seemed unhappy, including Harris, because they perceived it was done through tax increases. Even if the regular Ontarian did care, it was mostly because the deficits under the NDP had been so shockingly large that the province's most cherished programmes seemed to be in danger. For Harris and most of those around him, deficits had been unacceptable even back with Davis.

This portion of the CSR concentrated on jobs though, after outlining the frightening "facts": the debt had tripled over ten years to $80 billion, and it cost $8 billion a year to finance it. "It's obvious that immediate action is needed. The longer we wait, the harder it will be to stop the death spiral and begin paying off our massive debt." The CSR failed to mention that money would have to be borrowed to pay for the promised tax cuts and would, thus, deepen the 'death spiral' before the government even tried to pull out of it.

This may be the one area where the CSR does less to try and convince people why this is a good thing. Balancing the budget is presented as a good in itself. Other than stating it will help avoid future tax increases, but no explanation of why this is true, the CSR only makes the connection that a balanced budget will "stabilize the economy" and help create a "good jobs climate ... to attract new businesses and investment".

The document ends with saying that the Tories have $5.53 billion in cuts proposed, but that $500 million more are needed, and asks people to contact them with suggestions.

We believe this plan represents the best way to reach our destination – more jobs, lower taxes and less spending. It is the result of four solid years of work by thousands of people from all parts of the province. We are proud to put it on the table.

This is only the beginning. We want this document to stimulate an open, vigorous and honest discussion about Ontario's economic future. Let us be very clear .... we are unconditionally committed to reaching our goals, but we are very open to discussing how we get there. If there are better ideas out there about how to cut spending, reduce waste and improve efficiency, we want to hear them!

When this plan is implemented it will mean major change in Ontario. It's a Common Sense Revolution in the way our province is run. That's precisely why we have released the details of the plan now – so that you can think it through, ask questions, and perhaps help us find other, better ways to reach our goals.

We want you to join the Common Sense Revolution. If you believe that it is time to put Ontario on a different track .... If you believe we urgently need hundreds of thousands of new jobs.... If you believe that the way to get there is by cutting spending, balancing our budget, and giving you your money back in tax cuts so that you can be free to work, compete, create and achieve -- then this fight is YOUR fight.

That's what the Common Sense Revolution is all about!

Join the Common Sense Revolution.

Call us, toll-free, at 1-800-903-MIKE.

Though the CSR presented literally dozens of ideas for voters to cogitate, it may have been most successful for displaying a coherent philosophy throughout. Many political platforms present proposed programmes and costs, and they usually have segments that are reasoned and logical, but they're designed to appeal to some voters here, some there. The CSR set a whole new level of cogency for these. It had such a high level of ideological *purity* that it stands out stylistically as well as in substance. Even if average people did not understand it, or read it from front to back, any one part of it might well have impressed them. Even if the media only reported it in "bites", much of the consistency would still get through.

This is also true for the apparent concern it showed for people. Yes, there was hard-edged economics with a tone that certainly was threatening to some, but there was also a continuing recognition of the stress and strain that people had endured over the past years. Hard years had been sandwiched between two recessions, and voters wanted someone to say they understood what people had gone through. The CSR delivered not just ideas but empathy.

Normally, people expected this type of kindhearted feeling from the NDP, the party of conscience and of the worker and his or her family. However, after almost five years of withering abuse and constant struggle, they didn't seem they had any more tears to shed.

2. End-Game NDP

If the NDP campaign strategy was a subcompact car, it was one that misfired on all cylinders while trying to climb an exceptionally steep hill.

By the time it was over, the car had stalled and rolled backwards into the ditch. From the start, it was based on a premise that was just plain wrong. The New Democrats might be able to win or, at least, thwart crushing defeat.

The NDP refused to make promises and ran on their record, one of which they claimed to be proud. It was the height of foolishness, though I don't suppose they saw any other choice. As Bob Rae said in his book, "We would run on jobs, fighting for Ontario, and the capacity we'd shown for making difficult decisions."[2] The caucus felt this was the way to go, and most pushed for a spring 1995 election, afraid to wait until fall, which would have taken their mandate to its last day – a plan that usually reeks of desperation.

The strategy they did choose, however, came out little better. Running on their record, with no promises, left the impression that the government had no plan for another term. As Thomas Walkom, the *Toronto Star* columnist, wrote shortly into the campaign ...

> ... *Like Peterson in 1990, Rae refuses to be specific about how he would exercise this leadership if re-elected. Rae says he wants to continue as Premier because he has much that he wants to do. But he never says what. His government says it will have to cut spending dramatically if re-elected. But it won't say where. The Premier talks of defending medicare against Ottawa's cutbacks. But he doesn't explain how. ... Indeed Rae kicked off his campaign by saying it would be irresponsible for him to be specific about what he might do in a second term. This kind of trust-me strategy sometimes works for popular governments seeking re-election. But it's not clear it will work for a government that is at 20 per cent in the polls.* (Toronto Star, "NDP campaign reminiscent of Peterson's", 4 May 1995, p. A27)

Nevertheless, there was talk of another NDP platform booklet, like in 1990. However, given that *An Agenda for People* was now a printed record of broken promises, it must have seemed a poor idea to remind too many of it with another written list.

It was Arlene Perly Rae, the Premier's wife, who would write the government's epitaph. She "felt that a 'no promises' campaign left voters with the sense that (they) had run out of steam and had nothing more to offer." "'Your approach has tons of integrity and no politics' (she told her husband). She was right."[3]

What the NDP leadership seemed to miss was that they had alienated their own supporters with the Social Contract and they had scared most other voters by driving up debt and taxes. Perhaps the saddest aspect was that even many of the very poor rejected the New Democrats. The Tory promise of a 'hand up, not a hand-out' gave them the hope they didn't see expressed in the NDP's lifeless campaign.

To misuse Thomas Hobbes' most famous phrase, their campaign was solitary, poor, nasty, brutish, and short. Solitary in the sense that Bob Rae seemed almost alone in the defence of his party. Poor in that it did not seem to have a lot of money, or friends, behind it. Nasty in that it took the brunt of vicious barbs from both the Tories and Liberals. Brutish by being run on a coarse, ill-conceived strategy. Short in that most of the NDP seemed to give up at least a couple of weeks before the election.

Though it is easy to say in retrospect, the NDP might have suffered a lesser defeat had they simply conceded that defeat, in private to themselves, at the beginning and focused on winning their core urban ridings. Instead, the Premier fought a very regular campaign, crisscrossing the province, speaking to crowds that often had as many protestors in it as friends. In this case, fighting the good fight probably made the NDP's defeat even more complete.

3. Liberals on cruise control

So what were the Liberals doing as the NDP term in office came ever closer to expiring? They were counting their chickens, so to speak. To put it simply, they thought the New Democratic victory in 1990 was a fluke caused by David Peterson's mistakes, and their *40-year rule* would be soon restored. And there were few observers who did not expect them to win the election. The party was, and had been, floating around 50% in the polls for some time. Though leader Lyn McLeod was not well known, it was thought she would firm up apparently already-strong support from female voters. Truth is ... few of the campaign team thought she needed to be known. Who was going to beat them?

However, these seemingly terrific poll results masked some serious difficulties the Liberals were experiencing. Their days as Official Opposition had done nothing to fill the party's empty coffers. The central party might have been out of debt, but it didn't have anything close to enough to fight a full election. Though, for some time, it had appeared very likely they would shortly be forming the government, neither individuals nor the corporate community warmed up to them to any degree. Middle-class voters were getting beat up by the extended poor economy and were in no mood to part with their hard-earned cash. Most riding associations were still in debt from 1990. The general mood of negativity meant membership had fallen from hundreds, or even thousands in some associations, to dozens. A handful had even collapsed, without enough people to run an executive. And corporations were not attracted to what they saw, a party that might have seemed to be leaning to the right-of-centre but still didn't walk-the-walk of a pro-business party, as the Tories did. Though a Lyn McLeod government might not have seemed reminiscent of the Peterson regime, who they had identified as spendthrift and anti-business, they were unconvinced that the Liberal leopard had changed its spots. As a result, the Liberals were in no position to fight anything but a fiscally meagre campaign, especially at the local level.

As well, some Liberal associations made terrible decisions in choosing candidates. Fourteen of the 130 were MPPs defeated in the 1990 election. Perhaps this is the observation of a political scientist, but it doesn't take much research to find that, once an elected member is defeated, they are almost unelectable again. Whether their times are seen to have passed, or the character and history of a local member is more important than a central party will admit, it is unclear why they usually lose ... but they do. (In two different Liberal meetings prior to the 1999 election, and another in late 2001, the attendees were told the local candidate is just 15% of the reason voters choose a party. This may be so ... it may not be ... but, in a close election, it may well be the determining factor.) In this case, just one of the 14 was actually victorious, and six of the 13 who lost did so by more than 10,000 votes ... in ridings that were more winnable than most.

But there's no question the biggest problem for the Liberals was over-confidence. They knew the NDP was on its way out, and they didn't take the Tories seriously.

And so the Liberals waited, fat and expectant. Elated by their healthy lead in the polls, they dreamed pleasant dreams of power, measured the government offices for curtains, mentally doled out the cabinet posts among themselves. (Toronto Star, "Harris wins gamble voters were looking for a straight talker", 9 June 1995, p. A16.)

They expected to win the election by doing nothing beyond the ordinary, and that's pretty much what they did. They planned for a typical campaign, not taking risks, preparing to drop 5-8 points in the polls while being attacked by the NDP and Tories, then rebounding when voters realized how insubstantial were the promises of the other two parties. It didn't happen that way.

Critics of Harris don't like to give him and his people much credit, yet they really stole the election from the Liberals. Of course, the Liberals were accomplices in the "theft". Some ink was spilled on pointing out how the Liberals blew the election through a series of gaffes, such as an 82-page policy book with 143 promises. In effect, it said so much that it said almost nothing anyone could understand. But what it did say seemed to mirror the Tories' CSR. And the Liberal's sloppiness in policy wasn't new. For example, the one serious mistake that came to the fore during the campaign came from McLeod, when she couldn't explain her complete turnaround on the issue of benefits for gays and lesbians.

The NDP had tried to put forward a package on legal recognition of same-sex pension benefits, and adoption for gays and lesbians, in 1994. In an April 1993 by-election in the St. George-St. David riding in downtown Toronto, the new Liberal leader, Lyn McLeod, had offered her support and that of the Liberal caucus for same-sex rights. She even wrote a letter to Bob Rae asking for his government to entrench these rights in law. But when this bill was put forward in May of 1994, one of its provisions permitted adoption rights, as well. Since it was to be a free vote, McLeod knew a number of her caucus would vote against this, both for personal reasons and because the Tories had just won the March Victoria-Haliburton by-election by opposing such rights[4]. Whether or not she personally opposed the bill seems questionable. At any rate, she said the proposed legislation should be limited to work-related pension benefits and dental coverage, not adoptions, and refused to support it. Then, when Rae offered to remove this provision, she still refused, apparently without reason. As a result, the bill died on Second Reading, when the Tories, 12 NDP and all but three Liberal members went against it.

Then, come the 1995 election campaign, McLeod had softened her stance even further. She was now no longer willing to have a government of hers present any legislation on homosexual rights, saying she wouldn't stop a private members' bill though, but knowing full well private members' bills succeed about as often as the Chicago Cubs. It was not that the public disagreed with this attitude, as much as it was that the change in Liberal party stance seemed to come on the wind, without reason beyond caucus timidity.

This public uncertainty about McLeod wasn't helped by her second day of campaigning. She stood in front of reporters and pointed out boxes of postcards that supposedly were responses about auto insurance from a

concerned public. Instead, they were mostly cards about health care. And
she backed off on a commitment that a government of hers would bring
down rates 15%-20%, saying she would make sure rates didn't rise by that
much.

While it is clear she made bad decisions on these issues, was sloppy,
and/or she received horrible advice – and it clearly damaged both
McLeod's and Liberal credibility – it was the Tories who brilliantly
pounced on them and turned the mess into a memorable TV commercial,
reminding the voters of the stereotype that Liberals were like weathervanes
... they simply went with the wind, standing for nothing. (Interestingly,
this was a rip-off of a commercial used against Bill Davis in 1981.) On the
other hand, they, the Conservatives, had real beliefs. All you had to do
was read their promises and you'd see that. And that was very impressive
for many in the electorate, who had tired of politicians who stood for little
and seemed to govern by polls. Even if you questioned the Tory beliefs
(or didn't understand their ramifications), you had to respect them for
having convictions.

But the Liberals did offer tangible policies. Taking a shot a Bob Rae for
not saying how the NDP would govern in a second term, McLeod unveiled
her party's plan, which laid out a timetable for commitments to be kept in
increments of one month, three months, and one year. On the economic
side, they committed to cut $1.7 billion, or 5%, in provincial income tax,
cut spending by $4.1 billion (though with $660 million in new spending),
business would receive tax breaks of $417 million, but would lose $114
million in grants, there would be a tax break for first-time home-buyers,
and 170,000 families with less than $50,000 in taxable earnings would be
able to deduct $1,000 for each child under 5, if they had spent that much
on day care, at a cost of $350 million per year.

McLeod said that welfare recipients, except the disabled and elderly,
would have to do volunteer work, take training, or go back to school to
collect their full benefits. Refusal would mean a reduction in their
cheques. Funding for health and hospitals would be frozen, but there
would be no user fees. One Cabinet minister would be appointed to coordinate all children's services in the province. There would be public
scrutiny of senior civil service and university president salaries. The MPP
pension plan would be replaced with an RRSP, and double-dipping by
former MPPs (taking a pension and a government job at the same time)
would be stopped. Lobbyists would have to register with the government
and publicly declare for whom they were working. University and college
tuition increases would be limited. Emission testing for cars would be

brought in to catch bad polluters. The distribution of violent video games, videos, computer programmes, and serial killer cards would be restricted. Also, Go Train service would be extended to Guelph, Kitchener, Barrie, and Peterborough.

As to the Liberal position on actions taken by the NDP government, some would stay and some would go. Assistance to build four subway lines in Toronto would continue. The law to ban *scab* workers during strikes would be kept, but with exemptions to exclude companies with under 20 workers, and permit work to be contracted out at a different location. They would also keep the drug plan for the working poor, and the NDP promise to cap school trustee's salaries and bring in a standardized report card. The Liberals were going to return to a quasi-no-fault auto insurance system with a cut of the added 5% tax. They would scrap the plan for a government takeover of home care and homemaking services, cut some commissions and jobsOntario. They would restore international trade offices closed by the NDP, return out-of-country OHIP coverage to a maximum $400 per day, and reverse the law that cities could ban basement apartments in certain neighbourhoods.

The problem was that many of these policies were quite similar to those of the Tories, just watered down to make them more acceptable. At least some Liberal strategists thought they were acceptable. Other Liberals were actually concerned that this resemblance was dangerous, not to mention that some of the pledges were not something Liberals should support. Mike Harris himself noted several items seemed taken from the pages of *The Common Sense Revolution*. The Tories had promised mandatory workfare. The Liberals responded with "mandatory opportunity". The Tories had their 30% tax cut. The Liberals came forward with one of 5%. The Tories would rid the civil service of 13,000 workers. The Liberals 12,000. The Tories would balance the budget in five years. The Liberals would do it in four. The Tories would dump NDP labour laws. The Liberals would just reform them. In short order, the Liberal red book was dubbed "Blue Lite" and the point was made that it might be better to vote for the real thing rather than the pale imitation.

The Liberals, perhaps because of their expectation of victory or maybe because the people running the campaign weren't the best qualified (by now, a number of strategists had moved on to work for the federal Liberal government), could not seem to counter the Tory punches. They saw the poll numbers drop, as expected, but they watched as the numbers kept going down. They had no strategy to deal with this, and the campaign floundered. As the swells got bigger and did more damage, many senior

Liberals simply stopped bailing water and hoped they could hold their breaths long enough to swim out of their sinking boat. They couldn't.

4. *Hot buttons*, sharp knives

The "Mike Harris Team" as they preferred to be called (disdaining *Progressive* Conservative), made perhaps the greatest use of *hot button* issues that has ever been seen in Canada. Hot buttons are issues that seem to rile up people, in many ways, irrationally.

In the last months of the NDP government, its members were determined to make a last ditch stand for their beliefs. (For some of their supporters, this was far too little, too late, and they weren't shy about saying so.) For some, this was the New Democratic team conceding the election but hoping to stave off the kind of slaughter the federal Tories had suffered in 1993 by rallying their traditional supporters. For others, it was the NDP showing themselves as the *party of justice* – the vision they had of themselves – in hopes of pulling out a long-shot win. Yet instead of making it a big promise for a re-election campaign, they passed a bill, just before the election, guaranteeing province-wide employment equity for women, visible minorities, natives, and the disabled. Since it would not come into effect until September, you had to actually vote NDP to make sure you'd get it. It was symbolic – a sort of left-wing pledge to unionists and voters of social conscience to bring them back into their camp.

The Harrisites, however, portrayed it much differently. To them, it was not only something that personally offended their neo-conservative sensibilities, but it was incredibly stupid given the present economic situation. They termed it the "quota bill" and pointed to it as proof the NDP had no idea what it was doing. It would "breed mediocrity", "ignore merit", and "compromise excellence". It would undoubtedly cost the government more money and, given a projected $8 billion deficit, that was insane. It would cost business more money, thus destroying much-needed jobs. And it would give preferential treatment to certain segments of society and, if society wanted true equality, no one could have that.

Who knows if somewhat better crafting of the bill would have made any difference. Though no hiring quotas were stated, the bill was heavy on numbers and statistics, and it gave critics a lot of ground to suggest that quotas were hidden inside it or, at least, quotas were really the intention of the NDP and would eventually appear. To say that reaction was fair would be wrong. There was no requirement for a 50% hiring target for any of these groups. There was no requirement to hire unqualified people simply to make up numbers in occupations that lacked equal representation of these groups. In fact, the legislation gave two full years for employers to come up with a plan for their operations, without hiring a soul. In the end, the *Employment Equity Act* was pretty fair. It just didn't fit with the prevailing mood.

Did it matter it wasn't the bogey the Tories portrayed it as? No. At a time when young, white, middle-class men couldn't find work (and the perception was even worse than the reality), it seemed almost an insult to them and their parents. A sexist or bigoted view? Absolutely, but it just didn't matter. It was a visceral issue that played directly to those from whom the Conservatives sought support – white men and their families. This issue did not come from the CSR, but it was still manna from heaven for the Tories.

Could the NDP government not have seen this overwhelming criticism coming? Apparently not. In his book, all Bob Rae had to say on the subject was "we underestimated the Tories' willingness to run a vicious campaign that appealed to public fear and emotion".[5] Sun Tsu said know your enemy and know yourself. Clearly the New Democrats didn't have a good handle on their own minds, for they certainly did not understand the depth of their opponent's amorality.

Perhaps the biggest hot button issue was welfare and welfare fraud. In a long recession, people worry more about themselves and less about others. In other words, self-interest is the prime concern. The Harris strategists understood this and played to it unmercifully, even if that meant stretching the truth well into a lie. They claimed up to 5% or more of all welfare money was being paid out fraudulently. They had no proof of this. In fact, most experts in the field believed it was 1% or less. (Almost all research backed up this view.) And even their numbers in the CSR worked out to less than 1%.

The real problem was that most people believed they knew someone, or knew of someone, who was a welfare cheat. There was always a house or apartment where someone had a party the day the welfare cheques came out, or showed up with a taxi full of groceries. It didn't seem to matter that poor people often can't afford their own cars and have to get a cab for large purchases, nor that they usually have to buy a lot at once, because they can only afford the cab once. Nor does it matter that the revellers may have friends who can afford beer, or that partying household includes just one cheat in a neighbourhood of several thousand inhabitants. People believe what they believe and, when the economy has been bad for five years, as it had been by 1995, catching cheats is a remarkably popular pastime. The Tories were relentless in playing up the need for tightening this system, one portrayed as full of corruption and incompetence.

It is also certain that the error of the Hulgaard incident did not change the beliefs of the Ontario Tories. Come election time, they were again suggesting it was necessary to cut welfare benefits, as the NDP had increased them to the point where, they hinted, people were moving to Ontario to collect such benefits. Far less subtly, they again indicated that those on welfare preferred to stay on it because it paid much better than working. These were both ludicrous statements yet, despite the opposition parties saying as much and the Hulgaard affair proving part to be untrue, the media never really called the Tories on the claims. While Ontario's benefits had risen to highest in the country under the NDP, they were lower compared to cost-of-living. And though the Tories promised to *only* cut them to a level 10% above the national average, by 1999, benefits were just fifth-highest compared to average income, and this still didn't consider Ontario's higher cost-of-living.

Harris also pledged to make people on welfare work for their benefits. In this way, it would be "a hand up, not a hand-out" as Harris loved to say. People would gain dignity, and experience they needed to get real work. To most Ontarians, who had been suffering from the prolonged slump in the economy, this seemed very fair. Even the NDP had brought in a system that required many on welfare to return to school to get their money. There is also no question that many currently collecting welfare benefits favoured Harris' plan. For the first time in years, a politician was apparently offering hope. He recognized that many of these people had been stuck on welfare for years, and *workfare* would allow them to get the training they needed for real jobs ... or so he said.

The Tories loved to hold up the state of Michigan as the shining example of welfare reform and workfare. There, rolls had dropped by 90,000 single adults and 80,000 families over the first term of Republican governor John Engler. But what Harris and his candidates failed to point out was what Michigan had done to gain these seemingly impressive numbers. Elected in late 1990, at least in part, to reform the state's welfare system, Engler had wasted little time. By autumn, he ended General Assistance to over 80,000 single, able-bodied individuals with no dependents, leaving them with no recourse but to find jobs, become dependent on their extended family and friends, move out of Michigan, or starve.

However, along with this rather malevolent act, Engler had other real reforms. By the middle of 1992, the state established the inelegantly-named programme "To Strengthen Michigan Families". It was based on four principles: promoting self-sufficiency for welfare recipients by encouraging employment; targeting support to those who needed it most; increasing personal responsibility; and involving communities to help recipients. It allowed an increase in both the amount of money that welfare recipients could earn and the number of hours they could work without benefits being reduced.

In October 1994, the state created the *Work First*, work-for-welfare, programme. It required all recipients of cash assistance to work, undertake education and/or training, or volunteer for 20 hours per week to remain eligible for benefits. Food stamps were reduced by 25 percent for recipients who did not comply with employment and training requirements, and non-compliance for a year resulted in a recipient losing their benefits entirely.

In fact, the State of Michigan was actually spending more on social assistance than they had before workfare, even with many fewer collecting benefits. This was because of the new programmes to pay for child-care, transportation, and further subsidies for those on welfare to return to school. And though the CSR also said extra money would be spent, the Ontario Tory campaign actually said their work-for-welfare programme would save money overall. This was because they had no intention of setting up these extras and were just going to cut benefits. For them, it would free up considerable money they needed to help cut taxes. The bonus was that it seemed to be extremely popular with voters, and it fit nicely into the Harrisites' neo-con thinking – it was up to each person to sort out their own problems.

Another hot button was photo radar. The NDP had brought this forward in April 1994, ostensibly as a safety measure. Ontario drivers are notorious speeders, and this was supposed to slow them down on highways, particularly in-and-around Toronto. (Get on Highway 401 between Windsor and Toronto someday. The slowest cars are almost always those with American licence plates.) Bob Rae's caucus felt this was one way of dealing with accident rates (which were not rising, by the way) and congestion. For others (including myself), it was another fee being added onto taxpayers' backs. During their term, the NDP were terrible for introducing new fees for one thing or another. It was their way of trying to hide tax increases, I suspect. Between 15 August 1994 and 30 June 1995, these fines brought in just $19 million[6], however, far below expectations.

So when the Tories promised to get rid of photo radar, it was hugely popular. The fact that a study of the safety effects of photo radar was going to be finished in a few months didn't deter them. (The study was never finished, and cancellation of the photo radar programme also included a refusal to ever release the information the study collected.) In fact, once Harris was elected, ending photo radar was his first promise kept.

The final hot button issue of the election was regarding young offenders. There's no doubt that most Canadians and Ontarians have always had a problem with the federal legislation that limited the terms for criminal offenders under 18 years-of-age. It doesn't really matter if you are 15 or 50 if you murder someone. The result is a dead person and a family and friends who will always carry the pain. Though the feds believed that sending a young person off for 10-25 years with hardened criminals was a bad idea, society in general disagreed, and ignored that you often get an even more hardened criminal when they come out of prison. And most people believe if you give them a slap on the wrist for a fight or a stolen car, these delinquents will just get worse if they don't appreciate that severe punishment comes with crime. Did the Tories care they might create more dangerous characters? No. Did they care that the provincial government has no jurisdiction in the matter? No. They knew what the public felt, and they felt it , too.

As a result, they proposed boot camps for young offenders under provincial jurisdiction, with sentences of less than two years. And they went to great lengths to say that these delinquents should suffer a far greater wrath than prescribed by the *Young Offenders' Act*. The problem with that was they had no jurisdiction over it. Another federal matter they howled over was gun control.

There is no question that these hot button issues were at least as important as those raised in the CSR and, to some extent, mirrored them in attitude. All told, they presented a political party that had vision, believed wholly in that vision, and was not going to go soft once they got into office, even if they ran into trouble implementing the vision. Did people actually believe in it themselves? Not really. During the election, Mike Harris continuously ran into people on the street who said they liked the ideas, but didn't trust him to bring them to pass.

I seriously doubt most voters ever even saw a copy of the CSR, let alone really knew what was in it. The electorate, or 44.9% of those who cast ballots, heard the jargon-esque slogans of the CSR and heard the

Conservative party's positions on these *hot buttons*. They got summaries of the platform on TV clips and in newspapers. They had a positive gut feeling about the Harris Tories and they went with it. The NDP had blown its chance. Between the Conservatives and the Liberals, the former was the party that was offering simple, seemingly substantive, promises, and it was doing so with an attitude that fit the times.

There can be no doubt that the Tory campaign was the most energetic. From Day One on, Harris was the focus, even while he moved about the province from one stage-managed event to another. Initially, he was tense and awkward, and he tended to run off at the mouth. In London, a city with one of the province's largest universities, he commented that tenure for professors should be scrapped. Who should be guaranteed a life-time job? Nobody else was. However, as things wore on and the Tories rose in the polls, he became far more relaxed and comfortable with his scripts. He was able to stay *on message* and avoid further embarrassments.

In the meantime, both McLeod and Rae were having further troubles. At a campaign event, the Liberal leader stated that a woman should not be forced to abandon her home when abused by her husband, the abuser should have to go. The next day, a *Toronto Sun* headline screamed, "Yell at your spouse and lose your house". It was unquestionably unfair, but it flustered McLeod further and gave some the impression the Liberals were going to be just as *holier-than-thou* as the New Democrats were perceived to be. And the Premier, knowing the end was nigh for his government, began to increasingly lose his temper and concentration. At a rally in London, he halted in mid-speech to chastise a reporter for chatting with someone. At the National Rubber plant in Toronto, he proclaimed how his government's $7.9 million grant had saved the jobs of the workers, only to have it later pointed out it was the Peterson government that was responsible.

In the end, the fact that the CSR was mostly a mass of prejudice, exaggerations, and assumptions made no difference. The appeal was in the simplicity of its ideas and the fact that seemed to reward the *virtuous* while punishing the *malignant*. If you work hard and look after yourself and your family, you will be rewarded. If you expect society, through government, to look after you ... you're in for a big disappointment!

5. The blue tide sweeps in

Frankly, it was all over before election day. The polls showed definite and growing support for the Conservatives by the fourth week of the campaign. Tory advertising had spread their vitriolic message far and wide and it had turned passive ill-humour into more active discontent. Essentially, Harris was saying *kick the leftie leeches in government by voting for us*, and a plurality were in the mood for a good ass-kicking.

But there was another side, as well. Many of the disenchanted simply said a pox on all your houses and stayed home. Voter turn-out was a sad 62.3%. In effect, only 28% of Ontario's eligible voters actually selected the Harris Tories, yet they ended up with 63% of the seats, or 82 of 130, 44% of the popular vote, and an undeserved majority.

The election saw the province break up into discernible political regions. Historically, this wasn't unusual. Throughout the glory years up to 1985, the Tories had held much of northern, central, and eastern Ontario, and the Toronto region. The Liberals did well in southwest Ontario, the Golden Triangle around the horn of Lake Ontario and into Niagara Region. The NDP were particularly strong only in Toronto and Hamilton, and northern Ontario. When the Liberals came to power, their strong regions remained, along with serious advances in Toronto, the GTA, and eastern Ontario. Then, in defeat to the NDP, they turned over ridings in all these areas, with the victors dominating in all but eastern Ontario and the GTA. When the Harrisites were elected, they won in every region except northern Ontario and the Ottawa area. But what was noticed, particularly, was their total control over the ridings in the GTA, which the media erringly referred to as the 905 because these ridings fell under that telephone area code.[7]

However, at the risk of disputing conventional wisdom, these ridings had been Tory for most of the post-war period, so their return to that fold was hardly as surprising as commentators in the media made it seem. In 1981, the Davis-led PCs took nine of ten suburban Toronto ridings and, in 1985, even Frank Miller's poor showing still gave the Conservatives six of the ten. There can be no question, however, that the principles of the CSR seemed to resonate strongly in the GTA and 905. This area is mostly suburban and wealthier than much of the rest of Ontario, and survived the recession in a much better position than most of the rest of the province. When a party came forward saying people should look after themselves, and get tax breaks, it was a natural fit. Suburbanite Torontonians were very much the landed gentry of the 1990s and saw their self-made wealth as being in spite of government, not because of it. Yet it would be wrong to say that this was the only factor that helped the Tories, or that it applied to every voter in the GTA/905.

Another factor in the suburbs was ethnicity. The fast growth in these areas was also due to the number of immigrants who had come to the area over 30 years or so. Some had made good livings and were moving out of the burgeoning city and others were people setting up their own businesses and interests where land was cheaper and opportunity more apparent. Loyalties with immigrants are often formed with the party in power at the time they get to their newfound home. This had certainly helped the provincial Tories over time, as it had the federal Liberals. However, this changed somewhat in the late 1980s and early 1990s. As with all partisan affiliations, parties were losing their hold on ethnic segments. Many immigrants were arriving in Canada with more wealth than their predecessors, from countries where they had been anything but the oppressed poor. For these, supporting a party that upheld the interests of the better-off was in their self-interest.

Finally, there were ethnic communities that had seen their opinions overrun by larger ethnic groups in ridings. Whereas some Toronto area ridings had large numbers of Italian Canadians, and the active amongst them had managed considerable influence over many years, other ethnic groups had seen their differing opinions squashed by being out-voted. Naturally, over time, they gravitated to other parties so their opinions could be heard, and many had moved into the ring ridings surrounding the city.

So, in the 1995 campaign, the Tories had support from wealthier Ontarians, immigrant Ontarians who had moved away from the Liberals and NDP over a decade, and others who were still loyal to the provincial Tories from the 1960s and '70s, when they had come to Ontario. These were boosts that gave the Harrisites somewhat stronger than typical support, particularly in the GTA.

That having been said, it was probably just as important for the Conservatives that they were able to almost sweep southwestern Ontario. In the Davis majority of 1981, the Liberals bucked the trend and took 12 of 24 seats, the Tories with 11, and the NDP with one. It was a region the Grits had controlled for many elections before, and would again in 1985 and 1987, with 15 and 17[8] seats, respectively. However, in 1990, their stranglehold was broken, as many of the three-way splits resulted in NDP victories. The results were interesting, as the New Democrats took 16 of these seats. Most of these ridings were won by the Liberals in 1987, yet they became NDP-held ridings in 1990 which, in turn, became 14 Tory ridings in 1995. In fact, 10 went straight from the NDP to the Tories, apparently upsetting conventional wisdom.

Why have the Liberals lost their southwestern former fortress of support? The apparently obvious answer is that they no longer offer ideas that appeal to people who are primarily rural and small-c conservative. Yet, having said that, the policies of the Ontario Liberal party are not significantly different, in an ideological sense, than they were under the David Peterson government. Perhaps the leadership of the party is more restrained, and its economic views are more bridled. It might be argued that people in this area are more conservative, and that the Liberals became too liberal for their tastes. But they elected mostly New Democrats in 1990, who were obviously more liberal yet. In fact, this isn't the question. Clearly, these people have been thinking along the same lines as many in the rest of the province.

What needs to be considered is why people in southwestern Ontario were more supportive of the Liberals during the Tory dynasty. Did they not see the Tories as *progressive* conservatives, or did they not support this balance? It might be argued that many here preferred conservative progressives, or more traditional *business* liberals, who preferred the self-reliance of the farmer and small business owner. They didn't like being told what to do, and hated when government interfered with things that directly affected their lives. It was still very much the liberalism of Mitch Hepburn, and it pervaded much of the Liberal party right up through the 1970s. When Stuart Smith, a Montreal-born psychiatrist, took over after Robert Nixon, Brant County farmer, it must have been quite a shock. But it was the 1980s that began to alienate many from generations of party loyalty and, once it turned out David Peterson was very much like a John Robarts' Tory, some of the more conservative Liberals no longer saw the party as their exclusive home.

At the same time, the southwest was changing. Yes, much of it was still farmland, but increasingly few people made a living from agriculture. People were moving into the larger communities and, because of population growth, these were becoming the centres of political ridings. Urbanization was leading many away from a traditional voting pattern. Many were, in reality, becoming just as demanding of progressive change as Torontonians. When Peterson stopped delivering, it led them to the

NDP, then the Tories. The Liberal fortress had been breached, probably for good.

And then there's central and eastern Ontario, Tory bastions for decades. Or perhaps not. While the ridings that surround Lake Simcoe and southern Georgian Bay have been extremely solid in supporting Conservatives, the east has been much more a split between the Tories and Liberals. While it was fertile ground during the dynasty years, eastern Ontario has gone mostly Liberal since, with the exception of 1995. Of course, the Liberal success has been centred in the greater Ottawa region and Kingston, while most of the more rural and small-town areas remain primarily Conservative in support.

The one area where the Harrisites could not break through was in northern Ontario. This had been a region where they and the NDP had dominated for many elections. That is, until 1987, when the Liberal sweep crushed the Tories, dropping nine 1981 seats and seven 1985 seats to just two. In both 1990 and 1995, (and in 1999, for that matter) that was just one – Mike Harris' Nipissing riding. So why have northerners remained cool to Tory charms? The answer would seem to be that northern communities are much more dependent on government than those in the south. The promise of slashed programmes and civil service translated into fewer jobs and income, not more. What good is a tax cut if you have no job and very little chance of getting a new one? The Harris prescription for good times would, for many, mean leaving their homes and moving south. And there was no way to coat that pill to make it seem attractive enough to swallow.

The regionalisation of Ontario in 1995 was more re-run than original. Certainly, the *new* Tory coalition including the GTA was anything but. If there was any great change, it could be argued that the northern ridings actually deviated from the norm, not the GTA nor Toronto. During the Tory dynasty, much of Toronto supported the Conservatives. Voters there supported the Liberals when they won, the NDP when they won and, despite what time has made people think, they voted for the Harrisites in 1995, too. It would only be in 1999 when the majority of seats didn't go with the winning party.[9]

The fact is, most of the so-called regions of Ontario usually support the winner. By my estimate, every area has supported the election winner a majority of the last six elections, with the exception of the north which has only done so 50% of the time. The GTA has supported the winning party five of six times, with the rest south of North Bay having done so four of six times.

Probably more important than any regional divide, though, is the social cleavage the 1995 election started. Shortly after he was elected, Mike Harris stated that his government had not been elected to represent all Ontarians, just those who voted for them. This is known as narrowcasting – appealing to your core voters – rather than broadcasting – appealing to everyone. It is usually the option of a political party in trouble, trying to shore up its support. As a rule, parties want to expand beyond their centre to draw votes in from those who might support the competition. The bigger the tent, the more voters that can be under it. Many would say this is the thinking behind the Liberal party (leading to the accusation Liberals stand for nothing because people on one side of the tent may think the opposite of people on the other side).

It was unique for the party-in-power to govern with this attitude. Normally, one would expect to alienate some of the people who voted for you over your term. In order, then, to maintain your margin of victory, you need to replace those you lose. As a result, you need to widen your attractiveness to those who did not support you. The Harris Tories rejected this.

Strategically, it could be argued this was a smart move. Instead of *weakening* their message of revolution to make it appeal to others, they bulldozed their opposition, never even considering that those who didn't vote for them might have valid points. Of course, this was quite risky. If Tory voters changed their minds, even in modest numbers, the government could easily be lost. That meant it was necessary to deliver them significant benefits to keep their loyalty. And who were these people?

Polling has shown the core Tory supporter is a middle-aged-to-older male, with above-average income. They live all over, but especially in suburbia. Tax cuts were aimed right at them, as was every bit of the *fiscally-responsible* dogma of the Harrisites. As well, the personal responsibility agenda – not relying on the state – is attractive to those who are wealthier and more individualistic. In essence, the Tories writing up *The Common Sense Revolution* were appealing to themselves and no one else. However, had it not been that some others came along for the ride, they would never have succeeded.

The 1995 election signalled more than just *us vs. them*, it saw the possible beginning of the end of a political party that had fundamentally altered the Ontario scene over 50-some years. When the Cooperative Commonwealth Federation, or CCF, fought its first Ontario election in 1943, it ushered in an end to Conservative vs. Liberal and made possible the domination of the Tories, as some Liberal supporters were drawn to more radical change. But this arrival also heralded the beginning of *Progressive* Conservatism and the pattern that so accurately fit with the people's attitudes. That was then ...

The alliance of the CCF to labour may not have instantly changed the minds of voters as to the New Democratic party's legitimacy, but it did fundamentally alter the substance of the party and for what it stood. In my mind, this association both helped and hurt the NDP electorally, yet it was only when they finally came to power in bad times when this alliance was sufficiently tested to demonstrate it wasn't really there at all.

It is somewhat ironic that several months before the 1995 election, the NDP prepared briefing books to assist the next government as it came to power. They had received no such thing from the Liberals, and they felt it had contributed to their stumbling out of the blocks when they had taken office. Had they known it was the Harris Tories that would be elected, they might have reconsidered any assistance.

There is no doubt Bob Rae resented losing power to the Harris Tories.

We railed against the Tories, pointing out their 30 per cent tax cut would mean huge cuts in health care, insisting that classroom education and human services would suffer, decrying their latent appeal to resentment and prejudice. None of the Tory numbers made any sense. Nothing added up. (Rae, p. 307)

In the meantime, Mike Harris was proceeding apace with his revolution in Ontario. As each of his ministers went further down the path of the true believers, I took no great satisfaction in knowing that this is what I had predicted. Every cut, every slash, every anti-welfare taunt, every ritual scapegoating was a manifestation of the right-wing extremism that had taken hold of the Tory caucus after 1990. (Rae, p. 314)

Perhaps he also failed to recognize that his objectives and that of his supposed allies were not really the same, at least until it was far too late.

We never stopped fighting for jobs and work We refused to single out the poor and the needy for punishment. We refused to fire tens of thousands of public servants. We expanded health services, and strengthened the province's commitment to the environment, to equality, and to all its citizens. We insisted on partnership between business, labour, and government. We saved jobs, and tried to build a province ready to celebrate its diversity and tolerance ...

I am always learning again that life is too short to be bitter or to look back with recrimination or second guesses. The people have spoken, a new government with a very different perspective has been chosen, and we shall all have to live with the results. (From defeat speech, Rae, pg. 310)

Not that I would take issue with Bob Rae, only he knows what he was feeling on the night of his government's repudiation, but his words do seem to exhibit some bitterness, regardless of what he said. I'm sure he did indeed know what a Mike Harris government would do ... basically undo everything his government had worked to do for almost five years. If that didn't make him feel somewhat bitter, he's an exceptionally forgiving human being.

In a strange way, the unions assisted the Tories to bring about *The Common Sense Revolution*. When they decided that the Rae NDP had *done them wrong*, they mercilessly attacked them in the media, again and again. They withdrew support. Even come election time, they refused to stop the feuding, apparently blind to the threat posed by the Tory agenda. Then, with the Harrisites in power, they took the bait and went on strike, sandwiched on either side by one-day strikes known as *Days of Action* in nine cities. This is exactly what they should have known the government wanted. The only possible conclusions are that the union leadership was out of control and acting without thinking, or they didn't care about the results. Both sound ridiculous, but one or both must really be true.

In my opinion, it was a combination. The anger that affected Canadians and Ontarians was not exclusive to non-union members. Both public union membership and leadership were profoundly resentful of government that seemed to have done nothing but put them down. Getting the right to strike simply gave them an obvious route to follow to fight back against this perceived oppression. The logic of this muscle-flexing was entirely lacking ... or they honestly believed they could make an openly hostile government back down, which seems almost too naive to accept.

The other reality, one which I'm sure most would not admit to, is that union leaders are there to represent their members, and only their members. Once you cease to be a member, the union no longer holds any responsibility to help you. As Bob Rae said, in describing his *crucifixion* for the Social Contract ...

I learned that the leadership of the public-sector unions were more interested in the "sacredness" of contracts than they were in the importance of jobs, more concerned with protecting the full benefits of the survivors than the fate of the people tossed overboard. (Rae, pg. 246)

This seems to be a perfect description of the result of the March 1996 strike, as well. The union leaders knew job losses were coming. Instead of trying to save as many as possible, with pay cuts or work-sharing, they basically gave the government *carte blanche* to slash away. Those that remained retained their full pay and benefits. Those that did not could live off their severance and then apply for Employment Insurance, if they couldn't find a private sector job. Those that kept their jobs might feel badly for their unlucky colleagues but it's probably better than losing pay.

The Liberals took the 1995 defeat much better, outwardly at least. The ramifications were terrible though. The party instantly spiralled downward, losing members, organization, and donations. Two elections in a row they had been at 50-plus percent in the polls going in and had lost. How could this have happened? What happened?

For the Tories, victory was to be an orgy of power. Finally, for Harris and a few others, all those years of being outcasts had ended. This was their first opportunity to actually have any influence at all, let alone run the government. And run it they would. They would run amok.

Part 2 Endnotes

1. This was somewhat of a *fooly* for the media. While the central party might have been in the black, most of the ridings owed significant sums, especially to the central party.
2. Rae, op.cit., p. 305.
3. Rae, ibid.
4. This is the way it was portrayed in the media, at least. There are those who believe it was a small issue among many and was blown out of proportion by the Toronto newspapers.
5. Rae, op.cit., p. 307
6. Ibbitson, op.cit., p. 116
7. In fact, the Liberals and NDP won a sparse four 905 ridings, but none in the GTA, defined as those in Durham, York, and Peel regions.
8. In 1987, redistribution had actually dropped the area to 21 seats.
9. The Tories took 19 and 11 of 30 in 1981 and 1985 though, in the latter election, the NDP took 10 and the Liberals 9. The Liberals won 25 of 31 in 1987, the NDP 18 in 1990, and the Tories 17 in 1995. In 1999, the Liberals won 11 of 22, to the Tories' 8 and the NDP's 3.

Part 3

"Doing more with less"

Making promises to get elected is usually fairly easy, but actually keeping them is often difficult. Mike Harris was determined to make sure his government kept its promises, and as quickly as possible. And while that may have been a laudable goal, it led Ontario down a dangerous path it is still on. Instead of doing business as parliamentary rules demanded, they simply ignored or re-wrote those rules to suit their rush to action.

Keeping a promise, more than anything else, establishes legitimacy in the minds of those to whom you made your promise. If you do so quickly, not only is legitimacy created but it is greatly reinforced. Did the Tories realize this or were they just in a hurry to make changes? Perhaps a bit of both.

When Harris went ahead with pledges to do away with employment equity, photo radar, and make cuts to welfare benefits right away, he established a high level of trust with the voters, especially those who had voted Tory, but even with others. It was a credibility that would reinforce Conservative support right through the term and the next election, and get the government down a very rocky road largely undamaged. It also seemed to salve any doubts people might have had that the rules, and their rights, were being trampled upon in the process.

During the election, the governing New Democrats contended the deficit for 1994-1995 would be $5.5 billion, down by a third from their first year in office. As memory serves, both the Liberals and Conservatives rejected this as too low. Nevertheless, the Tories claimed surprise when they found out this was not an accurate assessment. As a result, more desperate measures were required ... or so said the Premier at the Walkerton inquiry, six years later.

Shortly after assuming office we were notified by the Ministry of Finance, all of us, the deficit was now projected to ten point six billion dollars ($10,600,000,000). And the Ministry of Finance, in conjunction with Management Board, made a request that we couldn't wait. We *had to immediately address this situation. So that was the context for these first reductions that we asked of everybody.*

In effect, a whole round of financial cuts that had not been planned was undertaken, almost immediately. It created a rush that came with some consultation with the ministries, but was mostly just the arbitrary application of cutting. Finance minister Ernie Eves' emergency measures were made up of a combination of CSR promises and knee-jerk moves. The reduction of welfare benefits, the end of jobsOntario and business subsidies and grants would not wait. Toronto would lose funding for one of its new subway lines. Ministries were told to immediately find a half-billion dollars in things to be cut. Municipalities would have to pay part of the costs of child care. School boards were to lose 1% of their funding. Low-income women would lose pay equity funding. As of 21 July, the Tories were almost $2 billion closer to their target.

But to bring off such sweeping change in such a hurry left the Tories with a problem. There was no doubt they anticipated delay tactics from the Opposition parties. While their strategy to get elected had made them some friends amongst voters, it had also made much of the rest of the population wary and fearful, and they must have realized such swift manoeuvring might actually spur the Liberals and NDP to attempt to bog them down in legislative rules. Regardless, I'm sure they felt this was no time to be delayed or distracted. Instead, they took the bull by the horns and planned a pre-emptive strike.

1. The omnibus bill

The practice of putting many bills together into one, in an attempt to pass them all at once, is known as an "omnibus bill". Historically, omnibus legislation has been seen negatively because of the tendency to pack so much into such a bill that it cannot be given careful consideration by either elected representatives or the public. Passing bills of an omnibus nature is often seen as a method of trying to slip covert measures past people rather than as an efficient use of time. For example, when the Mulroney government used this type of legislation to enact the Free Trade Agreement with the United States, most elements were so little discussed that they still cause concern, such as selling water. Unfortunately, omnibus legislation is being used more and more often and, as a result, people's contrary reaction has been dulled.

On 29 November 1995, the government brought forward its first economic statement. Though they had already made $2 billion in cuts, this would be the first ones that were actually planned. Minister Eves announced transfers to municipalities, school boards, hospitals, universities, and colleges would be slashed by $3.5 billion in the coming fiscal year, and another $2.5 billion over the following two years. Municipalities would lose $706 million over two years for programmes like recycling, libraries, and transit. School boards and post-secondary institutions were to lose $800 million in the first year. Hospitals were being cut $1.3 billion over three years.

As well, Eves pledged to see to it that Legislative office spending would be reduced 20%, internal government spending by 33%, and payments to agencies, boards, and commissions would be chopped 28%. At the time, the impression was given that these were across-the-board cuts, but that was not the case. In fact, some ministries would almost escape cuts while others would be eviscerated.

Given the Tory agenda and the speed with which they felt it needed to be implemented, Eves brought forward his laundry list of cuts in a massive omnibus bill, Bill 26, the *Savings and Restructuring Act*. He also stated his expectation that it would be passed by 14 December, prior to the Christmas break. Given the sheer size of the proposed legislation, nearly-one-foot-thick, the time-line guaranteed there could be no effective debate, which is undoubtedly what the government wanted. Included in Bill 26 was:

a) Ontario Loan Act, 1995 - Finance ministry legislation to authorize the borrowing of $5.6 million over 1996;
b) Income Tax Act and Corporations Tax Act amendments - Financial ministry legislation to implement changes already made by the NDP, but never enacted;
c) Public Sector Salary Disclosure Act, 1995 - Finance ministry legislation to force the disclosure of the salaries and benefits paid to public sector employees earning $100,000 or more per year;
d) Pension Benefits Act amendments - Management Board changes geared to take surpluses from the Ontario Public Service Employees Union (OPSEU) Pension Plan and the Public Service Pension Plan;
e) Freedom of Information and Protection of Personal Privacy Act and the Municipal Freedom of Information and Protection of Personal Privacy Act amendments - Management Board changes to limit Freedom of Information appeals and increase user fees for those making requests;

f) Toll Highway legislation - Transportation ministry bill to allow for tolls on the new Highway 407;

g) Municipal Act and related statute amendments - Municipal Affairs and Housing ministry changes to promote municipal amalgamations and annexations by permitting the Minister to order such changes, as well as permitting more service and licensing flexibility;

h) Ministry of Correctional Services Act amendments - change to reduce the quorum for the provincial Board of Parole from three to two to improve efficiency;

i) Pay Equity Amendment Act, 1995 - Ministry of Labour legislation to repeal the NDP's so-called "quota bill";

j) Interest Arbitration Amendment Act - Ministry of Labour changes to the Police Services Act, Fire Departments Act, Public Service Act, School Boards and Teachers Collective Agreement Act, and the Hospital Labour Disputes Arbitration Act to impose new criteria on arbitrators to effectively limit wage settlements;

k) Health Services Restructuring Act - Health ministry legislation to create the Health Services Restructuring Commission, and give it the authority to restructure or close hospitals;

l) Ontario Drug Benefit Act amendments - Health ministry changes to require recipients of Ontario Disability Benefits to pay part of the costs of drugs, restrict billing access for those involved in fraudulent billings, require the use of only the lowest cost brands, and deregulate the amounts that can be charged for drugs;

m) Health Insurance Act and related amendments - Health ministry changes to try and alleviate physician shortages where such have been identified, as well as authorizing new powers to permit the Minister to access doctors' records to recover over-payments from OHIP;

n) Physician Services Delivery Act - Health ministry changes to try and stop the Ontario Medical Association from acting as the negotiator for all doctors, and end the government paying for doctor's insurance premiums;

o) Game and Fish Act amendments - Ministry of Natural Resources changes to direct Game and Fish Act revenues directly toward ministry costs;

p) Public Lands Act, Forest Fire Prevention Act, and Lakes and Rivers Improvement Act amendments - Ministry of Natural Resources changes to remove the requirement for mandatory permits for such things as open burning, dams, access roads, docks and boathouses;

q) Conservation Authorities Act - Ministry of Natural Resources changes to cut provincial involvement with conservation authorities and download funding responsibilities onto municipalities;

r) Mining Act amendments - Northern Development and Mines changes to allow mining companies to self-regulate mine closures and reduce their liabilities for abandoned mines.

On their face, these bills and amendments had nothing in common. But there was one thing: money. They all raised or created new fees for services or cut services and/or regulations that cost money to administer. Even considering the $1.9 billion in July cuts, this was truly the *enactment* of *The Common Sense Revolution*.

However, in their rush to get the bill before the Legislature, the Tories had not taken sufficient time to write it up properly. Political and bureaucratic staffs supplied facts and figures to Guy Giorno (a 29-year-old lawyer turned speech-writer turned policy advisor) who, in turn, packaged them up and sent them along to the Ministry of Finance to be written into legislation. When first presented to the Legislature, it was a confused mess of contradictory measures, careless mistakes, and indiscreet power-grabs. In the end, they were forced to present 160 amendments just to repair the errors in their own bill and, then, force each one of them through individually.

Though Tony Clement, then the parliamentary assistant to the Citizenship minister, would blame the bureaucrats for adding in measures so they could assume a laundry-list of powers they had wanted for years, the truth is that the power-grabs came because the Tories wanted them. In health alone, the controversial measures were not at the behest of ministry staff, but of the minister himself. Jim Wilson wanted a commission to close and cut hospitals, he wanted the power to search doctors' records, and he wanted to force doctors to work where the government told them to work. It was only the sounds of *screaming* that had them back down on most of the heinous measures.

The Liberals and NDP were determined not to let this bill pass quietly, just as the Tories feared. But given the problems with Bill 26, the time-line put forward by Ernie Eves was stretched to the limit. It was clear the slightest difficulty might well collapse the government's plans. On Wednesday, 6 December, they got their trouble. The Opposition chose not to vote on a routine motion. When Speaker Al McLean ordered Liberal Alvin Curling to leave the chamber, as he is required to do, he refused. Other members surrounded him and there he stayed, even though the Sergeant-at-Arms was charged with removing him. In fact, he remained until just after 10:00AM the next morning. Since the rules state a sitting cannot begin after ten o'clock and the Legislature doesn't sit on Fridays, it was effectively shut down until Monday. Then, with the Christmas break scheduled to begin the next Friday, the government was faced with sitting through Christmas or waiting. It was also clear that the Opposition could try further filibusters and continue to delay passage. When the opposition House Leaders offered Eves a compromise, he took it. January would be dedicated to public committee hearings, whereupon a Legislative vote would be held near month's end. But it was an unhappy saw-off for the government. Bill 26 would not pass in 1995.

The Tories were forced to listen to 367 individuals and groups during these hearings, pretty much all of whom roasted them for one thing or another. And though the Liberals and New Democrats had agreed to this deal, it didn't mean they had to make it completely easy. Each of the Tory amendments had to be discussed and voted on, causing ill-humour and embarrassment amongst the government members.

Ironically, in their determination to get started on their agenda, the Tories broke their first promise. In the CSR, they had explicitly said no new user fees. The omnibus bill permitted the creation of dozens. Using the argument that representatives of the municipal, university, school, and hospital sectors had requested more "autonomy" in decision-making, Eves permitted them to begin collecting a variety of user fees, from an annual $100 levy on Ontario Drug Benefits to dispensing fees on drug prescriptions to 15%-20% hikes in post-secondary education tuition. Municipalities were given the authority to implement *cost-recovery methods*, such as library, park, and garbage fees. Of course, the Opposition parties chided the government for breaking this promise, and the Tories denied they were, arguing that "co-payments" were not the same as user fees. Unfortunately for Harris, he had taken David Peterson to task during the 1990 election for allowing health care co-payments, which he had then said were nothing but user fees.

At this time, the Harris Tories also chose to mirror a rather foolish attitude displayed by the Mulroney Conservatives, especially during their second and final term in office. Whenever they did something the public disliked, and another poll came out showing they had dropped even further in the public's estimation, Brian Mulroney or one of his toadies would proudly announce that their lack of support was a sign they were doing a good job. Only bad governments are popular because they won't make the tough decisions.

The "bully bill", as it was dubbed by the media, was this exactly for the Harrisites. The government was soon bemoaning all the nasty things people were saying about it. Between September and January, the Conservatives dropped in the polls from 50% to 34%. Finance Minister Eves said it was due to opposition fearmongering. Both he and other Cabinet colleagues agreed the public didn't understand the changes and, for the first but far from last time, they would comment "we have to do a better job of getting our message out".

That was obvious. Along with the omnibus bill, Tory ministers had been shooting themselves in their collective feet. Community and Social Services' minister David Tsubouchi suggested people on welfare should buy dented cans of tuna to save money, while he paid $1,200 a month to an image consultant. He went so far as to say that if they couldn't find them at 69ø a can, they should negotiate for a better price. Bob Rae asked him when the last time was he had bartered for food. Tsubouchi also insinuated these people might consider moving to British Columbia, where the rates were higher and the weather more temperate, though it was more of a trick question by a reporter that he fell for. Transportation minister Al Palladini said roadside emergency telephones were no longer necessary because everyone had a cellular phone in their car. He also said that the proposal to get rid of Cabinet minister's limousines and drivers was wrong, because he needed his to get to work. And to make things worse, he said there was no reason his ownership of a car dealership should stop it from bidding on government contracts. Municipal Affairs' minister Al Leach did not know the contents of the portion of the omnibus bill he was in charge of shepherding through the Legislature, as he said it did not allow for poll taxes when it did. But the authoritarian use of the rules to make so many changes at once seemed to truly focus the displeasure of Ontarians, for a short time anyway.

The Harrisites didn't learn their lesson from this trouble. What should have been shameful, yet edifying, wasn't at all. In fact, the omnibus bill became another badge of courage for them, and pushing it through, 160 amendments and all, was *revolutionary change*. "Bill 26 didn't serve as a warning to the government. It served as encouragement."[1]

2. Kicking the poor while they're down

There is no question that the attitudes of many people permitted what was to come, when the Harris Conservatives were elected. From Day One, the Tories seemed nasty and mean-spirited. But so were a lot of Ontarians at that time. Recession had come, then come again, and its aftermath

lingered. A lot of people were unemployed, many of whom had been that
way for months or even years. Most others had seen their jobs hanging by
a thread for several years, never sure that their next day at work wouldn't
be their last. And wages had stalled, so no average person dared spend any
money to replace aging cars or on houses that needed repair. Gloom had
pervaded people's minds for most of the NDP years, and they seemed
quite glad to send them on their way.

The cut to welfare benefits almost appeared cathartic ... like a salve gently
stroked into a wound. This reduction was a promise to a weary populous
that wanted to see someone else suffer as they had. It was a vengeance
exacted on those whom many thought had laughed their way through this
tough period on the government dole. If they hadn't been petty, vindictive,
and cruel, the cuts might have been worthwhile just for their psychological
benefit. But they were petty, vindictive, and cruel.

The CSR promised benefits that were 10% above the national average, and
the Tories were determined to keep this promise fast. But it wasn't just
that. They needed the money, and they enjoyed the idea of sticking it to
those they saw as indolent cheats. The haste in their actions and the clear
delight they showed in making the cuts demonstrated that attitude. They
thought that by making life unbearable on welfare, they would force the
recipients to finally get a job (as though there were thousands from which
to choose).

On 21 July, seven weeks after their election, they made good on this,
cutting benefits by 21.6%, or $469 million per year, they said. It was a
major change which brought widespread condemnation by activists and the
socially-concerned who feared that many of these 600,000 poor had now
been sentenced to an even worse fate. Yet it also brought nodding
approval by many citizens who agreed with the feeling that welfare was
nothing more than the lazy robbing them through their taxes. They even
ignored the fact that the government was not telling the truth about the new
rates being 10% above average. They were actually calculated leaving out
Ontario and the Territories. If these had been included, benefits were in
fact well-below average compared to most of the rest of the country. It
was only in the text of the CSR that they had referred to the 'average of all
other provinces'.

But the critics of this move never let up on the government. It didn't take
a rocket scientist to see that, for every cheater who lost their ill-gotten
money, hundreds, or perhaps thousands, of those who really needed it
would suffer terribly.

The other thing was that no one seemed to notice that a cut of 21.6% to 600,000 people would save the government far more than the $469 million it claimed. An individual recipient could receive $663 per month, or $7,956 per year in benefits. This was being cut to $520 per month, or $6,240 per year. At that rate, a cut of $1,716 per year, even if the entire 600,000 were individuals, the government would really save just over $1 billion annually. They admitted to this in the CSR. And given that most recipients were actually mothers with children, the savings were clearly higher yet.

The whole concept of welfare became the government's hobby horse, as they continually came back to it to either do a little more kicking on these poor or to keep trying to justify why they kept at them. For example, in April 1996, 17,000 college and university students were cut off welfare and told they could get student loans. Why should they get a *free* ride? Throughout the term, the Tories continued on with how so many people had been helped by the benefit cuts and workfare. The problem was they couldn't prove it. But that didn't stop them. They hired a polling firm to look up 5,441 people who had left the welfare rolls in one month of 1996 to show that they had found jobs and were now *productive members of society*. Unfortunately, they couldn't find 3,282 of them, and a disproportionate number that they did find were better-educated, and had recent job experience, meaning they weren't terribly representative of the whole. Also, most of those contacted could afford both telephones and housing. Many others who hadn't found work had returned to school, were now on Employment Insurance, or had changed living arrangements which made them ineligible to collect benefits.

Nevertheless, the Harrisites persevered. Based on the 2,159 people they did find, the government suggested that 60% of those who had been on welfare now had full-time jobs. They simply disregarded the 3,282 who couldn't be reached. In fact, their survey ignored what seemed obvious to others ... many of those who had left welfare were now begging help from friends and relatives or were sleeping in the streets and in hostels.

In 1997 they tried another survey, this one by mail, thus eliminating the problem of those who lacked telephones. It was an unmitigated disaster. Surveys were mailed to the last known addresses of 1,000 former recipients. Just 59 people responded, with 35 of them saying they were back on welfare.

In the 1999-2000 Social Services' ministry business plan, the Tories claimed they had saved the public $100 million by catching 14,800 cases of welfare fraud. It was an impressive claim even though, as 1.3% of the department's budget, it seemed small compared to their election claims of 5% or more. Of course, the truth was it was even smaller than that. Forty million dollars was actually "future costs avoided", and many of the cases were of misuse, not fraud. In fact, there were only 747 convictions for fraud in 1998-1999, down by 297 from the year before. That was about 0.1% of the total cases. And these 747 frauds had cost taxpayers about $8 million, or just over a tenth of one-percent of their budget. Of course, if you subtract the costs of the extra administration to catch cheaters and prosecute them, the total was likely zero, or less than zero. But that wasn't something the Tories wanted to advertise.

In fact, the Harrisites were so convinced that a high percentage of welfare costs were as a result of fraud that they brought in the internationally-known Andersen Consulting to help them catch the perpetrators. Unfortunately for the Tories, this *private sector application of sound management principles* would cost the Ontario taxpayer over $200 million, ending up with savings of less than $20 million per year.

The whole affair had its genesis in two things: the Harris Tories' belief that the welfare system was rife with fraud; and, the neo-con notion that anything done by the private sector is more efficient and effective than anything done by government. In the case of welfare fraud, the Harris Conservatives believed government had proven to be anything but effective in rooting it out, so it was necessary to bring in a private company to do the work for them. In January 1997, they hired Andersen Consulting to create a new social services' computer system to catch fraud and duplication. They estimated savings of $300 million a year.

Somewhat ironically, the Rae NDP had come to a similar solution, as they were looking for a private partner to assist them in reconstructing the social assistance computer system about the time they were swept from office. Many American corporations had become involved in similar schemes there, and took contracts based on being paid a percentage of savings rather than normal payment. This was supposedly the private sector profit motive in evidence – the better the job you do, the more money you will make. Of course, it was also premised on there being sufficient fraud that government would actually save money. The Harrisites continued on with the NDP plan, but would elect for a greatly expanded project.

Why they selected Andersen Consulting over other companies only they know, but it may have been because Andersen had done similar work for the New Brunswick government in the mid-1990s, which had allowed that provincial government to reduce staff by 125. There is no question Andersen had a wealth of experience in designing computer systems. They also had a plethora of critics and dissatisfied customers.

The auditor for the State of Nebraska said hiring Andersen to streamline their welfare system was like "pouring money down a deep, dark hole". The state paid them $30 million to design the computer system, then another $8 million to teach staff to use it. In total, it was a cost overrun of $24 million. The Canadian government had hired Andersen to write up a new payroll programme. They fired them when they missed the deadline while, at the same time, Andersen was requesting a doubling of fees. The consultant had a contract with the State of Texas for a computer system to track child support payments for $12 million. They billed for $75 million. And the New Brunswick government ultimately paid Andersen $2.9 million to get out of a contract for a consolidated justice computer system when cost estimates suddenly went from $60 million to $144 million.

But these would pale beside the contract Andersen worked out with the Ontario government. A new social assistance computer system was going to pay the consultant up to $180 million over five years, with Andersen permitted to bill for up to $575 per hour for the project director, $85 per hour for data entry clerks. As auditor Erik Peters pointed out in his November 1998 report, these wages were six times the going rate. They didn't even compare well with supposedly overpaid government wages, as a similar provincial clerk made $28 per hour. Harris and then Community and Social Services' minister Janet Ecker replied to critics that, even though these wages may have been negotiated at too high a level, money would be saved regardless. Ecker added that she hoped to renegotiate this part of their agreement.

That didn't happen. Thirteen months later, in Peter's next report, he again commented on the deal, saying almost nothing had changed. "There could be better value for money for the taxpayer in this whole process." "The ministry cannot say 'No' to those (billing) rates under the current agreement. That was clearly a mistake of the original contract."[2] He added that the $346 million in reputed savings the government was claiming (downgraded from $300 million per year) was "somewhat doubtful". As well, Andersen had been paid for savings that were actually the result of actions taken by Ministry personnel. However, there had been one change. Andersen had increased hourly billing fees by 3% for most of their personnel, as permitted in the contract.

Before being shuffled out of this ministry, Ecker kept her word about looking into the terms of the agreement, sort of. She had hired another consultant to examine it. This person came back with an assessment that Andersen's fees were fair. It must have escaped the minister that one consultant wasn't likely to pan high fees by other consultants. The new minister, John Baird, reiterated the government's hope that fees could be renegotiated. Of course, this was a year later.

By late 2001, Andersen Consulting had become Accenture and had been paid $193 million, $5 million more than they were supposed to have been paid, and with four months left on the deal. In fact, some fees had been renegotiated, but not until the year 2000. Total savings were estimated at $89.5 million, just 6% of what had been promised over the five year period. Baird said that savings had, in fact, been more than $350 million but with what was paid to Accenture and one-time costs, the number had been greatly reduced. However, he added another reason. "We're a victim of success, the declining caseloads make it even more difficult to find the savings."[3] Of course, if a decline in numbers hadn't been anticipated, as cheaters were discovered, then someone was really asleep at the wheel, so to speak. Baird added that he expected the government would save $200 million per year once the contract was up, but that makes no sense. Excluding the $40 million or so Accenture would not be receiving, the *savings* were less than $17.9 million per year, and should decline further if more frauds were found. To think that the government will be saving anything by 2002 is almost ridiculous. But it does say something about the way the Tories calculate. If $100 in fraud is found in one year, it is assumed that money is *saved* every year afterward. After five years, it is said $500 is saved. In fact, the only saving is $100.

If there was one criticism of the whole deal that must hurt the Harrisites, beyond the financial one, it is that the new computer system supposedly fails almost as much as the old one did. One thing is clear, however. People on social assistance needed the $193 million more than Andersen/Accenture.

3. "Mike the Knife"

A core promise of *The Common Sense Revolution* was to cut the number of civil servants. Now there's no question that the business mantra of the '90s was to cut staff to cut costs. Reducing wages was the easiest way to improve the corporate bottom line. The problem was that many companies cut well beyond excess staff into those they needed to do the job. As a result, they undermined their own efficiency and many made themselves less competitive. But the Harrisites were determined to apply business management principles to government. I'm sure it never occurred to them some of these doctrines might be flawed.

And cutting staff fit perfectly with their view of bureaucrats. They believed most civil servants were simply union members doing as little as possible for the highest wages possible. Here is Mike Harris' attitude, as expressed at the Walkerton Inquiry. In reference to an OPSEU memo that suggested Environment ministry cuts would endanger public health, he said:

Well, every change, I think, that was being made, there would be somebody who would say it would have a consequence. I would expect OPSEU, their role is to make sure that -- that everyone in their primary job, every one of their members continues in the job and there should be no cutbacks, that was, I think, a clear position and that -- that should be their position, that's ... their role. So, certainly we got -- this is the kind of reaction I would expect ... from the union representing the workers, that they would raise concerns.

And cutbacks in the number of civil servants had to come if the government was going to balance the budget and pay for tax cuts. There just wasn't enough money available through revenues presently available. But there was a problem. Legally, the government had to give proper notice of lay-offs, which was some six months. If more than 20 workers were being dispatched, notice was eleven months. With bumping rights, this could expand the time-line up to almost two years, as notice would then have to be given to the bumped workers. There was no way Harris *et.al.* were going to wait that long. Financially, they couldn't wait.

Fortunately, they had one advantage, and they realized it from the beginning. Civil servants had not had a pay-raise in five years, and the Social Contract had temporarily cut their wages and made them quite angry. The Harrisites had rubbed salt in the wound by exempting public servants from successor rights when they repealed Bill 40 in October 1995[4]. Everyone expected a strike. The Tories prayed for it.

The Rae New Democrats had hoped to appease their union critics by granting public service unions the right to strike in 1994. It was something the latter had wanted for a very long time, and it was hoped this might convince them to stop attacking the government and support it, once again.

There are those who also believe that the New Democrats, had they been re-elected, would then have demanded union concessions themselves, and giving them the right to strike was the only way to get them. Perhaps they thought this, though one must wonder if they truly had the political spine to actually do it. Regardless, this measure was left to their successors to make the cuts they wanted.

Under past rules which excluded the strike option, public service unions had to settle for binding arbitration when it came time for contract disputes to be worked out. Typically, arbitrators would not find entirely for one side or the other, but would compromise, meaning the unions would usually get at least part of what they wanted. With the right to strike, there was no longer binding arbitration and everything was up for grabs. So when Ontario Public Service Employees Union members began agitating for a strike, it gave the Tories exactly what they needed – the opportunity to propose the cuts they wanted.

The CSR had promised to cut the number of provincial employees by 15%, and the Harrisites egged the union on by demanding that bumping rights and a number of other provisions which protected union jobs be eliminated from a new contract. And they wanted to cut the amount of contributions being made to union pensions. They knew this would never be acceptable, and it would be like fanning the red cape in front of an angry bull. But they wanted the union members stirred up and looking for a fight.

So even though the public sector unions knew what was coming, it didn't seem to make them any wiser. The OPSEU contract had expired in 1994, followed by the Social Contract in the spring of 1995. The membership was angry and wanted to make up for perceived injustices. Though there were a hundred or so matters for discussion, the big ones from the union perspective were the restoration of successor rights, a guarantee of bumping rights, a massive re-training programme for laid-off workers, and access to pension benefits to help those who lost their jobs – a provision which had existed until Bill 26. It was as though the union chose to oppose everything they knew the government wanted.

OPSEU had three possibilities. They could have proposed renewing the old contract, tried to drag out negotiations on a new one and, therefore, maintain what they had, or they could go on strike. Either of the first two options might have forced the government into the role of *bad guy*. The Tories needed cuts. If they couldn't readily get them, they might lock-out their own employees. Government services might grind to a halt and cause public upset. But these would not have satisfied the union membership.

Leah Casselman had just taken over the presidency on the platform of getting back what had been lost. She was not about to recommend anything but aggressive action.

When they walked out on conciliation talks in February, they played right into the hands of the Tory government, and their able negotiator, Management Board Chair Dave Johnson. The Harrisites were on a deadline. The fiscal year would be ending on 31 March, and they wanted to know how many lay-offs they could manage in 1996-1997 in short order. Once OPSEU gave up on contract talks, they got a strike vote of 66% and lit the fuse to a strike to begin on 26 February. They now recognized that the government had no intention of making concessions, and apparently they felt only a labour disruption would pressure the Tories into this.

So 55,000 OPSEU workers went on strike over the last week in February. Few Ontarians had any sympathy for these people, as they too had suffered with no pay increases and massive job losses. They saw *bureaucrats* as highly-paid, not terribly over-worked, and atypically secure in their employment. This was just them "getting theirs". This lack of empathy did not help. However, what the union really miscalculated on was that, because some 12,000 civil servants had been declared as essential, and there were still managers in place as well, most citizens barely noticed a loss of services. It was soon clear to all that OPSEU negotiators had no leverage.

However, once again, the government caused its own trouble. Someone in the Premier's Office had been toying with the idea that replacement workers might be needed. The day before the strike began, this leaked out as a media report that senior government sources were planning to hire 5,000 strike-breakers. The next day, just to make matters worse, Premier Harris said the strike was the fault of the Rae government because it had given the union "this candy, this new tool ... and they are determined to go and use it and try it, and I'm not sure there was anything we could have done to stop them". It certainly now appeared the government had wanted a strike all along, just so they could *break* OPSEU.

But it didn't matter. People thought the strike was wrong, and most services continued with little change. Had the weather not been fairly moderate or had the strike dragged on for a very long time, this might have been seen differently and the public view might have changed. As it was, the union was on the *wrong side*, and it had no way of improving its lot. Regardless, they felt they needed one massive show of their resolve to make their case.

The Legislature was due to resume sitting on Monday, 18 March, having been on Christmas break with the exception of the one day it took to pass the omnibus bill. Some 5,000 protesters flooded the grounds of Queen's Park, determined to make their point and to stop MPPs from getting inside. What they didn't know was that Speaker Al McLean had other plans.

Security at Queen's Park was a combined responsibility. The building itself was under the control of a half-a-dozen OPP officers who coordinated the actions of 50 security guards. These OPP constables answered to both their superiors and to the Speaker. The grounds themselves were the purview of the local Toronto police. In many ways, it was a stupid arrangement but this was overlooked because protests at the Legislature were usually small and peaceful.

But there had already been two serious demonstrations in the ten months since the Tories had taken power. In September, protesters had anticipated the vicious cuts to come, and had been there to show their disapproval of the Throne Speech. In February, a small group of the 800 secondary and post-secondary students who had shown up to protest education cuts and tuition hikes had become violent, broke into the building, and vandalized barricades outside and doors, walls, and furniture inside to the tune of $20,000. It was no doubt because of this that McLean chose to make certain it didn't happen again. The problem was he didn't bother to tell anyone other than the OPP.

When the pickets began to delay MPPs and staff from entering the only available entrance to the building, the OPP Crowd Management Unit decided to *bash a few heads*. Alleged to have said they were going to "whack 'em and stack 'em", people were pushed around by police with plastic shields, soaked in pepper spray, and hit with truncheons. It was a complete change of tactics that took everyone by surprise. Even the Toronto police were shocked by the turn of events.[5]

Though some in the public were astounded by this and the shine came off the government's actions, it didn't make any difference regarding the OPSEU strike. The union had gained little influence and, though some government services were beginning to buckle under the strain, there had been no widespread problems and none appeared likely in the near future. And the union had one other difficulty. The 5,000-member Association of Management, Administration, and Professional Crown Employees of Ontario, which was also on strike, had settled ... and their deal was not along the lines of what OPSEU wanted. With this seeming to set a pattern for settlement and the union having to borrow money for strike pay, the end was nigh. Despite Casselman's claim that OPSEU had made "major gains", in fact, they had been utterly defeated. Thirty-four days of strike had yielded a slight gain in severance pay. That was all. The government got what it wanted. Successor rights were gone. The union lost most of its bumping provisions. Massive numbers could now be fired.

One of the biggest examples came in the Environment ministry. It was decimated, as 36% of all staff were axed. The budget was reduced by an incredible 42%. How could you get rid of this many people and this much money and expect the ministry to do its job? The only way was to slash the size of its job. Regulations had to go, and this was done to "eliminate government barriers to job creation, investment, and economic growth", as promised in the CSR. Not only were cuts being made to save money, but they gave the Tories what they needed to implement the neo-conservative philosophy of smaller government.

This labour dispute turned out to be the best thing that ever happened to the Harris government. The unpopular strike ended with the government in complete control, able to lay-off anyone with minimal notice. They would take full advantage of this. Almost immediately, lay-off notices started going out. By the end of fiscal 1996-1997, over 11,000 civil servants had been sent packing. By 2001, that was over 16,000. The number of public servants was reduced by more than 20%. And the Tories drop in the polls reversed itself completely, as they shot up from 34% to 54%, surpassing their earlier *honeymoon* numbers. At that point, union members may have been wishing they could return to the days of the Social Contract.

* * * * *

The move to efficiency was not without internal bumps. When it was suggested in the CSR that Ontario had too many politicians, *even MPPs*, there were few critics. After all, almost no one likes them and most believe they are overpaid and under-worked. When it was suggested that a great deal could be gained by cutting the number from 130 to 103 to mirror the new federal constituencies[6] , it seemed like *common sense*. However, when a number of MPPs realized this would mean their own ridings would be radically realigned or even disappear, there was some upset.

In one case in southwestern Ontario, three ridings would be reduced into two. The difficulty was that all three were held by Tories, meaning one would have to go. An internal debate raged for some time. The hope was that one would take a patronage appointment and free the field for the others. Whether or not no specific job was offered, or it wasn't good enough, no one took the hint.

Now there was a favourite to be gone. Bruce-Grey MPP Bill Murdoch is an outspoken man who had been a Liberal prior to losing that party's nomination in 1987. A week later, he was the Conservative candidate. Defeated in that election, he was victorious in his next try, and became a true believer of the CSR. However, on several occasions, he had criticized his own government and was not considered to be a pal of the premier. (I should note, he has never actually voted *against* his government.) Perhaps it was his good fortune that he was in the most easterly of the three ridings and was considered fairly popular there for his individualism. It was unlikely either of the other two could have beaten him for that nomination.

Then, eyes turned on Helen Johns, a seeming lightweight from the riding of Huron. I use the term 'lightweight' despite her qualifications. She has three university degrees, a Bachelor of Arts from York University in 1975, a Bachelor of Commerce in Accounting from the University of Windsor in 1980, and an MBA from Simon Fraser University in 1987. As well, she had 15 years as a business controller, as well as experience in consulting and as a college instructor. Regardless, the local perspective was that she was an unimpressive MPP who had risen as far as she was going to. Though she had initially been chosen as the Parliamentary Assistant to the Minister of Health from July 1995 until April 1997, she was then shunted to the much smaller Ministry of Environment and Energy as PA responsible for Energy issues. She remained when the Ministry was restructured as Energy, Science and Technology.

However, it would seem that the powers-that-be had other plans for her, as she would move into Cabinet in 1999. In the end, it was Bruce MPP Barb Fisher who walked the plank, as she was defeated by Johns for the nomination. While Fisher was well thought-of, the new territory had been mostly in John's old riding, and Fisher waited too long to challenge her rather than Murdoch, and couldn't recruit support in the new area. Perhaps, as well, it was as simple as the fact that she had won her riding in 1995 by just 2,000 votes, while Johns had won by a margin of 6,300. Johns was simply the safer bet.

A far nastier battle took place between Chris Stockwell, then Speaker, and backbencher Doug Ford. Stockwell was much better known, but wasn't much liked by the Tory hierarchy who saw him as a troublemaker. Ford, on the other hand, was little-known, but was seen as a team player who would support party policy without question. Both took turns calling each other a liar, with Ford attacking Stockwell over his true allegiance to the party, while Stockwell criticized Ford for not standing up for his constituents. In the end, Stockwell won.

When all was said and done, the Tories lost five sitting members who were defeated for nominations by other sitting members. If there was a saving grace, it was that all were in fairly safe ridings, where the Tories could expect their candidate to be re-elected, even if a few feathers were ruffled.

This was not necessarily the case elsewhere. It was not just the Tories who had a few difficult choices. Probably the nastiest fight of all came between two Liberals when they both decided to battle for the same riding nomination. Monte Kwinter had the higher profile, having been a former Peterson Cabinet minister, but Annamarie Castrilli was also seen as Cabinet material in a future Liberal government, not to mention she had run for leader in 1996. However, for whatever reason, the party hierarchy chose not to intervene to give any hint of preference or lay out any rules or alternative options. The matter simmered for too long and led to a bitter dispute that Castrilli lost. Ultimately, she took the defeat so badly she ran for the Tory nomination in Parkdale-High Park, won, and ended up running against her former colleague Gerard Kennedy. She was soundly thumped by Kennedy in the election.

The other side of this internal cutting was pension reform for MPPs. When the Harrisites came to power, an MPP who stepped aside or was defeated received a pension based on number of years in the Legislature, as long as they had been there a minimum of five. Once they were out of office, they were eligible to begin collecting at any age, as long as their age and years of service equalled the number 55. According to the CSR, this was a "sweet deal" that had to end.

They brought in a new system that would pay MPPs through RRSPs, just as were available to ordinary people. Each member would receive an annual contribution of 5% of their pay of $78,007 from public funds, along with the amount they themselves contributed. As well, once they were out of office, due to retirement or defeat, they would receive a severance package, based on time in the Legislature. And tax-free allowances were eliminated. This was all seen as very fair, though I'm sure more than a few MPPs grumbled that it was hardly reasonable compensation given the short careers had by most elected members.

However, even the cost-conscious Tories felt the need to cushion the blow, at least for long-serving MPPs. For anyone elected prior to 8 June 1995, *locked-in retirement accounts* were created so that the pension earnings they had been permitted would be protected. These LIRAs would be based on time as an MPP but just up to 1995. Or, as an alternative, they could take advantage of a *life income fund*. This would take the same money, and pay it out as a lump sum once the MPP retired or was defeated. It meant that Premier Mike Harris and Finance minister Ernie Eves had access to either payments on, or the whole of, more than $850,000 each, once they left office.

But cutting MPPs was not the main thrust. While Ontario had 130 provincial representatives, there were thousands at the local level, municipal and school board, all of whom received wages and expenses. Given that the Conservatives felt there would be great savings by cutting 27 MPPs, the potential in slashing school trustees and municipal councillors was enormous.

It does not seem the Tories had a particular number in mind to slash, but they knew how many locally-elected officials there were – 1,992 school trustees and 4,586 municipal councillors. The easiest way was to simply make this part of all the other changes. As part of Bill 26, they gave the Education minister the power to restructure school boards – and cut trustees – and the Municipal Affairs' minister the authority to amalgamate municipalities – and cut council sizes. Once the school board amalgamations had taken effect, boards had been reduced 44.2% in number, with a concurrent drop in trustees of 70.5%, to 589. And maximum pay for a trustee was limited to $5,000, regardless of the size of the board. In terms of towns, townships, and cities, 815 in July 1996 had been cut to 447 by January 2001, a cut of 45.2%. Councillors had gone down to 2,804, a drop of 38.9%. For the Conservatives, this has been a tremendous success that has saved taxpayers many more millions of dollars.

But what of democracy? It doesn't seem to have been a question that ever entered the minds of the government members. Though there were some critics of making these cuts, they came from the constituencies the government felt were their enemies, so any concerns were seemingly ignored.

As I mentioned earlier, about the sewers of Creemore, when municipalities are amalgamated and councils condensed, it becomes more difficult for citizens to actually get the same level of representation. The same holds true when councils are simply cut. If a city of 100,000 has 16 councillors and that is cut in half, it means each remaining council member must represent an extra 6,250 citizens. That may not seem like much of an increase, but it means 12,500 have half the opportunity to contact or receive representation from their councillor. Now imagine what that would mean in a city of over two million. When the Tories decided to amalgamate Toronto, this would be pointed out.

4. The Hospital Closing Commission

Though *The Common Sense Revolution* document promised there would be no cuts to health care, it seems reasonable to conclude the Harrisites had no intention of *increasing* health spending either. It also doesn't seem they came to office with a plan for restructuring health delivery services in Ontario. The furthest their thinking seems to have gone was to create a royal commission to study change, while actually cutting back on *excess* in hospitals. Since the days of Frank Miller as Treasurer, there were those convinced that there were too many beds and too many staff for those beds. This was what the CSR termed as 'waste' and 'mismanagement' and the commitment was made to 'rooting (it) out' and re-investing 'every dollar we save'.

So hospitals were aggressively restructured, and an idea for a plan of change was created by this commission. However, while government members talked about some of these ideas, and some pilot projects have been set up, the reality is that *reform* has gone little beyond chopping hospital care and, because these *reforms* stopped with the end of the commission, the system was left unfinished. It's as though a car got a new engine, but the mechanic failed to hook up all the wires but can't understand why it sputters and stalls.

One of the off-shoots of the omnibus bill was the March 1996 creation of the Health Services Restructuring Commission (HSRC). It was a seven-member panel, headed by then Queen's University Dean of Medicine, Duncan Sinclair, charged in its mandate ...

1. *To make binding decisions on the restructuring of hospitals*
2. *To make recommendations on the restructuring of sectors or other elements of the health services system, including advice about reinvestment needed to restructure hospitals and enhance other health services*

3. To foster the creation of a genuine, integrated, co-ordinated health services system

It appeared to make good on the CSR commitment of the Tories to find financial savings in the health care system for re-investment, but also went beyond that by helping the government to establish a *vision* of health care for the future. The commission ended on 28 March 2000, having completed most of these tasks. Perhaps with the exception of those people connected to the HSRC, few others were unhappy to see it go.

In its final report, *Looking Back, Looking Forward: A Legacy Report*, the members of the HSRC knew that it had achieved a mixed level of success. While the members seemed satisfied with the restructuring of urban hospitals, they were less sanguine about most other results. It wasn't that they felt their job had been in vain, it was that they wished it could have been done differently and under different circumstances. They even identified the problems that plagued them right from their first days.

The government had already announced it planned to reduce transfers to hospitals by 18% over three years. With a mere four years to do all their work, there was no time to be lost doing their research and implementing their plans. Though they had an "arms-length relationship" from the government, they inappropriately recognized most of the *dirty work* would have to be done during a short "window of opportunity", perhaps only two years, well prior to the next election. Yet this relationship was also seen as a negative, in that they couldn't expect much assistance from the Ministry of Health. As well, it would make it difficult for provincial politicians to support their work, support they could have used given the natural resistance that was expected regarding hospital closings.

What the HSRC members didn't seem to realize was that an 'arms-length relationship' was exactly what the government wanted. The ploy was a simple one: if the Harris government didn't want to take the blame for closing or reducing community hospitals, the responsibility had to be laid on a body completely independent of it. The commission had to be virtually cut off from the rest of the government. So when the inevitable shouts of disapproval were heard, Health minister Jim Wilson could simply say all decisions were up to the HSRC.

Making the HSRC work even more difficult, since hospital cuts had already been announced and it was the commission's first duty to deal with urban hospitals, was the widely-held public perception was that these changes were "being driven solely by financial considerations". And this belief ran deep, especially given that, while people may have harboured concerns about the health care system, they weren't dissatisfied with their "individual experiences with the system". For many citizens, this call to reform hospitals was greatly concerning. Over the years, people have become very attached to their hospitals, even in communities that had multiple facilities. (These were the first the commission focused on.) Hospitals have been the core of a community's health system for a very long time.

But the commission faced even further troubles starting out. It wasn't just ordinary citizens who were leery about changes. Health care workers of all stripes feared that the HSRC was simply the Harris government's tool to pare back wages and slash jobs. Similarly, those running health facilities feared the commission was just the government's way of telling them how to operate, including how much they could spend and on what. Put simply, virtually everyone held reservations about what the HSRC was actually going to do.

In *Looking Back, Looking Forward,* the commission members make it clear they wished they could have dealt with the *vision* matter first, including how to pay doctors, instead of hospital restructuring. Basically, they had been forced to go at it backwards. If they could have come up with a comprehensive plan for what the health system should be, they could have *sold* it to the public and health providers first. Then, people might have understood that what was intended was to shift the focus away from "hospital-centred care" to "patient-centred care", an idea that also demanded shifting some funds away from hospitals into long-term and home care. It would likely have greatly reduced resistance to change. However, since the government had made them agree to tackle hospital reform first, this wasn't possible.

So the commission ploughed ahead. Once they began making what they called "directions", or orders, for hospital change, they got into trouble, despite a public relations' campaign to get out the message. Many found the recommendations based on troubling mathematical calculations that weren't easily fathomed. What was understood was that, in most cases, both the bed capacities and staffing levels of hospitals were being reduced. The loyalty people felt for their hospitals very quickly overcame the commission's meagre attempts at public consultation.

The HSRC also faced a number of court challenges, usually due to directions that affected who would actually operate amalgamated hospitals. In January 1997, the Sisters of St. Joseph of Sault Ste. Marie, the owners and operators of the Sudbury General Hospital sought a court-ordered stay to stop the commission from ordering their hospital's union with two other acute care hospitals in Sudbury. Their argument was that the HSRC was forcing them to give up their administration, and this violated their freedom of religion protection under the Charter of Rights and Freedoms. The Ontario Divisional Court refused to grant the stay, saying that the public would be harmed more significantly than the Sisters if the restructuring was delayed. In the end, there was no appeal, as an agreement was reached to permit the Sisters to have a role in the new regional hospital's administration.

An even more contentious amalgamation occurred in Pembroke. The non-denominational Civic Hospital was ordered closed, with its services transferred to the newer and larger Catholic General Hospital. The concern was primarily that the Catholic hospital refused to offer certain services available at the public institution, that is, abortions and other services related to reproductive health and, thus, these would no longer be available to the public at large. Again, the Divisional Court chose not to intercede, though it was hardly a strong approval.

The Legislative Assembly ... and the government ... gave the [HSRC] a very strong mandate to restructure the Ontario hospital system . . . . The court's role is very limited in these cases. The court has no power to inquire into the rights and wrongs of hospital restructuring laws or policies, the wisdom or folly of decisions to close particular hospitals, or decisions to direct particular hospital governance structures . . . The law provides no right of appeal from the HSRC to the court. The court has no power to review the merits of the HSRC's decisions. The only role of the court is to decide whether the HSRC acted according to the law in arriving at its decision. (Decision of Mr. Justice Archie Campbell, as quoted in *Looking Back, Looking Forward*, p. 111.)

The HSRC considered this quite a victory. The public was far less sure. In fact, the Pembroke General Hospital did indeed stop delivering abortions, forcing women to travel to Ottawa or further for the procedure. To this day, there are many who believe their rights have been violated by the alleged reform.

There were many other legal objections, including Wellesley Central Hospital in Toronto, a public institution ordered to relinquish itself to St. Michael's, a Catholic hospital; Doctors Hospital, also in Toronto, which was to relinquish itself to The Toronto Hospital; the *Hôtel Dieu* Hospital in Kingston, which was to be taken over by two other hospitals and closed; Douglas Memorial Hospital in Fort Erie, which was to be amalgamated with eight others to create a Niagara Region network. In all these cases, the HSRC won in court. However, they did lose once.

Hôpital Montfort in Ottawa was the only hospital in Ontario to offer services primarily in the French language, as well as in its teaching and training. Regardless, the HSRC ordered it closed in February 1997 and its services amalgamated with three other city hospitals, convinced that French language services could be delivered by them, particularly the Ottawa General Hospital. By August, due to "submissions received", the HSRC relented and said Montfort could remain open, though with reduced services. Its 252 beds would become 66, including the loss of surgical and acute-care beds, and it would lose its emergency department and cardiac unit. This was not acceptable to the administration and they went to court, arguing that Charter-guaranteed equality rights were being violated by the diminution of French health services, the unwritten protection of minorities, and that there was no assurance that other hospitals would maintain French language service levels. The Divisional Court heard the case in June 1999, releasing its decision in November, rejecting the constitutional contentions but accepting that the HSRC order violated minority rights. The commission "had seen these needs only in terms of the provision of bilingual services, and failed to address the necessity for homogeneous Francophone institutions". The court quashed the HSRC's order, which the province appealed after the commission's demise. On 7 December 2001, in a unanimous verdict of the Ontario Court of Appeal, the judges upheld the lower court decision.[7]

If the provincial government finally follows through on the recommendations of the HSRC, its actions have resulted, or will result, in the amalgamation of dozens of hospitals, the closure of 31 public hospitals, six private ones, and six provincial psychiatric hospital sites, four hospitals being taken over by other hospital corporations, ten joint committees having been established to administer multiple organizations, the institution of 18 rural/northern hospital networks, and the creation of child health networks in Ottawa, Toronto and London, regional rehabilitation networks, and, a French language services network in Ottawa.

However, in *Looking Back, Looking Forward*, the commission members identified a number of issues that they were concerned were being delayed or ignored by the government, as their mandate was coming to an end. Most were related to the Ministry of Health hedging on re-investments or not acting to resolve impediments to the further transfer or "re-balancing" of services, in the areas of mental health, rehabilitation services, community care access centres, chronic care hospitals, long-term care facilities, and home care.

And the HSRC went out making seven recommendations to aid the
continuation of reform.

ACTION 1:   *Build on the implementation of hospital restructuring and*
             reinvestment in other health facilities and community
             services.

ACTION 2:   *Articulate and communicate a vision of the future health*
             services system in Ontario .

ACTION 3:   *Clarify and define the role of government as primarily*
             responsible for system governance and leadership.

ACTION 4:   *Develop a comprehensive health information*
             management system.

ACTION 5:   *Implement a new model providing comprehensive*
             primary health care.

ACTION 6:   *Foster and support greater integration and co-ordination*
             within and across the system by:
             - Building on community efforts to strengthen integration.
             - Strengthening academic health science
                centres/networks.

ACTION 7:   *Develop and implement a process for improving health*
             system accountability and performance.

(HSRC. *Looking Back, Looking Forward*, p. 137.)

Clearly, Action 5 on primary health care reform is the most major issue
lacking in all the work done by the HSRC during its four years. However,
it did make recommendations on what needs to be done in this area. The
main proposals deal with people enrolling with group medical practices of
doctors and nurse practitioners, who will offer a defined range of
comprehensive primary health care services, 24-hours-a-day, 7-days-a-
week. Depending on the service provided, these groups would be paid by
fee-for-patient, or capitation, as it is known, sessional payments, and an
incentive system for meeting agreed-upon targets. These are controversial,
expensive suggestions, which probably explains why the government has
acted on almost none of them, going no further than a handful of pilot
projects.

Conclusions regarding the HSRC are difficult to determine, though it is
probably fair to say its results were uneven, at best. If there were three
flaws with the HSRC, the first was the perception that it was actually the
Hospital Closing Commission which, functionally, it was. The second,
and more important I think, was that no one bothered to explain to the
public why health care reform was needed, and convince them of it. The

Harris government just let the HSRC walk into a situation in which no one had been prepared for the debate to come. People resisted changes to their hospitals, or their closing, because most people didn't perceive the need for change. No one bothered to prepare the intellectual soil for tilling. The third was that, where there were multiple hospitals in one area, the commission seemed unwilling to accept any other model than one that created *big box* health organizations. It ignored uniqueness and differing administrative styles and realities to arbitrarily force organizational unions that the public opposed.

Perhaps the reason the government and the commissioners failed to recognize the lack of public agreement with change was because, when the Tories took power, there were a number of local initiatives underway in different areas to consolidate hospitals and health care services, in general. It may be they took this as an implicit popular acceptance of reform. If so, they were wrong.

Ultimately, the other failure of the HSRC was its inability to hold the government to its word. The financial savings from health restructuring were supposed to be re-invested in the system. Now there is no question funding increased. Between the fiscal years 1995-1996 and 1999-2000, the government budget for health increased from $17.4 billion to $20.2 billion. However, the re-investment that was supposed to go into community-based services, such as long-term care and home care, did not appear in any great amount. In fact, such services were also being cut. In 1996, the minimum requirement for 2.25 hours of care for each nursing home patient was dropped. (By 2001, it averaged 14 minutes per day.) It is not clear whether the Harris government expected the HSRC to determine what amount of re-investment was needed – probably not – but it tried.

However, it must be said that the arms-length relationship, while difficult for the commission, became almost equally so for the government. In setting up a board that could act with Ministerial power, it did so ... occasionally to the political detriment of the government. Ministers Jim Wilson and Elizabeth Witmer found themselves trying to explain away a number of decisions, though they themselves had no part in making them. In fact, ministry officials consistently sent letters to the commission asking its members to reconsider decisions, such as the one on Montfort.[8]

Eventually, however, enough was enough. It had been the HSRC's intention to issue directions to rural and northern hospitals, once they finished with the urban ones. However, it wasn't long before they began to do just this, and the government found itself facing a reality they hadn't anticipated. As much as they wanted to get rid of hospital over-capacity, they clearly hadn't considered what this might mean in rural areas ... ones that were in the heart of Tory ridings. The commission was ordering cuts to small hospitals, and was running into criticism that patients could well face death because of the travel distances to other hospitals. The Harrisites wasted little time in ending the arms-length relationship. In June 1997, Wilson intervened to change the commission's rules, such that rural hospitals could not be closed or amalgamated. Then, in April 1999, his successor, Witmer, prohibited the HSRC from issuing any further hospital orders, and they decided, from there on, the commission would only provide advice to the Minister of Health on this subject. It was a cop-out, no doubt precipitated by the coming general election.

The true *hangover* left for the government was the HSRC's actions to reduce hospital over-capacity. As much as the closure of hospitals caught headlines, it is the reductions to those that are left with which the Tories have to deal, especially those in rural and tourist areas. Many now operate at *capacity*, but this can mean being extremely short of staff and beds at various times. The definition of capacity was more based on *average* than anything. In areas where tourists flock in for a few months, then vanish, averages can be seriously thrown off. So, in some areas, limits were set, only to be far lower than was needed at times of greatest use. This is particularly true for emergency services, especially in under-serviced areas.

I have doubts that history will judge the Health Services Restructuring Commission positively. Making massive changes to the health care system without first having a comprehensive plan was a mistake. Not being able to make certain the government followed a plan after the commission was terminated was also a mistake. Of course, neither mistake was made by the commissioners, as they had no say in the matter. That belonged to the government, mostly due to its desire to stay *arms-length* from health care cutting decisions that were innately political.

But there was another side to health care change, where the government was quite hands-on, sticky fingers and all. As mentioned, the omnibus bill contained provisions to seriously affect doctors and their wages. Bill 26 would have given the Ministry of Health the power to dig into doctors' records to search for over-billing or over-treatment, to limit billing numbers in areas where doctors were plentiful in hopes of forcing them to practice in under-serviced ones, to increase medical school tuition, and to take away the Ontario Medical Association (OMA) as the doctors' representative in contract talks, as well as taking away its ability to set fees for doctors. The idea was that if each different group of doctors, be they specialists or general practitioners, were forced to negotiate separately, their strength in negotiations would be diminished. However, when the government failed to slip the omnibus bill by the watchful eyes of the Opposition and the light of day was shone on these provisions, the Minister abandoned most of them.

But Jim Wilson wasn't done yet. With his section of Bill 26 gutted, yet still determined to restrain these wages, he ended the government's $36 million subsidy of physicians' malpractice insurance. By March, obstetricians and gynecologists announced they would not, for fear of lawsuit, handle difficult births. Angry words were exchanged, and the Tories backed down in the face of fearful expectant mothers.

Then, a few months later, in July, the 6% clawback that the Rae government had imposed on billings was raised to 10%. In Promised Land, John Ibbitson suggests "this was a remarkable decision for a Harris Conservative" in that market forces influence wages, even in a "socialized" system.[9] However, it may not have been out of character, at all, for this government. For the CSR agenda to be implemented, the Harrisites needed enemies: people on welfare; civil service unions; teachers. It seems to me that doctors were initially identified for this list.

Throughout this period, there was an ongoing threat that doctors would go on strike. This potential must not have seemed entirely regrettable, as the 1986 doctors' withdrawal over the loss of extra-billing had actually made the Peterson Liberals more popular. However, instead of striking, the doctors elected to stop taking new patients. Bad enough that many general practitioners and specialists carried through with this action, but the optics were much worse because obstetricians and gynecologists did as well. When the media began showing pictures and telling stories of frightened women in their eighth and ninth months of pregnancy and no doctor, the public was angered. Perhaps the government felt this would boomerang back on the doctors but, for the most part, any backlash whipped the Harrisites and Wilson, in particular, and ministry officials sat down with doctors' representatives to discuss a new contract.

In mid-fall, a deal was reached in which the government conceded cuts to clawbacks in favour of getting doctors into under-serviced areas. However, the OMA negotiators apparently didn't realize the resentment all the government fumbling had created amongst physicians. Wilson himself made matters worse. He demanded the College of Physicians and

Surgeons punish those doctors that withdrew services. The ratification vote failed by a 3-1 ratio. Doctors said they wouldn't force their younger colleagues to practice where they wouldn't. They felt the clawback was too high, if not entirely unfair. It meant they were working too many hours for free. Specialists still maintained they were under-paid. It was felt many simply wanted more services de-listed from OHIP so they could charge whatever *the market would bear*. At this point, many doctors escalated tensions by cutting back their hours and making themselves unavailable at night.

It was at this point that the government found its way out, though certainly not intentionally. Jim Wilson is known as a man with a serious temper, one that he had great difficulty restraining during these tough days. He consistently made disagreeable comments about the doctors, which just made them more angry and determined. On 5 December, his communications' assistant, Brett James, suggested to a reporter that Dr. William Hughes, the Vice-Chair of the Specialists' Coalition, was the top-billing doctor in Ontario[10] . Presumably, this was supposed to embarrass the man, as he was one of the leaders of a group organizing a province-wide withdrawal of services planned for the 13th. Given that it would break privacy rules to have or disclose this financial information, James had to resign. However, the question was *how did he know how much Hughes billed*? Was it just an off-hand comment made without proof, or did he actually know? And if he knew, did Wilson? Wilson had to go, too, at least until an investigation was done.

Harris took this as his chance to escape the no-win situation into which his Health minister had got the government. As such, he appointed his recently-anointed golden boy Dave Johnson to cover health for the interim. Johnson wasted no time in getting a deal. No doubt with the approval of the Premier, he laid down for the doctors, conceding to virtually every one of their demands. The clawback dropped to 2.9%. New doctors practising in over-serviced areas would receive 70% of fees, increasing each year to 100% after three years. The billing cap would be increased for family doctors. The only negative for the physicians was that specialists had to eat a decrease in their billing cap. That was temporary, as was the agreement.

On 31 May 1997, a three-year contract was ratified that allowed for 1.5% annual pay hikes for all doctors and the elimination of the clawbacks. Nurses, in particular, were incensed, as they saw this as taking money out of front-line services. Jim Wilson was back at the helm by then, having been cleared of any wrongdoing. He said the deal would cost $300 million over three years. However, other critics said the cost would be closer to $1 billion, given the loss of revenue from the clawbacks.

Perhaps when he had been sitting on the sidelines, Wilson learned from Johnson the benefits of concession. In some ways, this was the first real defeat of the Harris government. They had identified a problem – money spent on doctors salaries – and had decided to take it on. It was much the same as with the civil service and the teachers. But when they went at it, they were outflanked and outwitted. In the end, instead of saving money, the government ended up spending more as the price for peace. As it was, the Harrisites left the doctors alone from there on, and one group was dropped from the government's enemies' list.

5. 'Who Does What ... To Whom'

For many, the Tory government's foray into *disentanglement* made little sense. While it was true that the division of responsibilities between the provincial government and municipalities had become increasingly complex and occasionally irrational, the Harrisites had so many things on their plate that it seemed strange they would choose to bite off such a big chunk of something new, just at that time. The CSR carried one line on the topic. Under the 'Less Government' section, the document said 'We will sit down with municipalities to discuss ways of reducing government entanglement and bureaucracy with an eye to eliminating waste and duplication as well as unfair downloading by the province'. It was far from one of their more significant promises, and hardly one of their firmest, yet it would prove to be one of their most devastating decisions.

Education vs. Welfare

Simply, the Tories were forced to delve into the morass of disentanglement due to their desire for money. With cuts to be made, the government had to address the areas of expenditure. Since health care had been declared as off-limits – at least directly – that left welfare and education as the next obvious targets. Now the CSR had been very clear on the Tories' position on welfare. Cuts were going to be made that would engender significant savings, yet not nearly enough. That meant the education budget would have to be hit, as well. But how to do it and not make people fear that their children's education was being compromised?

As John Ibbitson well points out in his book, in effect, there were five *wanna-be* education ministers in Mike Harris' Cabinet – the real one, John Snobelen, and four others who had all been school board trustees, Elizabeth Witmer, Dianne Cunningham, Cam Jackson, and Harris himself.[11] Each saw themselves as knowledgeable on the subject, as well as agreeing that the education system was in trouble. What better way to hide their *thieving* from its budget than to re-construct it with the province in charge, and with the local authorities as powerless husks that would do little more than continue to sop up public criticism.

And this last point must have been a significant factor amongst the four former trustees. School board trustees have been targets for tremendous abuse over the years, particularly as their remuneration crept up. Undoubtedly, Harris, Witmer, Cunningham, and Jackson remembered malignancies and curses directed at them during their years in that position. It must have been reasonable to think that any ill-feelings engendered by changes to the system would continue to be directed at school boards.

However, initially, Minister Snobelen favoured doing away with these boards entirely. There were 129 school boards in the province, counting those in English public, French public, English separate, and French separate. For most people, including the Minister, each ran as a mini-fiefdom fuelled by the power to hike property taxes at a whim. Though they may have been accountable to the voters at election time, they were less than 50% accountable to the province because less than half of their money came in transfers from it. There were few boards that hadn't been attacked for building *Taj Mahal* headquarters and having trustees and staff that took far more in pay than they returned in work. Doing away with them, figuratively-speaking, and taking over total control of education would mean savings from massive employee cuts, the divestment of unnecessary infrastructure, and an end to board-to-board duplication. For all intents and purposes, each school would become a board unto itself, with the principal in charge ... just like the old days.

As well, the teachers' unions had seemingly found a way of constantly enhancing their wages. Every year or two, a handful of school board union locals would go on strike and eventually settle or be forced into binding arbitration. This would result in modest gains, but gains in fact. Other boards would use these settlements as models, and teachers across the province would get wage and/or benefit hikes. Again, perception was not reality. Between 1985 and 1995, teachers in Ontario received an average wage increase of 40%. However, the cost of living had gone up about 40%. In essence, they were no better off and just maintained what they had. Of course, when most other people had their wages frozen, cut back, or they became unemployed, during the 1990-1995 period, they had little sympathy.

But there was another reason for the Harrisites to axe school boards. *They clearly weren't doing their job.* Annual per student funding in Ontario tended to be higher than in the other provinces. In 1994-1995, it was the second-highest in the country. To the Tories, the problem seemed to be value for money. In the limited testing that came from occasional national and international assessments on a variety of subjects, Ontario students usually did no better than average, and often worse. In other provinces spending less, test results were at least as good or even better. If that was the case, surely per student funding could be cut without making anything worse?

Snobelen's view was one based on economics, while the other *education ministers* took in the added dimension of *what was wrong.* They saw the testing results as an abomination and felt Ontario students needed a tougher curriculum and regular testing to prove that they had indeed learned the material. This was, essentially, the final rejection of the child-centred education model brought in under Bill Davis. It might have seemed ironic for Tories to reject something on which one of their predecessors had *made his bones.*

The Tories wanted to take $1.4 billion out of the education budget. This would reduce it, but to the alleged national average. And with the property tax now making up so much of the money being spent by school boards, per student funding was beginning to vary greatly from board to board, especially in rural, northern, and Catholic boards. Snobelen felt that doing away with the school boards would allow the province to then fund by an equal amount per student, though no one was promising the average wouldn't be lower than before.

As part of the November 1995 economic statement, education was cut $400 million, or about 3%. While even the Tories thought it was unfortunate that this hit the school boards that received less funding from property taxes – typically the assessment-poor boards – speed demanded quick action. And while the omnibus bill gave municipalities the opportunity to raise funds from user fees, it did nothing for the school boards. In place of that, Snobelen promised them a "tool kit" that would be filled with ways of helping them reduce their costs. Unfortunately for him, the other four so-called education ministers would steal the batteries for his tools.

Snobelen, on advice from some trustees, wanted to re-open collective agreements to permit the boards to remove certain benefits from teachers, such as compensation for class preparation time and accumulated sick leave. This would have saved the boards millions of dollars collectively and, the Minister was assured, would be enough to get them through these cuts more-or-less unscathed.

However, Elizabeth Witmer, in particular, objected, when he presented this tool kit to Cabinet. She felt that this was simply trustees trying to get the province to do their dirty work for them. Better the school boards force this on teachers, as they had agreed to these benefits originally. Why should the provincial government become the villain and take the heat more deserved by the trustees?

It seems likely that Snobelen saw the problem Witmer didn't. The school boards were not about to go against the teachers. Not only did they not want to upset them, since they were the main employees of the boards, but a significant number of trustees had been teachers at one time. If it was left to them, they would never try to renegotiate contracts and any cuts would indeed end up coming from the classroom.

The Minister was surprised when Harris agreed with Witmer at the February 1996 Planning and Policy Committee meeting, as did the others in attendance. Though they relished the thought of a show-down with unions, they recognized they were already facing one with the provincial civil servants and "even Mike Harris was reluctant to conduct labour wars on two fronts at once"[12]. Instead, it was decided there would be a moratorium on capital spending by boards, but that they would actually get a little more in operating funds. As well, they would be advised that they could seek to reduce teachers' benefits, if they wanted to try. "In essence, the boards were being given a year to put their houses in order."[13]

It was Snobelen who now had a two-front war of his own. Not only did he have to come up with a billion dollars more in cuts, but he could now see he wasn't necessarily going to get the easy blessing of his colleagues. It is often hard to get changes past a Premier, but if he had to compete with Cabinet members as well, he was in great trouble. It didn't help that the media made fun of him for introducing an empty tool kit.

In fact, there were hopes that the school boards would *do the right thing* and finally take the knife to their administrative structures. The provincial and municipal governments had to do it. The hospitals had to do it. Why not the boards? Well, they didn't. Instead, 78% of the boards raised property taxes to make up for the initial cuts. Snobelen and Harris were incensed. And while it reinforced the Minister's belief that the boards had to go, his more radical approach also resurrected Snobelen's status with the Premier.

Yet some of the criticism of school boards was unfair. The proportion of provincial funding had been dropping for many years for most boards, which had forced them to increase property taxes to maintain standards. From 1985-1995, the education portion of property taxes rose 133% in the province, while the provincial government's share dropped up to 33%. Also, there had been a rise of 20% in student enrollment and a 38.4% increase in inflation over the same period. In fact, it turns out, virtually the entire increase in school board property taxes was simply to cover significantly higher costs.

With Snobelen's reputation having improved, the Minister returned to his idea of single-school school boards. If there was any question that the abolition of school boards was unconstitutional because it would violate Catholics' right to control their own system, this would eliminate it. However, it would also create a problem the man apparently didn't want to face. Such boards had been all meshed together originally because it was nearly impossible for the government to deal with thousands of schools on an individual basis. Going back to such a system would re-institute what most considered a nightmare. As well, any complaints about education would be coming straight back on the province, and what MPP wanted to deal with that?

It's not clear where the idea came from, but it must have had instant appeal. Leave the boards alone, just take away their powers. Run the system from Queen's Park, but leave trustees as straw men to take the blame for things people didn't like. Take the tax money and dole it back on an equalized basis, with the boards having no ability to raise their own funds.

But, even with seemingly great ideas, there is a price. In this case, the province taking over the school system would transfer the $5.4 billion that was raised on the property tax into the provincial income tax. And even with the property tax being cut by the same amount, the Tories didn't believe that people would recognize the saw-off. They feared people – especially their own supporters – would see the provincial budget rise and think they had tossed their election promises out the window.

The truth is that this uploading could have been the most progressive move this government would make. Given the regressive nature of property taxes, moving these costs to the income tax would have been more than fair. By regressive, I mean that property taxes are not based on one's ability to pay them. Imagine, for example, a retired widow on a small pension of $15,000 living in a nice brick house in old Toronto that she and her late husband owned. This house is assessed at $300,000. At the same time, a working couple with a combined income of $150,000 live in, and own, a larger split-level bungalow, on a bigger lot, in Markham. It is also assessed at $300,000. *Common sense* would seem to dictate that it is fair they both pay the same tax on their residence. However, that's a regressive tax. The widow may be property rich, but she's income poor. In effect, having to pay the same amount as the couple penalizes her for having a home which has been kept up and is in a nice neighbourhood. If the education portion of her property tax was increased, then she would become even less able to pay it. At a certain point, the penalty could easily become the loss of her home, as she would be forced to sell it and move somewhere cheaper. Income tax is considered progressive because it is based on a person's ability to pay it. The more you make, the more you pay (in theory). If the couple's income tax was increased to finance education, they would be much more able to handle it because they are income rich.

But the Harris government wasn't about to be progressive. And it had another problem. Janet Ecker, then Community and Social Services' minister, having replaced David Tsubouchi, was suggesting that welfare be uploaded to the province, as well.

Upper-tier municipalities such as regional and county governments administered general welfare assistance (GWA), help for able-bodied people temporarily out-of-work (after the exhaustion of federal unemployment benefits) and had to pay for 20% of its costs. The province picked up 80% of this, plus administered and paid 100% of the costs of family benefits (FBA), considered long-term assistance, usually for single mothers with children.

The province was still working on its plan to impose a work-for-welfare programme on all able-bodied men and women, people who were primarily collecting GWA. This meant they would have to get these upper-tier municipalities to cooperate, either by coercion or *bribery*. Neither was especially palatable, given that municipalities were signalling they didn't want to be involved and unions were threatening to boycott any organization that used workfare workers[7]. So Ecker proposed taking over GWA and its total costs, and having the province run it. If it had control, it faced no opposition and those on workfare could *do their time* with provincial government offices and affiliated agencies.

It might have seemed an elegant plan had it not been that these costs would have uploaded another $5 billion onto the province. On top of what Snobelen was proposing, this would have been out of the question, right from the start, if it hadn't been that the Ministry of the Solicitor-General wanted to dump policing onto municipalities and the Ministry of Transportation wanted counties and regions to take over responsibility for most provincial highways. A discussion began on a revenue-neutral swap between municipalities and the province, one that would *disentangle* a number of services.

It didn't take a chartered accountant to realise it couldn't be done, however. At best, the downloading of policing and highways would send $2.9 billion to the municipalities, while the uploading of education and welfare would cost the province $10.4 billion. This would hardly be revenue-neutral. And while provincial politicians and bureaucrats debated what to do, they could not seem to come to a resolution.

Meanwhile, the *Who Does What* commission had been appointed in May 1996, for much the same reason, to disentangle provincial and municipal services. John Ibbitson suggests its purpose was to co-opt local government officials by inviting them in on the process. Such *luminaries* as former "Tiny Perfect" Toronto mayor and Mulroney Cabinet minister David Crombie and long-time Mississauga mayor Hazel McCallion were appointed to the panel. The difficulty here was that it is hard to put independent-minded people on a committee, even if they were all pretty much Tories, and expect them to just rubber-stamp whatever you come up with. It might also be fair to say this group worked a might faster than expected. Within months, they were also proposing the uploading of education and welfare to the province.

There was no way the government was going to risk taking on a significantly larger budget, even if the revenue existed to do so. The Harris Tories were there to shrink government or, more precisely, shrink the provincial government. In the end, the *solution* to the conundrum came from an unlikely source, the "ever-diminishing-in-stature" minister Al Leach.

Leach might have proven he was an able bureaucrat in his time with the Toronto Transit Commission, but he hadn't proven much worth as a politician or Municipal Affair's minister. Inside of a year in office, there were Tories who were wishing the man would disappear, either through early retirement or by Harris dropping him from Cabinet. Regardless, he still held the ear of the Premier and many of his colleagues.

Though neither education nor welfare were under his purview, he chose to stick his nose into the question of disentanglement, perhaps because it would affect municipalities. He was clearly not a man who accepted the old adage that hard services, like roads and sewers, were best delivered by the municipalities and the soft services, like welfare, were best coming from the province.[15] The argument here was an easy one. Hard services cost a predictable amount of money per year. As a result, property taxes could be calculated on a solid set of numbers, which would keep it from jumping around. On the other hand, soft services could vary greatly from year to year, and property taxes are difficult to adjust for rapid fluctuations.

Leach began to lobby his colleagues to accept the uploading of education, while entirely downloading welfare. His argument was more simple. Education was something that affected everyone, especially those with children. Welfare affected a very small number of people. Leaving it to be dealt with on a local level only made sense.

Between Snobelen and Leach, both the senior of Ecker in Cabinet, they carried the day. This was despite her objections that it would be almost impossible to make municipalities cooperate on the implementation of workfare, and that the property tax usually dropped when times were bad, just when welfare rolls were normally on the rise. What she may have missed on this latter argument was the widespread belief amongst her colleagues that welfare rolls went up because of cheaters, not need.

Snobelen was to get his way. Boards would be reduced in number and stripped of most of their powers, though they would continue to negotiate contracts with teachers. Funding would come entirely from the provincial government through the income tax, no longer any from property taxes. And Leach got his way, mostly. GWA and FBA would be amalgamated and entirely administered by municipalities, while being funded 50% by them. To top it all off, the province would off-load any financial responsibility for water and sewers, most highways, public transit, long-term care facilities, health units, and public housing. In the face of expected opposition, a billion dollar adjustment fund was to be set up to temporarily cushion the blow. And the Tories could afford it. Despite the claim that this exchange was completely revenue-neutral, the truth was closer to the municipalities being forced to eat an extra billion dollars or more per year.

But as the government prepared to introduce its solution, there was another problem, one even more the creation of the Tories themselves. It had to do with a *simple* change to Toronto ... amalgamating it with its neighbours.

6. 'Me-gas-i-ty'

"Megacity", pronounced 'meg-a-cit-y': a great or large and important town.

"Megacity", pronounced 'me-gas-i-ty': the mess now named Toronto.

In many ways, this was an issue that ambushed the Harris Tories. In their drive to make government more efficient they, as was their habit, failed to do their homework, and they failed to consider they might offend someone. Many think they knew they would cause offence and didn't care. Perhaps this was true once they felt public pressure, but I don't think they intended to irritate right from the start. I think they just fell into a hole they failed to see ... again.

As mentioned earlier, the Conservative party had a history of amalgamating municipalities as a way of seeking efficiencies, so it wasn't a great leap for the Harris government to contemplate the same for the burgeoning and expensive Toronto. And I'm sure that Ministry of Municipal Affairs staff did little to hold them back, as they had been busy during the NDP's term promoting such unions in a variety of smaller areas. So, when Premier Harris suggested that Toronto amalgamation with its neighbours was a good idea, I doubt the Tories had any grasp of the wasps' nest at which they were poking.

Creating a greater Toronto was not a plan of the CSR, though the concept of municipal reorganization was mentioned, indirectly.

> *Canadians are probably the most over-governed people in the world. We do not need every layer – federal, provincial, quasi-governmental bodies, regional, municipal and school board – that we have now. We must rationalize the regional and municipal levels to avoid the overlap and duplication that now exists.*

In fact, the reason to take on such a job was, again, alleged common sense.

The Tories felt that eliminating a municipal layer would save money, which they needed. There are those that think that the *attack* on Toronto was simply Mike Harris' revenge for people there not supporting his government's policies. And there is little question that Harris himself was tired of dealing with the latent dislike and mewling he and his government received from Metro Toronto-based politicians. Perhaps this made Toronto the target, but I doubt it was the impetus for reorganization. It is seldom the case that you want to make changes that conjure up a stronger opponent.

It is unclear that the Harrisites had any real intention to act on this front at all. Beyond a throw-away election utterance by Harris to get rid of the Metro level of Toronto, they had not really committed to municipal *reform*. However, they were drawn in by a leftover of the Rae administration. Too late in its term to do anything about it, the NDP appointed a task force, headed by then Toronto United Way head Anne Golden, to look into governance in the Greater Toronto Area. When the report was issued in January 1996, it caused some stir, as it recommended doing away with the upper tier level of government, both in Toronto and in the surrounding regions, as well as promoting property tax reform. The lower-tier municipalities would remain, and be given more powers to deal with their concerns. The only remnant of the upper tier would be a council made up of relevant municipal mayors which would coordinate area-wide planning.

Al Leach instantly hailed the report and promised to get on its recommendations, as soon as possible. No doubt his enthusiasm was due to the fact that its recommendations seemed to fit so exactly with both his, and the premier's, own perspective. However, this was in the middle of the debate over the omnibus bill, so action was going to be delayed. But before anything could be done, circumstances changed. Almost right away, abuse was heaped upon the report by local politicians out of the 905 area. It was not so much based on abolishing the regional governments, as it was on Golden's proposed changes on taxes.

All across Ontario, property taxes were a mess. They varied on houses of equal value from place to place, making them apparently unfair. While some homes had been re-assessed in the last few years, there were others that hadn't been in 50 years. The Golden Commission proposed a virtually unchanged system, except that reassessments would be done regularly, and sharp rises and falls in assessment would be evened out. But the change seen as a problem would be to pool education property taxes paid by businesses in the GTA so that companies moving into the suburbs to avoid high City of Toronto property taxes would not be able to drain funding from city schools. Well, this was like a declaration of war for suburban politicians, and the provincial government was not anxious to be in a fight with people who should be their friends.

The other thing that changed was that Mr. Harris went to Asia. Mike Harris had just returned from southeast Asia as a member of the ubiquitous Team Canada, trying to open markets for Canadian and Ontario companies in that part of the world. Apparently, when Ontario delegates, and Harris himself, were asked where they were from, answers like Scarborough and Etobicoke, and even Ontario, met blank stares. Once they said Toronto, everyone knew where they meant. Apparently, it set the Premier to thinking. Maybe their ideas for the GTA were backwards.

It took several months, but the Tories worked out their response. Much to the chagrin of Anne Golden, they went the other way, proposing to do away with the lower-tier municipalities and keep Metro and the regions. Again, Al Leach was the front man, changing from Golden booster to Golden critic. His logic was that keeping the lower tier with service agreements to cover region-wide concerns was much less efficient than just eliminating the cities and boroughs and going with region-wide government. He proposed the creation of a super-sized Toronto.

In Promised Land, John Ibbitson suggests that Harris could have been expected to oppose amalgamation, given his philosophy of favouring smaller government.[16] However, I think this is a misinterpretation of Harris' beliefs. In fact, the man seemed to favour centralized, centrally-controlled government. Going back to his closing of the Tory headquarters in 1990 and his running the party out of his office, he had shown a propensity to concentrate control whenever possible. And, with the debate over education at this time, he was also showing a preference for centralizing that, as well. In any event, Harris took to Leach's plan.

The government's arguments in favour of this kind of change were basic. "We propose leaving behind the overlap and duplication, escalating costs, confused priorities and conflicting mandates. And too many levels of government", said Leach. The number of duplicated departments and services were repeated endlessly, as was the argument that taxpayers would save money. According to a government-commissioned KPMG study, this would amount to about $300 million per year. Other arguments were that political responsibility would now be clear, rather than leaving citizens confused as to whether something was Metro or city, a unified city would be better able to create a climate for growth and business, community councils would ensure neighbourhood concerns were dealt with, and this was an inevitable evolution of government in Toronto.

In December 1996, the Tories introduced Bill 103, the *City of Toronto Act*, forcing the amalgamation of the six lower tier municipalities – Toronto, Scarborough, North York, Etobicoke, York, and East York, along with the upper-tier metropolitan government. The "Megacity", so nicknamed by *The Toronto Star*[17], was to eliminate waste and duplication. The line went that "one is cheaper to run than six", or seven if you included Metro.

Now there are those who believe that this was actually the Harris government at its best, recognizing the uncoordinated governance of the area and how it was negatively affecting business and planning, much as it had, in a different way, back in the 1940s when Leslie Frost had chosen to act. The aforementioned *Toronto Star* was one flag-waver for the megacity. If one accepts two aphorisms, that *the end justifies the means* and *one is cheaper than six*, this may be true. However, if one prefers the high road and rejects the *common sense* of amalgamations, then this may have been Harris *et.al.* near their worst. Apparently, a good portion of Metro Toronto residents thought the 'worst'.

The major organized opponent of the megacity initiative was *Citizens for Local Democracy*, a group of concerned people, quickly put together and led by former Toronto mayor John Sewell. Not only was Sewell an opponent because he disagreed with their stand on Toronto, but he was still fuming about the Tories having savaged the *Planning Act*, a statute that had been redesigned by a Sewell-led commission under the NDP. But C4LD, as they came to be identified, opposed the government for more visceral reasons.

C4LD had three fundamental objections to amalgamation. The first was that 106 Metro and local councillors were going to turn into just 45, including the mayor, which would leave people with less representation and less access to their representatives. As well, they argued that "small towns" inherent in Toronto – the ancient suburbs that had been amalgamated years before, but had retained much of their characters – would be *bulldozed* in the supercity. Unique services would be lost, and differing service levels would have to be eliminated for the sake of uniformity. The other problem they had was that the government couldn't prove its claims of financial savings. Urban guru Jane Jacobs, a resident of Toronto, and the mother figure of all left-wing city philosophers, made a convincing case that smaller cities are better able to respond to local needs, while being more innovative and retaining a sustainable, livable city.

Unfortunately, the case against megacity was undermined, unintentionally, by many local politicians. While most of them also opposed amalgamation, they kept reserving their criticism in certain ways. Too many, like North York mayor Mel Lastman, defined the *uniqueness* of their community by how often it had garbage collection. And Toronto mayor Barbara Hall, while resisting the proposed union, demanded the municipal elections be delayed for six months so that there could be sufficient time to reconsider it. Many saw this as a call simply to give her longer to prepare to run for megacity mayor.

But the Tories were having none of the reproval, stiffened their backs and prepared to move ahead. At the same time, they had their programme for disentanglement ready to go. They elected to combine it with their work on Toronto and present them in a "mega-week" of announcements in January 1997. Just as a year before with the omnibus bill, they hoped to overwhelm the opposition by the sheer number and importance of the proposals, and steamroll over it.

Yet those who opposed the amalgamation had their own plans. In a desperate attempt to change the minds of the government members, they pulled out a weapon the province had mentioned during the election campaign – referenda. Many Tory MPPs, especially those that were also in sympathy with the federal Reform party, were supporters of the idea that the people should be able to present the government with policies through referendum or plebiscite – a direct vote by citizens. The Metro mayors decided to use this against them, hoping a negative vote would make the Tories reconsider.

The second Monday of January was the beginning of mega-week. John Snobelen announced Bill 104, the *Fewer School Boards Act*. It proposed significantly reducing the number of boards and trustees. As well, it would limit trustees to a maximum remuneration of $5,000 per year, no matter the size of the board. On the tax front, the education portion of property taxes would be eliminated and the province would assume 100% responsibility for education funding. The Minister also announced the government's intention to write up a tougher curriculum and bring in standardized report cards.

On Tuesday, it was Janet Ecker's turn. She outlined the funding changes on welfare, completely shifting it to the municipalities, along with 50% of the cost. In addition to this, the municipalities were told they would have to pick up half the cost of local subsidized day-care, as well as total responsibility for public health administration and programmes and all of public housing.

Wednesday was a tag-team of ministers: Transportation's Al Palladini; Health's Jim Wilson; Culture's Marilyn Mushinski; and Attorney-General Bob Runciman. Palladini announced the province's downloading of most highways, public transit, and GO Trains to the municipalities. Wilson told them they would now be responsible for half the cost of long-term care. Mushinski ended grants to libraries. Runciman announced an end to public subsidies for local policing.

Mega-week ended on Thursday, with Finance minister Ernie Eves letting the public in on the province's intention to bring in Actual Value Assessment for property taxes, as recommended by the Golden Commission, though it would apply province-wide. This would mean that all homes would have to be re-assessed regularly.[18] Of course, assurances were made that the swaps would be completely revenue-neutral. Even if that was true, which seemed questionable, it didn't mean the exchanges were entirely fair. For example, there can be little doubt that the new city of Toronto would suffer, having to take on extra costs for welfare, while the neighbouring suburbs would be relieved of some of these costs.

Meanwhile, the *Citizens for Local Democracy* were doing their best to make life hell for the government. Not only were they able to pack halls with people spitting venom, but they were filling the public hearings, trying their best to put the fear of God into the Tory MPPs, especially those from Toronto ridings. At first, they were somewhat leery of getting involved with the municipal plebiscites, apparently because Sewell didn't trust the local politicians. However, that changed as it became more obvious people were going to vote overwhelmingly against amalgamation.

And they did. The votes were held on 3 March. The question put forward was "Are you in favour of eliminating [*name of municipality*] and all other municipalities in Metropolitan Toronto and amalgamating them into a Megacity?" Obviously, it wasn't a very neutral query. Toronto went 73.4% against. Scarborough, 81.5%. North York, 79.4%. Etobicoke, 69.7%. York, 71.2%. And East York, 80.8%. It averaged 76% against, with about 380,000 people voting. Though the Harris government was perfectly correct in questioning the results, as they varied from Etobicoke's traditional poll vote to North York's phone-in vote to the other four municipalities using mail-in ballots, it didn't matter. In this case, the overwhelming numbers dictated legitimacy, fairly or not. The provincial government was on the run, but was not willing to concede.

Leach offered a few minor amendments. Instead of creating a council of 45, it would be 58. Community councils would have most of their powers defined by the city council, not the province. As well, the trustees that were to be appointed to oversee the transition would not be free from legal action should they violate any laws. He also went to the Association of Municipalities of Ontario to ask it for any advice its members could offer.

But their troubles continued. When Bill 103 moved to the committee stage, after Second Reading, the opposition parties presented 11,000 amendments to it. The NDP had come up with a *form* amendment that demanded the residents of each of the roughly 10,000 streets in the six municipalities be canvassed for their opinions on amalgamation. It was a canny move that forced the government into a 24-hour-a-day session, until they could vote down all the amendments. The parties worked in teams to make sure they could continue. This was much easier for the Tories since their caucus was so much larger, and particularly difficult for the NDP with just 16 members. And even with this, the Tories weren't paying complete attention and allowed one of the NDP amendments to pass. When a final vote came due, the three parties agreed to allow it in teams, as well, and the Tories repaired their error. It took two weeks but Bill 103 finally passed on Friday, 11 April. As of 1 January 1998, the amalgamation of Toronto would take effect.

By comparison, Bill 104 on reducing school boards passed without difficulty, 12 days later. For whatever reason, the Opposition made no move to filibuster it. Perhaps it was because there weren't thousands of people to give it the same kind of media coverage. Perhaps the MPPs hadn't caught up on their sleep.

But that wasn't the end. Municipalities continued to complain that they would be bankrupted by welfare costs should the economy slide again, so AMO came up with a compromise. Instead of the province taking all of education costs off the property tax, they could continue to collect 50% of them from it. In exchange, the municipalities would only have to pay 20% of welfare, plus 50% of administrative costs. As well, the province would re-assume responsibility for long-term care, and 80% of day-care funding. Lastly, the province would grant municipalities $200 million to cushion the downloading of public housing repairs.

In August, the Tories blinked again, and ordered the GTA municipalities to share the costs of region-wide child-care, GO Transit, subsidized housing, and welfare. When city politicians complained there would be $103 million in extra annual costs, along with $61 million in one-time expenses, they agreed, in January 1998, to loan the new City of Toronto $200 million over two years, along with a $50 million grant. This money was to cover transition costs, but it came with strings. Though the first $100 million was guaranteed and came interest-free, the second $100 million was contingent on the city showing it could find savings, that it really needed the money, and after it agreed to repayment terms. The grant was limited to the purchase of communications' equipment for the police and fire departments.

I think it's fair to say that disentanglement was really *re-entanglement*, a complicated re-ordering of the mess that already existed. The Harris government had its chance to be truly progressive by uploading both education and welfare and getting them off the property tax system. Instead, more now comes out of it than it did before. This, in combination with the megacity exercise, wasn't so much "the mistake that ate the agenda", as Liberal strategist John Duffy said[19], as much as it was "how to spin your wheels and spend a lot of time and money doing it".

Toronto amalgamation, as with all similar municipal restructuring, was a mistake because it was based on the whole *one is cheaper than six* theory. The flaw in this thinking is that it isn't – 'one' costs just as much or more than 'six'. Amalgamations end up costing more in the end, in virtually all cases. The examples are legion, and are basically caused by the same reasons. The Harris government argued that there were 2.4 million people in Metro Toronto, with seven governments supposedly looking after their interests. If this could be made into one government, overlap and duplication would be eliminated, along with excess staff and infrastructure, and save significant amounts of money.

But that's not how it works. The problem with this type of *common sense* thinking is that it is based on the false premise that *one is less than six*. The reality is that the sum population of the megacity, at the time, was 2.4 million, just as the sum populations of Toronto, Scarborough, North York, Etobicoke, York, and East York was 2.4 million. If services are being delivered to the same number of people, before and after-the-fact, then it will require virtually the same number of people to deliver them. Yes, it might mean the odd manager or department head is no longer needed, but it will not substantially reduce staffing levels. It may well increase them, as more people need to be hired to increase service levels to one or more of the component municipalities. And in the case of infrastructure, most was built to service a given area. That service will continue, regardless. On occasion, it might be that a firehall or some such building is no longer required because of service area overlap, but it also may well be that service agreements already existed that meant fire fighters would cross these boundaries. It could also be that the divestment of one small hall requires an expensive addition to another to bring it up to the higher standard of the new municipality.

And speaking of higher standards, it is usually the case that higher staff salaries are the result of amalgamations. Typically, the municipalities to be consolidated have different wage scales, some often being in unionized environments where others are not and must become so. Thus, it is necessary for wages to be equalized, and that seldom means being reduced. On occasion, it may mean they are equalized over a period or three or four years. Regardless, they increase at a much faster rate than they might have otherwise.

As well, if six municipalities have 500 kilometres of streets or roads before merging, they will still have 500 afterward. So if they had ten snowploughs and ten sanders before, they'll still need ten of each afterward. It may, in fact, be that equipment has to be purchased to handle higher service levels, or to replace equipment that is worn and not up to handling a bigger service area.

I have a bit of a history myself on this issue, having studied the restructuring-amalgamation-annexation battle between the Sarnias, city and township, as well as being an interested observer in the London annexation and Simcoe County amalgamations. I have no doubt in stating that there has never been an amalgamation, anywhere in the western industrialized world – certainly not in Ontario – that ever saved money. Yet, saving money is almost always the reason that the provincial government amalgamates municipalities. This was most definitely the prime reason for the Tories to propose uniting the Toronto region, as with smaller ones it would foist on other municipalities. It just seemed like common sense.

But it would be unfair to say everything the Tories did in their first term was based on the concept of common sense. In one instance, it was anything but sense, common or otherwise.

7. The inquisition begins

The most irrational move by the Harris Conservatives, without doubt, was picking a fight with teachers. It seemed to come out of nowhere, for no particular reason. Traditionally, most teachers had been steady supporters of the Tories, at least from the days when Bill Davis was Minister of Education. It was a loyalty that may not have gone to the bone, but it was more than skin deep. And for most of the rest, they went to the New Democrats.

Yet Harris and his lengthening line of education ministers all seemed determined to anger, alienate, and annoy as many teachers as possible. The first, and most obvious, example came from John Snobelen. The only way to describe him is as an incredibly successful businessman who should have stayed away from politics. After some years in waste management trucking and transportation equipment manufacturing, he had made himself into a millionaire and was likely drawn to politics as a new challenge. The public might have seen an irony in the challenge. You see, Snobelen was to become Mike Harris' first education minister even though he had dropped out of high school after completing Grade 11. The irony, however, did seem to be lost on Snobelen himself. There can be little doubt Harris appointed him based on his business smarts.

In their books, Promised Land and Hard Right Turn, both John Ibbitson and Brooke Jeffrey offer an interesting observation. Traditionally, Cabinet ministers act as advocates for whatever ministry they look after. Perhaps they would even have some experience in that sector. Not under Harris. He built his Cabinet specifically with people who would not feel any allegiance to their departments. Quite the reverse, they would actively move to cut their ministries.

Snobelen seems an obvious example of this. His knowledge of management methodology was to be used to redesign the huge department, presumably to save money and to make it more efficient. However, it is probably safe to say his business acumen permanently stalled his political career almost from the start. Within months, a videotape came to light that showed Snobelen lecturing officials on how to improve the education system. His theory was that if you refer to schools as being in worse shape than they really are, you will create the conditions which will allow for radical change. "Creating a useful crisis is part of what this will be about." "... We need to invent a crisis and that's not an act just of courage, there's some skill involved". The conclusion of this was obvious and no one really tried to explain it away.

After a public dressing-down by the Premier, probably borne more of embarrassment than disagreement, Snobelen moved ahead with changes to re-write curriculum, introduce province-wide testing of students, and radically reduce the number of school boards. It wasn't that any of these things were inherently needless or evil. The changes, however, were handled clumsily, and set off the beginning of tumult that would last years, cause the government no end of headaches, and alienate most teachers.

There are those who try to personalize this government's apparent distaste for teachers to Harris himself. Some suggest that, as a failed teacher, he wants to punish those who have succeeded, as some kind of perverse need for vengeance. However, many of his former colleagues in teaching in North Bay suggest he wasn't an inherently bad teacher. He just wasn't willing to put in the long hours necessary because he enjoyed socializing too much. Some have suggested that his dislike of teachers comes from his days as a school board trustee and chair, when he had to negotiate with their union leaders for contracts. He obviously didn't like the way they squeezed additional pay and benefits out of boards while getting less work. Unfortunately for this theory, the Nipissing Board of Education was not especially tight with cash under Harris' leadership. Not only did the teachers not have to extort the money, but neither did trustees, as they gave themselves significant raises, as well. (Another irony, given Harris' later conversion to *trustee as volunteer* and only being worth $5,000.)

But the reason Harris supposedly left the profession was because he did not like the fact that benefits came from seniority rather than ability, and he was either morally outraged or insufficiently patient to wait his turn. Of course, as we have seen, in his youth he was hardly patient about anything. But how this would make him want to bully teachers is unclear. Perhaps he would want to alter the system that rewards them, but that's not the same thing.

Frankly, there is no evident reason to take on teachers except one. Teachers have strong unions and people like Mike Harris and his caucus do not see union members as anything but a protected special interest. Union strength has resulted in the concept of promotion by seniority rather than ability. Labour negotiation rules permitted public sector union members like teachers to benefit without individual effort. For someone who feels *self-made* like Harris and many in his caucus, a teacher would not be someone he respected. His ilk would see someone like that as part of the 'government's bloated bureaucracy' that needs to be cut.

And cutting is exactly what the Tories had in mind for them. The July 1995 cuts took $400 million out of education, but that was at least a billion dollars less than what the Tories wanted to take out, supposedly to bring spending down to some alleged national average. The whole exercise of uploading and downloading had not made an appreciable difference. By the fall of 1997, the Harrisites were still well short of what they wanted from education, and they saw their chance to get it from teachers.

Even with everything the government had done up to this time – the introduction of a curriculum with higher standards and grade-level testing, the ending of Grade 13 by September 1999[20] , a re-introduction of *streaming*, standardized report cards, making junior kindergarten optional for school boards and cutting its funding, cutting the number of school boards and taking over full funding of them – they hadn't yet got to the one change they had planned for education – getting more money out of it. The Minister took care of that on an otherwise quiet Monday, three weeks into the school year. First Reading of Bill 160, the *Education Quality Improvement Act*, passed. The legislation was to extend the school year by two weeks for elementary students and three weeks for secondary students. It was to give the province total power to determine residential education property tax rates, put limits on class sizes, and reduce the number of teacher professional development days. But the two factors that would become the most controversial were a provision to cut preparation time for teachers and one to, at some point, set a new funding formula for schools and students which would equalize differences between public and separate boards.

For the Tories' purposes, it was the adjustment to prep time that was key. They had become convinced, as had the NDP before them, that teachers had managed to earn a deal with government that had become just too generous to be affordable. Teachers were required to spend just 3.75 hours per day in the classroom. This was the lowest amount in the country, yet Ontario teachers were the best paid. If the Harrisites could cut prep time by removing it from the bargaining table and simply make it a regulation of government[21], they could easily make up the money necessary to fulfill their desire for cuts. After all, if a teacher was in the classroom with students instead of preparing to teach, fewer teachers would be needed. Though Snobelen himself refused to give an estimate of how many teachers could be laid-off, he did say he preferred a 50% cut in prep time[22] . The unions suggested this could mean the elimination of 10,000 positions.

The whole situation balanced on one of two attitudes toward preparation time: either teachers had more than they needed and giving up some would allow them to spend more time teaching students; or, they had just enough to handle all the out-of-class work they had to do, such as course preparation, helping students, and marking, and a loss of it would mean they would either have to teach while ill-prepared or they would have to work some time each day for free. The government took the former view. The five teachers' unions and most of their 126,000 members took the latter one.

And that was the crux of the labour dispute that began five weeks later. Teachers walked out on a province-wide illegal strike to protest both over the proposed reduction of prep time and the government's attitude. Six days prior to the strike, a draft copy of the contract the government had offered to their new Deputy Minister of Education, Veronica Lacey, was leaked. It included a section that stated the government's expectation that she would come up with a "plan for the 1998-99 $667 million reduction" in education spending. It also anticipated an illegal strike and said she was to come up with a "joint legal strategy" with the Attorney-General's ministry to deal with it. A couple of days later, in a rare moment of outright political honesty, the Premier admitted these provisions were true.

Just as the Harrisites had counted on an OPSEU strike, so they also hoped for this illegal teachers' strike ... and for the same reason. They expected the people would oppose it, just as they had the other one. They figured this public support would permit them to make their desired changes with little opposition beyond the teachers themselves. However, once it came out they wanted a cut of two-thirds of a billion dollars, it seemed apparent that Bill 160 was simply the Harris government's way of sucking money out of schools. As a result, public support was much more up in the air.

On the other hand, it isn't a secret that many people aren't in love with the teaching profession. Hearing that the Tories wanted to take this money out of education was certainly not condemned by all. They agreed that school needed to be toughened up, and a few less teachers would hardly be a negative thing. The Tories had their supporters who liked the proposals, especially because of the cuts.

As I recently commented to a friend of mine, "50% of people like teachers and 50% don't. For many politicians, it is important to be with that 0% in the middle". It was a bit of a joke, but not entirely. Most politicians are afraid of going too much one way or the other, lest they alienate large numbers of people. But the Harris Conservatives, by this time, had made their bed with the half who denigrate teachers. Therefore, it may have been somewhat surprising, or not, that both the new opposition leaders, Dalton McGuinty and Howard Hampton, came out vociferously with the half who were in sympathy with the teachers. By the time it left office, many in the Rae government were no great allies of them. They had felt very stung by their lack of support and that their pay schedule was such a drain on the provincial treasury. Having said that, Hampton was busy trying to mend fences. An election was expected in about 18 months, and time was running out to get these people back on the NDP's side.

The bigger surprise was McGuinty's wholehearted throwing in with the teachers. Many inside his party wanted him to try and ride the fence between the sides, knowing how many liked and disliked the teachers. Others were uncomfortable with supporting any strike that was illegal. I knew of one very good party member who scrawled his complaint about this on a sheet of paper, along with his resignation from the party, and faxed it to Liberal headquarters. However, whether he felt the teachers were in the right, he was supporting the integrity of the education system, or he wanted his teacher wife to let him into the house, McGuinty was at the forefront attacking the government.

This was one battle John Snobelen didn't get to fight, however. On Friday, 10 October, Mike Harris shuffled his Cabinet. His hard-worn Education minister got the heave-ho and was sent to relative obscurity in Natural Resources, where he remains today. Dave Johnson, the man who had got them through the OPSEU strike and pinch-hit in Health to get a deal with doctors on a new contract, was given the Education job. It was a change he would come to regret.

Johnson took the line that the government needed a balance between its goals for high quality education and its fiscal responsibilities. The difficulty was that no one in the Harris administration had really enunciated anything specific to improve quality, while they were now on the record as wanting a 5% cut in spending.

The other argument made by the teachers' unions was that there was now little point in negotiating their contracts with the school boards. The trustees had been stripped of their powers and, with prep time and class size to be set by provincial regulation, there was little left over which to actually bargain. As a result, they wanted the government to set up province-wide negotiating. Of course, the Tories wanted none of that, given it would likely mean province-wide strikes. And that's part of the reason the teachers went out, to give the Harrisites the province-wide dispute they meant to avoid.

The strike began on Monday, 27 October and lasted two weeks. In fact, it might have gone on far longer, as most teachers seemed willing to stay out. Their anger had overcome any financial troubles they were facing. However, their union heads were beginning to sweat by that point. There had been a school of thought that the teachers should abandon their classrooms for a couple of days to make their point, then go back to work. It would display for politicians the might of teachers while likely avoiding any repercussions for the illegal nature of the work stoppage. However, when teachers showed little desire to return to work, the union stewardship soon realised they were on the hook for an increasing problem. Over two million students were out of class. Parents were becoming more restive, as their schedules were upset by the need to supervise their youngsters, and their older kids seemed to ignore studying in favour of playing video games or hanging out at shopping malls. Polls had shown a surprising number of parents were on the teachers' side at the outset, as they were identified as trying to protect education while the government was seen as trying to strip it of money ... which couldn't be good. The union leaders were fearful that this goodwill was dissipating as the strike dragged on.

But just as they had done with OPSEU, the government seemed to want to egg them on. Within days, Finance minister Eves was apparently suggesting too much of education costs came in the form of the $1.1 billion annual government contribution to the teachers' pension fund, and that education funding was being drained to pay for it. With this, however, came a coyly disguised threat. The government could always change the law to cut this payment. It was now clear to everyone the Harrisites would have no trouble opening up any contracts to make the necessary alterations.

The pension contribution came from actuarial tables that used a teacher who made $65,000 in their best five years of employment – the basis for their pension – and who retired at age 60. Males were judged to live, on average, to 85, with females to 90. That meant the pension fund had an unfunded liability and, in 1989, the Liberals had begun making monthly payments over 40 years to make up the difference, as they were legally required to do. But Eves decided to compare the amount he was putting in versus what the NDP had in 1993, and it was $1.1 billion higher. The difficulty was it was 12 months of payments compared to less than six. Part-way through 1993, the teachers had given the government a three-year *holiday* from paying this money as part of its Social Contract commitments. (In fact, in the months before the strike, they had offered the Tories another six-month holiday in exchange for giving up on some of Bill 160.) Clearly, the Finance minister was distorting the truth, but his point was pure Harrisite – teachers are over-paid and greedy. As people on welfare were to Community and Social Services, so teachers were to Education.

Yet even the government was not entirely consistent about its position. Before Snobelen was axed from Education, he backed off on extending the school year. It was widely theorized this was because it dawned on him it would cost hundreds of millions of dollars and the exercise was about *saving* money. And within days of the start of the strike, Johnson said the government would only cut prep time by a third, which should still have resulted in savings of nearly $400 million.

The strike ended when it was clear the government was not going to bend any further, and leaders from three of the five unions were beginning to fear the legal consequences of going on. It was clear that when teachers returned to class on Monday, 10 November, a good portion of them would rather have still been on the picket line. As it was, they continued their protest in other ways.

Rumblings of discontent continued right through the school year. Even months later, teachers were expressing to me their distaste at having gone back to work and not having dealt with the government once-and-for-all during the strike. It was an ominous tone, given that their contracts with a number of school boards would be expiring in the summer.

Bill 160 passed the Legislature on December 1st. What everyone then waited for was the funding formula that was to lay out just how equitable the new methodology would be. Many in Catholic boards and rural boards waited expectantly, hoping to see per pupil funding rise, while those in urban boards that would soon lose their rich property tax base were anxious. It wasn't a short wait, either. Johnson didn't unveil the formula until near the end of March, after many earlier suggested appearances were aborted.

Initially, as on the first day, the formula was seen as a *good news* announcement, and I'm sure Minister Johnson expected it to be taken that way. After all, money for education was to remain stable for three years, which would allow all boards to plan with some certainty. *Classroom spending* would now be defined. There would be 3,000 new teachers, even after the cut to prep time. And school boards would have to fill out annual "report cards" to prove they were spending money wisely. The only difficulty was that Johnson did not come armed with many specific numbers to back up his claims and, once they did filter out to the boards, even those that got more money started to question how the funding was being allotted.

Typical of the Tories, they had created a one-size-fits-all approach.

Boards with older schools, smaller schools, and extra non-teaching staff were penalized, while those with newer, bigger, less-well maintained ones were rewarded. This was especially hard on older cities, who, simply by sheer number, had a lot of older and smaller schools. However, the formula was also not good for the rural boards which were supposed to have benefited by the change. While they may have received more money per student, their core of schools, which tended to be much older and smaller, docked funding because they didn't meet the *cookie-cutter* regulations on square footage. They were also hit hard by the cuts to funding for transportation. The separate boards probably came out the best, though even many of them took a few punches.

There were those who referred to the problems with the funding formula as "anomalies". In many cases, I suspect they were actually planned. If a board had surplus space, it had to be used before the board would be allowed to build new space. On the surface, it made sense. Unfortunately, in many rural areas, this meant there was space in a school 50 kilometres from where more was needed. This caused a slew of schools to be closed, or planned to be closed, to eliminate the excess, so the boards could then turn around and build new schools where needed, even if this meant the closure resulted in overcrowding where the space used to be. The other result was that students began to be bused over wider areas to eliminate the surplus, even though there was no money to pay for this busing[23], meaning something else had to be cut. As for the students themselves, as someone who had to ride the bus over two hours each day throughout high school, I can say this travel is a tremendous waste.

Another significant problem was that small schools no longer met minimum-size requirements for funding for principals, secretaries, or librarians. Some were amalgamated with neighbouring facilities and lost their administrations. Most ended up with libraries open part-time, sometimes as little as an hour, two or three times per week. And funding to purchase texts has fallen, as well. It is very hard for students to make use of books under these circumstances.

And given that custodian services were not included in classroom spending, schools are no longer as clean as they used to be. It is not uncommon to hear that principals now spend part of their time cleaning toilets.

Many of the school boards' trustees, seeing that the numbers would not result in a better deal, perhaps panicked and instantly issued lay-off notices to thousands of teachers. They said they did this because time was so limited, under the contracts, that they barely had time to give notice and have it take effect before the next school year. On the other hand, they didn't do a lot of public musing about alternatives, either.

There was one area in which the teachers had come to agree with the government, though. The CSR had said the Tories wanted to cut teachers' numbers through attrition and many teachers, now becoming frustrated and demoralized, wanted to leave. As a result, they worked out an agreement to use the $10 billion surplus in the teachers' pension fund to pay for a reduction in the retirement number. Previously, a teacher's age plus years of work equalling 90 meant retirement with full benefits. This concord resulted in a reduction to 85 from 1 June 1998 to 31 December 2002[24]. So, for example, a 53-year-old with 32 years experience could now go. It was estimated this would mean up to 18,200 teachers would be able to retire early, if they wanted. If so, the province would save $500 million a year in pension contributions, and Ernie Eves suggested another $200 million, presumably in the difference in salary between a veteran teacher and a new one. Though both government and union officials hailed this as a win-win situation, it didn't stop the thunder of discontent that continued to roll through the ranks of teachers.

By the time the summer had ended, school remained out for tens of thousands of students, as teachers again went on strike, though this was just in some of the school boards where teachers were in a legal strike position. The crux of the dissatisfaction was with working hours. There had been a *phony war* of sorts during the summer months, as teachers' unions negotiated with boards that didn't have the power to solve the problem. The cut to preparation time meant that secondary teachers were being required to work 1,250 minutes per week, or 7 out of 8 periods over the course of a year. Elementary teachers were to work 1,300 minutes per week, though that was already a common occurrence. A big question became what exactly constituted classroom time. Did it include time to assist students who needed extra help, time for marking, home room time, time taken up supervising halls and schoolyards? Though this was to be negotiated with school boards, it was quite clear that its definition only mattered to the provincial government. Yet the Harrisites seemed reluctant to state what they intended this to be, at least before the school year began.

And matters were no clearer for school boards, either. With few powers to actually affect negotiations, and little extra money to allow for mutations on the provincial model, most were left to dicker over fine points. However, depending on the board, some of these points wore teachers raw. For example, in the Near North District School Board, which includes the

area from Muskoka to North Bay, they had to hire on more teachers to meet minimum class-size ratios, but could only afford it by getting teachers to agree to a reduction in their benefits, giving up leaves, and extra pay for being department heads or for having Master's degrees or PhDs.

While there were not full strikes in all boards, many had rotating strikes, lock-outs, or the withdrawal of extra-curricular activities, such as the coaching of after-school sports. As well, a couple of boards ordered students to stay home, figuring that schools could not operate properly under these conditions. Regardless of the increasing disturbance, the Minister stated the government had no desire to bring in back-to-work legislation, at least not until such time as the Education Relations' Commission determined the students' school year was at risk.

The government had been caught with its pants down by the strike the year before but realized the public was much more wary of more labour unrest this time around. And just to reinforce this anxiety, they spent $1 million on an advertising campaign to promote their changes to curriculum and teaching time. Included was a $25,000 *infomercial* by Mike Harris which aired just four days into the dispute. This time, they were determined to come out on the *plus side*.

After three weeks, the government was satisfied it had what it wanted. Parents, in particular, were upset at the second strike in two years. Even students, who had appeared to overwhelmingly support their teachers a year prior seemed less loyal this time. And while teachers themselves hung to the picket lines, their enthusiasm for the fight was manifestly lacking. Nevertheless, they weren't headed back to work, voluntarily. Johnson presented, and got passed, back-to-work legislation that put them back in class on Tuesday, 29 September.

But all was not well for the Tories. Advisories from a variety of sources were saying hundreds of schools would have to close across the province as a result of the funding formula. There can be no question the government anticipated a large number of closures and the resultant bad publicity. However, whether they failed to foresee how bad it would be, or it was their plan all along (which would have been out of character for this government), the Tories came up with an extra $200 million to keep schools open for another year. It was interesting that the Friday, 6 November announcement came from the Premier himself and not Dave Johnson, an action which Harris was known to do when he wanted to upstage one of his own ministers. His comments were to the point. "I cannot see the need for parents and children to have fearmongering hanging over their heads any longer." "What it does is give us a year to make sure ... that we get it right." More likely, it was a year to give people time to adjust to the idea schools were going to go ... and a lot would.

Many of the school boards would sign contracts that met the provincial dictates, more-or-less. Many others went against the expressed wishes of the Minister, signing contracts with teachers for less than 7 of 8 classes, or including advisory and supervisory time. In what, at the time, was a bit of a surprise, the government members bit their lips and these latter boards were not punished for their actions. It seemed possible the government had had enough. In effect, they had got what they wanted. Cuts were now in place.

8. Other matters

Along with these serious and huge issues were many that seemed to slip by with little attention, as the public was no doubt distracted. The Tories had many smaller promises to carry out and, even with their busy agenda, they took the time to deal with other things. One of the hot buttons of the 1995 campaign had been to deal with young offenders. Now even though this was mostly within federal jurisdiction, the province did what it could.

After much bluster, *Project Turnaround* was commenced. It established a privately-run boot camp of sorts near Hillsdale, just north of Barrie. The intention was to have 38 repeat youth offenders, 16 and 17 years-of-age, undergo strict discipline incarceration in a military-esque training camp. A company would run it under contract from the Corrections' ministry, with private trainers and guards. It was the feeling of government members that rigid order, study, and physical training would help these boys achieve the self-discipline they had been so sorely lacking.

The night before the official opening by Solicitor-General Bob "Mad Dog" Runciman, there was a power failure and escape by two inmates, who smashed through the perimeter fence in a camp van, destroying it, then disappeared into the bush. Though they were both caught within a few hours, it was quite an embarrassing start both for the government and the company running the camp. Immediately, union guards were ordered to take up positions at the facility.

Since its less-than-illustrious start, Project Turnaround has been little heard-of. Over time, it has become less disciplinary and more a school.

However, two more such facilities are now in the works, one each in eastern and southwestern Ontario, along with one for young men to be built in Harris' Nipissing riding.

* * * * *

In February 1997, the Ontario Government established a land use and resource management planning process called "Lands for Life". It applied to Crown land covering 45% of Ontario, mostly in the north and central areas. Three regional round tables of about a dozen appointees each were set up to make recommendations on the province's parks' system and protected areas, the land-use needs of the forestry, mining, and other resource-based industries, as well as those of nature tourism, including angling, hunting and other recreation. Though the government claimed that there were to be extensive consultations with industry, environmentalists, and aboriginals, each group was supposed to report by summer. However, the deadline was much too short, and had to be extended. It was the spring of 1998 before preliminary land-use options were announced, and July before the round tables' draft recommendations were submitted.

However, the members of these groups had been given no common framework for their reports, which meant Ministry staff had difficulty putting them together. This delayed the process further, as the three round table chairs were asked to do the work for them. The end result was 242 recommendations on the various topics, released in late October 1998, which, in turn, brought forward over 14,000 submissions from the public. Many were complaints that industrial concerns were seemingly more important than parks and protected areas.

Perhaps fearing further delays, and facing an imminent election, the government held discussions with representatives of the forest industry and a coalition of environmental groups called Partnership for Public Lands. This resulted in the "1999 Ontario Forest Accord: A Foundation for Progress", a document suggesting certain protected areas, along with a process to identify others, not to mention recommendations on the needs of the forest industry.

On 29 March 1999, just before the election, the Premier chose to do the honours himself and announce the land-use strategy, with a call for further public comment. There would be 60 new parks, 44 expanded ones, and 274 new conservation reserves. This time, another 8,200 submissions were received. The final document was released in July.

After the fact, the government spun the story to make it seem Lands for Life had been to create new parks and protected areas, right from the beginning.

> *There's the personal pride I feel knowing that my grandchildren will be able to visit parks that didn't even exist before today. There's the recognition that all of our children and grandchildren will benefit and enjoy these lands and waters. There's the knowledge that suns will set and rise over these protected forests and lakes, creeks and hills for generations to come. Through strong leadership, we have also succeeded in creating an historic and lasting partnership. A diverse partnership, including environmentalists, foresters, anglers and hunters, miners, and tourism outfitters. ... This partnership is without precedent. It is a model, not just for other provinces, but for other countries. I am confident of that.* (Premier' press statement.)

Harris' lack of humility aside, nothing could have been further from the truth. This was a front for the real purpose. The round tables had been instructed to only consider areas where logging occurred, not all Crown land. As a result, Lands for Life was simply an exercise to guarantee the forestry and mining industries long-term, guaranteed access to Crown lands.

For decades, Crown land had been open to forestry in exchange for royalty payments. In 1980, the Davis Tories were pressured by environmental concerns to change this. Clear-cutting with no replanting was leaving large areas denuded of timber, causing ecological devastation. The government came up with 20-year renewable management contracts in which the logging companies would have to agree to conditions which would see some level of regeneration. Should those conditions not have been met, the government had the power to take away a company's logging rights.

Many environmentalists believed, once the Rae New Democrats came to power, these forestry concerns would have to buckle down and meet far stricter commitments. What they failed to realize was that most loggers were unionized, and the NDP was not about to do anything that might cost jobs, especially during a recession. That having been said, in the dying days of the government, they did pass legislation to change these agreements to licenses, effectively doing away with 20-year terms and leaving the companies to log at the pleasure of the government. It was at the request of the forestry firms to review this that Lands for Life was set up.

As part of the initial round table recommendations, it was proposed that the licensing system be replaced with stewardship agreements. These would be similar to the earlier system, but would also compensate companies when land was removed from their use by government, be it for parks or protected areas, or if government established new environmental regulations that would cost them more money. Lands for Life was to consider 45% of all the land in the province. In the end, just 5.4% was set aside. In other words, Lands for Life was intended as an exercise to pick a minimal amount of territory out of logging lands, so the timber companies could do as they would with the rest, and get paid for what land they did lose.

*****

During their term as government, the NDP set up the Family Support Plan. It's job was straightforward – to enforce support orders. The number of spouses defaulting on either child or spousal support had grown to epidemic proportions. The government decided that it could wield a bigger stick by ordering these people to make payments to the province. The money would be deducted directly from an employer or another income source, and the authorities would disburse the money to its recipients. If someone fell behind on payments, the government would pay the recipient anyway, then go after the debtor.

The Harris government made some changes. Between August and December 1996, as part of "reducing government", the FSP's eight regional offices were closed and resurrected in one location, in Downsview. As well, *The Family Responsibility and Support Arrears Enforcement Act* was passed, changing the name of the Family Support Plan to the Family Responsibility Office, and making some minor changes for voluntary opting out, and more support provisions. Practically, the office consolidation resulted in staff cuts of 40%, from 340 to 200. As well, a backlog of changes to personal and financial information and unanswered correspondence increased to more than 90,000. Recipients found that it was almost impossible to get through to the new office, as the staff reduction left nothing but the telephone system to put callers on hold.

The result was chaos and significant media criticism. The government, uncharacteristically, responded by hiring temporary staff to clear up the large backlog. Then they hired back permanent staff, eventually restoring it to the early 1996 level.

However, that didn't entirely solve the problems. As of the end of March

1999, the Family Responsibility Office had over 170,000 registered cases, with about 128,000 of these active cases in arrears. As of the end of March, five years earlier, its predecessor had 126,000 cases with 96,000 in arrears. As a percentage, those in arrears was virtually the same. However, the total amount in arrears had risen 28% from $700 million to $1.2 billion, or an average of $7,291.67 up to $9,375.00. And this was at a time when income and employment was increasing so excuses for letting these amounts rise were fairly indefensible.

* * * * *

There were still other issues for the Tories during their first term. The surviving Dionne quintuplets, after being refused compensation for their suffering at the hands of the Ontario government as children, received $4 million, but only after a massive public outcry. The Harrisites, finally following through on the pre-election promise to bring in legislation to assist the disabled, presented a meaningless list of voluntary hopes for improvement. The outrage from the disabled and their advocates caused the government to let it die on the order paper. It would be the second term before they would pass similar legislation, also roundly denounced by the disabled as toothless. All it does is require public institutions to identify barriers to the disabled, not to do anything about getting rid of them. And there isn't even this much to make private facilities more accessible.

Throughout 1998, the federal and provincial governments sat down to discuss compensation for those infected with Hepatitis C through the blood system between 1986 and 1990, when testing was available but the Red Cross didn't avail itself of it. Initially, the Harrisites took the position that compensation should be limited. Reports suggested Ontario's position was hawkish on the subject, denying national Health minister Allan Rock's attempts to make a more generous settlement. At the end of March, a deal was worked out to offer $1.1 billion in compensation to about 6,600 (then thought to be as many as 22,000) victims. Both those affected and the public felt the deal was miserly and made their concerns loudly known. However, it was more generous than the original positions of several provinces, including Ontario. Then, suddenly in late November, the Harris government turned 180° and Health minister Elizabeth Witmer announced Ontario would go it alone with a $200 million package for those infected before 1986 or after 1990. In fact, the Premier went so far as to then criticize the deal with the other provinces and the feds. For some, this turnaround was welcome, if somewhat belated. For a few, it was a sign there was an election coming.

The Tories' first term was one of divisive confrontation. They firmly believed that taking the time to consult with people would weaken their resolve and delay their actions. As a result, they chose to roll over any opposition, no matter what it took to bring their quasi-revolution to fruition. Because they felt those who disagreed with them were simply the forces that had bankrupted the province while making themselves fat and happy on the largesse of taxpayers, they could ignore them. In fact, they could attack them at every opportunity. The Tories had been elected to represent the interests of those who had not benefited, or didn't believe they had. They had been chosen by voters desperate to bring common sense back to government.

Their version of common sense is unlikely to be found in any dictionary, however. It involved slanting the tax system to benefit wealthier Ontarians and business, cutting regulations that protected ordinary people, and ridding the government of those most important to actually doing the work. It meant limiting democratic debate, trying to hide significant changes, and changing the electoral system just enough to give the Tories the upper hand for re-election. And despite what many might have thought, they wanted to be re-elected very badly. And it wasn't because they needed to set the *revolution* in stone. They hadn't yet set up their golden parachutes for retirement.

Part 3 Endnotes

1. Ibbitson, op.cit., p. 147
2. Toronto Star. "Some consulting service fees higher, ministry confirms", 10 December 1999, p. A12.
3. Toronto Star. "MPPs slam provincial welfare deal", 12 October 2001, p. A2.
4. Successor rights are those that allow salary and benefits to be taken from a public sector job to one in the private sector, as well as any job guarantees that might exist.
5. Normally, the Speaker would have informed them of any such change. Al McLean told no one but the OPP.
6. As of 1 January 1998, federal redistribution occurs, as it is supposed to every ten years.
7. The province has not yet said if it will appeal to the Supreme Court of Canada.
8. Ibbitson, op.cit., p. 197.
9. Ibbitson, ibid., p. 198.
10. According to John Ibbitson, James claims not to have said this, though the reporter has a different version.
11. Ibbitson, op.cit., p. 222.
12. Ibbitson, ibid., p. 229.
13. Ibbitson, ibid.
14. The unions would take a different tact eventually. By the spring of 1998, union leaders were suggesting that those on workfare be unionized to give them some rights. The government took the possibility so seriously it passed legislation to bar them from unionizing or striking, even given its dubious constitutional legality.
15. "Hard" services are sewers, water pipes, road paving, snow clearance, and the like. "Soft" services are planning and welfare.
16. Ibbitson, op.cit, p. 247.
17. Toronto Star, "Harris favors plan for megacity", 30 October 1996, p. A1.
18. The first province-wide reassessment was done in 1998, using 30 June of the year prior as the date to determine property value. These will be done annually, beginning in 2003 for the 2004 taxation year. In 2005, assessed value will be determined by averaging the current and previous years. Beginning in 2006, it will be the current and two previous years.
19. Ibbitson, op.cit., p. 240.
20. This was delayed until September 2001.
21. Normally, this was something to be negotiated. The Harrisites were

the first to turn it into a mere regulation.
22. His successor, Dave Johnson, would settle for a third.
23. The government did not consider busing a classroom expense.
24. This has now been made permanent.

Part 4

"Dalton McGuinty ... he's just not up to the job!"

The Tories won the 1999 election before the campaign ever started. In early November 1998, the Conservative party paid for television ads to personally attack Liberal leader Dalton McGuinty. They questioned where he and the Liberal party actually stood on health care, using the lack of specific party policy to suggest he stood nowhere. It was a return to the weathervane-type of ad they had used against Lyn McLeod in 1995, but it had a far nastier edge. The commercial ended with "Dalton McGuinty ... he's just not up to the job!" The ads played for two weeks, then a couple more weeks leading into the election. Given McGuinty's low public profile and the unflattering portrayal of him in the ads, it's little wonder people, even many Liberals, began to question his ability. This view was reinforced when the media overwhelmingly determined him as the loser of the leader's debate, halfway through the campaign.

1. The Common Sense Evolution

Given the CSR heralded such a sea change in the way Ontario was run, it was not surprising that the media and Tory opponents thoroughly expected *The Common Sense Revolution, Part II* for the next election. Perhaps this was unrealistic, given the Conservative platform had pretty much been fulfilled by 1998, and the last 12 months of their first term had been much quieter than the first 36. As well, how does one follow up *revolutionary* ideas with more of the same in such a short time? By definition, as such ideas are implemented, they are no longer revolutionary, no longer ideas but realities, and they need to be administered.

The Tories weren't prepared to go that far, but neither did they have more radical change in mind. They had simply carried out their agenda in such short order that there was little else to do but carry on to make certain it was completed. However, even Harris himself denied they were ready to settle in and be "managers". The revolution continues, he said. He had to say it, as it was the heart of their strategy to be re-elected.

There would be no CSR II, at least that's not what it would be called. In fact it didn't get a name until the election was imminent, something that truly seemed to irk the media. My guess is they were looking to either praise or pan it, and hated that they wouldn't get much time to examine it sufficiently to do either. The reason it didn't get a name earlier, however, was not because the Tories were trying to hide it. They had intended to call it *20/20*, but the Liberals beat them to it as the name for their platform.

And it was actually the Liberals who came out with their ideas first. The *20/20 Plan: A Clear Vision for Ontario's Future* was a fairly traditional platform document that hit the high points without being too detailed. The party overlords were still stinging from the criticism of their 1995 attempt. Health and education were the focal points. A Liberal government would hire back 10,200 nurses, offer financial incentives and free tuition for young doctors who would establish practices in northern and under-serviced areas, guarantee patients emergency room assessment within 15 minutes of arrival at hospital (originally an NDP idea), guarantee cancer patients radiation treatment within four weeks of diagnosis, guarantee new mothers a minimum 48-hour stay in hospital after child birth as well as home follow-up by a nurse, restore Women's College and Montfort Hospitals, and establish a five-year funding plan for all hospitals.

On education, they promised to reduce early grades' class size from 25 to 22, restore funding for junior kindergarten province-wide, as well as for arts and music, committed to cutting university and college tuition 10%, restore loans for part-time students and re-regulate professional degree tuition, restore full funding for special and adult education, and provide evening tutorial and remedial programmes for students who needed extra help.

But the Liberals offered other significant commitments. On the environment, they said they would have Ontario's five coal-burning electric generating plants converted to natural gas, set the toughest standards for air pollution in North America, as well as higher standards for water and the disposal of hazardous waste, re-hire 100 environmental enforcement officers fired in the cuts to the Environment ministry, reduce pollutants in gasoline, and put more money and effort into cleaning up the Great Lakes.

On social concerns, the Liberals promised to restore funding to women's shelters and services for abused women and children, restore rent controls, create a new Ministry of Children as part of their *First Steps* initiative to directly deal with the needs of children, introduce a tax benefit to assist with shelter, clothing, and food for poor children, create 7,500 new housing units for people with special needs and former psychiatric patients, and establish new rules and regulations for Children's Aid Societies. As well, they would set a minimum two-year jail sentence for drug-dealing or carrying a weapon within five blocks of a school.

On financial matters, the Liberals were somewhat less specific, stating they would not support new tax cuts until the budget was balanced, would stop downloading provincial cuts onto property taxpayers, upload ambulance services the Tories sent down, and put more money into the aforementioned areas. The $2.5 billion in promises would be paid for by existing fund re-allocation and growing revenues from the booming economy.

The media reaction seemed positive, if somewhat muted. If there was criticism, it was the seeming repetition of the idea that the Liberals would simply *do better* than the Tories. However, the lack of financial specifics instantly sent the Tories into a frenzy, attacking the platform as another example of Liberal largesse with the taxpayers' money, just at a time when the Conservatives had done all the hard work to get provincial finances under control.

Regardless, on the last day of April, ten days after the Liberals presented *20/20*, the government party presented its own platform. In some ways, *Blueprint* was intended to appear as CSR II. What it lacked was the originality and impact of the CSR, mostly because it reaffirmed its neo-conservative principles but with little that was new. And the Tory strategists could read polls. While they had consistently shown that a majority of people believed the government was "on the right track", they also showed that the government was seen to have moved "too far, too fast". But one difference between it and the CSR was that the latter left most of the hot button issues as campaign points. *Blueprint* included them in the body of the document. Perhaps this is why the 1999 platform was twice as long as its progenitor.

Blueprint opens with the typical kind of political rhetoric one expects – comments that misdirect, say nothing, and outright lie.

> *Blueprint*
> *Mike Harris' Plan to Keep Ontario on the Right Track*

Note that it is referred to as 'Mike Harris' Plan'. The continued focus on the leader had taken on even greater status, this time around. They had gone as far as dropping the party's name from election signs, preferring just the *Mike Harris Team*, along with the party logo. His popularity still out-distanced that of the party, though I don't think it can reasonably be said the Progressive Conservative label was still 'radioactive'.

> *As we look ahead to the year 2000, Ontario's promise is unlimited. This province and its people can aim for the top in those things that matter most to all of us:*
>
> *- A healthier, safer, cleaner province*
> *- Lower taxes to create more and better jobs, particularly for our young people*
> *- Stronger skills and better futures for our children through quality education*
> *- A framework of roads, schools, hospitals and technology links for today and tomorrow, and*
> *- Government which is leaner, more sensible, more efficient and genuinely concerned about serving you.*
>
> *This is all possible, but will take strong, focussed (sic) leadership. It won't come easily, but it can be done, and it will be worth it.*

Note that this is referred to as a future achievement – 'This province and its people <u>can</u> aim for the top' ... ' it won't <u>come</u> easily'. Presumably, this is the government giving goals that they will attain *if* they are re-elected. A cynic might suggest that the Tories were covering themselves should anyone say they were actually claiming they had accomplished these things already.

Four years ago, my team and I were proud to take office with a plan to get Ontario back on track.

While many people doubted we could do it, and some fought against us, still more agreed that it was time to turn Ontario around. That meant making tough, deliberate choices to achieve our goals. As Premier, I've learned that leadership is about creating a clear vision of what needs to be done, setting priorities, then doing what it takes to reach our goals.

Ontario's turnaround in the past four years didn't happen by accident. Thanks to your hard work and some key decisions, we were able to get rid of the roadblocks that held us back:

- As promised, we cut the provincial income tax rate by 30% and put $1,385 per year back in the pockets of a typical Ontario family (two earner couple with two children and income of $60,000 per year).

'... Still more agreed that it was time to turn Ontario around.' This was one of the fictions Harris liked to spread around. He always made it sound like the majority of Ontarians were with him in his *revolution*. Perhaps it gave him some psychic feeling of well-being to believe it, even if it wasn't true. However, there's no question they made 'tough, deliberate decisions'. I am doubtful most were the correct ones.

- We tackled the skyrocketing $11.3 billion deficit and we're now on track to balancing the budget in 2000, right on schedule.
- We not only kept our word on health care; we made the tough decisions others wouldn't to put the system back on firm ground. We increased health care funding by $1.5 billion and put every penny we found in waste and duplication back into patient services.

Here we see another debt number from 1995, inflated for popular ingestion. And in fact, the Tories had actually changed their promise to balance the budget in four years. They reverted to the CSR pledge shortly before the election, probably because it was too soon to say they had succeeded. I'm sure

Bob Rae would dispute that the Tories were the first to make tough decisions about heath care. In fact, his government actually cut health spending through a programme of altered priorities, which the Tories chose to ignore.

> *- We scrapped job-killing payroll taxes, unfair hiring quotas and unbalanced labour legislation. Since 1995, Ontario has seen the biggest job increase on record, with more than 540,000 new jobs. That means we're ahead of schedule in our five-year plan for 725,000 jobs.*

And, as one observer noted at election time, 540,000 over four years is 135,000 per year. At that rate, the five-year total would bring the Tories up 50,000 short, not 'ahead of schedule'. Of course, Harris has said government doesn't create jobs anyway ...

> *- We overhauled a welfare system that clearly wasn't working by getting able-bodied recipients to earn part of their benefits and by bringing in work-for-welfare. Today, there are nearly 400,000 fewer people trapped in a cycle of welfare dependency.*

Perhaps this is nitpicking, but 'trapped in a cycle of welfare dependency' seems to say that anyone on welfare is ensnared in a system from which it is almost impossible to escape, rather than receiving help to get them through a rough time. It sounds like anyone collecting these benefits is doing so long-term, which doesn't stand up to research. Most people who collect these benefits are off them in a year or so.

> *- We put the emphasis back on teaching in our classrooms, and increased aid for post-secondary students. Now, more resources are spent on classroom education and we have more students in post-secondary education than ever before.*

'... Increased aid for post-secondary students' *– we'll loan you a little more because we've made it cost far more.* This was truly a venomous distortion, given that their tuition was permitted to rise 60% over these four years. '... More resources are spent on classroom education' – untrue, as per student funding had dropped in virtually every public school region in the past decade and this was certainly clear going into the campaign.

Common sense. Solid progress. A strong foundation.

But creating a better province with more jobs and a better quality of life is not a sprint or even a marathon - it is a never-ending challenge, one that requires strong leadership and a clear vision. We live in a highly competitive, complex, and fast changing world. We either keep moving forward or risk sliding back and losing our ability to support vital programs such as health care.

'We either keep moving forward or risk sliding back ...'. This is an innate understanding that Ontarians want progressive government, but it's redefined. Perhaps they should have said *we ... risk sliding back into government dependence.*

After all the progress we've made together, we can't risk it all by returning to the old style of politics that left Ontario in such a mess four years ago.

And this basically says that 'the old style of politics' was not progressive.

We believe Ontario should continue to move forward to better times, not slide backward to high debts, high unemployment, runaway spending and low expectations. Today in Ontario, we can look to the future with hope and confidence. Let's not lose that.

That's why we believe in this plan - the Blueprint for Ontario.

In Blueprint you'll find a balanced, straightforward, no-nonsense plan for our future. The foundation for this plan is a strong, growing economy. With economic growth, more people are working, providing for themselves and their families. It also gives us, as a society, the resources we need to support a better quality of life - higher quality education in the classroom, more secure communities, dependable and sustainable health care.

This is why we focus so clearly in Blueprint on keeping our economy competitive, growing and strong. Ontario needs a realistic plan for reaching our potential, and proven, experienced leadership to make that plan work.

'Proven, experienced leadership' – Harris, not the new Liberal nor NDP leader. Of course, this would have been an argument against him in 1990 and 1995.

This is our plan. I hope you will take the time to read it, consider the options, discuss it with your family, and compare our plan with those of the other parties. In the end, it's up to you to make the decision to keep

Ontario on the right track to a better future.

Mike Harris

In other words, Ontario is already on the 'right track' and to vote for either of the other parties would mean a worse future.

It's pretty basic, but it does touch on the things the Tories wanted to get across. Again, the focus is on Harris, his popularity being the party's main advantage. It reiterates the "promises made, promises kept" motto of the campaign, and runs through how things are better, with the Tories innately taking credit for this. Interestingly though, this introduction doesn't exhibit the same message of ideological consistency that was in the CSR. And unlike what Harris says about leadership 'creating a clear vision of what needs to be done, setting priorities, then doing what it takes to reach our goals', *Blueprint* is far from visionary. In fact, it is very much more like the Liberal's *20/20* plan. There can be no question it lacks the essence of the CSR.

As to the specifics of *Blueprint*, the Tories laid out their seven big promises, then outlined them in somewhat more detail. Provincial income taxes and the provincial part of the residential property tax would be cut 20% over five years. There would be a 20% increase in health care spending over five years, along with a Patient's Bill of Rights. There would be more student and new teacher testing, more financial assistance for "advanced education", and a "guarantee that classroom funding will continue to match rising enrollment". A $20 billion "SuperBuild Growth Fund" would be established for infrastructure renewal, but as a private and public sector partnership. People collecting welfare benefits would face drug and literacy testing, and workfare would be expanded.. The debt would be reduced at least $2 billion over five years by a 1% cut in spending. As well, on top of the 725,000 new jobs they had promised in 1995 to deliver, there would be 825,000 more over five years.

One of the habits the Tories had acquired over four years was the tendency to repeat things over and over like a mantra, presumably to make people think that repetition must make them true. *Blueprint* was a prime example of this. These major commitments were repeated tirelessly, along with graphs to demonstrate their "accuracy", four of which were also repeated.

The document was laid out to reinforce the "successes" of the Tories' first four years, then hammer home their new promises. Under "Cutting Taxes", they stated they had reduced taxes 69 times, including the 30%

income tax cut, which "produced dramatic results" – 540,000 new jobs. They will cut income tax a further 20%, because it "is the most effective way to help create even more jobs for Ontario" – again, a statement of *fact* without any proof. And this $4 billion will create another 825,000 jobs. The 20% cut in the provincial share of property taxes, $500 million, will "provide relief to every homeowner and renter in Ontario". The relief for commercial and industrial property taxpayers, "businesses in Ontario's highest taxed areas", will come in the existing plan to cut these taxes $500 million. And they pointed out they had scrapped the land transfer tax for first-time home-buyers, eliminated the "job-killing" employer health payroll tax on the first $400,000 of payroll, had cut almost 20% off workers' compensation payroll taxes, removed 140,000 low-income people from the tax rolls, and ended the $50 corporate filing fee.

They pledged a Taxpayer Protection Act, to force any proposed increase on any "major provincial tax", or the creation of a new one, through a province-wide referendum. They promised to fight the federal government over employment insurance premiums and, since Ontario income tax was increased any time the federal government increased income taxes overall, they said they would remove the province's collection system from theirs, to eliminate this. And they said the small business corporations' tax would be halved.

Blueprint then moved on to "Strengthening the Economy". It claimed the deficit had been $11.3 billion when they had taken office – or $1 million an hour, as the Harrisites liked to recite. It was now "on track to zero", or $3.6 billion in 1998-1999 and projected at $2.6 billion for the coming fiscal year. For this reason, the government was promising to legislate a balanced budget, which would penalize the present or any future Premier and Cabinet members that dared run a deficit by cutting their pay.

Barriers to job growth had been removed, such as "unfair job quotas", and more than 1,000 "un-needed" regulations. This *success* meant the Red Tape Review Commission was going to be made into a permanent watchdog. A computerized registration system had been set up for businesses, to cut time "from 3 months to 20 minutes". Workers had been given a secret ballot for union (de)certification, and work weeks would be redesigned to allow "more flexibility". Hydro rates had been frozen (though it didn't mention the freeze had been cut off early and the Minister was stating rates would have to raise to pay its debt).

Under "Getting People Back to Work", the document repeated the government's success in getting almost 400,000 people off welfare "and put(ting) their lives back on track". "That's the fastest drop in welfare dependency ever recorded in Canada ..."

As a result, **Ontario has gone from having the highest number of people per capita on welfare in Canada to the lowest.** *But some people need more help to trade the welfare trap for the pride and self-sufficiency of a new job.*

They had established work-for-welfare, stopped jail inmates from collecting benefits, and established a welfare fraud hotline "which has uncovered 15,000 cases of abuse and fraud and saved taxpayers nearly $100 million this past year alone". They had cut "excessive welfare rates" yet allowed recipients to work and earn back the difference "without financial penalty". They had set up the Learning, Earning and Parenting programme which required teen parents to stay in school and take parenting courses in order to receive benefits, as well as having established a whole new "more generous" programme for disabled people. And it wasn't just welfare for people they had toughened up. Two-hundred, twenty-five million dollars in grants to corporations had been cancelled.

Remedial training would be required for welfare recipients who failed a "basic language and math test". In this way, they would be job-ready. Drug treatment would be required for those who failed drug testing. "You can't get off welfare and hold a job if you're addicted to drugs." Permanent bans would be put in place for those convicted of welfare fraud. Welfare case workers would receive advanced training to give them a new focus, putting people back to work. Workfare positions would be opened in the civil service in parks and road maintenance. Incentives and penalties would be adopted for municipalities meeting or missing work-for-welfare targets.

For "Making Government Work Smarter, Better & Faster", the Tories had cut 130 MPPs to 103 saving $11 million, eliminated tax-free allowances and "the gold-plated pension plan" while cutting their pay 5%, reduced the civil service by 16,000 for savings of $650 million per year, cut the cost of government administration by 35% saving $300 million, and reduced municipalities and school boards, cutting 2,200 local politicians.

They promised to cut more waste, though they gave no specifics as to how. They pledged to set new and higher standards for public servants, to make government younger, "smaller, quicker, less bureaucratic, less expensive, and more responsive". They also wanted to improve "customer service and satisfaction" with a Declaration of Taxpayer Rights, which would include the right to be treated with courtesy and respect, as an honest and law-abiding citizen – unless proven otherwise, to know why you or your business is being contacted, audited or inspected, and a timely response from government. There was also another pledge to "sell things we don't need".

Finally, *Blueprint* broke out of economic matters. It started with health. The Tories said they were fully committed to the principles of the *Canada Health Act* and, to prove it, they had increased spending in this area despite $2.8 billion in transfer cuts (an accusation they repeated on the next page and the page after that). As to the $900 million extra they were about to get from Ottawa, they promised to put "every penny of it" back into health. They promised to increase health funding 20% more over five years. As proof they would keep their word, they reiterated their 'promises kept' mantra – $1.2 billion more for long-term care, 260,000 more breast cancer screenings, a pneumonia vaccine for the elderly and very ill, a 'Healthy Babies, Healthy Children' programme, $225 million over two years to reduce emergency room waits, $67 million in extra high-growth hospital funding, and a new university nursing programme, along with "more jobs for nurses".

Their Patient Bill of Rights would guarantee 15-minute patient assessment, a 60-hour minimum stay for new mothers with telephone and home follow-up with two days, a 10% reduction in ambulance response times, and cancer radiation treatment within four weeks. They also promised to assess care through hospitals' "customer surveys" and report cards, and eliminate waste, fraud, and abuse through "smart cards" which would hold a patient's medical information. They committed to further "powerful" incentives to get doctors to go to northern and under-serviced areas, such as free tuition if the physician stayed put for a minimum of five years. On nurses, they said they would spend $375 million more in 1999-2000 to hire them, culminating in 12,000 new nurses over three years.

Even for hard-core Tories, it was difficult to miss the similarities of these commitments to the Liberal's *20/20* booklet. It was as though they simply lifted the Liberal health promises and improved on a couple. The Patient's Bill of Rights came from the NDP. Most of the rest of the platform was uniquely Harris Conservative.

They were delivering "A Safer Ontario" with new and tougher parole standards and drug testing for parolees, a province-wide sex-offender registry, making parents financially liable for property damage done by their children, as well as having to pay for their legal aid if they could afford it, and the establishment of an Office for Victims of Crime to offer programmes for such victims. After all, they had already put 1,000 new police on the street with "modern law enforcement equipment", were building new and better jails, had started 90-day on-the-spot licence suspensions for those failing sobriety tests, expanded the province's DNA crime laboratory, applied to have more paedophiles declared dangerous offenders, and put more money into the Special Investigations' Unit to keep police accountable. They also offered tougher restrictions to fight domestic violence, drug dealing, "aggressive panhandling", and a desire to make criminals pay for the cost of their custody.

But Ontario was not just safer, but it was "A Cleaner Ontario". *Drive Clean* had been established to test automobile emissions, with the intention of cutting smog by 22%. A Water Protection Fund of $200 million had been set up "to help municipalities clean up their water and sewer systems", as well as $5 million for something called the Great Lakes Renewal Foundation. They said they had set "strict emission standards" for all hydro producers, and they were challenging neighbouring American states to clean up on cross-border pollution.

Their new environmental promises were modest in number. The Lands for Life initiative was about to see the creation of 378 new provincial parks, and additions to 44 others, in northern Ontario, covering 2.4 million hectares. As well, polluters would face doubled fines for first and second offences, and industry would be irregularly audited by "environmental SWAT teams" to make certain they were living up to the standards. Environmental laws would continue to be reduced and simplified. Their commitment to make hunting and fishing a right enshrined in legislation was less seen as an environmental promise than a sop to this traditional Tory group who had been upset by the ending of the spring bear hunt in January.[1]

On "Giving All Children a Good Start", the Tories also appeared to be stealing Liberal ideas. They had already appointed a Minister Responsible for Children in October 1997[2] . They were also committing to an Early Years programme, based on the study they commissioned in 1998, one co-chaired by Dr. Fraser Mustard, a noted expert on childhood learning, and Margaret Norrie McCain, a child advocate and former New Brunswick Lieutenant-Governor. They pushed for the creation of early child development and parenting centres to help kids, the further crackdown on 'deadbeat' parents who were not making their child support payments (including the use of private collection agencies), the continuation and expansion of divorce mediation, and provision to allow employees of companies with 50 or more workers the opportunity to take ten unpaid-leave days to look after a family crisis.

In "Education for the 21st Century", they pledged another tenet, the Charter of Education Rights and Responsibilities for students, teachers, and parents. "Respect and responsibility" would be taught in class, part of which would be the daily singing of *O Canada*. A "Code of Conduct" would be established for behaviour, as would a dress code imposed by parents, and province-wide student testing on core subjects in every grade. Staff would have to undergo criminal background checks, and teachers would enforce the Code of Conduct by imposing detentions and suspensions, while principals and vice-principals would be given the authority to expel students. Teachers would also face testing of their skills, training, and knowledge.

Blueprint made it sound like a negative thing that previous governments had allowed post-secondary students to *only* pay 20% of their education. The Harrisites had "restored the balance" by increasing it to 35% over their term. In turn, they claimed student loans had been increased 33%, new scholarships had been created, and tax credits had been provided to help pay these loans. And they committed to further scholarships. The Tories also mentioned that many traditional degrees were no longer getting jobs for students and, while "learning for its own sake is an admirable goal", it was their intention to tie some funding to "job placement results".

As to SuperBuild, the province decided to put all of its capital assets together into one fund – $10 billion over five years – and seek an equal amount from the private sector in order "to build and renew our roads, schools, hospitals, and technology links", not to mention colleges and universities.

It was on the subject of the economy where the Tories pushed the difference between themselves and the Liberals. They were being specific on economic promises. The Liberals wouldn't say how much all their promises of restored funding would cost. (Of course, the Tories didn't lay out a lot of numbers on their non-economic promises, either.) The Liberals responded by saying that the Harrisites were still short on their promise of 725,000 new jobs, as only about 540,000 had been created. In retort, the Tories pointed out they still had another year on the promise. There was some criticism that commitments were to be paid by new money coming from Ottawa and money *saved* by the Tories. As Harris put it, they did all the hard lifting and the Liberals were going to take advantage.

The NDP didn't seem affected by the pre-election presentations of platforms by the other parties. They chose to wait until the campaigning was on before releasing their plans. Unlike the pre-1995 past, theirs lacked the most detail of all.

Echoing the 15-minute emergency room evaluation, and the hiring of nurses and health-care workers for $375 million, their only other health care promises were to set higher standards and ban the ownership of any new nursing homes by private interests. On education, they, like the Liberals, committed to a 10% tuition cut, making junior kindergarten mandatory, and permitting school boards to again raise taxes and make spending decisions. They promised to hire 500 new environmental officers, and cut chemical emissions by electrical generating stations by 83% within three years. On social matters, they were a bit more expansive, promising 16,000 affordable housing units over four years, 14,000 new housing units for people with special needs, psychiatric patients, and those with addictions, they would restore rent controls and extend it to vacant apartments, and increase shelter allowances for those on welfare to 85% of the average rental cost in their community.

On finances, the NDP were probably the most conservative. They committed to rolling back the 30% cuts that had gone to those earning more than $80,000, but said there would be no increase of the deficit to finance $1.5 billion on their other promises. As well, a modest $30 million would be spent to save resource industry jobs, and a new fee on vehicle licences in the north would be dropped. There was also a rather vague pledge to keep wealth generated in northern Ontario in northern Ontario.

For the most part, the New Democrats didn't focus on policy, and neither the Conservatives nor the Liberals focused on their policies, either. Frankly, neither expected the NDP to be much of a factor.

But all three parties seemed to miss that *Blueprint* was full of holes. A lot of the history of the Tory term was revisionist, to say the least, and, I'm sure, can be traced to them not being shy about blowing their own horns. Why not blow up a modest success into a gigantic one, or a defeat into a victory? Perhaps had the Opposition tried to point this out, it might have made some difference. However, the Liberal focus was on health and education, almost exclusively, and the NDP's came to be on attacking Liberals.

The 540,000 jobs new jobs created in Ontario over their term was not, in fact, "the largest job increase in the country's history", nor was its pace.

The Peterson Liberals had governed during a time when over 700,000 jobs were created, but why let the truth get in the way of a good story. The 30% income tax cut was the "first real increase in take-home pay for the average Ontario worker in a decade". Only problem here is that, while these people might have had bigger cheques going home, once they paid new government fees and hiked property taxes, they were no better off than before. Many were much worse off. Even in 2001, the average family's income has risen only a couple of hundred dollars, which puts them thousands behind given inflation, and this Taxpayer Protection Act would not stop even more fees and municipal taxes. And when the Tories promised a "Made in Ontario" income tax rate to save provincial taxpayers from federal tax hikes, they were being disingenuous. In fact, Finance minister Paul Martin had pledged to cut federal tax rates. This was going to cost the province revenue. In breaking from the same collection system, the Harrisites actually stopped Ontario taxpayers from fully benefiting from national cuts. And SuperBuild, the project to guarantee new capital spending, was actually a massive reduction in provincial capital expenditure of more than half over five years.

The Tories would hire more nurses ... many of whom were the same people they had sent packing two or three years earlier. More was to be spent on water and sewerage, while regulations were being cut to undermine oversight of water and sewerage. 'Stricter emission standards' had been set for the former Ontario Hydro, yet its coal-fired plants were spewing out never-before-seen levels of pollution. Neighbouring American states were being 'challenged' to clean up their acts, while Ontario cut regulations which meant more pollution here than ever. New York State estimates were that Ontario was headed for nitrogen oxide emissions three-times that allowed for eastern American states during summer smog season. Of 3,000 air pollution violations in 1998, there were two prosecutions. The Tories were spending as much on the environment in 1999 in real terms as was the Davis government ... in 1971.[3] Ontario now had the lowest per capita welfare rate in Canada and, undoubtedly, the highest number of people living in the streets. People on welfare needed testing for literacy even though most of them could no longer access schooling through welfare. People on welfare needed testing for drugs even though there might well be a higher percentage of MPPs who are drug abusers.

One thing *Blueprint* failed to mention was the government having deregulated professional degrees from tuition limits. In other words, universities could now charge whatever they wanted for such programmes as MBAs and medical schools. It effectively meant some students were now being charged as much as 200% of the cost of their degrees. They also didn't mention that repayment of some student loans was tied to how fast the government felt a degree was likely to get you a job. In all cases, it was now expected more quickly and at a higher rate. But this document did boast they were working with the federal government to create the Millennium Fund for Students, "the largest student assistance program in Ontario history". In reality, they were hindering this totally federal programme by clawing back every cent a student was granted through the Millennium scholarship if they also received Ontario loans, which were already capped at $7,000 per year.

Yet the truth is that the Tories didn't trust *Blueprint* to be the main plank in their re-election strategy. Yes, it re-affirmed the Tories' revolutionary changes and their desire to continue on it that vein, but another move was much more demonstrative in the real Conservative strategy. Despite denials, they intended to *buy* the election.

It couldn't have seemed a bad idea. After all, the Tory coffers were overflowing from four years of being the best buddies for which business could have hoped. They had roughly eight million dollars but election laws were such that they wouldn't be able to spend more than perhaps a third of that during a campaign. The easy answer was to re-write the law to see they could spend more of it.

The Liberals had been the last to update the rules on running elections in 1986. However, they and their predecessors had always done so with the cooperation of the opposition parties. The Tories didn't really care if they had it or not. They initially proposed shortening the minimum length of campaigns from 37 to 28 days, increasing constituency spending limits from about $51,600 to $98,000, and to raise the maximum that an individual or corporation could donate to a party from $4,000 to $7,500. These were obvious moves to advantage the Tories at the expense of others. The party-in-power with its greater number of incumbents would generally gain from a shorter campaign period and, given the Conservatives were able to raise more money, they would benefit greatly from these spending and donation increases. The Liberals and NDP opposed these changes, though they were somewhat red-faced that they had members on the Commission on Election Finances which had endorsed them.

Chris Hodgson, the Management Board Chair, was responsible for seeing the proposals came to fruition. His arguments favouring the legislation were minimal. Increasing spending limits to $98,000 was simply making up for inflation since they were last changed in 1986. However, the reality was inflation would have brought them to less than $72,000. As well, with the ridings now going to be larger – the same as federal ones – the increase was necessary to be fair. However, federal limits had been about $62,000 per riding during the last election in 1997.

When Bill 36, the *Election Statute Law Act*, was presented, Hodgson had relented somewhat, with limits set at 96ø per voter. With an average of about 65,000 voters per riding, each party would be limited to around $62,000 per riding. Limits on corporate donations would rise to $15,000 from $7,000. Individual contributions to ridings would increase to 75% of the first $300 of donation, and 50% on the next $700, to a maximum $1,000 donation. In an election year, this would actually double, as these contributions could be made both to the riding association and the riding campaign.

But another change was that central party spending would be permitted to rise 50% to 60ø per voter, meaning this could go up to over $4 million per party. As well, election polling, research, and travel expenses would be exempt from limits. Given that the parties usually spent over $500,000 on these, the combined exemptions could mean upwards of $2 million more in *free* spending. Every move benefited the Tories, given their greater ability to bring in money and their greater cash reserve from which to spend it.

The other change that would have a significant effect was doing away with the process of enumeration and going with a permanent voters' list. This had been a proposal of Warren Baillie, the Chief Election Officer, and was not obstructed by the opposition parties. Part of the reason for change was the cost of enumeration for each election. Part of it was that computerization meant records could now create a reasonably up-to-date voters' list, or so they thought.

The Liberals and New Democrats were very clear in their opposition to higher spending limits, though they did not have similar positions. The New Democrats were against any increase and said so. The more each candidate could spend, the more unfair any campaign would be. It was a self-interested position, but one based solidly in principle. The Liberals, on the other hand, did not take a self-interested position ... surprisingly. Quite the opposite. For the party that was worst off for cash, they accepted that raising limits was reasonable. However, since ridings had been made the same size as federal ridings, the limits should be the same as federal limits, not significantly higher, as was originally proposed.

There were some in both the Liberal and NDP camps who differed from their parties' stands. Many Liberals concerned about democracy, as well as those who were worried about their lack of finances, thought that going along with raised limits was the height of stupidity. Higher limits meant elections were becoming about money and buying your way to power, not about ideas and issues. And some in the NDP liked higher limits, as they felt this might assist them in ridings where they were in tough fights with the Liberals, given that they still had significant support from union dues. Not that any complaints really mattered, given that the Tory majority was going to force through the changes. However, it is instructive to note how few actually stood up for the democratic side.

Another position where both the Liberals and NDP agreed, though, was in their disgust that the changes were going to be made without their approval. In the past, such legislative changes to election spending had been agreed to by all parties in the Legislature. In this case, the Harrisites simply forced it down their throats. They rejected public hearings and used time allocation to limit debate to three sittings over 15 days. No amendments were permitted.

The outcome was very predictable. The Tories spent early and often, starting with the television commercials attacking Dalton McGuinty ...

2. The Liberals just can't express their true Liberalism

To say that the Liberals had learned their lessons from 1995 would be flattering. In fact, many of the same conditions applied as they had four years earlier. The party had less money, as its debt had risen from loans not yet paid from the last election and the leadership campaign, and they couldn't seem to attract many donors. The new leader, Dalton McGuinty, had been chosen in 1996 with little fanfare and less public attention, something he and the party had done little to remedy over the previous two years. And a lack of organization still pervaded, from the ridings right up to the central party.

There had been great hope that jettisoning Lyn McLeod would lead to success. Fairly or unfairly, many inside the party blamed her for the flip-flops that gave the Tories momentum during the '95 campaign. They felt that, once she was gone, a new leader would come with a new reputation and the party would get a clean slate. That having been said, McLeod stayed on until late 1996, impressing people far more once she announced her resignation. She was looser and more relaxed, and came across as much more earnest in her attacks on the Harrisites than she had appeared against the Rae NDP.

The leadership fight seemed remarkably restrained and pleasant on the surface. And while it never became as bitter as many, there was a definite undercurrent of unease and split within the party as a number of people all chose to seek the position.

Gerard Kennedy had been head of the Daily Bread Food Bank in Toronto before being elected in the May 1996 by-election in York South, which had opened up with Bob Rae's resignation. Winning it made many Liberals feel better than they had since their defeat almost a year earlier. Naturally, many New Democrats were annoyed because they lost the riding ... and they saw Kennedy as someone far more left-wing than the Liberals deserved. Unfortunately, some Liberals felt he was much too left-wing, period. Regardless, in just a matter of months, his out-going personality and energy made him a favourite to replace McLeod.

And, in fact, there were no other favourites. Gerry Phillips, the long-time Scarborough MPP and Liberal financial whiz, had been the preferred choice, but he had backed out of the race months before because of an irregular heart beat. Yes, there were other candidates, but none grabbed the attention of the media and the public the way Kennedy did. What it quickly meant was that those in the party who weren't enamoured of him began to coalesce around ABK – Anybody But Kennedy. Annamarie Castrilli, Joe Cordiano, Dwight Duncan, John Gerretson, and Dalton McGuinty were all MPPs and all seemed competent choices with differing bases of support. The seventh, Greg Kells, was an Ottawa businessman who, like many so-called fringe candidates, just wanted to have his say.

Along with the core of Toronto, Kennedy's support, perhaps surprisingly, seemed to come from the party establishment. Gerry Phillips, former leader and Treasurer Bob Nixon, and "Rainmaker" Keith Davey all were in his camp, as was *The Toronto Star* editorial board[4] . Many were attracted not just to him but to his message that this should be the *liberal* Liberal party. Whatever the reason, Kennedy entered the convention with 720 committed delegates.

Cordiano had the most experience in the Legislature, having been first elected in 1985. He came in with a good portion of suburban Toronto and Italian members. He argued for moderate policies, yet was the only one of the seven to promise a repeal of the 21.6% cut to welfare. He went into the convention with 496 delegates. McGuinty had an Ottawa region base, and had garnered the support of many of those who would have backed Murray Elston, had he run again. (He had lost to Lyn McLeod in 1992.) He had worked diligently to meet members across the province, yet went into the convention with just 413 delegates. Duncan came from Windsor and brought with him extreme southwestern and labour supporters. He strongly attacked Kennedy on a TVO debate over his plan to cut the work week and discourage overtime to create jobs, arguing it would scare away business. Of course, it would also have cut union wages. Early delegate selection had him in third, but he dropped to fourth with 383 delegates once the numbers from the north, Toronto, and Ottawa were counted. Gerretson had been mayor of Kingston, and attracted some eastern Ontario and municipal support. He argued experience was necessary for the new leader, that the party couldn't afford "on-the-job training", which was interpreted as a slight to Kennedy, in particular. He went in with 132 committed delegates. Castrilli was new, Italian, from Toronto, and attracted some female support. She aimed her barbs mostly at the government. However, only elected in 1995, she had no firm base and attracted little interest.

The convention was not without surprises, the first of which was a rather nasty letter circulated by members of Kennedy's own riding executive, recommending delegates not support him. Apparently, they had supported an opponent for the by-election nomination, then didn't like that he didn't take advice from them when in office.

After the fairly tame run-up campaign, the next surprise was the vehemence of some of the speeches, particularly that of McGuinty. Perhaps trying to set himself out from the crowd, he spent most of his 20 minutes questioning Kennedy's ideological stand, his qualifications, and his lack of time in the party, while promoting those qualities in himself.

The third, and most unwelcome, surprise came when the convention opened three hours late, then the first ballot was dragged out for six-and-a-half hours. There were problems with appointing alternates, then the voting. It was buffoonery at its worst, and it cast a pall over the whole process. When the results were finally released at about 7:30PM, Kennedy was first at 770, with Cordiano next at 557. Duncan had 464, McGuinty 450, Gerretson 152, Castrilli 141, and Kells just 24. Only Kells was off, and the second ballot went ahead with all others remaining. The numbers remained remarkably the same. Kennedy, Cordiano, and Duncan added a handful each, while McGuinty, Gerretson, and Castrilli bled a little support.

It was at this point that bad feelings came more to the fore. Gerretson went to McGuinty, likely because they were both eastern conservative Liberals, as did Castrilli. It was suggested by an aide this was because she saw him as "a fellow outsider", and she didn't like Dwight Duncan who had the support of other MPPs who didn't care for her[5]. The question was whether or not these two could take their delegates, about 10% of the total, with them.

The answer to that came two hours later. It was now after midnight. Kennedy still led, up to 803, but McGuinty had indeed inherited the lion's share of these moving votes, jumping past Duncan into a tie with Cordiano at 601. The Windsor MPP had 509 and was eliminated. Then, the next surprise came.

Dwight Duncan would receive a great deal of criticism for his action, especially from his own supporters. After being disparaging of Kennedy before the vote, he crossed the convention floor to join him. This caused anger, confusion, and near chaos in some quarters. Many of his supporters felt sold out and refused to go with him. Cordiano's people had expected him to come to them, and they were staggered by the move.

Observers speculated that Duncan must have been *bought off* by the promise of a high Cabinet post in a Kennedy government. That may be. However, in the end, it may have been that Duncan simply recognized that he and Kennedy had the most in common. They both explicitly supported re-investment in health and education, and might have been considered to be more alike than different. Cordiano had made a virtue of being moderate, perhaps to the point of not taking stands on too many issues. McGuinty was also seen as being somewhat more right-wing. Cordiano was in his fourth term, McGuinty his second, but neither had done much to give the appearance of being leadership material. They certainly didn't exude the charisma of Kennedy. Perhaps it was this simple for Duncan, though it certainly was not for his supporters.

He was only able to deliver 165 votes to Kennedy. The fourth ballot gave him 968, while McGuinty picked up 159 to move into second place with 760. Cordiano had gained 95, but fell off the ballot with 696. Ninety or so of Duncan's supporters from the third ballot didn't vote.

There were some who thought Cordiano would go to Kennedy. They were both Torontonians, and many of his supporters were thought to want to support their fellow resident. However, Cordiano and McGuinty had been in caucus together for six years, and they had more views in common than those on which they differed. The MPP for Lawrence crossed to his colleague from Ottawa, and took 445 votes with him. It was apparent to most that the final ballot was just a formality. For the first time, and at the worst moment, Gerard Kennedy was no longer in first. He lost to Dalton McGuinty 1,205 to 1,065.

In his book, John Ibbitson suggests that McGuinty was victorious because he appealed to delegates who wanted someone "solid, pragmatic, (and) dependable", someone who "would push the Liberals as close to the Tories ideologically as the party could get without disappearing up the Tory platform".[6] I cannot help but disagree. Though there is no question a few delegates felt going with a conservative leader "seemed the safest place to be", I would ultimately suggest McGuinty's selection had little to do with ideology and much more to do with geography.

No one should kid themselves – Gerard Kennedy lost the leadership more than Dalton McGuinty won it, and there were three reasons Kennedy lost. Yes, there were those who saw him as too left-wing and opted for McGuinty. And then there were those who saw Kennedy as too inexperienced. This was certainly a larger number. Many actually liked him best, but felt he needed seasoning and time in the Legislature. He would be a *leader-of-the-future*. And Kennedy had good support, as can be seen by his leading right up until the final ballot. But the most important reason contributing to his defeat was that he was from Toronto. In probably all three major parties in Ontario, there is a visceral dislike of Toronto. The city is, in my mind unfairly, seen as controlling and atypical of the *Rest of Ontario*. Even most of those from urban Ontario outside Toronto see the world through the eyes of traditional, small town values, and suspect Toronto as somehow being the unified Sodom and Gomorrah. In the end, many delegates from the *Rest of Ontario* would unite around whoever was left standing to face Kennedy, and that turned out to be McGuinty.

The obvious contradiction is that I have said most of Cordiano's support came from the Toronto area, and many wanted to go with Kennedy, in the end. But he took about 80% of his first ballot support with him to McGuinty. The truth is they were very loyal to their candidate and they hung with him. It may be they too recognized McGuinty was more like Cordiano than Kennedy. It may also be they felt Kennedy needed more experience. Regardless, at 4:25AM, McGuinty was pronounced the winner.

His first promise was to shake up the party. The new leadership brought in new people, many of whom were really old ones who had been minor players in minor roles under Peterson. With them came the desire to regain power but, perhaps, also the lack of understanding as to why they had lost it in the first place. They would show a remarkable inability to advance membership, cut debt, or come up with a substantial election plan.

That's not to say that the powers-that-be didn't try to improve things. There was certainly more of an attitude that the senior party people were paying more attention to the membership, and there seemed a true desire to make policy that was more decisive and honest. Unfortunately, this may have been more smoke and mirrors than reality.

Though many party organizers worked for several months to ask regular members what they thought needed to be said, the strategists who wrote up the platform again fell into the same old trap. The Liberals led the polls. *Do nothing controversial to upset people and you can cruise into government.* It was stupid and cowardly, ignored past history, and alienated many ordinary members, not to mention those who had actively participated in the policy creation process in good faith. More importantly, the *20/20* platform was another mishmash of bland commitments – far blander than the ones put to the party by the membership – and promises to do better than the Tories, or that's how it was seen and portrayed, and little was done to dissuade that view. Did people vote NDP or Conservative as a result? I doubt it. I don't doubt some people who could have been expected to be Liberal supporters stayed home, though, and didn't vote at all.

There was also concern before the election – appropriate concern, it turned out – that the central party was overly shy. When the Tories were in the process of their resurrection, they carefully curried favour with those they saw as sympathetic to their philosophy. As well, new people with new ideas were invited to pass along their attitudes to the senior party people. However, the Liberals neither sought out friends for cash nor for ideas. From 1997 to 1998 in particular, they seemed almost timid and fearful. Perhaps it was as simple as the people at the top were so inexperienced they didn't really know what to do, or were too afraid to ask for help lest they look inexperienced. While it might be unfair to say this further undermined the party apparatus, it would not be to say it didn't help make it better.

There was more than this lack of organization that ticked off many in the ridings. The party was determined to clean up its finances, and it started off by telling the riding associations that they would have to pay back every cent owed to the central party before they would be permitted to choose a candidate for the next election. Treasury-wise, it was probably a good idea, but it did contain a dark shadow which few seemed to recognize until later.

Many riding leaders were very upset. Not only were most told their associations still owed thousands of dollars from loans from the 1995 campaign and unpaid annual commitments that, in some cases, stretched back almost a decade, but they would also be required to pay back debts some had been told by party officials were settled. In a quiet revolt that accepted the party did indeed need money, the ridings went along with most of these conditions but forced a motion that eliminated the consideration of anything owing from prior to 1995. For the most part, this got rid of any questionable debts and just left the ones that could be verified. Still, this debt repayment scheme required most ridings to spend most of their time and effort simply trying to pay back what they owed at the cost of election readiness.

The unintended result – the 'shadow', if you will – was the length of time it took before ridings began nominating candidates. The central party people seemingly did not recognize that the ridings were equally as poor as it, and it would take some time to raise the money to pay what was owed. Regardless, they would not be permitted to nominate a candidate before paying their debt. In the end, though an election was expected in the spring of 1999, few ridings were able to nominate candidates prior to ... the spring of 1999. The lucky ones were the ones that had their choice in place more than a few weeks before the May election call. (Maybe it shouldn't be surprising, but incumbent Liberal MPPs were exempt from paying back the debt prior to nomination, though they still were supposed to pay it. As of late 2001, some haven't.) When the party finally recognized that many ridings were short a candidate, they had no choice but to let them pick their person because time had simply run out.

3. The NDP wanders down the garden path ...

For the New Democrats, matters may have been much worse. Falling from government to third party in June 1995 must have hurt a great deal. Never budging up in the polls between then and 1999 must have been horribly worrisome. Taking increasing flak from significant union leaders must have been extremely annoying. But the biggest difficulty New Democrats suffered was that they couldn't seem to come to terms with their time in power. The membership couldn't reconcile its actions as government with the promises it had made to get elected.

Whether federally or provincially, from its inception in 1961, the NDP was always characterized as the party with a social conscience. It was the moral centre of the people and parliament, always there to remind them of the plight of the poor, workers, women, the injured, the disabled, and all those who weren't given a fair shake by society. Yet once in power, many of the party's own supporters felt this tenet had been violated ... a principle they had always felt was inviolable. To have done so was sacrilegious, so to speak. As a result, they were unwilling to return to the party or even consider voting for its candidates.

Practically, this meant the NDP suffered a divided caucus and a divided party. Some felt they had actually done their best as the government, balancing support of their friends with what needed to be done for the province as a whole in a horrible recession. Others saw their 56 months in power as a waste and a sell-out, where supporters were pushed aside to benefit the traditional friends of government. In the wash, it seemed to play out in their leadership campaign ending in June 1996.

Bob Rae's departure from politics was a quiet one. Though he didn't decide to quit right after the election, his memoir leaves one to believe he was leaning that way. Toward the end of January 1996, he made his decision to go, and wasted no time in doing so. On 7 February, he resigned and, on the 8th, he started a new job as an international lawyer. As it was, though, he had left his party asea, without any real healing from the election. They were defeated and directionless.

Four candidates came out of the woodwork, all former Rae Cabinet ministers. Peter Kormos, the fiery rebel who had actually been fired by Rae, was first out of the blocks. His candidacy was straightforward. He wanted to represent the people who thought the Rae NDP had turned its back on its socialist ideology, and he wanted them to return to being the party of conscience. Next came Frances Lankin, the one of this group who had held the highest portfolios in government. She was instantly proclaimed the frontrunner. Both she and competitor Howard Hampton defended the NDP-as-government, clearly delineated a desire to see them become the government again, and promised to see to it a future New Democratic regime would bring back such policies as anti-scab legislation and employment equity. The final candidate was Tony Silipo. While well-liked, he had little support, perhaps because he didn't seem to stand for any particular point-of-view.

The battle seemed to be between just two – Lankin and Hampton. Lankin set herself out more middle-of-the-road, concerned with consensus-building and being pragmatic. Regardless of the fact she was the most outgoing and likely the smartest of the four, this style was the most like Bob Rae's and it hurt her. And because she had held the most senior positions of the four, and been praised the most by Rae, she was accused of bearing more responsibility for the government's failings. On the other side, Hampton was more dogmatic, arguing it was a dog-eat-dog, us-or-them world, and the NDP had better get on board the bus with the *have-nots* so as to fight back against the neo-cons and their support of the *haves*. He moved away from the defensive posture that the Rae government hadn't been so bad to one that said it didn't go far enough to help people. In effect, the leadership race was a contest to determine the direction of the NDP for many years to come: moderate, managerial party trying to prove to voters it could again govern; or, left-wing party seeking to show its former friends it could again govern but for them. Yet it might be fair to say that few seemed to realise the two perspectives are not mutually exclusive. After all, they won the 1990 election by being that left-wing party championing responsible, conscientious government. Regardless, the outcome was quite divisive, even if the campaigning itself wasn't.

The result would not set a clear path. Hampton would surprise most observers and win, leading throughout the 13-hour balloting. In fact, it was many union members defying their leaders who supported Lankin that put Hampton over the top. But Hampton's 55/45 margin was so thin that the party was virtually divided into halves, and the new leader did not do the best job in trying to heal their wounds. Though he made Lankin[7] his party's Health critic, many of her supporters were pushed into the background.

As the 1999 election approached, the NDP faced another rather nasty opponent – not the Tories nor Liberals, but an idea. Many people, including intellectuals, Liberals, and unionists, saw the flaw in the Ontario system that had seemingly brought the Tories back to power. Between the two opposition parties, they got about 55% of the 1995 popular vote but lost the election. Splitting the majority of the electorate guaranteed they both lost. And though the NDP was extremely weak in the months leading up to the election, they held enough support (about 15-20%) that they might again assure a Tory victory. That possibility meant even some loyal New Democrats started to think the unthinkable. It might be necessary to vote Liberal to get rid of the Tories.

The concept is called strategic voting. In this case, if you're a voter, you look at the New Democrat and the Liberal candidates in your riding and determine which one is more likely to defeat the Tory candidate. Even if you're an NDP supporter, if the Liberal is likely to do better than your candidate, you should vote Liberal. This was a popular refrain of Dalton McGuinty's. (While he usually accepted that Liberals in some ridings might need to vote NDP, he didn't push that nearly as hard.) In effect, hold your nose and vote Liberal for the good (or perhaps lesser evil) of the province.

It was an idea that seemed to frighten and anger Howard Hampton. If the electorate embraced it, there was a good chance the NDP might be wiped out, especially if New Democrats voted Liberal but Liberals didn't vote NDP. This worry probably led him to the ridiculous claim that the NDP were actually stronger than the Liberals in about 60 ridings[8]. On the other hand, the New Democrats might well benefit from strategic voting in a number of marginal ridings. Nevertheless, no one likes hearing others, especially alleged supporters, telling other supporters to bail out and vote for an opponent. This is exactly what happened between Hampton and Canadian Auto Workers president Buzz Hargrove.

Hargrove is a vehement opponent of the Harris *revolution* and he wanted it ended. He even convinced his own union to support strategic voting, going against decades of explicit support for the New Democrats. Given he was one of those unionists who had fallen away from the Rae government, his promotion of strategic voting seemed anti-NDP, and that's what Hampton apparently believed. The two made no secret of their differing views and the quarrel was soon a public one.

However, while Hargrove may not have been the favourite of his fellow unionists, he wasn't alone in his support of strategic voting. OPSEU supported it as well and, while the Canadian Union of Public Employees did not, it also did not put much money into supporting NDP candidates in strong Liberal ridings.

Did Ontarians opt to vote strategically? Not really. Yet, in the end, Hampton almost faced his worst fear. If part of the message got through to the electorate, it was *voting NDP is wasting your vote*. Though the Liberals couldn't stop the Tories being re-elected, they did benefit from a definite move away from the New Democrats. As badly as the results had gone for them in 1995, 1999 was much worse. Not only did they drop to just 9 seats from 17, but their percentage of the vote fell from 20.6 to 12.6.

And if anyone thought that this disaster ... and it was a disaster ... might lead to rectifying the unacknowledged split in the party's reason for being, it didn't. You see, the party leadership did not seem to recognize, or willfully ignored, that there was a problem. The provincial party's trouble seemed to mirror that in the federal party, and the whole debate of what the NDP should be seems to be waiting for a national decision on its future direction.

4. The *phony* campaign

As I said, the campaign began and, in many ways, ended before the writ was issued. The Tories wasted no time in making sure they did what they had to do to get re-elected. The polls throughout most of 1998 had indicated an upsurge in Liberal support, so the Conservatives went right for the one thing that distinguished the two parties most – their leaders.

The Tory TV ads began on 10 November 1998, but the shots at McGuinty had already begun. A day earlier, Harris had written an opinion piece in *The Toronto Star* attacking McGuinty for not having a firm position on health care. (Undoubtedly, it went to *The Star* to work on the minds of traditional Liberal supporters.) As well, Minister of Long-Term Care Cam Jackson held a press conference to do likewise, and distribute a pamphlet for the same purpose. Then, the ads appeared, showing the Liberal leader's face surrounded by question marks, suggesting that his vagueness on health was because the Liberals secretly planned to hike taxes to pay for changes.

McGuinty and his handlers tried to put the best face on the assault, suggesting that free publicity was good publicity. And there were many who felt the Tories weren't helping themselves by increasing McGuinty's almost non-existent public persona. But the Tory strategists looked at it differently. The Liberal leader's profile was low but, according to Conservative polling, it was rising and, for most who had an opinion, they liked the man. As Leslie Noble said, it was time "to bomb the bridge".[9] The Tories might have to absorb a negative reaction at first, but it would pass. In retrospect, it seemed this assessment was right on, for the most part.

As Ian Irquhart suggested in his *Toronto Star* article the day the ads began, this tactic was called "branding". McGuinty was being branded as weak and dishonest and, though this might appear initially unfair, "it will make voters more susceptible to later appeals".[10] And repeated often enough, it would have the effect of making any mistake or slip-up by McGuinty seem to reinforce this brand. It turned out to be another successful strategy for the Harrisites, especially because the Liberal braintrust didn't want to bring out their platform too soon, lest the Tories steal it.

This was a point that was bandied about the party for months. The policy process that the Liberals had put in place was supposedly finished in September, October, November, and December, yet nothing came forward from either the party headquarters nor the leader's office. Furious discussion began about why the party was holding back, as word spread before Christmas that the platform was written and waiting. The debate seemed to centre on whether bringing it out early would simply give the Tories more time to steal its provisions. Waiting until the election would stop this.

That was apparently the view of those in the uppermost positions. I know from my perspective and that of those in my riding and many of the ridings around mine, there was a clear difference of opinion. Many expressed the view that the sooner we got out our ideas, the sooner the public would identify them as ours. If the Tories stole them, that would make the Liberal party seem all the more legitimate. We lost the argument, and the *20/20* plan did not appear until mid-April.

If there was any part of the Tory strategy that didn't work it was the promotion of Howard Hampton and the NDP to counter McGuinty and the Liberals as to whom was the *real* opposition to the government. Beginning with the op-ed, Harris would comment on the clarity of the New Democratic message compared to the weasel-words of the Liberals. Of course, he would slam the NDP's message as wrong and explain why, but he consistently suggested this was better than waffling and being unclear. This part of the strategy failed completely, at least in this way. People still remembered the NDP as government and wanted nothing to do with them. Even if you questioned McGuinty, the choice between Liberal and NDP left few doubts as to which to pick, at least pre-writ.

Up to the election call, the Tories had the advertising pretty much to themselves. The other parties simply didn't have enough money to fight it out with them. Once the writ dropped, the Liberals decided to fight fire with fire, and came up with their own attack ads. They were intended tell voters the Liberals would save medicare and education, while reminding them of the chaos and hard feelings created by the Harrisites, particularly in their first two years. While they succeeded at this, they really never hit at those who had supported the Tories. They simply reminded those who hated Harris why they hated him but they did nothing to try to change the minds of those who didn't mind kicking the poor or the unions.

There were also criticisms that these ads failed to promote McGuinty, as not even one of them showed his face directly. At best, his name was mentioned or it came up on the screen at some point. Meanwhile, the Tories focused their entire campaign on Harris. Just as in 1995, it was the Mike Harris Team, not the Progressive Conservative party. He appeared strong. McGuinty's absence played into the branding of weakness.

The NDP took a similar tack to the Liberals, with sombre black and white scenes of Tory hospital, housing, and university malfeasance. However, instead of identifying the ill-doing as Conservative, they added the Liberals to it, stating both were the same under the skin.[11]

The campaign itself was called on Thursday, 6 May. The day-to-day travel, press scrums, and news clips seemed ordinary with the exception that the focus on McGuinty continued. Instead of the Premier having to defend his record and his government's mistakes, he quietly went from staged event to staged event, touting the party's message, one theme at a time. Perhaps more disciplined by four years as premier, he avoided gleeful, dangerously unscripted, retorts to tormentors, and went about the business of being re-elected. On the odd occasion when he did go on the offensive, as when he charged McGuinty with having a secret deal with unions to exchange votes for favours, his relish was still curbed. Asked about details, he responded with, "Who knows? When you cut a secret deal, it's secret." Past behaviour might have suggested he would continue on. He did not. It was almost as though he had practised his answer with handlers before making the accusation.

If the Liberals had expected Harris to hand them a few points with loose lips, they hadn't planned on losing some from their own troubles. The Tories released their budget on 29 April as a lead-in to the election. Instead of McGuinty raising his profile through a spirited attack on it, he got laryngitis and had to leave the critique to Finance critic Gerry Phillips. Then, a couple of days into the election, he got the numbers wrong on education spending promises and had to be bailed out, again by Phillips. Then, former leadership contender Annamarie Castrilli won a Tory nomination.

But it was the weakness of the Liberal's economic platform that shone through consistently. While McGuinty continually said the tax cuts the

Tories had enacted were wrong while the province was still running a deficit, he also said a government of his would not repeal them. Too much it seemed like the Liberals wanted to have it both ways, just as the Tories always accused. However, many people recognized that promising tax *increases* during an election was akin to blowing your own party's brains out. Saying you would overturn cuts was pretty much the same.

Meanwhile, the New Democrats were having little effect, perhaps because they were harping on the same basic issues as the Liberals, attacking the same Tory targets. The only two differences that were evident was the NDP's promise to roll-back tax cuts for those earning more than $80,000 per year and that this would fund increased social spending, and how few people were listening, likely due to the party's anaemic polling numbers. Leader Howard Hampton tried to get some of the spotlight, especially when several youths were supplied pizza and beer at a Conservative event, but it ended up a non-starter.

At mid-campaign, Hampton and the NDP changed tactics and joined Harris in attacking McGuinty. The polls consistently showed the NDP might be in extremely serious trouble, as the Liberals were perceived by voters as the alternative to the Harrisites. So, just before the halfway mark of the campaign, Hampton turned his attention away from the Tories and directly onto McGuinty. During the leader's debate, he referred to McGuinty as "Mike Harris II", accusing the Liberals as liking most of what the Tories had done and saying they would just continue on with the Harris policies of helping the rich, hurting the poor and workers, and dividing society. It was a desperate strategy to save the NDP from oblivion.

There can be no question, throughout much of the campaign, Hampton was more dynamic than McGuinty, and he was temporarily able to hang this albatross around the Liberal leader's neck. On the other hand, this didn't benefit Ontarians. The attacks on the Liberals simply stopped them from gaining any momentum which might have held the Tories to a minority and, ultimately, have seen them turfed from office much as the Miller Conservatives were in 1985. Instead, the NDP message was that the Liberals were just as bad as the Tories, their numbers just as "phony". But instead of getting voters out for his party, all Hampton seemed to do was convince them to stay at home and not vote at all.

Though opponents of Mike Harris probably found his re-election, with a renewed majority, the most distressing part of this campaign, for me, however, it was on a par with the reality that his victory was only due to the support of just over a quarter of eligible voters. For the second election in a row, voter turn-out was poor. Only about 58% of electors actually voted. Given that the Tories received 45.4% of the vote, this means just 26% actually chose Harris. Who knows? Had the other 42% voted, he might have won by more. However, as someone who has examined many elections, I find this doubtful. Usually, the higher the turn-out, the more likely it is that the party in power will be turfed out. I personally had hoped for a turn-out of over 70%. In my mind, this would have virtually guaranteed a Tory defeat, or at least a minority, which would have quickly led to some sort of Liberal-NDP cooperation. As long as *The Common Sense Revolution* was stopped, I would have been happy. In spite of the fact that many people had suffered through his term, there was little the Tories had done that couldn't have been repaired. With a second term, that was going to be much less likely. Unfortunately, Ontarians seemed awash in a sea of apathy.

If there was any *tide* washing in or out for the parties, it came during the leaders' debate for the Liberals ... and it went way out. When it was all over and television clips were on the newscasts for all those millions to see who hadn't actually watched the live event, they saw Mike Harris and Howard Hampton talking over Dalton McGuinty, most of the time. They were basically crowned co-champs simply because, it seems to me, they yelled louder.

Regardless, the media named their winners and the campaign changed. Hampton had been seen as a non-entity until his debate performance. This changed completely, and he began to get far more air-time. This *success* would be his party's undoing. In rather short order, he came to be asked questions for which he was ill-prepared or ill-suited to answer. He characterized McGuinty as Norman Bates, the serial killer from the movie *Psycho*. Had he said he looked like Anthony Perkins, the actor who played Bates, that might have been one thing. But framing McGuinty in the guise of a serial killer had people wondering about Hampton. When he answered a reporter's question as to which party he would support should there be a minority, his witticism of Dalton McGuinty being Mike Harris II came back to haunt him. If they were the same, how would the NDP choose whom to support? When Hampton said he could indeed support Harris, every criticism that he had made of the Tories over the previous years paled and made him look so two-faced that the NDP bounce in support dropped like a rock into a river off a bridge.

Liberals did not understand how the media had so quickly crowned Harris and Hampton as debate winners, and they were not prepared to respond.

McGuinty supposedly looked weak and Harris strong. To those running the campaign, it apparently seemed that the Tory attacks were now sticking. In fact, this was already a great concern, especially regarding the Tory accusations that this was the free-spending Liberal party of lore, and could not be trusted. Just days prior to the debate, McGuinty announced that no Liberal government of his would raise taxes without first asking voters for permission through a referendum. It was a huge blunder, as it played right into the NDP argument that the Liberals were still 'Blue Lite'. It wasn't Liberal policy, it was Tory policy, and it played right into the other accusation that Liberals stood for nothing.

In July, at the Liberal Provincial Council after the campaign, I had the opportunity to talk to McGuinty about this. He said that polling showed people believed we were free-spenders and we had to counter that image. When I suggested it was a mistake, that Liberal volunteers had walked away because we were suddenly promoting Tory policies, he got defensive and eventually said the action had been taken at the campaign manager's insistence. All I wanted was a *mea culpa* that showed he was a leader prepared to take responsibility. I didn't get it.

The election campaign quickly floundered. Given the debate declarations and the lack of money, the Liberals drifted through the last week or so, unable to staunch the Tory momentum. And once Hampton did in his own party, a majority victory was basically assured for Harris.

The Conservative campaign had been fairly consistent throughout: attack McGuinty and spend money. It was very good at both. Unlike the CSR document, which had been printed in small numbers over many months and was virtually non-existent by election-time, 1995, the Tories had one million copies of *Blueprint* distributed, mostly in newsprint form, during the campaign. As well, they bombarded people with television and radio, as well as newspaper ads, regarding their strengths and the opposition deficiencies. And the strengths were portrayed as many, even though they may not have been entirely accurate.

The economy was humming along better than it had been since the 1960s. Voters appreciated the sense of relief it gave them after years of anxiety. Mike Harris proclaimed his party's tax cuts as being responsible. As was said in *Blueprint*, "The debate is over – tax cuts create jobs". Rubbish. The vast majority of self-respecting economists disagreed, but the Premier was convinced. Indeed, there was a relationship, even if it was a spurious one.

The American economy was also doing extremely well, and exports to it, such as from the auto industry, fed economic growth in Ontario. And this was fertile ground for the Americans to come shopping. With a dollar in the mid-60-cent range, the exchange rate made our manufacturers far more competitive than most domestic factories. However, instead of the Harrisites accepting this as the reason for economic growth, they refused to accept anything less than the dogma that tax cuts create jobs. In fact, anywhere trickle-down economics had been implemented, even most conservative economists had declared it a failure.

5. A view from *on the ground*

There is little more depressing than being in a riding election campaign office in the midst a one-sided defeat, except perhaps if you've had hopes of winning and you're seeing them dashed. I had no illusions we were going to win the Simcoe-Grey election in 1999. I was the office manager and policy chair for the campaign, and I had watched what seemed to be a better-than-expected start stall, then decline. Yet, I still had hope for the overall provincial campaign. That was gone soon enough, but not immediately.

The campaign headquarters opened just two days before the election was called. Like most Liberal ridings, we chose our candidate later than we should have. Given that we were taking on a Cabinet minister who had been in the Legislature since 1990, it was far too late to build up any profile for our man.

At first, we seemed to find a number of people who were willing to volunteer – not enough for a full campaign, but more than I had expected. Unfortunately, few wanted anything to do with knocking on doors – a goodly percentage of them were teachers and didn't want potential confrontation – and even fewer wanted to take on senior positions in the campaign. There aren't many people nowadays who seem to have the time to commit to things political, especially for intense periods. The result was too few people trying to do too much and not getting it done well enough. I myself put in 90-plus-hour weeks and still I felt I wasn't doing enough.

The early days seemed to go well. Criticism of the Tories was everywhere, and the people I met seemed enthusiastic about putting them in their place. (Of course, their fans weren't dropping in to meet Liberals, were they?) There seemed a real popular discontent with our local member, Jim

Wilson, as well. He had been anything but a good constituency representative. In fact, it was a rare occurrence when he left Toronto to deign us with a visit. His Alliston constituency office, which had been the main one before redistribution, was seldom open and, even when it was, the telephones were even less likely to be answered. And many blamed him for the growing troubles in the health care system, as he had been its Minister when the Tories took office and the slicing began. However, he did seem good at arriving with large cheques for the local hospitals, just in time to avoid disaster.

Of course, any hope we Liberals had for success had to be tempered with the reality that most of the riding had been held by the Tories since the time of Mitch Hepburn. Perhaps that's why a little hope went a long way. It was unusual for there to be any interest in the Liberals here. (I can only imagine what it's like to be a provincial New Democrat here, as they normally get 10-15% of the vote. Federal ones get half that.)

We had more problems than hope, though. While we had enough money to start the campaign, the prospect of getting more was limited. Most of what had been donated had come from individuals, and many had been generous. But that meant our motherlode was pretty much tapped out immediately, and lesser veins, like business, proved to be extremely limited, though three or four unions did come across with liberal donations.

And while we had volunteers to help, they were inexperienced in campaigning and needed a lot of supervision. With few people to show them, we didn't get enough done, and many, rightly so, began to quickly drift away. I'm afraid that we just didn't have things well enough organized to keep them busy and interested.

It also didn't help that our candidate, Norman Sandberg, was a rookie. Yes, he had served on a town council for just over four years, but his knowledge of provincial politics was limited, and he really didn't understand what had to be done to win. He refused to tangle with his opponents, preferring to be seen as a gentleman, above the fray. An example came from the day of the biggest all-candidates' meeting, in Collingwood, his home town. One fellow had worked diligently to get the per student funding numbers from the Simcoe County District School Board. As we thought, they showed a decline every year from 1991 to 1998-1999[12], with a projected decline for the next year. MPP Wilson had been arguing the reverse, and we were pleased to get the ammunition to *shoot him down*. I personally put the information in our candidate's hands and, as policy chair, told him he had to use it when Wilson made his claims.

He didn't. Chained to my desk, I couldn't attend, but I did see the debate when I got home. I had taped it on local cable television. Our guy went first, and made his statement that per student funding had dropped. Wilson almost instantly cut in to decry the prevarication and reiterated that funding had gone up. It was then I expected the numbers to come out and Wilson to be put in his place. Instead, our man simply said the Tory was wrong but he "didn't want to argue numbers". I groaned, cursed, and lasted a few more minutes before turning the television off and going to bed. When I asked, the next morning, why he hadn't used the proof to nail Wilson, he explained his theory on how *good guys finish first*. However, as one spectator at a later all-candidates' meeting put it, "people in Markdale (a village in the riding) prefer their politicians to get in the muck and be dirty". To some extent, I must agree. People expect politicians to make their points at their opponents' expense (without becoming personal). When McGuinty attacked Kennedy during the Liberal leadership, he made himself stand out. When he failed to be forceful in his condemnation of Harris and Hampton during the leaders' debate, the media declared him the loser.

Also, Norman didn't understand that campaigning was a long process, and demanded meeting people face-to-face. After winning the nomination, five weeks earlier, he failed to get out at all during the pre-writ period. Then, during the election, too many of his mornings were spent learning policy and too many of his evenings ended with dinner with his family. I would never question he's a good family man – far too good for politics. As well, there's no question he didn't get to 50 doors during the 28-day campaign. His preference was to *mainstreet* the business sections and meet shoppers. Fine. But not day after day.

At first, it seemed like we were in a real horse race, but the signs went bad soon enough. The night of the leaders' debate was the beginning of the end. As office manager, I felt I had to stay at the headquarters and, since the building was not equipped for television, we were left to listen to it on radio. It was strange how the people there reacted differently than those who actually saw the debate. For us, it had been three-way action, where no one really seemed to better the others. However, for those who saw it, especially the media, Harris and Hampton had been even while McGuinty had seemed to let the others talk over him to make their points. Maybe the sound was better, or worse, on radio? Who knows? Once McGuinty was declared the loser, most of our volunteers suddenly found they were busy, and the office quietened significantly. I suspect this happened across the province.

The last ten days of the campaign were surely the most depressing. Defeat was in the air, though I'm sorry to say the candidate didn't see it coming. It was the size of the defeat that surprised us all. A solid thumping by 17,000 in 1995 turned into a hammering rout of 19,000 in 1999. It was disheartening, to say the least. It seemed that nothing that we had done or said had made the slightest difference. Had we lost by half that total, many of us would have looked on it as a good start toward the next election. As it was, all we had done appeared to have been for nothing.

In the end, it was hard for most who had opposed the Harris Tories to understand how so many voters had just seemingly been conned into giving them another term. There were the provincial income tax cuts, but most had come at the price of increased municipal property taxes and higher fees on many services, necessary services that had been slashed, not to mention people living in the streets of big cities. There was also the months of blatant advertising, using taxpayers' dollars, to promote the government, with some clearly aimed to denigrate Dalton McGuinty. And the Conservatives had made a great show of having kept so many of their promises, but that had come at the cost of misery for so many, not to mention that many other promises were broken completely. There was also the slaughter of the NDP, but not the collapse that was needed to help Liberal candidates.

But the Tories had taken every advantage, and the Opposition parties had played to them badly. Aggressive campaigning was tempered by fear of offending voters and a lack of money. And both parties nominated far too many candidates far too late. They may have been gems, but the voters didn't have time to find out.

Perhaps what was truly offensive to me was that both the Liberals and NDP tried to re-write history by misstating their expectations, after the fact. The Liberals had great hopes of victory in the months before the election, yet within four weeks of the defeat, both leader and deputy leader were telling party faithful at the Niagara Falls' meeting that government had never been the objective, and that they were so pleased to have improved the Liberal standing in the Legislature. And though New Democrats had missed the Official Party Status of 12 seats, they simply bended on one knee and begged the government to let them have it anyway. (Which they did.) Frankly, I found both somewhat pathetic.

The other large question was over the new voters' lists. With the coming of the permanent list, it was now the responsibility of people to get on it themselves. Many did not or did not pay attention to the errors in it. And there were many, many errors. People were missed. Addresses were wrong. Entire blocks were not listed. Husbands were listed, wives were not. People who had voted for 50 years were not on the list. This helped lead to chaos on election day and many voters being driven away from polling locations without casting a ballot.[13]

Simcoe-Grey was one of the worst ridings for problems, I dare say. Several polls in the town of Angus were closed for three hours due to a bomb scare. As well, poll officials failed to arrive at one location in the Town of the Blue Mountains for four hours, as they spent that time in the wrong location in the wrong municipality! As a result, these polls were kept open two extra hours.

But it was the people who were sent away from the polling booths that were of most concern. I personally received several calls from voters who had dutifully gone to the polls, only to be told by officials they were at the wrong one. When they went where they were told to go, they were then told they had been at the right one in the first place. Most didn't vote. One was told she was in the wrong riding, when she wasn't. Several were refused ballots even though they could show the necessary identification to prove residence. All-in-all, it was a farce. I have no doubt voter turn-out was driven down several percentage points, as a result. As great as a permanent voters' list sounds in theory, people move around too much – apparently 10% of homeowners and 30% of renters per year – to make it practical. With luck, a future government will return to doing it the *hard way* through enumeration.

But one thing which hurt right from the beginning was the new 28-day campaign. With all the pre-writ advertising done by the government, there was no way for opposition parties to make much of a dent in four weeks, particularly in a rural riding and in a personal, face-to-face, way. Even if we had been able to mount a reasonable door-to-door effort, I am dubious that we could have got to more than 10-20% of households, and that's not assuming anyone was home. Of course, with the party's lack of money, we weren't right out there with the *20/20* plan to show people either. We received 88 copies of it for a riding with over 70,000 voters. When I called to find out when we would get more, I got an apology. It seems we were supposed to have received 100. But when would we get more? One-hundred was our entire allotment for the campaign. (We never did get the other 12.)

It was a frustrating campaign for many of us, and we swore it would never happen that way again. Of course, much of what will happen is out of our hands. And while we can try to affect the decisions of the strategists and those at the top, they will ultimately do what they want ... as they did in 1995 and 1999. Hopefully, their choices will be better ones in future.

Part 4 Endnotes

1. Cancelling the hunt was itself seen as pandering to the environmental movement, just before an election. The government offered a compensation package to outfitters reliant on the hunt.
2. This was Mississauga MPP Margaret Marland. She was dropped from Cabinet in February 2001 and replaced by John Baird, the rabid right-winger from Nepean, who also holds the Community and Social Services portfolio.
3. Toronto Star. "Ontario can't afford more air pollution", 13 May 1999, p. A24.
4. Toronto Star editorial. "Kennedy for leader of Ontario Liberals", 23 November 1996, p. C2.
5. Toronto Star. "Marathon vote reveals splits, pettiness in party", 1 December 1996, p. A6.
6. Ibbitson, op.cit., p. 208.
7. In July 2001, she resigned to become head of the Greater Toronto United Way.
8. In 1995, the NDP ran second behind the Tories in 14 ridings.
9. Toronto Star. "Tories anything but conservative with ads", 21 November 1998, p. A6.
10. Toronto Star. "Risk for Tories in attack on McGuinty", 10 November 1998, p. A15.
11. And let me tell you, many Liberals were offended by this. A couple I know, who were going with their local NDPer, to vote strategically, then decided not to, as a result.
12. Before 1998, school boards were funded according to the calendar year.
13. Also, about 1,000 of 63,000 district returning officers and poll clerks failed to appear for work. Some claimed to have been threatened. Others were so poorly trained they claimed not to know where they were supposed to go.

Part 5

The *agenda of ideas* wanes,

Second term, 1999-2001

There is no question that the second term of the Harris Tories has been remarkably quieter than the first. Most of the reason is simply that the government has run out of ideas. The CSR was pretty much fully legislated by the spring of 1998, and most of what was left was simply to continue on in certain areas on the same path and *fine tune* results. "Squeegee kids" needed to be dealt with, as did tinkering to make welfare even more onerous. Hydro deregulation had to be finished. Taxes had to be cut further to create more jobs.

But a lot of this term has also been spent on dealing with the ramifications of earlier changes. The *chickens have come home to roost* on many issues. The half-done reform to health care has meant they've needed to throw more money at it but they've done so while scrambling, without any thought. The half-baked ideas on disentanglement meant things were no longer being done that needed to be, and now the Tories are trying to take back some of these responsibilities, like GO Transit. The clumsy attempts to hide cuts to education have resulted in fewer, less-experienced teachers, increased class-size, and higher transportation costs and significantly more useless learning materials. The government tries to hide this with more and more testing. And, of course, the cuts to environmental regulation may have contributed to the Walkerton water contamination and deaths.

While Term One was practically the personification of action for the Tories, Term Two has been one of inaction or reaction ... and it's being handled far less well. Perhaps the problem of the Tory renewal need go back no further than the basis for their 1999 re-election document, *Blueprint*. Having got most of the so-called revolutionary reform out of the way the first time around, there was little new to be packed into this, and it showed. *Blueprint* seemed to be little more than regurgitated ideas expressed in the familiar terminology of the neo-con. The problem was ... this didn't actually give the government a blueprint for governing and, without one, it couldn't seem to do much but react to trouble ... most of which they created themselves. Of course, that didn't mean the Tories changed their proverbial stripes.

The one thing that has become clear is that Mike Harris was right when he said his government members would not be managers. The administration of public affairs has existed mostly as bluster and blather by Harris and his ministers, as they take credit for everything that has gone right and blame others for everything that has gone wrong. However, their works have set wheels in motion that will cause more troubles, some that are evident to all but Harris Tories, and others that are hidden, some on purpose.

1. Budgeting for Dummies

One of the great prevarications that will likely never come clearly to light is how much the provincial government has played with budget numbers to make them appear much different than they really are ... usually higher. The Harrisites are masters at manipulating accounts so that it appears more is being spent on things like education, when spending has actually been cut, and a lot more is being spent on, say, health care, when per capita spending has increased very little.

For example, at different points, they began to count teacher pensions, post-secondary funding, vocational training programmes, and TVO/TFO funding into education spending, without any clear mention that any year-to-year comparisons then become almost useless. In fact, probably the only statistic that mattered was per student funding, especially given that the CSR had promised not to touch classroom spending. Yet it was the one stat they don't seem interested in, busy as they have been parroting the line that it's increased, it's increased! Well, it hasn't, and the decline in education seems obvious to all but the government and its supporters.

In fact, between 1995 and 2000-2001, province-wide per student funding had declined 1.39% in absolute terms and 1.76% in real terms. Though overall funding increased about $600 million, that does not take into consideration a 12.34% increase in inflation and a 77,533 student, or 4.05%, increase in enrollment. Given these, per student funding dropped from $6,773 in 1995 to $6,654 in 2000-2001 in real dollars.[1] Projections for 2001-2002 suggest the government may get back to 1995 levels, but it is too early for that to be confirmed.

You see, the Harrisites love to make projections in their budgets which don't come true in actual revenue and expenditures. And the Tories have a bad habit of using the budget numbers well after they have been proven wrong. Between 1994-1995 and 1998-1999, Ernie Eves claimed a $2 billion increase had occurred in provincial income tax revenue, $14.8 billion up to $16.8 billion. But this was based on budget projections, not *actuals*. The actual income tax revenue increase was practically zero. The reason for the difference was that tax cuts had eaten up any increase. So, though the economy was causing revenue to spike, the government was actually taking in no more. As well, projections compared to actuals saw the deficit go from $4 billion for 1997-1998 to $4.5 billion. Yet the Tories reported the budget's projected $800 million drop to the public, not the actual $500 million rise.

As well, Auditor Erik Peters has criticized the government for a tendency it has recently shown to sign contracts in one year for multi-year funding programmes, then book all the costs of the funding to that first year. The result, as in the 2000-2001 budget year, was that $1.1 billion in revenue was effectively moved back a year, so that a possible deficit in 1999-2000 could suddenly become a surplus. Ernie Eves, then Finance Minister, triumphantly announced on the same day that the government had balanced two budgets in a row. Critics have suggested that the Tories balanced budget legislation is the cause of this creative accounting. Given that Cabinet ministers would have to take a pay cut in the event of a deficit, it seems reasonable they think this is something to be avoided.

But the Harrisites are guilty of much worse accounting sins. Another financial artifice of the Harris government is to blame all its woes on the federal government. It is a time-honoured method of provinces to pick a straw man and fight with it. Historically, the target of this has been the Government of Canada, though it was only with Bob Rae that Ontario became a proponent. Of course, Mike Harris has elevated it to high art. He blames the Liberals for not giving Ontario its fair share of transfers for health, education, and social services, then spends the money on completely different things or uses it to fund tax cuts.

The Harris duplicity came to light with the $3.5 billion fund set up by the federal government in 1999 for the provinces to spend over three years and again with the $23.4 billion over five years in September 2000, just before the federal election. After years of raging about the cuts to transfer payments – cuts he approved of when in Opposition – the provinces managed to finagle more cash from Ottawa for health care. Given the mewling by premiers that they needed more money for health, the intent was this money would be to alleviate the health funding shortage. Remember, this was the time when there were daily stories on ambulances trying to find hospitals with spare beds, cancer patients were being sent to the United States for treatment, and there was a shortage of beds for the elderly and chronically ill.

Ontario got $1.4 billion more money in 1999, and the Harris government committed to spend it all on health, along with another $200 million. It didn't. After one year, the province had increased spending $643 million. The Minister claimed the remaining money was being kept back for future need. This was a questionable justification, given the obvious immediate need. Then, in 2000, they received $1.2 billion extra, yet health funding increased just $770 million, meaning that $430 million was actually pocketed by the province, presumably to help cover the revenue losses from tax cuts.

Just now, in November 2001, Mike Harris has again gone on the offensive against Ottawa, demanding more cash for health, ranting that the federal Liberals "are the single biggest threat to universal medicare ... that refuses to fund its fair share of health costs". The Prime Minister responded that, had the Harrisites not decided to cut their taxes, they would not need more. While I am no great defenders of the federal government, the Premier's argument that Ontarians are getting the short end of the stick ignores reality. The Tories claim they spent $21.8 billion on health in 2000-2001, and they will spend $23.7 billion, this year. (Of course, Harris government claims should be taken with a grain of salt. In his final budget, in 2000, Ernie Eves said they were already spending $22.2 billion.) Given the extra $1.2 billion going to Ontario from Ottawa for 2001-2002, the Harrisites will only fall $700 million short of the $23.7 billion. With other tax cuts occurring, it basically means that Ottawa paid for it. In effect, the taxpayers of other provinces subsidized a cut for business and wealthier people here. And with the feds committed to pass along another $445 million to Ontario next year, it may well be that people in Alberta will be paying to balance our budget.

When Ontario was crying poverty on health spending because of Ottawa cuts, the truth was a little fuzzier than they liked to admit. First, the Harrisites chose to ignore tax points that Ontario had been given by the federal government over the years. For example, in his 2001 budget, Ontario Finance minister Jim Flaherty claimed the Canada Health and Social Transfer from Ottawa for 1999-2000 was $4.722 billion, including supplement. The federal government lists it as $11.198 billion. The difference is about $6.5 billion. For 2000-2001, the difference is $7 billion. For 2001-2002, it is estimated at $7.1 billion. How can the numbers vary this much? The province does not include tax points while the feds do. Does it matter, in the end, from which level of government it comes? I'm sure it does to politicians. However, it matters only in the fairness of the complaints about cuts to transfers. I suspect the only reason the feds don't make a bigger deal out of Ontario's unfair criticism is that it is not entirely unfair. The 41ø the Canadian government transferred to the province 30 years ago for health is now 34ø.

But there are other, non-health-related, examples of the Tories and their *fuzzy math*. For many, there is an illusion that "across the board" tax cuts benefit everyone, since the same percentage is given to all. Of course, this is nonsense. The more you make, the more you benefit, as you have greater disposable income. Someone poor pays little-to-no tax, so they receive little-to-no benefit of a tax cut. Of the Harris cuts to-date[2], 50% of the cuts went to the top 20% of wage earners. Someone earning $255,000 a year saves $15,540 or 6.1% of their income. Someone making $177,000 saves $6,030 or 3.4%. If you make $54,040, you save $1,710 or 3.2%. Some earning $10,000 saves nothing. Ironically, some of the biggest losers are senior citizens who overwhelmingly vote Conservative.

And many others have lost, as well. The Fair Share Health levy, that was to guarantee wealthy Ontarians paid their 'fair share' wasn't really designed to be fair. Each person earning $50,000 or more was to pay $100, with the 'rich' paying even more. In reality, this was not initiated as a tax but as a cut to the income tax surtax. It kept the top 10% of wage earners from getting their entire tax cut. However, in the last budget, the Tories cut the surtax for the wealthy, and there is a move afoot to end it entirely.[3]

Yet, as much as this playing with the numbers may irk the Auditor or some citizens, it is the entire financial programme of the Harris Tories that has led Ontario onto dangerous ground. The reality is that, if government revenues are not allowed to rise during good times – given away, if you will, in the form of tax cuts – then services can never improve and, quite importantly for economic conservatives, the debt will never be paid. Tax cuts have cost the Ontario treasury $45 billion in lost revenue since they took office. Given that they also increased the debt $20 billion by borrowing to finance their tax cuts, the debt could be as little as half what is was in 1995, with $5 billion a year less in interest payments.

Borrowing money to pay for the tax cuts of *The Common Sense Revolution* was like the landlord of a 100-unit apartment building going to a bank and taking out a $120,000 loan, then coming back to the tenants and dropping their rents $100 per month. For awhile, to the tenants, it seemed like a great thing, but that was before the free laundromat in the basement became $1 per wash and $2 per dry, the carpets stopped being vacuumed every week and became every month, the garbage was removed every other week instead of every week, and the elevator started to break down because it was serviced only every third year rather than every six months. The parking lot pavement started to break up. The building got colder in winter because the thermostat was turned down a few degrees. The water started to taste funny because the treatment service was cancelled. And then there was no money to fix the lock on the broken front door, or replace the bricks that were disintegrating over the entrance. Over time, most of the tenants realise they'd rather pay the $100 extra.

And if higher revenues are bled off through tax cuts while expenditures have been allowed to rise, what happens when the economy declines and revenues cease to go up? There is no room to move. That is what is now happening. Despite all the talk of the CSR and the $6 billion in cuts it said were to be brought in over three years, the Harrisites now spend more than any Ontario government has ever spent, including the Rae New Democrats. Expenditures for 2000-2001 were just over $61 billion, a full $8 billion more than the NDP was spending. However, with the economy in recession, or very close to it, every cent in revenue is being spent to maintain the *status quo*. Should this recession continue for long or get worse, revenues may actually decline. Then, we face deficits, higher taxes, spending cuts, or all three. The apparent return to fiscal health will be exposed for the mirage it has been.

2. Mikey hates everything ... or how I learned to stop worrying and love the Big Lie

One thing that didn't change in their second term was the Harrisites' penchant for the *Big Lie*. The best example of the Big Lie is in denying that Nazis slaughtered millions of Jews and others who did not meet up with their concepts of racial purity. For some people, like me, it is beyond stupid that there are people who can deny the existence of the Holocaust. There seem only two reasons to do so: an innate inability to deal with the reality that human beings can commit acts of such barbarity, as to make them unthinkable; or, they hate Jews so much that they approve of their genocide and want others to believe no Holocaust occurred so they won't be prepared to stop it from occurring again.

Though the Harrisites have never propagated racial hatred, they have certainly used the Big Lie to convince people that their acts are justified. As a University of Toronto student, Guy Giorno, now the premier's chief of staff, once wrote "never question the efficacy of the Big Lie".[4] In other words, the *desired end* justifies whatever you have to say to get there. And throughout their first term, they did. *Welfare was rife with cheaters.* Except even the government's numbers disputed this. *People weren't safe in the streets.* Yet crime rates were dropping. Regardless, the lies sold well amongst the public. So, in Term Two, why not just keep re-heating the same false rhetoric and people who bought it the first time will keep believing it. Whether it was welfare or crime or whatever, they just kept pouring it on. Perhaps these aren't Big Lies, but lies repeated often enough certainly take on the legitimacy of *common sense*.

Slave-for-Welfare

During the election, the Tories had declared the dubiously named *Ontario Works*, or "work-for-welfare", a huge success. The truth was it was a pathetic failure. They just refused to admit it and did everything necessary to hide the reality.

The one clear thing is that workfare is not a training school to get people jobs. Not only is it not getting them skills they need for long-term employment, but it is actually keeping people on welfare, denying them what they need to get off it. The government has created a pool of talent that can now be exploited. Though few groups were convinced of the efficacy of *using* these people, once municipalities were told to take larger numbers into the programme, they were nearly forced to start getting these people out into "community placements".

The province began giving the relevant municipalities quotas for people collecting welfare benefits to take non-paying "volunteer" work in their communities. Given the hesitance most had shown to enthusiastically take up the programme, the Tories offered a *carrot*. If a municipality could exceed the quota it was given, it would receive a reward of $1,500 per person. On the other hand, there was also a *stick*. Fail to hit your quota and you would be penalized. As a result, it was incumbent upon Ontario Works' staff to find organizations willing to take community placements. Though many groups hesitated at first, those that did take up the offer have often become reliant on these people as free labour. In the voluntary sector, it might even be fair to say it is distorting the whole labour market.

The problem is that someone getting a job and getting off welfare does not get the municipality a bonus. In effect, there is no incentive to help people get off welfare, but to keep them on it in the workfare programme. As long as they are in community placements, the municipality will pick up its premium. And of course, the worse the placement the better. If someone on placement was to get useful skills, they might get a job and be gone. In the end, the municipalities will get their *bribe* and the province can claim there are *vast* numbers of able-bodied people who are earning their cheques with work-for-welfare.

I knew a fellow who was in this position. As a man who had suffered from poor literacy, he was needy and hadn't managed to keep a job. Recognizing this, he went to an adult learning centre, on his own, and learned to read and write properly. Once he had gathered his confidence, he wrote a manuscript, pursuing his interest in science fiction. His reward for his hard work? He spent a year on Ontario Works as a placement who vacuumed floors, washed mats, and dusted desks. At no time did he get any experience that would have helped him get a real job. When his placement expired and couldn't be renewed, his *generous* employer offered him ten hours a week at minimum wage to continue on. He had no choice. Turn it down and be thrown off welfare and, of course, he had to declare the wages to Ontario Works at the risk of having his cheque cut back. Workfare was nothing but a cage holding him in. After a couple of months of this, he passed away ... and while his illness had nothing to do with this work, I know he felt frustrated in those last weeks. Though I'm guessing, I think this feeling was caused by the future he hoped for seeming to be just out of reach ... where it had been long before his Harris 'hand up'.

And it is becoming increasingly difficult to even *survive* at a minimal level on welfare. A great portion of the 21.6% cut in benefits in 1995 had been the slashing of the shelter allowance. And the government has not increased it, even as they permitted higher rents to landlords. For a single recipient, it is $325 per month, even though the average 1999 rent on a bachelor apartment in Ontario was $561, and $672 for a one-bedroom. For a single parent with two children, the allowance is $554, though the rent on a two-bedroom apartment averages $785.

The Tories were not entirely honest about their CSR commitment to allow welfare recipients to earn back the cut without penalty. Under STEP, or the Supports To Employment Program, set up by the Liberals, a recipient can keep all of their net earnings, up to a certain dollar amount, without having their benefits reduced. Then, one can earn a further 25% before their monthly benefit is reduced. Though an individual recipient working a 30-hour week at $7 per hour would have their benefit cut back to near zero, they would still be eligible for other benefits like prescription drugs.

However, as of 1 October 2000, this changed somewhat. For someone who has had some earnings for one year, the 25% extra was cut to 15%. And for the poor soul who has been able to manage some earnings for two years, they are no longer permitted to earn anything without an equal clawback. And this is cumulative, so that the reductions kick in even with months of no income, once the thresholds are hit. As well, if a child was to take an after-school job, this would count against their parents' benefits. These changes mean that recipients now are cut off welfare at lower amounts. Before, a single person could earn $960 before losing all benefits. Now, after a year, this person could only earn about $840 and, after two years, just $722. In other words, the Tories have created a system that means that those least able to get off welfare will now be punished most.

And just to add insult to injury, speaking of clawbacks, when the federal government established the Child Tax Credit to help poor parents, the Ontario government began deducting an equal amount from parents on welfare. In effect, they are confiscating the federal funds, and stealing from the poor.

Other changes have also turned welfare assistance into virtual indentured servitude. A recipient cannot now own a car worth more than $5,000. If they do, they must sell it, then have their benefits ceased until such time as this money is gone, though they can buy a cheaper car. In a market where many ten-year-old vehicles are determined to still be worth $5,000 or more, most are left to unreliable vehicles which are often in need of costly repairs or are just plain unsafe.

And in a move that denies the whole point of government existing to help citizens, the Tories have begun to put liens on the homes and property of welfare recipients. As a condition of eligibility for basic financial assistance, an applicant who owns any property is required to give consent to the municipality from which they will receive benefits that a lien may be placed against it, immediately for any land other than a primary residence, but also a primary residence if the applicant is in receipt of benefits for a period of one year. In fact, anyone who benefits – a spouse, same-sex partner or dependent adult – is required to make property available for a lien. And just to turn the screw, in April 2002, a principal residence will be considered by anyone on benefits for 12 months out of five years.

Poking, prodding, and private schools

After the 1998 strikes, teachers were left with few options to protest their treatment and that of the education system. Most of the rules that governed both were now regulations dictated by the provincial government. Even negotiations over contracts were of little use because school boards had little authority to make changes to these directives. As a result, there was a widespread move to end teacher participation in extra-curricular activities. It was really the only thing left to them over which the government had no control.

Through the 1998-1999 school year, this withdrawal was haphazard, by most teachers in some school board areas to few in others. However, throughout 1999-2000 and 2000-2001, there were virtually no school sports nor clubs anywhere in Ontario, with minor geographic exceptions. In fact, the hold-out was so pervasive that Education minister Janet Ecker had legislation designed that would have made these extra-curriculars, or co-instructional activities, part of teaching and would have forced elementary and secondary educators to participate against their will. In my mind, Bill 74 was an ill-conceived response to having been, once again, outflanked by an intelligent, dogged opponent. As one newspaper editorial put it, it was an affront to the freedom of association and the right to equal treatment under the law, as well as a denial of natural justice.[5] Of course, one of the areas most affected was Durham, including Ecker's home riding. It was an ongoing embarrassment for her, to say the least.

The *Education Accountability Act* would have permitted the government to impose contracts on teachers, if it saw fit. If not, it allowed school boards to legally bargain in bad faith to get agreements. It defined a failure to carry out assigned duties, even voluntary ones like extra-curriculars, as a strike. This also included *work-to-rule* slow-downs, and just giving strike notice would be legally perceived as a full strike. The only carrot the Minister held out was that she might not proclaim parts of the legislation if the teachers agreed to play by her rules.

And if that wasn't enough, there was Bill 81, the *Safe Schools Act*. This one was to enact the much-vaunted *Code of Conduct* for students the Tories had been preaching about since the election. Students would have to sing *O Canada*, and might have to wear school uniforms, and would have to be on their best behaviour. But it went much further. Under the guise of doing criminal background checks on staff, the Minister was giving herself incredible new powers. She could order her own ministry or school boards to spy. "The Minister may collect and may by regulation require boards to collect such personal information as is specified by regulation from, or about, the classes of persons specified by regulation ...". This information could go far beyond criminal checks to include everything from an individual's sexual orientation to their psychiatric history to their financial transactions to their Social Insurance Numbers. And, not only would this information have to be turned over to her, she could pass it along to whomever she wanted.

Within six days in June 2000, both pieces of legislation passed, and they were both given Royal Assent on the 23rd, though Ecker did not proclaim the sections of the *Education Accountability Act* dealing with co-instructional activities such as sports, arts and special school activities. However, they remained in the legislation as "an insurance policy for our students". And that was the stick. The government would proclaim these provisions if the teachers didn't back off on their withdrawal from extra-curricular activities. And they didn't seem likely to, as a poll of 27,145 public high school teachers done in May had shown 99.4% were opposed to this legislation.

Other Damocles' swords were hanging overhead, as well. The government, as part of Bill 74, announced its intention to actually enforce the 1,250 minute secondary school week for teachers, in order to shut down the school boards' tendency to define it differently from what the province wanted. The Harrisites were banning school boards from running deficits, a move which would force cuts on many, as provincial funding did not match the rise in inflation, escalating busing costs, and the loss of the remaining transition funding that had helped the boards make changes, even though they were still ongoing. And teacher testing was in the offing. A promise of the Tories from the 1999 election, it had still not come to pass as these bills went through, but the threat remained. The teachers, and many others, saw this as punitive. While the government argued that teachers had to be up-to-date on what they were teaching, it rejected that the constant professional development done by them was the equivalent. Yet, when it was put to Tory members that, if this was the case, shouldn't lawyers, doctors, engineers, and the like also be tested, the question was usually tersely ignored. It seemed that the Harrisites were again pushing teachers to go on strike, and had sewn up any loopholes that might allow the school boards to get out of them. All options seemed to be leading to a labour dispute.

But a funny thing happened on the way to a disruption. It didn't come. The new school year came in September 2000 and nothing happened. The *status quo* prevailed. The teachers continued not to participate in extra-curricular activities, and the province did nothing to intervene. It was a strange turn-of-events, given the government's goading measures of the spring. In fact, the school year came and went with little more than quiet sniping.

What had happened? I think the government finally realized they had *beaten the dog* for so long it no longer had any fight in it. Most teachers had become content, if not happy, to do their job and go home. *Extra-curriculars were never going to come back.* And that's what the Tories feared most. They had made the *dog* lay in the corner, and there it had decided to stay.

The government couldn't live with that, which left two choices: get the stick back out in the form of proclaiming the forced co-instruction sections of the *Education Accountability Act*; or, concede. After Janet Ecker threatened and mewled and spat for months and nothing happened, the testing of teachers was enacted, along with dates and time-lines. It caused little more than a grumble out of teachers. Without further conflict, the government had no political justification to force the issue. Yet another school year approached and kids faced another year without sports or clubs.

And then shockingly in June 2001, the government backed off on instruction time. What had been so important at 7 of 8 classes was suddenly compromised as 6.67 of 8. Both sides smiled, announced victory, and the teachers returned to coaching and running clubs for 2001-2002.

Had the Tories waited another year or two to make a deal, I'm sure the teachers would have rolled their eyes and worked the longer hours. As it was, they didn't gain a lot, but still felt better that the government had backed off even a bit. Of course, with budget cuts coming for 2002-2003, it will be interesting to see if the Harrisites don't pull their whip back out to start at them again.

With the situation with teachers having quietened, however, perhaps the government needed to self-flagellate again. The farce that is the Harris government's education policy continues in a new context. If there ever was proof that it was not written in the Ministry of Education but in the Finance minister's office, it came with the May budget announcement by new minister Jim Flaherty that the government would extend about $300 million in funding to private schools. A tax credit of up to $3,500 for tuition for each child, to a maximum of two per family, would be given to parents whose children attended private schools. There was no meat put on the bones of the declaration, but it quickly became the centrepiece of the budget.

The surprise for many was that Mike Harris had rejected just such a scheme during the 1999 election campaign. The constant chaos his government had created in education seemed, to the suspicious, to be purposely directed at undermining the public education system (just as the chaos in health services seemed to be undermining universal health care), and this move played right into that. The Liberals, in particular, had claimed the Tories had a hidden plan to bring in charter schools or school vouchers. The Premier had rejected the accusation out of hand. In fact, most observers accepted his word, as it went against any of his pronouncements as far back as anyone could remember, and was not particularly supported by the government's actions. However, his words now rang particularly hollow, especially as private school enrolment had jumped 20% over five years, and this seemed very likely to make it even larger, and drain far more than $300 million from the Treasury.

Flaherty's proclamation seemed to come out of nowhere. The speculation was that he had favoured this kind of funding for some time and, now that he was Minister of Finance, he wasn't about to let the opportunity pass. Supposedly, a number of private school supporters had been to see him in the run-up to the budget announcement and had convinced him now was the time to bring such a policy forward. He, then, went to Harris and convinced him.

And the story went that the caucus was only told the morning of the budget announcement, and that included Education minister Ecker. The media badgered her to admit as much, but she refused. No matter what else can be said of Ecker, she has never been one to say anything that might rock the Tory party boat, and her leadership ambitions.

A task force was appointed to conduct hearings into details. Already, the Opposition had slammed the proposal, and even two Tory backbenchers had publicly questioned whether it should apply to all such schools or wealthy parents. However, instead of conducting a fair review, the committee was stacked from the start. It was made up entirely of Conservative caucus members, three of whom had already expressed their desire for few-to-no restrictions on the money, according to Ian Irquhart of *The Toronto Star*[6]. He pointed out the chair of the committee, Ernie Hardeman, has two large Christian schools in his riding, another has been a long-time proponent of private, religious schools, and a third is a neo-con's neo-con. The staffing for the task force was seconded from the Finance ministry, not Education, seemingly indicating concerns with the monetary side, not the educational benefits. The hearings were held *in camera*, presumably to avoid embarrassing comments that might make it into the media, and the only witnesses invited were from the private school sector, "the people who will be directly impacted by the tax credit", according to Hardeman. And a paper designed to set out the framework for the committee points to the need for private schools to provide academic information for parents so they can judge them. There was no mention as to whether or not a determination should be made on if this was a good expenditure of tax dollars, the content of curricula, if there should be a cut-off so the tax credit wouldn't go to subsidize the wealthy, or if this would negatively impact on public and separate school funding. As Irquhart said, "in other words, the tax credit is a done deal, for rich and poor, with no significant strings attached".

And, in fact, this was confirmed by mid-December, when Flaherty announced there would be few qualifications to be met. Private schools would not have to meet the same curriculum standards as public and separate schools. Private school teachers would not have to have the same qualifications as public and separate school teachers. Private school students would not have to pass, or even take, the province-wide tests given to public and separate school students. There would be no limit on parents' incomes to qualify.

This really shouldn't have been a surprising result. Perhaps the whole policy flip-flop was but, once it was made, the suggestion that this funding could have been applied to only poor and middle-class parents was unthinkable. The Harris government is consistent in one thing ... it bends over backwards for the rich. And had there been constraints put on curricula at private elementary schools, it would have been a shock. After all, the people who had gone to Flaherty to ask for this measure would not have accepted the money minus control of what was to be taught.

Management Board Chair David Tsubouchi suggested in November 2001 that the province is facing a deficit of up to $5 billion, due to the declining economy and the additional damage done to it by the effects of the terrorist attacks on the United States on 11 September. Though I doubt it is quite that bad, Finance minister Flaherty's response was to say that, regardless, the corporate tax cut of $2.2 billion and the private school tuition subsidy of $300-$500 million are safe. If they are willing to go ahead, it means the government is far more dedicated to this radical change in education policy than many believed. It suggests, perhaps, that the Harris Tories may be easily as right-wing, or even moreso, after Harris is gone.

There is little doubt that either the Liberals or the NDP will revoke such funding should they become the government after the next election. However, should the Tories hang around another term or more before succumbing, it might be next to impossible to do little more than modify it. Regardless, it is clear, no matter what the Tories say, that there will be an impact on public and separate schools. With almost no limits applied to this tax credit, it could mean a sea change in the way people see private schools, and tens of thousands of kids could move to them and away from a public system that might be creaky, but is still the best way of socializing the young to fit into the society in which they will live.

And one shouldn't denigrate the need for kids to fit in, and to learn. With the ever-increasing pace of life, it will be more important than ever for young people to learn their community holds a piece of their souls. We need them to understand this, and the price is that we are willing to help them. That means a strong public education system, and a superior post-secondary system.

The Harris government believes that excellence in colleges and universities comes with those institutions proving they educate students to get jobs. This goes against the beliefs of scholars going back thousands of years. A well-rounded education does far more than get someone a job, it raises the whole level of knowledge in society. An enlightened community does more to cause the progress and advancement of a society than annual income. Higher education for the masses reinforces a diverse and democratic society.

In March 2000, the Minister of Training, Colleges, and Universities, Dianne Cunningham, announced that student tuition would be capped at a "reasonable and affordable" 35% of the cost of education, with limited maximum increases of 2% per year over each of five years. With tuition having increased 60% over the Tories' first four years, this was little comfort to students, as many were already running into obscene debt loads. Student loans had been capped at $7,000 per year, with anything above that only to graduate students at universities willing to require repayment based on income-contingency. This is a system where loans are repaid based on the amount a person earns after graduation. The up-side is that those earning less can pay their loan off with smaller payments. The down-side is that smaller payments stretch the loan out, costing the recipient more interest, with the ultimate loan cost depending on the length of repayment. Poorer graduates end up paying more.

And this was a concern of more than just students and their families. Even former premier Bill Davis perked up on the issue. At a speech at the Ontario Institute for Studies in Education, he said that tuition concerns should not be allowed to keep anyone from getting a higher education. He said respect and trust needed to run between teaching professionals, policy-makers, and the public, and suggested communication between these groups was vital, adding it had never broken down during his time in office. His talk came on the anniversary of the introduction of the legislation that created community colleges.

Colleges were established in the 1960s for a simple reason: to offer training that was specific to a particular job, usually in the trades. And it was needed. High school offered little in the way of such specific skills, except for shop class, and university was geared to general knowledge. In many ways, colleges were good and bad. While professional diplomas created the likes of mechanics and nurses, their natural institutional tendency also moved them into areas not initially intended, like certification for municipal clerks and treasurers, and community arts' and crafts' classes. But the Harris Tories, in their drive to dump government responsibilities, chose to screw up even the good part.

In late 1998, they brought forward, and pushed through, legislation to partially deregulate the apprenticeship system. Arguing there was a serious, and continuing, shortage of skilled workers, then Education and Training minister Dave Johnson brought in amendments to force apprentices to pay tuition. After all, university and college students had to. Why not apprentices? As well, it deregulated wages for them, meaning they would have to negotiate pay with those who were giving them the training. The legislation got rid of ratios limiting the number of apprentices who could be used as journeyman labourers, ended minimum training limits of two years, and made minimum-education requirements flexible as to the type of training. Effectively, these changes meant kids, many of whom have not done well in the regular school system, would have pay far more for less training, a lower wage, and it meant they might be able to start with as little as a Grade 8 education. In effect, the government was setting out (a lack of) standards to create a situation where even fewer people will earn real skills.

In 1997, the government deregulated fees on some professional graduate degrees, such as medicine and business. Their belief was that, since these students were typically high wage earners upon graduation, they could easily pay back higher loans on higher tuition. It resulted in massive hikes. For example, in an *alma mater* of mine, The University of Western Ontario, tuition for the first year of medical school has shot up 122%, from $4,844 to $10,753. What the Tories failed to consider was that even facing a huge debt would be enough to scare people away, regardless of eventual pay-off.

But limits on all tuition may end. In the years before Harris, university leaders were some of the strongest defenders of a public system. No longer. Many have sold themselves to the *free market* of education, arguing that deregulated tuition fees would create an American-style Ivy League of higher education. Some have proposed to the province that tuition for all undergraduate and graduate programmes be deregulated completely. Amongst others, Queen's University administrators have proposed increasing undergraduate tuition for Arts and Science by 46% over four years. The government's response?   After several months of saying she was considering it, Minister Cunningham rejected the idea for now. However, more right-wing Tories like Jim Flaherty are apparently quite in favour.

The total insanity of this continuing spiral upward in fees is breathtaking. A mere 15 years ago, undergraduate tuition was generally about $1,000 per year at an Ontario university. Inflation over that period has been about 50%. Yet this cost is now 300% higher. Well, the Tories wanted to restore a student's responsibility to 35% of the cost of their education as it used to be way-back-when ... way back when colleges didn't exist and university was intended for the financial elite.

I am the first to agree more money needs to be put into the system, especially with the elimination of Grade 13 and the coming of the *double cohort*, when the number of first-year students doubles for one year. But the reality is, as the government says, we need a more highly educated and highly trained workforce for the present and future. How does forcing higher and higher costs onto students improve education, especially at a time when wages have been stagnating for over a decade? All it does is guarantee that fewer students will avail themselves of education and training, and a greater number will be prone to being victims of market declines. Far more will need to depend on government as a social safety net. At a time when it should be easier and cheaper to get into college and university, it is actually getting harder and more expensive.

As well, there is the shift of funding universities away from the province toward bequests by alumni and corporations. One night I received a call from UWO from a student hired to poll alumni for money. He told me of the, then, new plan by the government to match, dollar-for-dollar, any donation I would make, and how this could mean so much more for the school. So I sat down and explained to him why the opposite was more likely. Every dollar he raised from me would be a dollar cut from the provincial government transfer the next year. Raise $1, get $1 from the province, have your transfers cut by $2 the next year. The more successful such institutions were at raising cash like charities, the less they would get in transfers from the province, leading to higher tuition and bigger classes for students like him. As well, most of what he was collecting was going to capital infrastructure, not operating costs. This would mean getting a few classes in a nicer building, if there was someone to actually teach the class or clean up the garbage in the classroom. Sounding confused and a little concerned, he rang off.

As the Tories shift post-secondary education to more of a market-oriented system, there will inevitably be winners and losers. Some universities will become high-end, expensive but respected Harvards or MITs, while other universities and colleges will operate with lower-paid staff teaching poorer students. If government would just realize that higher education is more necessary to a well-qualified workforce than tax cuts, business would benefit far more by the province spending $600 million to eliminate tuition for the 150,000 full-time post-secondary students than it does by leaving most of them heavily in debt for years to come.

Bypassing health

The implementation of massive changes made to hospitals continued into the Tories' second term. The Harrisites felt they were necessary and, perhaps as a result, refused to see the undesired consequences of their actions. I have no doubt they felt that there was an excess of beds in most hospitals. Most studies had been suggesting this for 20 years. But they saw an excess of beds as an excess of staff. That had led to much of the hospital chaos of their first term. But the hospital restructuring was far from over, and it was the rush to bring it off that saddled the government with its most damaging public relations prior to Walkerton.

These changes have resulted in not just the closings of hospitals but also in fewer inpatient beds, increased ambulatory services, and the closures and downsizing of emergency departments. The problem was that the government failed to realize that the overcrowding of emergency departments that was a problem before change began was magnified during the process of change. As a result, severely ill patients have had to be trucked to and fro from one hospital to another in hopes of finding one with a spare bed. In fact, people have died.

As hospitals and emergency departments were closed, shortages in beds and personnel began to be experienced. A study was done to determine the impact of systematic hospital restructuring on emergency department overcrowding in 20 Toronto hospitals[7]. It found that over the period of 74 months before restructuring, severe and moderate overcrowding averaged

0.5% and 9% per month, respectively. However, during restructuring over the next 46 months, it was found that severe overcrowding was 12 times higher, while moderate overcrowding was just over three times higher. Neither severe nor moderate overcrowding was increasing before restructuring. During restructuring, however, both increased significantly, with severe overcrowding increasing 0.2% per month and moderate overcrowding of 0.5% per month. The obvious conclusion was that emergency departments were pushed to their maximums too often because change – cuts to beds and staff – was made too fast and with too few transitional resources.

The issue gained focus after a series of people died from a lack of timely medical care. On 13 February 1998, Kyle Martyn, an active five-year-old, died of streptococcal toxic shock, after waiting in the emergency room of Credit Valley Hospital in Mississauga for over three hours to be seen by a doctor. In fact, he and his father had to wait more than 90 minutes to just get the child's temperature taken. Kyle was transferred to the Hospital for Sick Children that night, where he died the next day. Though quick diagnosis and treatment still might not have saved the boy, public attention and concern focused on why an obviously sick youngster would have to wait so long for any attention. The answer was that many of the hospital's then 19 emergency beds were taken up by patients awaiting transfer to other departments where beds were not available. The coroner's jury recommended funding promised by the province to take care of a need for long-term care beds be honoured, no more long-term or acute-care beds be closed, and beds be re-opened as long as there was a need. But he was not the first to suffer the incompetence of cuts, nor would he be the last.

On 20 February 1999, 16-year-old Dana Whitmore of Belleville was critically injured in a car crash, just outside the town. Cuts in 1996 had taken away Belleville's ambulance dispatch centre, and that responsibility had fallen to the centre in Kingston, 75 kilometres away. It ordered an ambulance in Madoc to the accident scene, a 30-minute drive, instead of one from Belleville, though the hospital was a mere 5-7 minutes away. Another ambulance, heading into Belleville with a stable heart-attack victim detoured to the scene and the attendant did what he could for the three victims, but he could not take them to the hospital. A lack of familiarity with the area was blamed for sending an ambulance from such a distance. However, the reality was clear that, had Belleville still had its dispatch centre, Dana and her friends would have got to hospital faster.

In July 1999, Collingwood resident Joseph Lambe was diagnosed with a dissecting aortic aneurysm, a condition in which the lining of the artery separates into two layers. With his chances of dying increasing every minute, his doctor tried to find an available intensive care bed. Even using CritiCall, the central system for locating help for critically-ill patients, no bed could be found for about five hours. Given the bed was in distant London, it was 12 hours between diagnosis and surgery. Though he didn't die for two weeks, his doctor suggested that the long wait caused less and less blood to flow to his organs, which eventually shut down, causing his death.

Even more attention was focused on the problems when 18-year-old Joshua Fleuelling died in January 2000. Joshua suffered a severe asthma attack and was taken from his home by ambulance to nearby Scarborough Grace Hospital. However, it was on *critical care bypass* and was not accepting new patients. As a result, Fleuelling's ambulance was re-directed to Markham-Stouffville Hospital, which was 18 minutes away. By the time they got there, it was too late, as Joshua died shortly after. Though Fleuelling had not made his asthma condition better by smoking, it still seemed shocking to many that it had killed him. A year after a coroner's jury made recommendations to stop bed closures until community services were in place[8] and increase the numbers of ambulances and paramedics, his parents held a press conference to point out none had been carried out by the provincial government.

At the same time pressure was growing on the Tories over these deaths, other problems were becoming more clear. Though the HSRC had recommended that sufficient funds be put forward by government to pay for their recommended and actual changes by re-investing savings, the Harrisites did not come through. Though the CSR had stated a pledge that 'not a penny' would be removed from health care, the fact was that hospitals, restructured or not, had their budgets reduced and were not left with enough money to pay for all their costs. In November 1998, Long-Term Care minister Cam Jackson said $270 million in savings was to be re-invested in Toronto hospitals. However, the HSRC estimated savings were, in fact, $376 million. It was 1999-2000 before spending on hospitals equalled what it had in 1992-1993, and that doesn't consider 12% inflation between 1993 and 2000 and 1.2 million more residents. In effect, per person spending had dropped over 20%.

Regardless, the Tories and their minions at the Ministry of Health became convinced that they could simply tell hospital management to keep finding efficiencies, even as almost every hospital began running into deficit troubles because there were no more to be found. The response from hospitals was that some ran greater deficits, others cut services, many did both. And though, each year, the province was forced to come up with extra money to bail out these institutions, it has never sunk in that perhaps the transfers to hospitals are just too low. When the government took over the management of the Hamilton Health Sciences Centre in April 2000 because it was running a massive deficit, the Tory attitude to health care was obvious. Their plan to *save* the hospital was to cut one of three emergency departments even though they were already so inundated they had to turn away patients, cut one of the departments doing operations despite line-ups for surgery, get rid of three of the four out-patient clinics, one of the two rehab facilities, and reduce the number of acute care beds by 95. And all this would only cover a third of the deficit.

In early 2001, new Health minister Tony Clement announced the province would no longer cover these hospital deficits, estimated at $273 million for 2001-2002. Yet, within months, extra money was flowing and, just before he announced his intention to run for the party leadership in mid-November, he said all deficits would be covered. However, it seems, eventually, the government will really stop coughing up the extra cash and, when it does, hospital service levels will have to be slashed.

Part of the reason that money was taken from hospitals in the first place was because it was supposed to go to create new acute care and long-term care beds in other institutions, or so suggested the HSRC. In this way, chronic care patients taking up hospital acute care beds could be transferred to these new facilities and, thus, alleviate the burden on hospitals.

In fact, the government had already begun to move in this direction. First, in 1998, the Tories had announced their intention to see 20,000 new long-term care beds created over the next eight years. During the election, they had announced $1.2 billion was to go toward building new long-term care beds in new or existing facilities. However, it is now obvious that not all this money would pay for the beds and their staffing costs. Some is going for profit-margin. Nearly 70% of the government contracts for these beds have gone to private corporations such as Leisureworld, Extendicare, and Central Park Lodge[9], all of which run nursing homes. As well, these businesses are having some of their construction costs paid for by the government, presumably to speed up the creation of new beds.

The government was also moving on another front, as well. In January 1996, as part of the omnibus bill, the Ministry of Health was directed to alter Ontario's long-term care system by streamlining 74 Home Care and Placement Coordination programmes into 43 Community Care Access

Centres (CCACs). CCACs are not-for-profit corporations, run by volunteer boards, that offer *one-stop shopping* for long-term care community support services, as well as admission to publicly funded long-term care facilities. Over 400,000 Ontarians presently receive services through CCACs. Specifically, these include assessing clients' eligibility for in-home services, planning a programme of care, then arranging for the services to be delivered. These services include homemaking, nursing, physio-, occupational and speech-language therapies, medical supplies and equipment, social work, dietetic services, and a variety of others. For children with special needs, CCACs provide nursing, therapies, and dietetic services so they may attend public school.

However, CCACs were not intended to deliver the services directly. These are contracted out under what is called *managed competition* to non-profit and for-profit service providers, which may include community associations, groups, hospitals, or private businesses. They are required to give the contracts to the low-bidder. In fact, it is this last point that is leading to the effective end of the Victorian Order of Nurses in Ontario. Once a main provider of home-nursing services, they have tendered for, and lost, most of these contracts to private companies. As a result, the VON has had to lay off many of their nursing staff and now operates on a fringe level only.[10] Managed competition has meant a *race to the bottom* in standards, as low bids and staff turnover increases have forced a decline in quality of care.

Even with this public relations bump-in-the-road, it appeared the government was on the right track with the concept of CCACs. They proved an effective way of delivering services to people at home and they appeared likely to make a dent in the number of elderly taking up needed hospital beds. However, that was before the Tories began reversing their own decisions. Part of the HSRC exercise was based on the theory that hospital savings would be returned to health spending through long-term care. The provincial budget for CCACs had been just under $1.2 billion in 2000-2001. Then, they froze that spending. As Minister Clement put it, he wanted to "flatline" funding while a review was done to see if services were being delivered on a consistent basis. (Ludicrous, given that CCACs were not required to deliver services to a given standard, he already knew the answer.) Of course, this would mean a $175 million shortfall, with the growth in client numbers and inflation. This was not a concern for "Two-Tier" Tony, though. "There comes to a point where you have to live within your budget." To the response that services would have to be cut to stay within budget, and people were being hurt, Harris retorted, "We don't know if it's a shoddy ploy for more money or whether it's legitimate".

On top of the 11,000-person waiting list for home care, the freeze has specifically resulted in some people being turned away as not being needy enough, most clients having their hours for care or receiving services cut, and having to pay for all medical equipment, such as bathtub hand rails and intravenous tubes.

Costs for the CCACs had risen mostly because of much higher client lists. However, recently, part of the rise is also the result of higher wages to nurses, homemakers, and other staff. Hospitals, in particular, had been offering higher wages to entice some of these people back to them, and the CCACs were forced to compete. Higher expenses meant several had fallen into debt, debt which the government had been covering with "one-time payments". That ended with the freeze. But those weren't the only extra costs. The competitive bidding process was causing administrative costs to balloon, presumably due to the paperwork and possibly because contracts weren't going to the low bidder. However, this is not clear because the private bidders have been exempted from Freedom of Information legislation. Clearly, though, profit margins are involved in any bid, so the debate is on as to how private companies can offer lower bids than non-profits.

Clement gave responsibility for the review to his associate minister, Helen Johns (presumably so he would have time to campaign for Harris' job). Instead of a report, Johns came out with legislation suggesting many changes, based on there being "room for improvement". The *Community Care Access Corporations Act* proposes that CCACs are to cease being non-profit corporations and become statutory corporations, if so designated by the Minister. The government would appoint their boards of directors and executive directors through Orders-in-Council, with terms of 1-3 years, with two possible re-appointments, for board members, while executive directors would serve at the government's pleasure.

To make up for the lack of consistent practices, Johns suggested annual reports, performance reviews, financial audits, with a review of the legislation after five years. Annual performance agreements would be a requirement for executive directors. However, everyday front-line services would remain unchanged. Managed competition would continue. The types of services supplied would remain the same.

However, there are to be other changes. CCACs will have to be more accountable to the Health ministry by meeting performance standards, submitting standardized reports, and regularly scheduled operational reviews. This "new business strategy" will be implemented to give "a clearer sense of direction and priorities for operations and service delivery". Case managers will face added responsibilities. Along with having to assess the needs of individual clients and what services they receive, managers will have to consider the cost of these services within a specific budget before they can authorize services. Placement coordination will also be changed because of the expected increase in long-term care beds. Nebulous at best, it is possible this means eligibility will be terminated for the most serious cases, since they can always be warehoused in a new long-term care bed.

As well, a new body would be established. A Community Advisory Council would be responsible for the co-ordination and integration of local services between CCACs, hospitals, long-term care facilities, and community support services. In this way, each community could prioritize based on local realities and concerns. Unfortunately, it is not yet clear how or who will run these councils.

It is evident that these changes to CCACs are mostly about returning control to Queen's Park. The government could simply have enacted standards that CCACs would have to meet, then fund appropriately. Instead, they are choosing to centralize control back with provincial authorities, just as they have done with most every other service. Of course, there is the added bonus that overseeing who runs the CCACs means many more local patronage appointment possibilities. And who better to run health care delivery than loyal party brethren, who will do what they are told?

But CCAC service delivery may eventually go the way of the dodo. The Premier has signalled his government is not committed to the health of Ontario's seniors and long-term ill. In his duel for dollars with the federal government, he stated outright that their lack of health outlays to Ontario might mean the province would cut off seniors and the poor from assistance for home care and prescription drugs. Whether or not this is rhetoric only he knows and, with his imminent departure from the political scene, it seems unlikely he will ever be able to follow through on it, true threat or not. However, it is out there for his successor to make CCACs organizations to cut off services for the needy rather than supply what these people need.

It may be, though, that the feds don't take Harris seriously, and that might be understandable. His government has made empty threats on health care before, beyond the Health Services Restructuring Commission, at least. For a political party that seemed determined to make doctors *pay the price* as much as other health care workers in the early days, the concession to the physicians in 1997 signalled a total capitulation by the Tories. When the time came for the next contract to be negotiated in 2000, the government made no moves which appeared tough. Though the HSRC had recommended mandatory change to bring in group capitation, or network practices of family doctors and nurses offering 24-hour-a-day services, over six years, the government went no further than making it voluntary and using no extra money as incentive to get these doctors to go along. The agreement called for a better-than 8% increase in fees over four years, while some services not considered medically necessary were to be de-listed (though this term was never used)[11], freeing up money to pay the doctors as well as putting some services beyond fee restriction. Doctors were also to receive premiums for after-hours work, being on-call, treating patients over 75, and working in rural areas. As well, billing limits were increased $10,000. Unfortunately, this is about the only instance of Harris being weak-willed. His government's treatment of nurses has been nothing less than appalling.

When the first cuts came, they were a little earlier than the Conservatives had planned, yet the calendar wasn't really all that important. Cutting the budget was the short-term goal. Part of that included hospitals, both directly and through the HSRC. And the biggest expense in health care is salaries. Jim Wilson tried, and failed, to curtail doctors' earnings. But there are far more nurses than doctors. They may not make as much individually, but sheer numbers would make up any difference.

Of course, once hospitals were ordered to cut, staff were the first targets. And NDP changes had already seen nursing positions go, so it must have seemed simplest to continue on this path. The Ontario Nurses Association numbers said 10,000 nursing jobs were cut between 1993 and 1998. The Health minister disagreed, stating it was more like 3,700. However, by the time the 1999 election came around, Ontario had the fewest nurses per capita of any province[12] , and Health minister Witmer acknowledged 8,300 such positions were gone, though she blamed the NDP for 7,000 of those cuts.[13] Given the far more substantive cuts during the Tory years, this seemed a dubious claim. The Tory response was to promise funding of $375 million for 12,000 new nursing positions by 2001. A month before the year 2001, nursing groups were saying the government had filled just 2,000 positions while the government said 6,000, though they couched this as being during their time in office.

Regardless, the immediate result was a drop in the quality of patient care, despite what many would say. When people are asked to do 10%, 20%, even 50% more work, it cannot be reasonably argued that this does not affect the quality of what is done, especially over time. This was even more a question in the light of hospital amalgamations that were seeing nurses changing responsibilities, hospitals, governing structures. For those who expressed doubts that fewer nurses would improve health care, the Premier responded that those trying to save their jobs were like workers in hula-hoop factories.[14] His view was common amongst his caucus. Nurses were union members that grew fat and happy on the backs of taxpayers. It would not be long before government MPPs realized their practical error.

Whether or not Tory members changed their attitudes is entirely debatable. Their moves were ill-conceived and failed to recognize reality. Just at the time when more was being demanded of the system, they tried to strip it of its essential nature – health is about caring. People care for people. Take the people from the system and caring is lost. Again they took the wrong lesson from history due to their focus on all things financial. Between 1984 and 1992, health care spending had tripled in Ontario while only doubling in Canada as a whole. For this, there was a multiplicity of reasons: more people accessing the system, not just because of an aging population but because the end of extra-billing now permitted the truly poor full access to health care; a rising provincial population; increasingly expensive high-tech health technologies; and, inflation of 38.2%. They didn't see the reasons, just the spending numbers.

However, the error of this thinking was visually apparent by 1998. Patients were being stacked in hospital corridors because there were no longer enough staff to look after them properly and get them moving through the system. While the numbers of in-patients declined, those who needed to be re-admitted took an alarming rise. Family members were having to empty bedpans and change dressings because there wasn't a nurse available. Once the Tories were faced with daily stories like these, it finally dawned on them that hospitals and health facilities weren't hula-hoop factories. Though several hundred million dollars had been spent in severance to send nurses on their way, offers went out to these same people to hire them back. Some came, many did not. They had given up nursing, or left the province or the country in search of greener pastures.

Hiring back some nurses has not entirely helped, however. Though things seemed to have steadied, there is still a shortage of nursing staff which will get worse because of how many fewer people are studying to be nurses. Along with the clear morale busting that went along with the lay-offs and re-hiring, uncertainty continues because hospital funding is not stable and many of the positions being offered to nurses are part-time[15]. And as is common in administrative/Tory/business circles, these days, few seem to understand that part-time employment is the equivalent of functional poverty, especially when it comes from low-bid CCAC contracts or inadequate nursing home wages.[16]

Another problem is the lack of skilled nurses in such fields as cardiac care, critical care, dialysis, emergency nursing, and oncology. As more and more give up the profession (the average retirement age is 47), demand builds. However, because dollars are scarce, hospitals do not want to hire inexperienced nurses and train them. The result is many new graduates of nursing schools are casually employed or unemployed while there are openings for these specialized professionals.

It is as though the Tories do not understand that nursing is every bit as essential as doctoring. While the latter may diagnose the disease and transplant the organs, nurses supply most of the *caring* that patients need just as much. In fact, with the move to registered practical nurses to set the bones and sew up the wounds, it may be the understaffing of doctors will disappear because of a new recognition of nursing. However, governments must realize that nurses are just as important and begin to work to keep them in the profession longer and find new recruits to this most noble and worthwhile career.

Shelter? I have a dog house in the back ...

In 1993, the federal government, at the prodding of the provinces and to cut their financial responsibilities, ended any funding for new social housing. In fact, constitutionally, it had no responsibility for this but had become involved in the 1960s when many areas were desperately short of such housing. The federal government being involved in provincial jurisdiction had been a hobby horse of the provinces for decades, and this was one of the reasons it withdrew.

Shortly after the Harrisites took office, they cancelled all planned co-op and non-profit housing projects in the province – some 17,000 units – supposedly because of the need to make cuts, but also because of their philosophical aversion to government-owned and run housing. Then, as part of the disentanglement exercise, they downloaded responsibility for all 240,000 existing social housing units onto the municipalities. Some funds were made available to do repairs, but not nearly enough, or so said the municipalities, which claimed their governments could be saddled with over $1 billion in added costs.

The federal withdrawal from social housing was made official on 15

November 1999. Thirteen months later, the provincial government passed the *Social Housing Reform Act*, which transferred ownership and operating responsibility for all public housing in Ontario to the municipalities, though they had been paying the $770 million cost since the beginning of 1998.[17]

The reason for the Tories disdain of public housing may grow out of the troubles the NDP had while they were in government. While it's true Harris never did have much use for the whole concept of subsidized housing, Bob Rae's government was a big supporter of it, but never really had the money to do what it wanted in the area. Many social housing agencies across the province, notably the Metro Toronto Housing Authority, were being exposed for incompetence and wasteful spending, or that's how provincial audits made it seem. Suppliers were over-billing. Contracts were being offered for bid by dubious processes. Audited rent adjustments were found to be in error. In some cases, case workers had embezzled tenants' rent cheques. The Tories responded with demands that a moratorium be placed on new units.

Through the CSR, they suggested a new approach to public housing.

We will end the public housing boondoggle that profits only the large property developers and return to a shelter subsidy program for all Ontarians who need help in affording a decent level of shelter. This will eliminate the inefficiencies of government-owned and -operated housing. By spending money on people instead of bricks and mortar, we will be in a position to eliminate the two-year waiting list for affordable housing.

In fact, this wouldn't have been a bad idea. A shelter subsidy is used for rent-geared-to-income units that are either co-op, non-profit or housing corporation-owned units. Such a programme would have put the money for rent straight into the hands of those who needed it the most, though it would not have built new apartments.

The problem was the Harrisites do not seem to have had any intention of going through with this commitment. After they were elected, there were few questions of why the Tories had not gone ahead with their promise, given the number of plates they had in the air. However, it wasn't too long before Housing Minister Al Leach announced the shelter subsidy was on the shelf for the time being. As late as the day before the '99 election, he was still saying a plan was being worked on. This would be one of the CSR promises to be broken.

It is not entirely clear why the Tories decided to support a shelter subsidy in the first place, as it really did go against their neo-conservative sensibilities. More in line with their philosophy was the CSR promise to "develop a plan to sell the more than 84 thousand units owned by the Ontario Housing Corporation". Their stated preference was to do as Margaret Thatcher had done with council housing in Britain and offer it to those who were living in it.

Early in the 1900s, disease, poverty and bad housing were a common part of life in industrialized Britain. Though it was by no means easy to convince government to go along, affordable public housing was developed for working-class people, as a sickly workforce wasn't of much use. It was managed by local governments. After WWII, the economic boom helped improve this housing but, once it was over by the late 1960s, increases in council housing rents led to numerous rent strikes.

When Margaret Thatcher was elected, her government ordered that council housing be put up for sale to its residents. Most units were offered at reasonable prices with 100% mortgages. For those that could afford to buy their homes, it was a good deal. For those who could not, they were reduced to living in what was left, the housing in the poorest condition. Also, many thought they could buy and tried, only to find they couldn't keep up with payments and lost their homes to foreclosure. Meanwhile, the Thatcher government reduced funding for public housing, ended tenants' security of tenure, pushed market rent levels, and introduced a poll tax. She promised the private sector would build new stock. It didn't and the level of homelessness skyrocketed, leading to widespread squatting. Perhaps this is why the Harris Tories didn't go ahead with a public housing sale.

But they did go ahead with an undertaking not in the CSR. On 18 November 1997, the Tories passed the *Tenant Protection Act*, though its title was a complete misnomer given its contents. It did away with the rent controls that had protected tenants from excessively high annual rent increases since 1975, enacting a new system that retained annual limits on increases, but only for occupied units. Once the unit is vacant, landlords can increase the rents by any amount. As well, the new legislation set up the Ontario Rental Housing Tribunal to act as an arbiter of disputes between landlords and tenants.

The new law made it far easier to evict tenants. In the past, 60 days notice had to be given. That was reduced to 30. Instant eviction can be written into an agreement, so that a potential tenant can be faced with accepting the possibility of eviction without notice or losing an empty apartment. In a tight housing market, this is extremely unfair. As well, tenants can have their lease terminated for repairs or renovation of their unit. And while they may re-occupy it once these changes are made, this is only if they have given the landlord a written notice that they wish this right of first refusal. However, many people have no idea they have this opportunity. Without this notice, the unit is considered to have been vacated, so rent control no longer applies. In other words, a landlord could evict them to paint the walls, then double or triple the rent.

Many believed that the loss of rent control would become a significant election issue in 1999. It didn't. This was because rent *de-control* was still in its early days and had mostly affected the poor. Because poorer people move more often, they were the earliest to suffer the shock of increasing rents. They were also those in the worst position to publicize their new plight. It is only of late that middle-class tenants have felt the wrath of annual rent hikes that are now double the rate of inflation[18]. And many landlords are applying to the housing tribunal for increases beyond the legal maximum of 2.9% for 2001. In August and September of 2001, there were 663 such applications affecting just shy of 80,000 units province-wide, with about 55,000 of those – or 11% of all apartments – in Toronto. This was a 23.7% increase in applications from the year before. The reason behind most of these requests was because of higher heating costs from the past winter. (Does this mean landlords will drop rents next year with the drop in natural gas prices?) It is unclear why these applications didn't come when the prices actually went up.

Talk has swirled for some time that the federal government would get back into funding public housing. After abortive discussions, there was finally a minor agreement in late November 2001. Ottawa has pledged $25,000 per affordable housing unit built, up to $680 million nationwide over four years, and requested the provinces match these funds. Ontario refused to match their $244.5 million. Instead, Municipal Affairs and Housing minister Chris Hodgson stated the province would rebate sales' tax of $2,000 per unit. His ministry's thinking? They should get credit for money they were already spending ... just not on actually building affordable housing.

As well, the City of Toronto asked the legislature to consider a private bill that would have restored the power the Peterson Liberals had given municipalities to block the demolition of existing apartments. Many in the media were fooled when government members[19] let a legislative committee pass it. They took this as a sign the entire government would let it pass.

Instead, the Premier intervened to see that it will die on the order paper, never to be brought up for Third Reading. (Of course, Harris' successor could save this measure.)

It is only as time passes that the effects of the deregulated system have become evident. The Tories knew all along that what they were saying – the private sector would build new units once they could charge a fair price – was ludicrous. The average carrying cost for a new housing unit is $1,600 per month. Given the general guideline that no more than 30% of one's income should go to rent, that means that this tenant would have to make $64,000 per year. This effectively eliminates virtually all present renters from taking this unit, and means few such units will be built. Instead of ending a crisis in housing, the Harrisites have made it much worse.

3. Walkerton

If the Tory government is defeated in the next election, it won't be difficult for historians to trace the turning point, where the public finally began to question its veracity and competence. That point lies in the town of Walkerton.

I'm sure, for citizens of this small Ontario town, it must be truly irritating that its very name is now synonymous with bad water, widespread illness, and death. But like someone who comes down with a never-before-diagnosed disease, its just simplest to name it after you.

The ramifications of the tainted water tragedy are numerous, and I use the present tense, even though this event occurred in May 2000. Governments across Canada have been forced to take a fresh look at water standards. Waterworks and water pipes will have to be replaced throughout the country, at the cost of billions of dollars. Families must suffer the pain of deaths. People, especially many children, will have to deal with, and worry about, sickness caused by the permanent damage done. Politicians and bureaucrats will have to reconsider whether their prime concern is keeping government small and cheap or building infrastructure with higher taxes. Society must debate the roles of government at every level.

On Friday, 12 May 2000, a torrential rainstorm in and around Walkerton resulted in a good deal of run-off, causing town officials to take a water sample the following Monday and send it to A&L Laboratories Canada

East, the private lab they had contracted to do such work. Their faxed response on the Thursday indicated E-coli contamination. In this case, it was Escherichia coli, strain 0157:H7, a bacterium that comes from the intestines of cattle and usually gets into people through fecal matter or undercooked beef. It releases a toxin that travels to the intestine and causes the cells of the intestinal wall to die. In people with a healthy immune system, this bacteria is usually destroyed before it can do too much damage, but in those who are very young or old, with compromised immunity, E-coli can easily kill or do serious, permanent damage. The response of officials was confusion and inertia.

On the same day, a boy, 11, and a girl, 7, from Walkerton were transferred to the nearby Owen Sound hospital. Both were suffering from abdominal cramps, vomiting, and bloody diarrhea. The doctor attending both, Kristen Hallett, suspected E-coli. The next morning, she called the Grey County Medical Officer of Health, Dr. Murray McQuigge. He wasn't in, so she left a message, then called back later to insist the matter had to be dealt with before people left for the weekend. McQuigge called the Brockton PUC, the municipal government that looks after Walkerton, three times over that day and the next, hoping to find the source of the contamination. Each time he was told all was well. Also that day, the Environment ministry received an anonymous telephone call informing it of the feculence. After some difficulty contacting the local administrators, ministry staff were told that, except for minor problems, everything was fine.

It was only the next day when McQuigge decided the trouble had to be the local water that a widespread boil-water warning went out. The next Tuesday, public health tests of the water showed E-coli contamination. It was only then that PUC officials admitted their chlorination system had not worked properly in some time, and that they had known for five days of the bacterial corruption. The PUC chair, Jim Kieffer, admitted that his people did not seem to realize how devastating E-coli can be, and the Ontario Clean Water Agency assumed control of Walkerton's water system to fix the problems.

Seven people died and more than 2,000 others were made ill. Immediately, there were questions. What exactly had happened? How could this have happened? Who was responsible? Though the difficulties had clearly been local, questioning eyes levelled their gaze at the Premier. After all, his government had sliced and diced environmental regulation and staffing. His response? "At no time was any person downsized in a way that should have affected the delivery of any services of the Ministry of the Environment."

Harris blamed the NDP. Presumably as a measure to cut provincial costs, the Rae government had started charging municipalities for water testing by ministry labs. When some local councils complained about their added costs, the New Democrats gave them the option of using private labs instead, effectively downloading even more costs. Then the Tories closed down three of the four provincial testing labs. So the fact that the private lab doing Walkerton's tests had only told local staff of the contamination was Bob Rae's fault, according to the Premier. Thus, it was quite strange when recently-appointed Environment minister Dan Newman gave his unequivocal opinion that, had the provincial government been in charge of water testing, the alert would have gone out much earlier.

When demands came for a public inquiry, Harris suggested that investigations by the OPP, the coroner's office, the Environment ministry, and a legislative committee would be sufficient. That position didn't last long though. The pressure of the situation made it impossible to procrastinate. Twenty-two days after the boil-water advisory, Justice Dennis O'Connor of the Ontario Court of Appeal was appointed as the sole commissioner of a public inquiry into the Walkerton tragedy, with a wide-ranging mandate to examine not just what had happened locally but provincial government policies and actions as well. Though the media began to put together the events leading up to the E-coli outbreak, it was the inquiry that focused matters, especially public attention.

Perhaps because I am a biased observer, to me, the inquiry became an indictment of the Tories, more than that of local officials. As someone who had grown up in a rural municipality next to a village where officials' idea of water treatment was a bottle of Javex bleach once a month, I expected to hear horror stories. So when Stan Koebel, water manager for Brockton, and his brother Frank, an employee, admitted they had known the chlorination system was not functioning properly, they had faked tests, falsified reports, and that they did not understand their responsibilities, it was less than a great surprise. In effect, they admitted to being so ignorant that they didn't realize how ignorant they really were. While local residents were angered, they were at least satisfied that the pair had not tried to hide their culpability and had confessed the truth.

The reverse was true for the provincial government. If one thing became clear at the inquiry it was that a properly designed process of review by the Environment ministry would have caught the failing Walkerton water system and the Koebel brothers' incompetence before the outbreak could have become widespread. It might have stopped it entirely. My conclusion is that such a system had existed in Ontario, and had been dismantled by government cuts. Premier Harris would beg to differ, I'm sure.

A little background:

Up to the Tory assumption of power, water treatment plants were inspected by four-member teams of specialists from the Ministry of the Environment. Their job was to personally take water samples for testing, and document any concerns they had with the operations of those facilities. If problems were found, there would be one or more visits by an environmental officer to check on compliance.

In 1996, as part of the ministry's dissection, these teams were disbanded and their inspection duties became the responsibility of ministry environmental officers, who work individually. Their other duties include water and sewage plant inspections, landfill, hazardous waste disposal operations, PCB storage sites, and checking on pesticide and industrial pollution emissions, not to mention they are also responsible for chemical spill emergency response and clean-up. At the time of the Walkerton contamination, after the cuts, if a problem was discovered, it was up to the staff at the water treatment plant to provide the ministry with a written schedule of their plan to fix it, though with no actual proof of compliance. As one official said, "We then hope that they will meet their schedule. We then choose, based on our availability, the facilities that will be followed up closely by ensuring they meet the targets".[20] In Walkerton, their facilities were tested in 1998, and the official found chlorination problems, a lack of staff training and too few water samples taken for testing. No one had managed to get back and check on the situation prior to the contamination.

While the NDP government had instituted the beginnings of cutbacks, it is unlikely this tragedy would have occurred under the rules at that time. With the savage cuts to the Environment ministry that came when the Tories assumed power, inspections at the province's 630 water treatment plants dropped from 75% inspected in 1993-1994 to 24% in 1998-1999. In other words, water treatment officials that would have seen their facilities checked out three out of every four years saw that drop to once in four years. In my mind, this invited abuse.

Also in 1996, three of the four ministry testing labs were closed. They had a responsibility to immediately inform the Environment ministry compliance staff and the local medical officer of health of any problems with drinking water contaminated by bacteria. And though the private labs that succeeded them were also told by the ministry to report any unsafe drinking water results to provincial authorities, there was no requirement in law to do so. In fact, there were municipalities that instructed the private labs to report only to local officials, presumably so they could deal with any problems without ministry interference or punishment. Undoubtedly, the Harris government did not want to burden these labs or municipalities with legal *red tape*.

The effect on the public was considerable. Before this catastrophe, most Ontarians, even Canadians, took the safety of their drinking water for granted. Their reaction, particularly after the inquiry began its sessions, was one of shock and concern. How could such a thing have happened in modern Ontario? It was unthinkable that something as basic as drinking water could kill in this day-and-age. Drinking water is something so intrinsic that, to find it was not safe, while people demanded answers, they also questioned how government could let this happen.

To Canadians, Ontarians especially, there are certain things that are inherently part of government and people expect government to protect them ... to make certain these things are safe. Food should be fresh and free from contamination. Roads should be cleared of snow and ice. Water should be clean. It may be on this point where the Harris government made a fundamental error. They seemed to believe that their election in 1995, on the principles of the CSR – particularly cutting the size of government – meant the public now accepted that all things governmental were open to downsizing or even elimination.

When under cross-examination before the inquiry, Mike Harris said his Cabinet was not warned of the health risks of cuts to the Ministry of the Environment regarding drinking water regulation. In fact, the criticisms of him that came from this testimony centred on his refusal to acknowledge any responsibility for what had happened, his apparent lack of compassion, and the fact he made no attempt to apologize, even in a minimal way. For a politician of his experience, this seemed odd. However, this is a fact of his testimony that is even more elucidating of the thinking of himself and those in his government.

In saying there had been no warnings of health risk, the Premier was seemingly playing very fast and loose with reality. In laying out the effects of the first round of financial cuts, Environment ministry staff stated the possibility of problems in writing. In part of his testimony at the

Walkerton inquiry, inquiry counsel Paul Cavalluzzo made this point.

Cavalluzzo: *"Summary of impacts in general. The impacts of these reductions include elimination of staffing flexibility to fill necessary highly skilled technical positions and less monitoring, compliance, enforcing standard setting, et cetera, activities which may increase environment health and -- environmental --"* Excuse me: *"And health risks and increase the Ministry's exposure to charges of regulatory negligence."* And it goes on, and then in the final paragraph in that part it states: *"These reductions will have an adverse impact on the delivery of environmental protection service levels, which in turn will increase public health and safety risks. Impacts are expected to be compounded by the cutbacks imposed by the federal government on Environment Canada, the Ministry will monitor its programs to ensure that environmental protection is not compromised, to the extent possible."* Now were you aware that when the first target set by the government was met by the Ministry of the Environment, that the officials in the Ministry were describing that there were -- that the reductions, to use their words, would increase risk to health and the environment?

Harris: No, I wouldn't have seen this document. This -- this would have been an -- an internal document being prepared by the Ministry of the Environment and Energy, but certainly the -- the -- the direction that was given to the Ministry in preparing it, was look at all the impacts, look at all the potential impacts and be prepared to ensure that there is no risk to -- to health and safety. And they would have to answer that. And that's -- the Ministry would have to monitor it's programs to ensure that environmental protection is not compromised.

Cavalluzzo: So what -- what you're saying then is in September when the -- this program was approved, that neither the Minister of the Environment, Deputy Minister of the Environment or anybody on Management Board brought to your attention the impacts which are clearly described in this document or submission?

Harris: That's certainly at -- at no time would I have been briefed or would Cabinet have received any direction that -- that safety would have been compromised. At no time would that have occurred, no.

The Premier's conclusion is quite difficult to believe. Perhaps he wouldn't have been told, but to suggest no Cabinet members would have been briefed ... What of the Environment minister? This is certainly something civil servants *must* bring to the attention of the minister, threats to water quality included. If the level of government fell that fast under the Harris Tories, then it must be concluded Ontario has been mismanaged hideously since June 1995.

Later, the lead counsel continued, discussing the first business plan for the Environment ministry, 1996-1997. As originally written, it stated quite clearly that environmental standards might be undermined if the desired financial cuts went ahead. It was explicitly this portion of the plan that Cabinet, Harris included, chose to edit from the final edition. Clearly, this action shows some *mens rea*, or the 'guilty mind' that in law gets an accused criminal convicted. It shows a conscious act that is difficult to dispute ... except perhaps for Mike Harris.

Cavalluzzo: And the reference that I would make is to page 25 and -- and once again, the context for this business plan is that this is really the second round of cutbacks. We saw what they said in respect to the first round of cutbacks in the Sep -- September 1st document 1995. Now we're at January 22 of 1996, dealing with the second round of cutbacks and we have agreed in the evidence that the impact on the Ministry of the Environment in this business plan for the two (2) years is something like two hundred point eight million ($200,800,000) dollars. Now, in describing the impacts, or describing the key impacts on page 25 you will see in the third bullet down that the closure of the three (3) regional laboratories is part and parcel of this plan. And then they go on and they say: "The Ministries ability to monitor and assess environmental change and give early warning of long term serious threats, ensure compliance with environmental standards and regulations and develop policy and programs in response to emerging environment and energy issues will be reduced as a result of a number of items, including the closure of some air monitoring stations, reduce acid rain, urban toxic great lakes, disposition monitoring analysis"... And so on and so forth. I need not go through the rest.
Harris: Right.
Cavalluzzo: At the next bullet it says "The public may perceive that the government's ability to protect Ontario's environment has been substantially reduced". Next bullet: "The risk to human health and the environment may increase as a result of improper or illegal actions which are neither detected nor controlled through Orders and prosecutions as a result of decreased compliance and enforcement activities". And then a couple down: "The level of front line service will be reduced as a result of slower response times to complaints. A focus on compliance activities, rather than providing assistance with the abatement actions"... And so on and so forth. Next line: "Greater reliance in Ontario on the private sector for analytical testing services"... And then finally: "Approximately 750 staff will be let go

over the next two years". And the other part of the business plan, which I think is important for later questioning; if you refer to page 12 it refers to the regulation review, at page 12. In the middle paragraph it states: "The Ministry has also initiated a comprehensive review of it's 80 regulations to determine how effective these regulations are in terms of achieving the Ministry's objectives and whether regulations could be streamlined or amended or deleted to eliminate red tape, without lowering the quality of environmental protection. The review would also provide an opportunity for examining new environmental management tools that go beyond the traditional command and control approach as the Ministry's review would be fully coordinated with the government's recently appointed Red Tape Commission". And -- and we'll come back to that.

Harris: Okay.

Cavalluzzo: Now, in terms of the -- in terms of the impacts, you would agree with me that the Ministry officials clearly set out what the key impacts are in regard to this particular business plan?

Harris: Yes. As they were asked to do, to point out any -- any impacts or potential impacts and -- and they have done that.

We see here that the Premier has accepted Mr. Cavalluzzo's contention that the potential effects of the cuts to Environment have been laid out in the business plan. That was temporary.

Cavalluzzo: Okay. And then if you -- if you, for example, refer to page 4, the proposal concerning the restructuring of lab services is set out. And I'm going to -- just referring to that now, because I'm going to be coming back to the labs later in my questioning. Do you see that in the second proposal, Proposal 1.2: "Restructuring Ministry Lab Services."

Harris: Yes, page 4?

Cavalluzzo: That's correct.

Harris: Yes.

Cavalluzzo: Okay. And then the final reference is at page 8.

Harris: Yes.

Cavalluzzo: And it's under the -- under the title, 'Marketing Communications.' And it says: "Key Messages: While the Ministry will become leaner and more efficient, there will be no compromise on environmental protection. The Ministry will encourage new partnerships that emphasize expertise over writing cheques and greater use of private sector delivery. The regulatory burden on business will be eased, while clarifying standards to be met and municipalities will be given greater autonomy and needing clearer standards."

Harris: Yes.

Cavalluzzo: And then the comment of the central analyst: "Is excellent plan

overall, no major concerns." And then it just says: "More detail is needed on media strategy." Now the next step obviously is that there's going to be a P & P -- a joint P & P Board(,) Management Board meeting to deal with the approval of the business plan. Now if you refer to tab 20 -- ...

Harris: So from the potential impacts they were -- they were asked to identify, to the page 8 summary.

Cavalluzzo: Hmm hmm.

Harris: Which -- which indicated there would be no compromise on environmental protection, and the review comments were -- were essentially in agreement. It also -- there's important information there on strategies for change.

Cavalluzzo: Right.

Harris: On page 3.

Cavalluzzo: Well you said -- you said that it says here, how -- how the -- the environmental protection will not be reduced. Am I understanding you correctly? ...

Harris: That there would be no compromise on environmental protection.

Cavalluzzo: Right.

Harris: But on page 3 I'm just pointing out the rest of the document, page 3 points out on strategies for change, so that there would be no compromise and some of the strategies that the Ministry were planning to undertake, focussing on priorities, on regulation, on program reform, changing organizational structure, restructuring Ministry operations, restructuring internal administration, cutting government grants, which was part of the grants to others, so that the -- the rest of the pages went through, in the business planning --

Cavalluzzo: Right.

Harris: -- exercise, went through a number of the strategies.

Cavalluzzo: Right. But the fact -- the fact that you have strategies for change does not remove the fact that they're saying there's going to be increased risk to health and environment as a result of these reductions so, obviously, any risk is potential, but it's there, you don't remove it by saying, oh, we're going to do this, that and the other thing?

Harris: Well, let me say this, there's -- there's risks in everything --

Cavalluzzo: Hmm hmm.

Harris: -- but I can tell you at no time was it ever brought to Cabinet's attention, to my attention, that the implementation of these business plans would cause increased risk to health and safety of any citizen

anywhere in the province.
Cavalluzzo: *Okay. Well, let's go to the document that went to Cabinet then, the next tab, tab 20.*
Harris: *Yes.*
Cavalluzzo: *And this is entitled 'Presentation to P & P Board, Management Board, Ministry of Environment and Energy Business Plan, Confidential Advice to Cabinet'.*
Harris: *Yes.*
Cavalluzzo: *The first page, it just starts with saying, "Ontarions* (sic) *overwhelmingly desire a healthier environment." Second page says, "77 percent of Ontarions* (sic) *believe that strict enforcement of environmental regulation must continue, regardless of state of the economy"; do you see that? It's the question I asked you before that, if an Ontarions* (sic) *--*
Harris: *I'm sorry, could you --*
Cavalluzzo: *"77...", page 3.*
Harris: *Oh, page 3.*
Cavalluzzo: *Yeah. "77 percent of Ontarions* (sic) *believe that strict enforcement of environment regulation must continue, regardless of the state of economy."*
Harris: *Yes.*
Cavalluzzo: *And it goes on, "93 percent of Ontarions* (sic) *think that government should put a high median priority on government spending on environmental protection."*
Harris: *Yes.*
Cavalluzzo: *And then, if you go to the advice that's being given to Cabinet, you will see at page 10.*
Harris: *Yes.*
Cavalluzzo: *It says: "The Ministry proposes to close regional laboratories, close the air monitoring studies, reduce acid rain, urban toxic in Great Lakes, deposition monitoring, eliminate the inspections of closed waste sites, reduce proactive inspections of industries, devolve responsibilities for some local matters to municipalities such as noise, odour and dust and then shrink in-house scientific and technical expertise..." And then it says: "Impact. The risk to human health and environment may increase. Secondly, ability to monitor and assess environmental change will diminish." Now, you would agree with me that that is clearly setting out, and I just read it, the risk to human health and environment may increase and ability to monitor and assess environmental change will diminish; you agree with me, that's -- that's clear on its face?*
Harris: *Yeah, those -- those are -- yes, it is and -- and I would also say to you that, before this would be approved by Cabinet, they would*

have had to have satisfied – or the Minister that -- that there would
have not, they were able to manage any of these potential impacts.
Cavalluzzo: *Okay. And I'll come back to that, but --*
Harris: *Okay.*
Cavalluzzo: *-- you will see on page 12, it talks about marketing the*
business plan and it says: "1. We face a major communications
challenges, strong environmental protection is not seen to be consistent
with spending cuts."
Harris: *Yes.*
Cavalluzzo: *"We would want to build a positive public image of the*
new Ministry, but stakeholders and media will be sceptical and our key
message is Ontario taxpayers will be told that we will not compromise
on the environment. The Ministry will focus..."
Harris: *Right.*
Cavalluzzo: *Et cetera, et cetera "...on core activities." Now were you*
aware that this submission to P & P Management Board, that joint
committee was approved?
Harris: *This is probably the period of time when I was -- was away*
either on -- I guess back from the Team Canada trip and then I was
away on -- to Davos[21] , and to Hong Kong and Japan at the time. But
certainly I would have been briefed on that meeting of P & P.
Cavalluzzo: *And that meeting was on --*
Harris: *And would have been briefed on any issues that would have*
been brought forward to Cabinet.
Cavalluzzo: *And that -- that meeting was on February the 8th and we*
were advised by your counsel that you were out -- out of the country on
that --
Harris: *Yes.*
Cavalluzzo: *-- day. You are still Chair of P & P and would be*
responsible for decisions taken by decisions taken by that --
Harris: *Yes.*
Cavalluzzo: *-- P & P. You would agree with that?*
Harris: *I'm responsible for every decision taken by our government.*
Cavalluzzo: *Okay. Now if we move on to tab 22 we see that on*
February 28th of 1996 the Cabinet, full Cabinet approved the
Ministry's business plan. You see at the top there, Cabinet minute
meeting of Feb. 28?
Harris: *Yes, February 28th.*
Cavalluzzo: *1996?*
Harris: *Cabinet, yes.*
Cavalluzzo: *And it -- it -- just a couple of portions of the minute I*
would refer to. One (1) is the approval itself. Paragraph one (1):
"The Ministry be authorized to proceed to estimates based on the

Ministry's business plan, subject to working with Management Board Secretariat to develop prior to estimates, a contingency plan should savings from the Municipal Assistance Program not materialise."
Harris: *Yes.*
Cavalluzzo: *"Secondly, given the need to achieve the government's overall expenditure reduction objectives, the Ministry has committed to achieving at least the targeted savings identified in the business plan. Management Board of Cabinet will attempt to find substantial additional savings through the estimates process, in particular the Board will seek complete program elimination wherever possi – or feasible." That seems to suggest that the Management Board would be looking for more savings on top of what had already been approved. Is that correct?*
Harris: *They would be looking for savings in every Ministry at this stage of our --*
Cavalluzzo: *Okay. And finally on page --*
Harris: *-- our government.*
Cavalluzzo: *-- I'm sorry, on page 2 at the last paragraph, it states that:*
"The Ministry further develop the communication strategy for it's business plan in consultation with Cabinet Office and the Premier's Office. No announcements are to be made without the approval of Cabinet Office communications." Now, Premier, were you in attendance at this Cabinet meeting on February 28th which approved the business plan?
Harris: *Yes, I attended.*
Cavalluzzo: *And at this particular meeting, did you -- do you recall seeking the advice from anybody at that meeting that these risks were manageable?*
Harris: *No, I don't recall specifically asking that question. This would have been a Cabinet meeting to approve all the business plans, presumably amongst other business that was there. And --*
Cavalluzzo: *Do you recall -- I'm sorry?*
Harris: *And I don't -- I don't recall specifically asking that question. It may have been asked, it may have been asked by others. But I can tell you this, I don't recall the Minister or my Deputy giving me any indication that any of the potential risks that had been identified could not be managed.*
Cavalluzzo: *But you don't recall asking that? You don't recall any other member of the Cabinet asking about whether --*
Harris: *I -- I -- I can't recall, back six (6) years ago, whether those questions were asked or were not, no.*
Cavalluzzo: *And -- and I know that in the minute itself, there is not*

one (1) specific reference to the risks being managed or being
manageable. There's nothing --
Harris: No, there's --
Cavalluzzo: -- in this document --
Harris: No, there's -- there's -- this document is simply Cabinet
approving the -- the business plan that was presented and was looked
at by Management Board, by P & P, by the reviews that you -- you have
mentioned within the
Ministry and what the central agency.
Cavalluzzo: But there's nothing that says, we'll approve the plans so
long as you guys can manage the risk that you've told us about.
Harris: No, the minute doesn't say that but the plan says that.
Cavalluzzo: The plan says that it's manageable?
Harris: The -- the -- my understanding is that – that the plan identifies
the risks and there are several stages in the plan where it says that
these risks, by doing business differently, is -- we -- we talked about,
that – and certainly the whole raison d'etre of the business plan and the
-- the template that was sent out. You will have to ensure that these
risks are manageable. And that's certainly the indication I had from --
from the Ministers.
Cavalluzzo: Well, certainly we can read the business plan and
certainly I could find nothing in the business plan which suggested that
the risks were manageable. It talked about changing it's focus, looking
at core functions and
things like that but it certainly didn't talk about how the risk was going
to be managed, to my recollection.
Harris: Well, that would have been up to -- to the Ministry. I can
assure you of this, that nobody brought to Cabinet's attention or to my
attention, and I think you heard from the Ministers to -- to two (2) of
them, to their attention, that they were not manageable, by either the
senior staff of the Ministry of the Environment or any of my staff.
Cavalluzzo: And -- and neither Minister could show us anything in
writing which suggested where we could find how this risk was going to
be managed?
Harris: Well, I can assure you nobody brought it to my attention that
it could not.

After a discussion on how the business plans were shared with caucus, for
the first time, with a repetition of the warning by staff, the discussion of the
business plan moved to its perception by the public.

Cavalluzzo: Now, you would also agree me, Premier, that as we've
just reviewed, that the risks to the environment and health were -- were

clearly set out in the business plan as they were supposed to be --
Harris*: Yes.*
Cavalluzzo*: -- according to it's format. The question that I have with*
you is, why then in the public release of the business plan, were the
public not given this information concerning the impacts relating to
increased – possible increased risk to health and the environment?
Harris*: Because that -- that was all information for decision makers.*
As I indicated, it's the first time it had ever been done this way, it's the
first time the -- the sort of internal type discussions that would have
gone on in the Ministry to arrive at the estimates and -- and the
spending targets were actually shared with -- with -- with more of -- of
Cabinet, with Management Board, with committees. And in fact, rather
historic, actually shared with Caucus. So those were all the -- those
factors that went into the decision making of the -- the estimates for
each of the Ministries. The normal process before we were elected is
you just put out the Minis -- the -- the -- the estimates the describe the --
the -- the programs. The second thing that was new and -- and historic,
I would say, is that we did provide more information than ever, through
the business plans that we released to the public.
Cavalluzzo*: Hmm hmm.*
Harris*: The key directions that -- and changes, if you like, and the key*
priorities of each and every one (1) of the Ministries set out those
objectives, and then also how they could be held accountable for those
objectives, so –
Cavalluzzo*: Right.*
Harris*: -- it -- the purpose of the business plan wasn't to -- to release*
all the information that went through the arrival of the budget process,
the purpose was to put out those strategic objectives --
Cavalluzzo*: But I -- I repeat my question.*
Harris*: Yes.*
Cavalluzzo*: In the business plan they are described as key impacts,*
and I'm putting it to you, first of all the public wasn't advised of that
and you obviously agree with that because it's not in the business plan.
Harris*: Right.*
Cavalluzzo*: And -- and the second point I raise and I ask is don't you*
think that the public is entitled to that information?
Harris*: Well, no --*
Cavalluzzo*: They're not?*
Harris*: -- in the sense -- no, in -- in this sense, if -- if those impacts*
were determined not to be manageable, and you were going to go
ahead which we would never have --
Cavalluzzo*: Right.*
Harris*: -- then certainly the public would be entitled to know.*

Previous estimates that were released gave the public no information, just the spending levels. So this was more information than had ever been given before, and let me repeat that had I or the Minister of the Environment, and I'm confident both -- both Ministers that you heard from, or -- or senior staff believed that there's any risk in this plan to human health or any increased risk, I -- I -- I think I've got to repeat that --

Cavalluzzo: *Right.*

Harris: *-- there's risk in everything, there's risk in -- in walking across the street, that any of these actions would increase risk, had we believed that, we*
wouldn't have proceeded.

Cavalluzzo: *But -- but, Premier, the risk they are saying is being increased, whether that can be managed is another question. But these plans are saying from the officials, risk is increasing.*

Harris: *The potential is that they'll increase, I would presume somebody in the Ministry has -- has identified that as a potential risk, and -- and if you carried on doing business the same way, if you didn't have the private sector doing something or a municipality doing something, or if you weren't able to manage your -- your -- your funding more efficiently, or if you weren't focussing on -- on these key areas to make sure, then that would have been a potential impact. But we were about changing, we were about changing the way government operated, as well as we were about balancing of the books. And I -- I repeat for you. If -- if -- if there was any risk, if I felt --*

Cavalluzzo: *Hmm hmm.*

Harris: *-- there was any risk, and if it had been brought to my attention --*

Cavalluzzo: *Right.*

Harris: *-- we would not have proceeded.*

Cavalluzzo: *I'm putting it to you, Premier, that because you were aware that if the public -- that the public in terms of a balance between economic -- economic considerations and environmental considerations that they would opt for protecting the environment. And because of that, the Government decided*
not to release that information, because you knew it would be politically unpopular to the public?

Harris: *Well I -- I totally reject that, that -- that -- that was not the thinking at the time, and it's not my thinking today.*

Mike Harris' testimony in Walkerton was widely panned. It wasn't that his *performance* was poor. He knew his answers and he responded without becoming quarrelsome when challenged. It was his refusal to accept responsibility that annoyed many, and his lack of empathy for those who had suffered that angered most everyone. "Accountable but blameless" was *The Toronto Star* headline of the next day, referring to the Premier's seeming position on himself and his government.

His message had been a simple one. Cuts to the Ministry of the Environment were necessary because government inefficiency and regulations were strangling business and investment in the province. To a conference on green technologies in 1998, the premier had clearly expressed his view on the matter.

> *We need to challenge the assumption that the more money we spend, the more regulations we have on the books and the more people we have in the bureaucracy means more progress in protecting the environment. That kind of thinking got us where we are today – saddled with a huge and expensive regulatory burden with little certainty that our regulations are actually doing the job that they were intended to do.* (Toronto Star, "Harris defends slashing 'silly' environment rules", Thursday, 14 Nov 1996, p. A2)

Though bureaucrats had warned his government that there were some risks involved to safety, he contended his Ministers were told they were manageable, though he could offer no proof nor actually recall being told they were manageable. The risks were only potential, after all. He also said his government was not to blame for mistakes made. Those were local.

Residents wanted an apology from their Premier. Even if he didn't want to admit to culpability for decisions his government made, they wanted him to say he regretted the whole contaminated water crisis had happened. Even if he wasn't going to say he was responsible for their suffering, they wanted him to say he was sorry they had suffered. But he wouldn't. Though he stated he was "accountable to all the people of Ontario", he would not accept responsibility for any mistakes that might have been made. "I am the leader of the government, whether I knew about it or not."

On this score, the difficulty for Harris was that there was written proof his government had been warned of cuts endangering human safety. Cavalluzzo introduced the Environment ministry's initial 1996 business plan that had been submitted to the Planning and Policy Committee of Cabinet for approval. It stated that risks to human health and the environment might increase as a result of improper or illegal actions that are neither detected nor controlled, as a result of self-regulation and reduced staffing to check on compliance. It pointed out that 750 staff would be let go over two years and that, in some areas, front-line staff were being reduced substantially given the closing of a regional office, a district office, four sub-offices, and three regional laboratories. The ability of the Ministry to monitor and assess environmental change, warn of serious threats, and establish policy and standards would also be reduced. As well, there was concern that the public would perceive the government was less able to protect the environment because of these cuts and changes.

In my opinion, it is unlikely the government ever considered people could die from their cuts. It is likely the acceptability of risk from cuts came from their myopic view of government: departments were bloated in size and in budget by civil servants who were trying to protect their own jobs and *fiefdoms*. Making cuts was simply a way of getting rid of unnecessary regulation, which would, in turn, allow the downsizing of a number of bureaucrats and the amputation of ministry budgets. Thus, the taxpayer would save money at the same time that life would be simpler for business and government.

That having been said, there was no way a business plan that suggested there were risks to cutting drinking water regulation could be released to the public. Given the *liberal* press, who would undoubtedly blow these concerns *out of proportion*, it would be too dangerous not to delete the offending phrases. After all, *they weren't true*. The regulations were just red tape, and any risk was *manageable*, at least in the minds of the Harris Cabinet members.

There is plenty of blame to go around for the Walkerton water tragedy. The fact that the drinking water system was not properly maintained was negligence by both those in charge of doing the job and those who were supposed to oversee their employees. However, that doesn't let the province off the hook. The cuts to Environment ministry staff and the change of philosophy that made treatment plants virtually self-regulated guaranteed that somewhere at sometime water would be contaminated and people would get sick. The worst part is, while the Koebels may have been ignorant, the Harris government was willful. Had they not cut staff and changed operating procedures that weakened the safety net protecting drinking water, there is a very good chance that the Walkerton contamination would have been discovered before it got out of hand, local incompetence or not.

And they were aware they might have gone too far. In August 1997, a senior consultant with the Health ministry drafted a letter that was sent by then Minister Jim Wilson to his colleague, Norm Sterling, in Environment. It requested changes be made to the *Ontario Water Resources Act* to turn into law the guideline that medical officers of health be immediately informed of adverse drinking water test results by testing labs. It was said this should happen before the responsibility for drinking water was downloaded to municipalities on 1 January 1998. When Sterling responded three months later, it was to Wilson's successor, Elizabeth Witmer. He said the transfer of responsibility would not affect procedures. A year later, the Health ministry again warned Environment, this time that private testing labs were not informing MOHs of poor water results. No action was taken until after people died in Walkerton.

The other blame that came from the Walkerton tragedy was on farming. Agricultural fertilizer practices were censured even though the *fault* was dubious. It is fairly clear the E-coli contamination came from bovine fecal matter which leaked into one of Walkerton's wells, supposedly during heavy rains. The heavy use of manure as fertilizer was roundly decried, yet wasn't all that much different than it had been in years prior. In fact, had it been that the top of the well wasn't below the nearby ground level, this contamination would not likely have happened.

But this excoriation didn't stop. It came to be directed at farms, given the number that abut on the boundary of Walkerton. What little action there was on this front from the provincial government came in the way of their proposed *Nutrient Management Act*, legislation to set out standards for the use of "fertilizers, organic materials, biosolids, compost, manure, septage, pulp and paper sludge, and other material applied to land for the purpose of improving the growing of agricultural crops", as well as farm practices regarding these nutrients. Of course, given the habits of the Tories, they can never seem to make the correct move without balling it up. Instead of setting out the standards and practices in the legislation, it will be done by regulation, meaning at the whim of the government. And just to upset farmers, the statute, if enacted, will also permit provincial officers to trespass on their land at will. It doesn't help that 'provincial officers' are not necessarily officials of the Agriculture or Environment ministries. They can be anyone designated as such by the Minister, even someone competing in the same line of farming.

In fact, it is the environment that may finally turn out to be the area that has suffered most under the Harris neo-conservatives. Not only was drinking water affected, but this government's business incompetence has led to a serious increase in smog. Estimates by the Ontario Medical Association state that 1,800 people a year are now dying prematurely of smog-related problems. The public is tremendously concerned. This alarm is particularly palpable in the late spring and summer, as that is when we are now *treated* to a growing number of smog alerts. In 1997, there were three air quality alerts. In 1999, five over nine days. In 2001, this had jumped to 23 days. Meanwhile, the Harris government insists things are getting better.

But exaggerating about the environment is not something new for the Tories. In 2000, the Environment ministry claimed it had managed to meet a large portion of its 1996 target to reduce smog-causing emissions to 1990 levels by 2010, but it was obfuscation rather than truth. In 1996, they had subtracted 257 kilotonnes of nitrogen oxides and 260 kilotonnes of volatiles as "reductions or planned reductions" in emissions. In 2000, they subtracted these numbers from their total, even though their calculations included them already. This is not the only case of the Tory government claiming much and supplying less than nothing.

On 24 January 2000, then Environment minister Tony Clement held a press conference at the Ontario Science Centre to announce the government's new regulations to deal with air pollution. Their highlight was a new trading system that would allow polluters to buy credits from cleaner industries. The logic behind this type of system is that industries will want to clean up so they can make money selling credits. Of course, the reverse side was ignored – that heavy polluters will not try and clean up because all they have to do is buy credits in order to pollute to their heart's content.

It wouldn't take long for critics to get fuel for their concerns. According to the Ontario Clean Air Alliance, Ontario Power Generation's annual contribution to air pollution is the equivalent of five million cars.[22] So when Minister Clement announced that OPG would be limited to spewing 36 kilotonnes of nitrogen oxides and 157.5 kilotonnes of sulphur dioxides into the atmosphere each year, as of 1 January 2001, everyone saw how serious the government really was. This *limit* on the former was six times higher than the Ontario Medical Association recommendation. These were supposedly cuts of 5% and 10% respectively. However, when the 1999 numbers came out, OPG's coal-fired generators alone were 15.4kilotonnes over the 2001 limit, in fact a 35% increase. OPG responded by saying it would not be able to meet the 36 kilotonne limit, but should be able to make 50 kilotonnes. No caps were placed on arsenic or mercury, which also result when coal is burned.

Ontario's increasingly lax environmental standards were causing trouble internationally, as well. While an estimated 50% of airborne pollutants in Ontario come from the United States, an increasing portion of theirs comes from Ontario. New York State, in particular, is concerned that the province's coal-fired power plants are spewing more and more into the air which then passes over New York, causing illness in people while killing lakes and trees. It got to the point where they threatened to seek legal redress against Ontario, though some considered this simple posturing during negotiations to renew the Trans-Boundary Air Quality Agreement.

The biggest ally of the Americans was the Government of Canada, whose government members were embarrassed by the bragging of the Harrisites that they were the *saviours* of the environment, while air pollution statistics showed the opposite. Ontario was, in fact, the biggest obstacle to getting a deal with the Americans. Ottawa criticized Ontario again and again, but could not convince the Harris government to concede to more stringent standards. In late 2000, the feds gave up and agreed to American demands, despite the Harris position. Their plan is to somehow force Ontario to go along, before the agreement takes effect. Canada must halve nitrogen oxide emissions by 2007.

As I write this, Ontario Power Generation has decided to buy state-of-the-art equipment to cut plant emissions. However, both the federal government and environmentalists have rejected this as too little, as this would not guarantee necessary reduction levels. Both favour conversion to natural gas, and the Harris government has elected to convert the Lakeview plant to this by 2005. However, Lakeview is tiny compared to Nanticoke, which is responsible for 24 kilotonnes of nitrogen oxide emissions per year.

The Tories have tried to do something to help, or so it seemed. Going against type, the government created the *Drive Clean* programme. It is an inspection and maintenance (I/M) programme that checks vehicles more than three years old but less than twenty to make sure their emissions are not above a specified standard. Given the increasing air quality problems in southern Ontario, the plan initially got a lot of good publicity, as it is supposed to cut smog by 22%, and people support something that will make the air they breath cleaner. However, there's a lot less to Drive Clean than it might seem, especially things good.

It was initially mandatory for those in the GTA and Hamilton-Wentworth and, after 21 months, was expanded to cover an extended zone that included most southern urban areas. In July 2002, it will widen again cover the entire "smog zone" of southern Ontario (which is every county except Huron, Bruce, and Grey). Emissions' repair costs were originally limited to $200, and now increase to $450 two years after phase-in, which means that the worst polluters are free to keep polluting. For example, if it is found a car needs a new catalytic converter, which would easily cost more than $1,000, the car's owner doesn't have to buy one because it is outside the maximum limit. The Ministry explanation is that this is so poorer Ontarians do not lose their cars because they cannot afford repairs.

A vehicle must pass an inspection before the test is ever made, to make sure it isn't leaking fluids, amongst other things. If it fails this, the emissions test isn't done. The car must be repaired first but, unlike with emissions repairs, there is no limit on the cost of these fixes. This is why the claim that poor Ontarians won't lose their cars is just plain wrong. There are many who believe this no-limit pre-test inspection is why shops are willing to lay out $80,000 for testing dynamometers when they only get $20 of the $30 fee per test. And during the first summer of Drive Clean, another possible problem was exposed. The Automobile Protection Association conducted an undercover investigation of twenty such facilities, taking the same 1988 Pontiac Sunbird in for testing. Given that it had already passed inspection, they were surprised to find that it failed nine times, with scores that varied by as much as 800%. As well, the average bill suggested for repairs was over $500. If it wasn't for the preliminary inspection and faulty testing, shops really would have great trouble making money.

As well, there are questions as to whether or not testing personnel are well enough trained, or the public is simply being defrauded, as inconsistent results suggest owners are being cheated. Many people, even some shop owners, believe that qualified mechanics are conducting Drive Clean tests. This is often not so. The government requires a certified Drive Clean technician, not a mechanic. What many facilities have done is they have sent people with little-to-no mechanical qualifications to be certified by the Ministry, so they may conduct the tests while being paid minimum wage. For the shop owner, it only makes sense. Who would pay a mechanic $25 in wages for a half-hour test, plus $2 for test gases, only to get $20 from the test?

But even the main reason for having Drive Clean – to reduce air pollution – is now under question. Recent research shows that I/M programmes are actually ineffective at combatting automobile air pollution, The Environmental Protection Agency in the United States used a computer model to predict emission reductions from I/M programmes. It was this that Ontario used to predict Drive Clean's benefits, though the dubious gains of I/M were stated back as far as 1996. However, as more evidence came to light and the model was refined, it has suggested greatly lowered predicted emission reductions, to the point where the EPA no longer supports I/M as a method of reducing emissions. It is clear this point has not been lost on the Ontario Tories, yet the programme is expanding, not being cancelled or modified.

But the government continues to let on to the public that Drive Clean is improving air quality. By mid-2000, it was saying there had been a 6% cut in smog due to this programme. However, they have no way to prove that, and it would seem to be belied by the increasing number of days we face under smog alerts. It is another example of the Big Lie. Keep telling people Drive Clean is a good idea because it helps the environment and they will keep paying. Tell them that estimates now suggest virtually no difference is being made by the programme and they will get uppity, just as they did with photo radar. A tax by any other name would smell as bad.

And Drive Clean is little more than a tax for the province and federal governments, and a bonanza for a few garages. It does very little to improve our quality of air – which was supposed to be the point – but is about to bring the province significant revenue. Between its inception and 5 July 2001, "Drive Clean caused 410,000 repairs to be made, bringing approximately $120 million to repair garages ... (and) $10 million from repair sales taxes into provincial coffers and a similar amount for the federal government ... (in GST)."[23] It is estimated, once the programme expands next year to include the owners of 5.7 million cars, the provincial government will collect $155 million per year in fees and sales taxes for parts and service. As a comparison, photo radar took in $19 million.

If the government was serious about reducing air pollution, it would close the coal-fired electricity plants, which spew an increasing amount of pollutants into the air each year. Reports have said that switching three coal-fired plants to natural gas would cut air pollution the same amount as taking every car off the roads in the Toronto area. Imagine what closing them all down would mean.

As for cars and trucks, vehicle worthiness inspections would be much more useful than Drive Clean. These would get at the fundamental problems much more so than this programme. First, unsafe vehicles could be removed from the road entirely and those that are marginal could be repaired before deteriorating too much. Second, those deemed "gross polluters" – a vehicle emitting visible smoke for 15 seconds during a five minute test – could be fined and repairs made. Third, it would not be a tax applied to those who have done nothing wrong. As a writer in *The Toronto Star* put it, it's like the police ticketing every car owner $30, even though only 15% are breaking the law.[24]

The environment has been a weak point for the Tories. There is little doubt that they under-estimated its importance from the very beginning. Though decades of polling has shown people want to save the environment, it is only at high levels when the economy is good. When prospects decline, most feel it is more important to have a job than a clean environment. The Tories came to power when times were tough. Though they themselves saw environmental regulation as bureaucratic job security that was killing jobs for most, they also understood that people would accept cuts to get more jobs. What they didn't understand was that undermining it too far would lead to illness and death, and that is never acceptable.

It is my opinion that, had the water in Walkerton not been tainted, the Harrisites would have continued on in the direction of allowing the private sector to move more and more into delivery of such services. On the day the terms of reference were issued for the public inquiry, 14 June, Municipal Affairs' minister Tony Clement stated that the privatization of water delivery should be explored, as should all local services except police and fire. He said this was simply a matter of seeing how services could be better delivered for less money. The fact there was to be an inquiry was irrelevant, as was public opinion on the issue. By January, the Premier had his old friend David Lindsay, now President of SuperBuild, looking into possible private partnerships to run water and sewer systems. Had it not been for this tragedy, given this government's predilection for favouring business interests, it is quite likely they would have contracted these out already. As it is, should Clement, or one of his ilk, ever become Premier, it is probably just a matter of time before they contract out being an MPP.

4. Everything is run better by the private sector

In the 1960s and '70s, the Ontario Tory government decided to make nuclear power the base of electrical generation in the province. It was seen as a *clean*, plentiful alternative to coal and oil. However, while it didn't result in black plumes of smoke, it did create radioactive waste and it was very expensive. But with the national government pushing its CANDU reactors around the country and the world, it was believed costs would eventually come down.

When the Harris Tories came to power in 1995, they wanted to rid themselves of all or part of Ontario Hydro. It had not only built up a $38 billion debt, but it was a public monopoly, offensive to the neo-cons by being both public and a monopoly. However, if you wanted to sell it off, you had to convince the voters that this was a reasonable move. The obvious solution was to blame the massive debt on the fact it was publicly-owned and a monopoly.

The fact is that the $38 billion debt has nothing to do with that and everything to do with governments that refused to pass along the real costs of electrical power generation to the public. When the Tories chose atomic power, they chose the most expensive method, but they knew if they let rates rise to pay for the incredibly pricey nuclear plants, the public might well rebel. Instead, they simply let the Crown corporation run up its debt. This was true even for the Harrisites.

Ontario Hydro was founded on the axiom of *power at cost*. In this way, both individual and business consumers could benefit from the plentiful harvest of hydro-electric generation from places like Niagara Falls. The costs should have risen with nuclear development. When the Tories didn't let this happen, they ruined the utility, ran up an unnecessary debt, effectively lied to the public, and created the conditions for the Harris minions to wreak havoc.

Amongst the neo-conservative fans of the Harris Tories, there was much joy, and high expectations, when they were elected in 1995. The thought that someone might actually begin rolling back the tide of government expansion gave them no end of delight. And this *anti-government* government seemed ready to deliver. Part of the CSR stated their dedication to getting rid of government agencies or Crown corporations that they felt didn't need to be publicly-owned. Of course, from Mike Harris' talk during the election, it didn't sound like they thought any of these needed to be publicly-owned.

But the neo-cons quickly found themselves disappointed on this front. Though the government set up the Office of Privatization, which recommended many such sell-offs, when push came to shove, the Harris Cabinet found few actual possibilities. The Tories had mentioned TVOntario (TVO) and the Liquor Control Board (LCBO) as two prime candidates for sale but, upon investigation, their lustres were too dull and too bright, respectively.

Many old-time Tories, such as Bill Davis, worried that Harris would sell off TVO, Ontario's educational broadcaster. Davis had himself created it in 1970 while Minister of Education, and there was still a small segment of the party membership who would have been quite displeased had it been made private. It is clear that this attitude was communicated to the powers in the party. I would guess that this made it all the more tempting a target, as the right-wingers in charge of the Tory party seriously disliked their elder predecessors. It didn't help that many Conservative *apparatchiks* loathed TVO's flagship nighttime show, *Studio Two*. Many perceived it as openly hostile to the party and the government, as many commentators on the show were blunt in their criticisms of the Tories. Some questioned how a current events' show could be educational. Of course, it didn't help that host Steve Paikin earned almost twice what they did as MPPs.

However, there was a problem, as I see it. Who in the private sector would want an educational broadcaster with little chance of ever making money? TVO's mission is to educate Ontarians, especially children, on all matter of subjects. Even given changes to make it more commercial, the whole character of TVO would need to undergo serious re-branding.

For example, a typical Wednesday's schedule in August 2001 looked like this: 6:00AM Polka Dot Door; 6:30AM Teletubbies; 6:53AM Paper, Scissors, Glue; 7:00AM Arthur; 7:27AM Blue's Clues - Series III; 7:53AM The Hoobs; 8:25AM Mighty Machines; 8:22AM SAGWA, The Chinese Siamese Cat; 8:35AM Benjamin's Farm; 8:40AM Dream Street; 8:49AM The Wiggles; 9:11AM Maisy; 9:16AM Little Bear; 9:25AM Little Star III; 9:40AM P.B. Bear and Friends; 9:45AM Bear in the Big Blue House; 10:09AM Twinkle Toes; 10:14AM Simon In The Land Of Chalk Drawings; 10:24AM Polka Dot Shorts; 10:30AM Yoho Ahoy; 10:32AM The Adventures of Spot; 10:37AM A Child's Dream - Series 1; 10:40AM Animal Alphabet; 10:43AM Elliot Moose Short Animated; 10:55AM Thomas the Tank Engine and Friends; 11:03AM Timothy Goes to School; 11:17AM My Zoo; 11:22AM Fetch the Vet; 11:32AM Arthur; 12:00PM Zoboomafoo; 1:00PM More to Life; 2:00PM Studio 2; 3:00PM Dotto's Data Café; 3:30PM The Hoobs; 3:56PM Arthur; 4:23PM Rainbow Fish; 4:35PM Engineering '00; 4:35PM SAGWA, The Chinese Siamese Cat; 4:48PM The Magic School Bus; 5:14PM The Big Bang; 5:36PM Brilliant Creatures; 5:36PM Bod Squad; 6:06PM Space Cases; 7:00PM The Underground; 7:30PM Imprint; 8:00PM Studio 2; 9:00PM McCallum; 9:52PM E Shorts; 10:00PM Human Edge; 10:03PM Biker Dreams; 11:01PM Human Edge; 11:02PM Your Health; 11:30PM Studio 2; 12:30AM Saturday Night at the Movies: Best of Saturday Night at the Movies; 12:30AM Feature Films: Enchantment (1948); 2:12AM E

Shorts; 2:30AM The Global Family Series 8; 3:00AM Saints and Sinners:
The History of the Popes; 3:50AM Off Air.

It's basically kid's educational shows from morning to early evening, then
adult educational shows or British drama until midnight, then an old movie
and more adult educational shows until sign-off. For a private owner, it
would be unlikely you could revamp the station sufficiently to bring in
advertisers. After all, it is not the station's purview to show *Saturday
morning cartoons* 24-hours-a-day, 7-days-a-week. Even as of 1995, this
was the time when the Canadian Radio, Television-telecommunications
Commission (CRTC) was opening up the television dial to dozens of new
stations. Though some proposals for new stations were turned down due
to poor financing or competitive concerns, a great many succeeded in
being licensed, and the value of all independent stations must have
diminished. Cheaper to just apply to the CRTC for a new licence than buy
TVO and try to re-make it in a new image.

The LCBO was the opposite – business interests were lining up to buy into
a privatized operation. Annual liquor sales in Ontario are worth hundreds
of millions of dollars. As a result, many were pushing their government
friends to sell off the Crown corporation. Neo-con supporters also
supported this. Why should government be in liquor sales, when it could
easily, and more properly, be dealt with by market forces? As well, the
LCBO paid out handsome wages to unions. With privatization, this could
end, and booze prices could be cut.

But for the very reason the LCBO was a strong target of the private sector,
it was also a huge *cash cow* for the province. Public liquor sales earn the
Ontario government over a billion dollars a year[25], too much to just let go
of. As well, Alberta had privatized their liquor board a few years earlier,
and the consequences were not encouraging. As a public entity, alcohol
could be purchased on a large scale at considerable discounts due to
volume. Once the system went private, with multiple small owners,
volume discounts disappeared and prices increased. Tack on a profit
margin, and Albertans were paying significantly higher prices for their
liquor. As well, selection diminished, as this would have added to cost.
And just to add water to the wine, so to speak, crimes around the *corner
stores* now selling booze went up, as they were not perceived as being as
well-protected. Consumers and the Crown treasury paid the price for
alcohol privatization.

Some observers used the government's failure to privatize liquor sales as a
sign they were more pragmatic than they outwardly seemed. However, it

might be fairer to say that a government strapped for revenues wasn't about to easily let go of a *money machine* so geared to profit. Not until the economy had turned around, at least.[26]

However, the Harris Conservatives were striking out on the road of privatization. As I said earlier regarding the Andersen Consulting exercise, the NDP government had actually blazoned the way for public-private partnerships. Perhaps because it was later in their term that they actually picked up on this line of thinking, they really only brought off one such relationship. That was controversial deal for the building of Highway 407.

The New Democrats were looking for any way to make a dent in the unemployment rate. A mega-project would have been the traditional route but, of course, there was no money for huge investments. However, if the private sector could be brought in to do the actual work, there would be no need for up-front provincial cash. In Ontario, when one thinks infrastructure, one means highway construction.

The idea of a highway to cut across the *top* of Toronto had been floating around for many years. Highway 7 had served that function for a long time, but was now so built-up and fragmented by traffic lights that it was little better than one of the major east-west corridors downtown. Allowing the freer movement of traffic seemed something few would oppose. But that wasn't entirely true. While unions might be pleased about these new jobs, environmentalists were less than impressed. (And then there were those like me who understand transportation studies well enough to know that "if you build it, they will come". New highways don't alleviate traffic congestion, they make it worse.) Though there was already a plan in place to build the 407, this scheme would not see the new road finished until 2035. Speeding it up with the help of the private sector would create jobs right away.

It took a little time, but the government was able to put together a consortium of private sector interests willing to finance and build the new route. The cost to the public was to be tolls to pay off the $1.5 billion cost but, with payments spread out over 30 years, many raised eyebrows slipped back into place. As the Premier loved to point out, after that, the province would own a paid-off highway with another 70 years of life. Tolls would be collected by monitoring devices that would pick up a transponder signal from each regular user, or photographs would identify the licence plates of occasional users, though they would pay an extra fee for not having a transponder. The further one drove on the highway, the more one would pay.

However, the Rae government would not be around to see the fruition of its deal. By the time its first section opened on Saturday, 7 June 1997, Tory Transportation minister Al Palladini got to be on hand for the ribbon cutting.

The Tories almost immediately got a *bright* idea. Their re-election campaign was not many months down the road, and though the economy was rebounding wonderfully, a little extra cash for spending promises might just be what the spin doctor ordered to turn around the polls that showed potential defeat in the offing. Instead of keeping the 407 as a public highway, as the NDP had planned, sell it off for a big cash infusion. Yes, it would mean the first permanent toll road in Ontario, but privatization was something they wanted and had not delivered to any extent.

A new deal was made with the consortium, and announced just three weeks before the election. The private group would lease the 407 for 99 years at a price of $3.1 billion. The government would continue to police it and punish those who didn't pay their tolls by suspending drivers' licenses. The Tories sold it as a tremendous deal for the taxpayers, given the honking big profit of $1.6 billion.

But trouble soon came the government's way. Though the consortium was to directly collect their tolls, mistakes in billing and a constantly busy telephone meant they were reporting delinquent payers to the government who weren't delinquent. Instead, they were people who were over-charged, or had never used the highway, who could not get through to straighten out their bills. At first, the Tories warned the company to shape up. When the problems continued, the government bent to pressure and announced it would no longer suspend licenses.

Over time, however, things quietened, and the government permitted the consortium to raise its tolls, not once, twice or even three times. The fourth increase in 27 months was announced the first week of December 2001, to take place at the new year. From 8:00AM to midnight, rates would go from 11ø to 11.5ø per kilometre. From midnight to 8:00AM, the increase would be 6ø to 11.5ø. The latest Transportation minister, Brad Clark, was succinct in his comments. If users didn't like the hike, they could go back to the "free" highways. But the Minister also said that the government would again suspend licenses, based on his belief the problems had been worked out (though an arbitration process has yet to be completed). It also came out shortly afterward that if the company sees certain thresholds met, they will be allowed to set tolls to any amount they wish.

For critics, these increases went against the whole spirit of the lease. The highway was supposed to be affordable for ordinary commuters to use. Every fee hike made it more a route for the rich than for Average Joe. If one drove 50 kilometres, one way, to work on Highway 407, it was now going to cost the car driver $2,875 per year (assuming only one trip per day, five days a week, 50 weeks a year). Of course, the driver has free will. There are, after all, the 'free' highways. Personally, I hope the tolls go up to $100 a kilometre. Soon, no one would use it and the taxpayers could pick up the highway in bankruptcy for a few cents on the dollar.

However, the consortium now faces a problem of significant magnitude. Highway 407 users are launching a class-action law suit against them for, effectively, usury. If drivers using the highway fail to pay their bill within 90 days, they are charged a $30 late fee, regardless of the size of the bill. In one case, that was a 300,000% interest rate, and 60% is the maximum allowed by law. If the courts certify the suit, it could potentially cost the consortium millions of dollars. It is a controversial lawsuit, though not as controversial as the highway lease.

The CSR had mentioned another target for possible privatization. Ontario Hydro was a 'barrier to growth' to be removed.

A 5 year freeze will be placed on Hydro rates to give consumers, employers and industries guaranteed stability in planning their budgets. This may mean more changes at Hydro including some moves towards privatization of non-nuclear assets. The current Hydro Chairman has already begun to lead this huge corporation back in the right direction. We will work with him, and many others, to bring Hydro back to its proper role, providing reliable and affordable electrical power to Ontario.

Yet nothing was seemingly happening on this front, either. Initially, Energy was combined with the Environment in one department, and ministers Brenda Elliott and Norm Sterling appeared to have spent all their time slicing away at staff and regulation. It wasn't until the Ministry was split and Energy became Energy, Science, and Technology that action stirred.

Seemingly out of nowhere, the new minister, Jim Wilson, now demoted from Health, presented a White Paper, *Direction for Change: Charting a Course for Competitive Electricity and Jobs in Ontario* in November 1997. It announced that the government had decided to split up Ontario Hydro into five parts, sell off two of those, and deregulate the whole industry. This was not just going to apply to non-nuclear assets, but to the whole utility. Of deregulation, he said, "Customers stand to benefit most with greater choice, lower prices, and a safe and reliable power system".

This was at least somewhat disingenuous of Wilson, however. When the *Energy Competition Act* was presented in June 1998, Bill Farlinger, the Harris advisor who had been appointed Hydro chairman shortly after they took power, said that lower prices were anything but guaranteed. "Nobody really knows what the price of power is going to be when competition comes in. History will tell us price goes down but that's a leap of faith really." Regardless, the Minister insisted competition had been "a recipe (for lower prices) in every other jurisdiction".

The legislation set out these changes. Ontario Hydro's successor companies are Ontario Power Generation Inc., which owns and operates the power generation facilities, and Hydro One (which was originally called Ontario Hydro Services Company), which owns and operates transmission, distribution and retail businesses. As well, three others were created but, unlike the other two, these are publicly-owned. The Independent Electricity Market Operator is responsible for establishing a wholesale electricity market and for ensuring fair and open access to the transmission system by all utilities. The installation and inspection of electrical equipment is now the responsibility of the Electrical Safety Authority. These two are organized as non-profit corporations. And the Ontario Electricity Financial Corporation, a Crown agency, is to wind down Ontario Hydro's existing guaranteed debt and liabilities.

Essentially, privatization/deregulation will make the system of electricity purchasing infinitely more complicated. Before, you purchased your power from the municipal utility where you lived or Ontario Hydro, if there wasn't a municipal utility. That was it. Rates were set by the Ontario Energy Board (OEB), and the user paid per kilowatt hour. The new system will be much different.

Now, consumers will purchase electricity from any of the competing licensed retailers, who will re-sell what they buy in bulk on the market or from Hydro One at the rate of the Standard Supply Service, which is the market rate. This market rate will be determined by the buying and selling of electricity on the *spot market*, which works much like the commodities' market. The price will be made up of three elements: the cost of actually delivering the power; a charge for paying down the old Ontario Hydro debt; and, the amount the retailer wants for the electricity. The first two are set by the OEB. It is only the last part that will vary. This is the competitive portion of the bill.

Hydro One will offer this part at the rate of the Standard Supply Service. Though the competitive market has not yet opened, as of November 2001, the SSS is set at 3.8ø per kWh. The few retailers listing prices are offering their rates as 5.65-5.95ø per kWh. If the market opens like this, it would appear to be a no-brainer to go with Hydro One. The risk is that the market price will rise and fall precipitously. Businesses will find it difficult to predict their power costs, and they and individuals may find their bills spike in times of heavy demand. This is particularly true because this price will be determined on the spot market. A particularly hot hour or two on one day in summer could see prices quadruple that entire day's price. In other words, if this competitive portion rockets up to 15ø per kWh, the consumer will be charged that for the whole day, even if heightened consumption only lasts a few minutes. However, this SSS price will be annualized. That is, a consumer will pay based on the estimate that power will be 3.8ø per kWh. Even if this increased to 15ø for the entire month of July, the end-of-year cost would be about 4.7ø, still well beneath the what retailers are offering.

On the other hand, the re-sellers' prices are based on one-to-five year contracts. For the penalty of paying a higher-than-standard price, the consumer benefits by avoiding the prices spikes brought on by heavy demand. Which of these two possibilities would work out to less will entirely depend on hot and cold days and nights. However, as an added wrinkle, these private re-sellers also have clauses in their contracts that permit them to charge an unspecified monthly service fee with 30 days notice. In other words, to some extent, costing for consumers will be a crap shoot.[27]

But a question had weighed heavily in anticipation of this deregulation. *What of Hydro's $38 billion debt?* Why would anyone want to buy into a utility that owed so much money? The simple answer is *no one does*.

Explaining the finances of this new arrangement is where most people's eyes glaze over. The difficulty is that it hasn't been in the government's best interest to make an explanation that's particularly clear. Voters/ratepayers might get upset.

The *Energy Competition Act* was enacted in November 1998 and the restructuring took effect as of 1 April 1999. At that time, Ontario Power Generation's assets were set at $8.5 billion, made up of $5.1 billion in equity and a debt of $3.4 billion. Hydro One's assets were valued at $8.6 billion, with $3.8 billion in equity and $4.8 billion in debt. This left the matter of *stranded debt*. This is defined as "the portion of Ontario Hydro's existing guaranteed debt and liabilities that cannot be serviced by the new commercial companies and by dedicated revenue streams"[28]. That is, if you take the combined worth of OPG and Hydro One, and subtract Ontario Hydro's debt of $38 billion, you get the stranded debt, or $20.9 billion. The critics of these evaluations were muted only because of the complexity of the calculations.

Where had these numbers come from ... ones that seemed ludicrous, as nuclear power plants were assessed as being worth nothing. In fact, the entire generating capacity of Ontario Hydro – three nuclear plants, 69 hydro plants, 8 fossil-fuel plants – was assessed at a mere $5 billion. Darlington had cost $10 billion a decade earlier. I don't think they depreciate that fast. The logic behind this number was never disclosed.

The accuracy of the valuations notwithstanding, the Tories could not have made them too high. The higher the assessment as to worth, the higher the sale price of any of these facilities. While that might have seemed good for Ontarians, it would make it more difficult for the government to divest itself of the old Ontario Hydro. And just to add more incentive for the private sector to pick up these *garage sale goodies*, consumers have been left to pay off the stranded debt. An extra amount is added per kilowatt hour as a debt charge which all users must pay. The new private companies have no responsibility for this, whatsoever.

Though the Harris government has claimed many suitors have expressed interest in buying into Ontario's power plants, only one has consummated the relationship. In July 2000, British Energy, through a new subsidiary called Bruce Power Inc., leased the Bruce nuclear facility for 18 years at a cost of $3.1 billion. The deal meant Bruce Power would pay the province $400 million up-front, then $225 million will be paid in equal installments at four and six years, along with annual cheques for $62-$92 million. The rest will come through variable payments, depending on market conditions. Most commentators thought the deal was good, though it was next-to-impossible to tell if the British company was paying a fair price, and OPG is still ultimately responsible for decommissioning costs once it comes time to retire the facility. And while they wanted the *down payment* to go against the stranded debt, the Minister suggested part of it would likely go against OPG's debt instead.

Was this a good deal? Evidence in July 2000 was spotty. It is less so now. Recently, the State of Vermont stopped the sale of one of its oldest and smallest nuclear plants to a British Energy consortium because they weren't paying enough. In the end, the new buyer paid twice as much, agreed to capping rates until the year 2012, and will keep on all staff at current salary and benefits. Not in Ontario you say? Pity!

Bruce Power is leasing its facility for about one-tenth what similar-sized American facilities have gone for.[29] And, after bringing two Bruce "A" reactors back on-line, it will operate the six with one-third fewer staff than are working at the four reactors now running. In effect, that's a 125% increase in responsibility for staff by 2007.

The government seemed to have three models for their deregulation of hydro: a trend in other countries, especially the United States; the natural gas market in the 1980s; and, long-distance telephone service. The reality was not nearly so much fun as the fantasy, however. As time has passed, the natural gas market has seen significant price hikes, and many of the re-sellers have turned out to be less than honest in their dealings with consumers. High long-distance charges on phone calls were cut by stiff competition, yet people's bills have more than doubled. Long-distance subsidized local rates and kept bills down. Now, we are on the threshold of local phone competition. The result is that urban areas, with significant local activity in a small geographic area will see a slight rise in costs, while rural areas with lower activity and little economy-of-scale in infrastructure will see significant hikes. Paying for basic phone service is slipping beyond the ability of many of the poor. Wait for hydro.

Initially, the competitive electricity market was to have opened in November 2000, but this was delayed for six months when it was clear no utilities were going to be ready. When it was even more obvious that was pie-in-the-sky, too, the tentative date was put off until May 2002. Given time, the government focused its message. This marketplace will be based on four principles.

1. *Protecting consumers and offering more choice. A competitive market will, over the long term, offer the lowest possible costs and lead to better service and value for customers.*
2. *Creating a strong business climate with a reliable supply of safe, affordable electricity.*
3. *Protecting our environment.*

4. *Encouraging new ways of doing business and supporting the search for alternate sources of power.* (Source: Ministry of Energy, Science, and Technology.)

While the second point is undoubtedly the reason the Harrisites have gone to all this trouble – cheaper rates for their private sector friends – it seems that even this is far from assured by the redesigned system. There were some who suggested that, if Wilson was so sure deregulation would mean cheaper rates, he should enshrine it in legislation by either forcing private sellers to offer power at lower rates or by giving consumers a guaranteed provincial subsidy should it turn out rates went up. On several occasions, the Minister said this wasn't necessary and reiterated rates would go down.

As was now becoming all too common for the Minister, the veracity of his pronouncements didn't last. By the time the 1999 election had come and gone, and Wilson had been re-elected, he changed his tune. Now, rates would likely go up, but by less than they would have otherwise ... a claim impossible to prove. To this day, the public does not seem overly aware of the consequences of these changes, though the government certainly has slowed implementation, perhaps hoping that time will bring better days. It is only in the past few weeks, as we close in on the opening of the competitive market, that the media has finally latched onto the frightening possibilities.

I won't deny I have been a big critic of this move. Right from the beginning it seemed like folly and, given that Wilson is the sitting MPP in my riding, I was determined to try and get it on the agenda as a local election issue in 1999. Given the plethora of things to criticize, however, it did not catch on.

But I have persisted. This is an exchange of letters between the Minister and myself, as submitted to the Thornbury newspaper, the *Courier-Herald*, in May 2001, to show a number of the issues and the two different views of hydro restructuring.

Letter to the Editor:

One of the greatest threats looming over Ontario is electrical power deregulation, and we, in this area, should be very concerned, as our local MPP, Jim Wilson, is the Minister of Energy and the voice behind this change. In 1998, he announced that Ontario was entering a new era of electricity generation and distribution, as Ontario Hydro was to be split up and partially privatized. Consumers were promised "greater choice, lower prices, and a safe and reliable power supply".

*However, we are only on the cusp of this 'new era' and already Mr.
Wilson's words ring hollow.*

*Ontario Hydro has been divided into five new companies. Now instead
of having one public monopoly that was to produce 'power at cost' for
Ontarians, we have a hydro hydra that controls 90% of the power and
has no legal loyalty to consumers here, just to profit for their
stockholders. And though British Energy has chosen to lease the Bruce
nuclear power plant, the conditions were so beneficial that they don't
have to pay one cent of its debt. The taxpayers are still on the hook for
that. So much for more choice.*

*This type of deregulation has been brought to such places as Alberta,
California, and New York. In Alberta, hydro bills have doubled. In
California, rolling black-outs and brown-outs have become common,
causing economic instability and sky-rocketing prices. In New York,
officials now want to restructure their system, as costs continue to rise.
Mr. Wilson has said we will not face these troubles. California and
Alberta did not have sufficient supply of electricity to meet demand, and
we have a healthy supply. However, in 1999, Ontario Hydro had to
invoke a brown-out due to low supply. In fact, in California, supply
had been estimated as being 30% above demand before deregulation.
In Ontario, it's just 15% now.*

*We were supposed to get lower prices for electricity. However, now
even Jim Wilson admits prices will be rise due to "upward pressure
globally". Yet 'pressure' appears relative. Already 13 major
industrial users have been guaranteed lower prices in long-term
contracts. This leaves individual Ontarians to bear the brunt of any
increases.*

*In the United States, electricity is purchased from private companies.
In Detroit, consumers are paying 175% of what Ontarians pay and
that's with regulation. Is a private owner of our electrical generating
stations going to sell to us at 8ø per kilowatt hour or to them at 14ø?
Who would you sell to, when you're supposed to be trying to maximize
your company's profit? In other words, our supply will drop, perhaps
by a great deal, until our prices rise, probably by a great deal.*

*The Harris government's position? Stay the course, things are mostly
fine. Deregulation is coming. As well, the moratorium on selling off
the dirty, air-polluting, coal-fired plants is to end. And even though
one of these plants must convert to gas or close by 2004, the others will*

be allowed to increase the amount of pollutants they spew. In other words, in exchange for a slightly higher supply of power, Ontario residents and all of our neighbours can expect more smog and more illness and death because of respiratory diseases.

It is time for Wilson and his Tory brethren to recognize deregulation means guaranteed price hikes for consumers, guaranteed lower supply as we provision the insatiable American economy, and guaranteed profit for big business at the cost of ordinary people. Maybe they should look back to Adam Beck, the man who was the force behind the creation of Ontario Hydro, who believed that the people of Ontario should benefit from this huge natural resource, with power at cost. Oh, by the way, Beck was a Conservative, too.

Byron Montgomery

* * * * *

Editor,

Byron Montgomery's letter to the editor of May 2, 2001. "Electrical deregulation a threat", is misinformed and does not provide an accurate view of the government's initiative for restructuring the electricity industry.

Under the previous monopoly-based electricity system, the former Ontario Hydro had a debt of $38 billion while the average price of electricity in Ontario went from one of the lowest in Canada to the third highest. The Energy Competition Act is about eliminating an electricity system that was ineffective while instituting a system that provides consumers with choice.

Competition imposes cost discipline on electricity providers and encourages savings, new ideas and innovations. With customer service choice, competition will also promote demand for cleaner or green energy such as solar and wind power.

Ontario is not California. Recent price increases in California and Alberta were not a result of introducing competition. They were due to inadequate supply during a period of sustained and rapid growth in demand.

In Ontario, the Independent Electricity Market Operator (IMO) has *forecast that the province has excess supply and generation resources adequate to meet current demand. The IMO forecast does not include $3 billion in new generation, representing almost 3,000 megawatts, proposed by private investors. Nor does it include Bruce Power's announcement that it intends to restart two units at the Bruce A nuclear generating station. This will provide an additional 1,500 MW in generating capacity.*

The recent media focus on price hikes in California and Alberta has overshadowed the success of restructuring in other jurisdictions where electricity consumers have enjoyed reductions in power prices. In Pennsylvania, consumers are enjoying reductions of five to 15 per cent in there (sic) electricity bills. In Sweden, the price of the electricity commodity has decreased by approximately 40 per cent. In the UK, consumers savings are estimated to be £750 million per year, which is equivalent to about $1.7 billion per year in Canadian dollars. And in the Australian State of Victoria, it is estimated that market reforms have resulted in declines in the average real price of 24 per cent since 1981.

On the matter of electricity exports, U.S. customers will have no special rights to Ontario electricity under our restructuring plan. They will have to bid into the Ontario market in order to buy electricity and will be limited in the amount they can take by transmission limits. There are only 4,000 megawatts of transmission capacity between Ontario and its neighbours. That means less than 20 per cent of Ontario's electricity supply can be exported at any time.

Regarding industrial customers of electricity, the special rates they have had for almost a decade are being phased out over two to four years. Ontario Power Generation will forgo revenue and net income to ensure that other customers will not subsidize special industrial rates during the transition to market rates.

Our government's plan for opening the electricity market to competition is based on four key principles: protecting consumers and giving them more choice, ensuring a strong business climate with a reliable supply, protecting our environment and encouraging both new ways of doing business and new sources of power. We believe that the principles guiding our vision will be fully met by May 2002.

Clearly, we must ensure that Ontario's electricity supply remains safe and reliable, that prices remain competitive and that consumers get the best deal possible. A competitive market, once the excesses of the past have been eliminated, will produce this result.

I trust that this information will be helpful to your readers.

Jim Wilson
MPP, Simcoe-Grey
Minister of Energy, Science and Technology

* * * * *

Dear Editor:

I congratulate Jim Wilson, MPP, and Minister of Energy, on his quick response to my letter, 'Electrical deregulation a threat', 2 May. It is unfortunate, however, he felt the need to say I am 'misinformed' and 'not providing an accurate view of the government's initiative'. Indeed, I would suggest his letter is the attempt at spin-doctoring reality.

First, Mr. Wilson suggests the old system was ineffective and expensive, piling up a $38 billion debt. What he fails to mention is that it was Tory governments who chose to pursue expensive nuclear power and, then, wouldn't permit the utility to pass these costs along to consumers. Perhaps had we known the cost, we might have rejected nuclear power and not voted Conservative? In fact, Mr. Wilson's government continued an NDP rate freeze that delayed paying the Ontario Hydro debt. Nowadays, his view does seem to have changed, as he wants rate increases to pay this debt back faster!

Second, Mr. Wilson says the Independent Electricity Market Operator has forecast an excess of supply, and new electricity generation is planned. These two "truths" were also predicted in California before deregulation. Unfortunately, supply quickly vanished and private investors didn't build new generation. Demand for electricity is fairly inelastic, that is, it doesn't change appreciably. Homes must be heated in winter and cooled in summer. As a result, price does not change except when severe cold or hot weather causes spikes in consumption. In a supply and demand system, when demand increases, supply is supposed to increase to keep these prices steady and competitive. However, in California, electricity suppliers found that NOT increasing supply when demand increased caused prices, and their profits, to skyrocket. This, in turn, did not decrease demand much, as homes must be heated and cooled. Deregulation caused the market to fail consumers.

Third, Mr. Wilson suggests prices have dropped in many jurisdictions that have restructured, such as Pennsylvania, the United Kingdom, and Australia. What he fails to mention is that this includes corporate manufacturers that have signed long-term agreements at vastly reduced prices. What does the average person actually save? In Pennsylvania, electricity restructuring took full effect this past January and, already, suppliers are applying for hundreds of millions of dollars of rate increases.

Fourth, Mr. Wilson is correct in saying that the United States has no special rights to our electricity. They are limited to 20% of our supply, simply by the lack of transmission lines. Of course, that ignores that some U.S. border states are paying as much as twice what we pay for electricity, so unless private producers are patriotic or incompetent, they will build new transmission capacity to the States. As well, Mr. Wilson fails to recognize that, under the North American Free Trade Agreement, we are required to sell power to the United States as though its consumers are Canadian. We cannot turn them down as long as they offer the market price. That means you can count on that 20% limit being maximized until new lines are constructed, when our prices will rise to their market levels.

Finally, Mr. Wilson says favoured industrial rates are being phased out. However, there's nothing to stop the private electricity suppliers from making these deals and, thus, tie up supply with enormous industrial users. That would still mean higher rates for individual consumers.

I might also suggest Mr. Wilson check out his own Ministry's numbers. It lists a reference price, the Standard Supply Service, for the competitive portion of your hydro bill. Presently, it stands at 4.2ø/kWh. Yet according to listings by private suppliers, they are offering 3-5 year fixed rates of 5.79-5.95ø/kWh. That's 38-42% higher. For this long-term rate to benefit consumers, it means day-to-day hydro prices must rise more than 42%.

I hear Mr. Wilson is looking for job opportunities in the private sector. One can only hope he's not hired for his math skills. Perhaps public relations? He spins a good yarn.

Byron Montgomery

The Energy minister makes many points in his letter. However, time and review are showing some are less than accurate. Prices will rise, but moreso than Wilson lets on. A Merrill Lynch report on the coming system says that Ontario rates will rise to American rates, once private companies begin to compete. As to the Minister's statement that only so much power can go to the States, that will increase, too. Hydro One and Transenergie U.S., a subsidiary of Hydro-Québec, have applied to build an electrical transmission cable under Lake Erie. With a 975 megawatt capacity, it would be capable of sending enough energy to the United States to power 975,000 average homes, or 975,000 fewer Ontario and Quebec homes.

Speaking to Wilson's point that Ontario Hydro had accumulated a debt of $38 billion while the average price of electricity rose substantially, the reasons hardly call for privatization as a solution. The Peterson Liberals had opposed building the Darlington nuclear plant in Opposition and, upon taking power, inherited it about half done and chose to let it be finished, rather than waste the $6 billion that had already gone into it. Then, the Rae New Democrats chose not to pass along the cost of this plant to consumers because it would have meant annual double-digit rate increases.[30] This violated the premise Hydro was supposed to exist under, *power at cost*. The fact that the Davis Tories had chosen nuclear power, the most expensive option, was a decision for which they would never have to pay. In its early days, the NDP attempted to pass along some of Darlington's cost, with rate hikes that added up to about 30%. However, in short order, they lost their nerve and froze rates. So when the Harris Conservatives were elected and began to claim that this debt was because Ontario Hydro was an irresponsible public monopoly, they were being less than truthful. In fact, they had made the situation worse by continuing the NDP freeze on rates.

As well, there was the question of supply. In Ontario, supply had remained static after Darlington came on-line, yet demand increased somewhat over the 1990s. That is until Bruce "A" was shut down in August 1997, after a damning report suggested Ontario Hydro's nuclear plants were being run at "minimally acceptable" levels. Hydro chair Bill Farlinger announced seven reactors would be closed to focus on the newer ones at Bruce "B", the final two of which were closed in March 1998. That removed seven reactors from service, and made servicing demand more difficult. As a result, OPG fired up its coal-burning plants to make up the difference. The result is sufficient power, but at the cost of significantly dirtier air, as I mentioned earlier.

On Thursday, 13 December 2001, Premier Harris announced that

electricity competition would go ahead as of 1 May 2002. This is despite
the fact that 43 of 94 local utilities have informed the OEB they will not be
ready. As well, Hydro One will be sold through a public offering, which
estimates suggest will bring in up to $10 billion, making it the largest IPO
in Canadian history. Harris promised that any money raised will go
directly to paying down the stranded debt. (Of course, he won't be around
to keep the promise.) Suddenly, and probably a little too late, great
concern has been expressed as to the apocalyptic possibilities.

Those who oppose hydro deregulation have a small voice, at best. The
NDP has been the core for criticism, but coming from such a tiny group, it
resonates little. I am at odds with my own party on this one. On a number
of occasions, the Liberal caucus in the Legislature has voted with the
government to make changes to our electricity sector and to stop debate of
these changes. And while the party is now opposing the sale of Hydro
One, it is supporting the break-up of OPG. Personally, I am at a loss to
understand their desire to go along with alleged reforms that have failed
miserably in other jurisdictions, and are changes that Liberal polling
indicates are opposed by the public by better than a 3-1 margin[31]. I know
of few other Liberal members who support the change. Quite the opposite.

To me, this is an issue that clearly demonstrates both the government's
ideological bent and its pandering to commercial interests, who now see
the opportunity to make easy profits. But, moreso, it also shows that
elected representatives are supposed to actually oversee the work of Crown
corporations. At any time, had MPPs actually taken on the responsibility
to see that Ontario Hydro was supplying power at cost, and doing so
responsibly, including considering alternatives to nuclear power, the
dubious administration of Ontario Hydro and its unthinking allegiance to
nuclear power could have been avoided. Sadly, none did to any great
extent.

But the move to ending the hydro monopoly has not gone without pain. In
fact, I think it's safe to say that the Tories got caught with their pants down
in one area of this deregulation. Privatization applied to municipally-
owned utilities as well as Ontario Hydro. That is, these utilities would
cease to be municipal departments and would be spun off as private
companies. As a result, municipalities could continue to own them or they
could sell them. Many chose to sell to the highest bidder, to cover costs of
capital improvements or to get funds to make up for losses from
downloading. Some of the utilities simply bought up other utilities,
creating larger businesses over larger areas, with far too many selling out
to Hydro One. What the province failed to consider was that, once

privatized, these municipal operators would actually begin to act like private companies.

Privatized utilities were to be allowed to apply for rate increases. Though Toronto Hydro was still public, local politicians saw the chance to bring in extra revenue, presumably while making it seem the restructuring was to blame. So the utility applied to the Ontario Energy Board for a 6% rate hike. In short order, other utilities did the same, with proposals for hikes of up to 17%. The government saw it had opened a door, and the Minister chose to shut it quickly.

Wilson had promised rates would go down under a new system and, even if it hadn't taken effect, he wasn't about to let these others embarrass him. He introduced legislation to stop the hikes, and ordered the OEB to make "consumer protection" its main priority until the new law had taken effect. Unfortunately for Torontonians, it was too late to stop the energy board from approving the city increase.

As well, Wilson accused many municipalities of raiding their utilities. Since they were going to be privatized, it made sense to exorcise them of any financial surpluses, and Ontario's municipal utilities had $1 billion in such surpluses. The Minister said this money should be used in "holding down rates". Municipal leaders probably felt a private utility would be just as likely to turn the surpluses into shareholder dividends. Nevertheless, the province didn't stop the practice, and it only got worse once privatization took effect.

Municipalities began to vacuum money out of their utilities. Instead of just taking surpluses, they began set up funds from which cash payments would be made to the owner municipality in the form of debt for the utilities. Once the competitive market opens, they will be free to absorb this revenue. Toronto plans to take $980 million from its utility, Hamilton $137 million from its, and Mississauga $270 million, with another $20 million to the utility's partner, the Ontario Municipal Employees Retirement System. An Energy Probe estimate suggests as much as $7 billion could be extracted by municipalities province-wide. The obvious result of this will be higher prices for ratepayers.

Further to this, when OPG was set up it supplied about 80-85% of all electricity consumed in Ontario. Given that this kind of dominant control would hardly further competition, the government ordered that the company would have to divest itself of sufficient production to get down to no more than 35% of this within ten years. This was presumably to force some level of competition on the generation side. At the same time, in an apparent contradiction to this philosophy, many municipalities that chose to sell off their local utilities were permitted to sell them to Hydro One, actually increasing its dominant retail market position.

The win-win situation laid out for Ontarians regarding deregulated/privatized electricity is little more than a sham. The rationale for government to privatize is this: because private companies are geared to making profit, they must be efficient, whereas government faces no such demand. Therefore, if a service being offered by government doesn't absolutely have to be delivered by government, the public would receive more effective and efficient service-delivery by the private sector. This is based on two premises. The first is that business must be efficient. The second is that certain services don't have to be delivered by government.

The reality seems much different. *Business must be efficient.* If the last ten years or so have proven anything, it is that this statement is definitely not true. A simple example is Enron, the American energy monolith. Though it appeared to be one of the most successful power companies in the world, it was in fact built on lies, with questionable accounting practices and overblown profit statements. I use this as an example because Enron Canada was one of the businesses that, at one time, expressed interest in buying into the Ontario hydro system.

Certain services don't have to be delivered by government. That being the case, why did government begin delivering them in the first place? A hallmark of capitalism is that if a profit is to be made delivering a service, business will step in to supply it. Exactly right ... 'if a profit is to be made'. A few examples of where the private sector wasn't going to make money: widespread public electrical service, so Ontario Hydro was created for the advantage of individuals and, even moreso, business; the delivery of mail to addresses across Canada, so Canada Post was established; rail lines throughout Canada, so the Canadian National Railway was set up. These were enterprises that were seen as needed, but the private sector was either not interested because there was no profit to be made (e.g. Ontario Hydro, Canada Post), or they had shown that they were unable to make a profit with them (e.g. CNR). That's not to say that this condition is forever constant. CNR was eventually sold off because it was seen as something that could exist privately and make a profit. The Harris government determined that Ontario Hydro was also in this position. Unfortunately for taxpayers in Ontario, private profit can be exploitive. And the proof is that some 20 American states have now *stopped* their moves to deregulate because of massive price *increases*.

All this raises another point, which is ... is the service to be delivered in the public interest? If yes, does this override the logic of private sector involvement? In the case of the CNR, there was some gnashing of teeth as to whether or not it still operated more because of the public interest or just as a leftover of a bygone era. The fact that hundreds of short-line, unprofitable rails were shut down before it was sold off to private interests probably answers the question best of all. No private companies wanted it had they been required to assume this dead weight. The *discipline of the market* wouldn't have allowed it. Lines were closed, the CNR went private, and many farmers, manufacturers, and some of the public lost their ability to travel by rail.

The situation of Ontario Hydro is somewhat different. Because it had always acted as a sole monopoly, it had never faced any competition. And unlike a hundred years ago, the private sector now saw profit in supplying electric power to the public, probably because technology has improved sufficiently to mean they can make money at it. However, is it in the public interest?

The point of Ontario Hydro had been *power at cost* – literally, people would be charged no more than the cost of producing and delivering the power. In my mind, this was perfect sentiment. It was a *public good* that few in the private sector wanted to tackle because of the enormous capital costs of supplying it across the province. But then the Tory government of the 1960s got it in its collective head that hydro-electricity could not be expanded sufficiently to cover Ontario's growing need for power. As a result, nuclear power was selected as the option for the future. The reality was, however, that nuclear was extremely expensive to build and also to deal with the resultant waste. Politicians would not pass these costs along to ratepayers, probably because they feared it would mean a backlash against them at the ballot box. The result was debt that just sat and collected interest for the lenders. And this debt grew as more nuclear facilities were built.

So when the Harris minions come to office, here's a Crown corporation that's snowed under a staggering weight of debt, with no apparent way out from under the burden. Their answer is the neo-cons' answer: restructure it so you can privatize the parts on which the private sector can make money, and simply force the consumer to eat the debt. And you justify it by saying that this debt was due to it being a public monopoly.

Back to that nasty question of the public interest, though. The profit for the private sector will come from increasing rates. While the wealthy might not notice a few hundred or thousand dollars of extra cost per year, the middle-class and the poor will receive no real administrative savings and have to pay this mark-up. And as has occurred in Alberta, business has seen spot market fluctuation drive their costs through the roof, forcing them to operate only at off-peak times, causing them to *lose* money and cut staff. So the public receives nothing for the loss of the assets of this Crown corporation they owned, and they get higher rates to boot. How is that in the public interest?

And one final question: what of the costs of the nuclear facilities once they are decommissioned? If the Bruce deal is any precedent, the answer is that the taxpayers will be stuck paying the bill. In other words, the people of Ontario paid to build the electricity system in Ontario, and they will pay to shut it down. The private sector will simply be allowed to first scoop the cream off the top.

* * * * *

The alternative to outright privatization of some services has been contracting-out. Keep government control while hiring a private company to deliver the service. This is much more common than just selling things off. Another American fad the Harris Tories have taken up is private jails, or one, at any rate. It, in some ways, has been more controversial than hydro.

Provincial governments in Canada are responsible for people who commit non-felony crimes with sentences of two years less a day, as well as those being held while awaiting trial. These short-term incarcerations resulted in numerous jails being constructed, usually near court houses which were in the seat of counties. For many decades, they were the responsibility of local authorities, though the province had ultimate control over them.

That having been said, money was not invested to do any more than keep these facilities to minimum standards. After all, they were only supposed to be cages with few other amenities. As a result, most dated back to the 19th century and were simply falling apart 100-150 years later. The Harris Tories saw the need to modernize these jails. But doing a good deed wasn't enough. They had to let their neo-conservative, *cookie-cutter*, thinking rule the day.

On Wednesday, 8 October 1997, Solicitor-General Bob Runciman announced the government would construct two new 1,200-bed, no-frills jails to be in Penetanguishene, north of Barrie, and Lindsay, west of

Peterborough. This would be part of a $450 million investment to expand and/or refurbish existing correctional facilities, and to build new ones. These facilities were to be large, by provincial standards, yet they were not exclusively to hold those inmates with 729 day sentences. It was hoped construction of these *super jails* would begin soon, with completion by the end of 1999. However, perhaps due to other funding priorities, building did not begin until about the time they were supposed to open. The Penetanguishene facility took its first inmates in November 2001, while the one in Lindsay is scheduled to open in spring 2002.

Each is made up of a multitude of housing unit pods, each of which has six, 32-bed living units with a common area. Each pod also comes with an exercise yard topped with mesh wire, interview and visiting rooms, the reasoning for which is to restrict inmate movement as much as possible. Located in the centre of the pod is a guard station which looks into each living unit, along with what is called a sallyport door system that permits an inmate to step into a holding unit. When the door behind closes, staff can permit the one in front to open.

After the announcement of these new jails, the Tories were somewhat coy regarding details. Typically, they sold the idea as creating more efficient and effective facilities which would save taxpayer dollars while making them safer, as these jails would house inmates more securely. But they also floated a trial balloon that they might opt for private ones or, at least, privately-run ones. At the time of the original announcement, there had been no mention that the facilities would be anything other than publicly-owned and publicly-run. The possibility that they might be private caused considerable consternation amongst the locals, as media reports told of serious difficulties, like prison riots and numerous escapes, at such facilities in the United States.

As the 1999 election approached, the Conservatives wanted to quiet these fears, as both jails were to be built in ridings they held. In Simcoe North, where Penetanguishene lies, the Tory candidate, Garfield Dunlop, replacing the now retired and disgraced Al McLean, re-affirmed the jail there would be public, as did Chris Hodgson, who represents Lindsay. That is, until after the election. Once the Harrisites had been elected in both ridings, they changed their tune. While Lindsay's was to be public, the one in Penetanguishene would be publicly-owned but privately-run.

The people of this area, Huronia, were outraged, feeling duped by the Tories' duplicity. They went to Dunlop, who denied he had ever said it would not be privately-run, perhaps drawing a distinction between that and privately-owned. Rallies were held to damn the government's decision, and speakers were brought in to caution all of the evils of such privately-operated institutions.

Though not part of the passionate debate, there was a more practical side. Approximately 300,000 inmates travel to and from court each year. When jails were a few hundred metres or a few kilometres away from the courthouse, this was easy. These super jails were causing the shut-down of dozens of facilities, but the courts remained. Suddenly, municipalities were faced with hundreds of thousands of dollars of extra transportation costs. Though it took about two years of arguing, the province recently gave way on its stand that municipalities would have to pay and said they would cover these expenses. That has not diminished the fear that inmates will use this constant transportation to escape.

It is too early to know what the effect will be of this privately-run jail, and whether or not it will be the only one. Certainly the NDP and Liberals have said they would not continue a private contract should they be elected. However, time will undoubtedly tell if the Tories falter on their present stand. Should there be escapes because of there being too few private guards, as has happened in the United States, it would seem quite likely the government might *compromise*. Of course, giving even a little on an issue that affects unions might be asking a lot.

5. Alabama North

In the autumn of 1992, the Legislature passed the NDP government's Bill 40, amendments to the *Labour Relations Act*. Essentially, it changed the rules so that it would be easier for workers to unionize, harder for unions to be de-certified, and it stopped the use of replacement workers, or *scabs*, during legal strikes. It also gave farm workers the right to unionize. If you were a union leader, member, or supporter, it was finaliy a sign that the NDP might actually use its power as government to help working people. If you were a business owner, a stockholder, or industry supporter, you were worried that you were on a conveyor to higher worker wages and lower company profits. If you were a non-unionized worker or anyone else, you probably didn't care.

The Harris Tories certainly did care. They brayed like unfed mules that the balance of power between labour and management had been so shifted to the unions that the situation was *killing jobs*. The Conservatives swore to "re-establish what they saw as balance". In other words, they wanted to reverse the union advances. Once they were elected, they wasted little time. In October 1995, they repealed Bill 40.

In October 1997, the Tories again weakened labour through a wholesale restructuring of the Workers' Compensation Board. Renamed the Workplace Safety and Insurance Board, the government gave two reasons for the changes. First, they wanted to refocus the board on workplace safety, not injuries. Second, they wanted to deal with an alleged unfunded liability that could reach over $10.7 billion by 2014. Substantially, it cut the amount employers would have to contribute by about $6 billion per year, cut benefits to 85% of net wages from 90%, while severely limiting claims for chronic pain, and reducing claimants' ability to appeal decisions. It also ended indexing for inflation for 50,000 on permanent disability pensions.

In December 2000, Labour minister Chris Stockwell heralded final passage of amendments to the *Employment Standards Act* (ESA). He said these changes would permit necessary flexibility in the workplace, and benefit both employers and employees. Critics suggested that was a charitable view.

The amendments to the ESA permit work weeks of up to 60 hours, to average them so that overtime would come less often, and allow holidays to be taken in increments as small as one day at a time, meaning workers wouldn't have to be paid vacation time. These would come into effect through voluntary agreements between workers and their employers. Before these amendments, the maximum work week was 48 hours, with overtime to be paid after 44 hours. Anything over 48 hours required a permit from the Ministry of Labour. The new rules allow an averaging of 48 hours per week over four consecutive weeks to a maximum of 60 hours, or 192 hours total. In this way, a worker might have to work three, 60-hour weeks and one 12-hour week.

The original reason for shortening the work week was unemployment. As the Industrial Revolution improved productivity, it cost more and more people their jobs. Society's leaders were given a stark choice: watch as a growing pool of unemployed became more threatening to the finances and safety of the community; or, give away some of business' newfound profits by cutting the work week and employing more workers. But another reason was safety. As work hours were cut, labourers were less tired and prone to mistakes that caused injury and death, and poor quality products, for that matter. Safety is a big reason why critics fear this increase.

The obvious concern is that making these changes voluntary is irrelevant. Though it is illegal, employers have been known to intimidate workers who are trying to unionize. Is it unreasonable to think that they might do the same to extract serious concessions from workers, especially on a person-by-person basis?

There has been one area, however, where the Harris Tories actually advanced workers' rights, even if it was grudgingly. As part of the 2000 budget, federal Finance minister Paul Martin saw fit to extend parental leaves for new mothers and fathers from 10 to 35 weeks for all those working for that government, effective 1 January 2001. With 15 weeks of maternity leave, this made for a possible maximum of 50 weeks coverage. It would also lower the number of work hours required for these parents to qualify for Employment Insurance from 700 to 600 hours.[32] However, these changes were only available to people covered under federal law. For it to be available to everyone, provincial governments would have to amend their legislation as well.

There then came terrific pressure on provincial governments to go along. A few did quickly, but others stuck to the *status quo*. Ontario was left as a blatant hold-out. Comments by Harris MPPs ran along the lines of this was the feds wasting taxpayers money again. If a mother wanted to stay home with her child longer, that was her choice, but it was not something that should be subsidized by government.

One day I listened to two women, one with child, talking about how great it was going to be able to spend a year with her baby, once it was born. (She wasn't due until mid-2001.) Though I didn't want to burst her bubble, I explained that Ontario had not extended this coverage for women in the private sector, so she was stuck at 25 weeks. This did not go over well. She asked why the province didn't think it was a good idea, if the federal government did? I could only say she should call her MPP and ask.

As it turned out, a couple of weeks later, in late November, the Harrisites crumbled and announced they, too, would extend maternity leaves to 50 weeks ... but it was done reluctantly and without grace. A few days before the official announcement, Labour minister Stockwell said, "We may just go for the full-blown 50 weeks, period, case closed, and then a warning to the federal government, before you do this stuff again, maybe you should take some time to consult with us ...".[33]

The fact is, such a *bonus* was inimical to these Tories. They had spent five years reducing workers' rights, and they weren't pleased at being almost forced to give some back. However, it was not seemly to target pregnant women, as the Premier had found out in April 1998 when he had suggested his government's elimination of a $37 per month supplement for pregnant welfare recipients was so "those dollars don't go to beer". The fall-out had been instant and embarrassing, and a failure to extend parental leave might have been seen in a similar, if less vulgar, vein.

In another loss of workers' rights, the Tories removed the ability of the Labour Relations Board to certify a union even if the vote fails. The NDP had made changes so this could be done if it was determined the employer had used intimidation, like threatening jobs or closure of the business or plant, in the run-up to the certification vote. An example of this happened in May 1996, when the United Steelworkers attempted to organize workers at a Wal-Mart department store outlet in Windsor. Eighty-four members were signed up in the first two weeks, then just five more after store managers refused to permit pro-union staff to respond to anti-union comments to the workers by another member at a store meeting. As well, four company representatives approached staff to ask if they had questions, then, when asked if the store would close should the unionization succeed, refused to answer. The workers rejected the attempt, 151-43, but an arbitration board found that the company had intimidated them through these actions and that the union had shown sufficient support amongst the workers, so they ordered certification. Wal-Mart, never known to be friendly to unions, appealed to the government after failing to overturn the decision in court, and, on 29 June 1998, the Harrisites passed the *Economic Development and Workplace Democracy Act* which did away with the clause. The board now has the power to order another vote, but no more than that.[34] The Wal-Mart workers voted to de-certify at the first opportunity.

But the Tories recently suffered another setback on this front. The Supreme Court of Canada ruled that their denial of the right of farm workers to collective bargaining rights was unconstitutional. This was an appeal of lower court losses for a group of 200 mushroom farm workers who had been negotiating a first contract when the Harrisites pulled the rug out from under them. In an 8-1 decision, the Justices found that this was a breach of the Charter of Rights and Freedoms, though they recognized the possible deleterious effects on farming. They ordered the province to come up with legislation to allow these workers at least minimum protections on unionizing, collective bargaining, and organizing strikes within 18 months, or these workers would receive full rights just as those had by auto or steel workers.

Both Harris and Agriculture minister Brian Coburn panned the decision, claiming this could compromise the viability of family farms. However, this was never the intention. First, one or two workers cannot unionize, so family farms are hardly at risk. However, the large corporate friends of the Tories who run factory farms are.

Of course, the Tories often do not rely on courts to uphold their edicts. In the case of the Ontario Municipal Board, they made this board's decisions unappealable (which in itself is probably unconstitutional).

6. OMB - Ontario Megalomaniac Board

In my mind, the Ontario Municipal Board is the most important planning authority in the province, even moreso than the Ministry of Municipal Affairs. It describes itself as "an independent and impartial adjudicative tribunal".[35] Well, that might be a technical, and generous, description. An 'adjudicative tribunal', yes. 'Independent and impartial'? Not really. Like other boards that are appointed by the government-in-power, the tendency is for a governing party to select its long-time friends as board members, meaning that decisions tend to be skewed along ideological lines. The history of the OMB is proof enough of that.

Originally called the Ontario Railway and Municipal Board, the body's primary purpose was to facilitate the growth of railroad lines throughout the province in the early days of the 20th century. However, by 1932, with the laying of the lines long finished (and the failure of dozens of rail companies due to the Depression), the ORMB had its railway duties taken away and came to focus on more specific municipal matters. Over time, these responsibilities grew to include oversight of annexations, amalgamations, official plans, property tax assessments, zoning by-laws, plans of subdivision, severances, minor by-law variances, development charges, and gravel pit licences. However, as duty after duty was piled on the board, it took longer and longer to deal with issues and proceedings became exceedingly expensive. In 1982, the OMB lost jurisdiction over municipal boundary changes and, in 1998, they ceased to take appeals on assessments.

Due to the importance of the duties of the OMB and the fact that appointments were for life, board membership became increasingly attractive and, as a result, made it perhaps the prime patronage job in the province. However, given 42 years of Tory rule, it also meant that the entire board was made up of Tories. While some were more independent than others, the OMB became well known as a promoter of government dicta, especially in its consistent approval of almost all development, and an increasing tendency to simply rubber stamp any annexation put in front of it. Some of this criticism convinced the Peterson government to replace life appointments with three-year terms. However, that was not retroactive. And while the Liberals and NDP were in office long enough to replace a few of the Conservative appointments, they were not there long enough to upset the reigning mindset.

But it wasn't just the board members who demonstrated these attitudes, it permeated the entire organization, right down to hearing officers who were, more often than not, known friends of the Tories. The OMB earned a reputation for approving zoning changes denied by municipalities, allowing severances that sliced up rural land, and favouring the subdivision plans of developers even when they violated the tenets of good planning. So when the Harrisites changed the rules so that OMB decisions can no longer be appealed to the courts or the Minister (though errors in fact can be judicially reviewed), there was tremendous concern that this was just another way for the government to promote unrestrained development without having to take any responsibility for the OMB's decisions. One area of heavy growth has been north of Toronto.

If one were nasty, you might refer to the Tory government as the Oak Ridges' Morons, or Oak Ridges' Moraine Boys. These unflattering nicknames, though, may be indicative of a bad habit into which Harris *et.al.* have fallen since their re-election. The ridings that make up the Oak Ridges Moraine, an ecologically sensitive area that falls just north of Toronto, were entirely Conservative after both the 1995 and 1999 elections, yet the Tories seem to have taken them for granted. When questions of development versus the protection of the environment, especially drinking water, came to the fore in late 1999, the government reaction was one of deny, denigrate, and delay.

At first, they denied there was a problem. Development in the outlying areas of Toronto had been going on, almost non-stop, for 40 years. Successful, well-financed communities had been created, and there seemed no reason to change a formula that had been apparently working well. But that was only the case if you accepted that almost unrestrained development never did any harm. By the 1990s, however, this was no longer the view of many, even some of those who had moved into subdivisions built in these formerly natural areas.

There can be no question that the developers got caught by their own success. As more and more people were drawn to the natural area, more and more of them became annoyed at seeing it chopped up for new housing. Naively, I suspect, most home-buyers moved to the region thinking that theirs would be the near-to-the-last house built, and that they would forever enjoy the stand of trees behind their back yard and the greenery of the nearby fields. Instead, a year or two after moving in, the trees were clear-cut for more houses, and the only green to be seen became lawns. People's views about development began to change, I dare say, because development became a Not-In-My-Back-Yard issue, just as much as any landfill.

The suburban opponents of development seemed to arise out of the fight to stop amalgamation in Toronto. This municipal union somehow seemed to signal the renewed expansion of the city outward, as flocks of Torontonians were choosing to escape the burgeoning city. This outflow was not new, but the perception of it seemed to be renewed. The big concern was that water coming through the moraine feeds into 65 water tributaries, including virtually all those in Toronto. Preserving this land was critical. However, as was the Tory habit, they chose to denigrate their opponents rather than listen to their concerns.

As I said, development had been going on for decades and successful communities had been constructed right alongside trees and fields and rivers. What was wrong with that? That was the government line. For those who didn't like it, they were simply the same whiners who didn't appreciate successes like Lands for Life. However, instead of taking them on and getting into a public debate, the solution seemed to be to delay. It was easier to leave planning matters to the municipalities and the Ontario Municipal Board. Concerns over development had arisen before, then gone away. With luck, there would be no need to deal with anything if the government could just wait out the complainants.

The Oak Ridges Moraine is approximately 195,000 hectares of land that stretches from north Oshawa in the east to north Caledon and south Dufferin County in the west. It is mostly a mass of clay, silt, sand, and stone that was created 12,000 years ago when two floes of retreating glacier pinched together, crushing the earth underneath. This base acts like a sponge to hold and filter water, and it is the primary source of drinking water for much of the Toronto region. Above ground, it is a combination of treed land, natural areas, and farms. As Toronto spills north, this natural beauty and lower-priced real estate makes it a predictable destination for those who would rather live a suburban lifestyle.

Unfortunately, development has the direct effect of spoiling nature and damaging the moraine. Potentially, this urbanization threatens the source of water for half-a-million people. This is why the debate over the area's future has such serious ramifications.

In 1998 and 1999, a number of large, high-profile developments were proposed for virtually every part of the moraine, especially in York and Durham regions. The moraine makes up the northern half of the City of Richmond Hill. As one of these burgeoning areas, the municipality has become a centre of the demands to develop the rural area within municipal limits. However, local politicians have more recently been swayed by their constituents' concerns over unbridled growth and had placed a number of restrictions on development ... restrictions that naturally upset developers. In the fall of 1999, they went to the OMB to appeal those zoning controls.

Few municipal politicians like having their decisions appealed to the non-elected officials of the OMB and, whether it was because of this or a true concern for the moraine, town representatives passed an Official Plan amendment setting out exactly where development would be allowed and where it would be restricted or banned, including a number of ecologically-sensitive zones. The developers' appeal to the OMB suggested that these limitations were excessive and fundamentally expropriated private property without compensation by banning development on it.

The decision came down on 23 February 2000. The hearing officer was Ron Emo, a former mayor of Collingwood, a long-time and dedicated Ontario Tory, and a well-known friend of the development industry. He had been appointed to the board by the Harris government three years earlier. His decision was to basically throw out Richmond Hill's zoning restrictions and open up the land for massive housing growth. He said that it was beyond the jurisdiction of the town to limit or prohibit development. And he was backed up by Environment minister Tony Clement who said that the town had all the tools it needed to protect the moraine. In fact, the Emo decision said they had none.

That wasn't the end of it, however. In May, five large development interests, probably emboldened by the earlier decision, went to the OMB for permission to build 8,015 homes on 814 hectares of rural moraine land that included farmland, open land, and trees in northern Richmond Hill.[36] City councillors were quite upset at the Emo decision and immediately launched their defensive. As well, dozens of groups applied to make presentations at the hearings, most of which were turned down, including the City of Toronto. OMB Chair James Mills said the city representatives should mind their own business, as though the people there had nothing at stake.

As the tide of public opinion locally turned against development, and hardened, the Tories were left with little choice but to do something they hadn't appeared willing to do before – new Environment minister Chris Hodgson imposed a six-month moratorium on development in the moraine area in May 2001, much to the chagrin of the developers. As well, he announced the creation of a 14-member advisory panel to make recommendations on future land-use there.

Even environmentalists were impressed with this move, hailing it as a new beginning. The government had finally come around to their way of thinking. Political critics were much more sceptical. The proof this was not so seemed to be *in the pudding*. Not only was this panel made up almost entirely of pro-development people, but the moratorium conveniently expired after a by-election was to occur in Vaughan-King-Aurora, a riding in the heart of the moraine.

This riding had been won in both 1995 and 1999 by former Cabinet minister Al Palladini, who had passed away suddenly in early March 2001 of a heart attack. However, prior to that, it had been Liberal for some years, and that party decided to put up the retired MPP and former Peterson Cabinet minister Greg Sorbara, as their candidate. With the Liberals opposing mass development in the area, it must have given the Conservatives pause for thought. The moraine moratorium seemed more a way of defusing the whole issue while the Tories tried to keep the riding.

There are those that would suggest winning the riding was not that important. After all, it was just one constituency, and losing it did not affect the Tory majority. However, a year earlier, a Conservative backbencher from Ancaster-Dundas-Flamborough-Aldershot, in the Hamilton area, had resigned on a question of principle over the amalgamation of that city with its neighbours. The Liberal candidate, Ted McMeekin, the Ancaster mayor, massacred the provincially well-known Tory Priscilla DeVilliers. Most gave the victory to McMeekin based on his opposition to the amalgamation and DeVilliers' manifest confusion on most issues. This was a dent in the Tory armour in the 905 area, and Vaughan-King-Aurora threatened to turn a one-issue *accident* into the very real appearance that the Tories were fading in popularity. And, as Bob Rae said, politics *is* about impressions.

The battle for VKA was actually quick and decisive. Sorbara won by 9,771 votes, which was a 22.7% margin.[37] Whether the result was a commentary on development on the moraine is dubious. Sorbara is a well-known, well-liked fellow with ten years experience (1985-1995) in the Legislature, and he had held much of VKA during his time in Queen's Park. His Tory opponent was a medium-profile, regional councillor with no provincial experience named Joyce Frustaglio. As with the '99 election signs, hers marked her as a member of the *Mike Harris Team* rather than a Progressive Conservative. Some took her defeat as an omen that the Premier's personal popularity is not worth what it used to be.

A month after the by-election, Hodgson announced that all housing developments that had been approved prior to the moratorium would be permitted to go ahead. Most interested parties accepted this as being fair, though Liberal critic Mike Colle was merciless in his censure. He said this was just a sign of things to come. It wasn't long before chainsaws and bulldozers returned.

In August, the advisory panel handed in its interim report. Though the members claimed their recommendations would seriously limit or ban development on 90% of the moraine, the truth was rather more elusive. The panel divided up the moraine into four land-use categories: natural core; natural linkage; countryside; and settlement.

The *natural core* area would be made up of forests, kettle lakes, and wetlands covering 35%, or 68,250 hectares, of the moraine. New development in this area would be banned, except for agricultural land. Sand and gravel pits already in existence would be permitted to continue, but no new ones would be allowed. As well, new roads could be built, but only if they met certain environmental standards and only if there were no reasonable alternate routes.

The *natural linkage* areas would be mostly woodlots, wetlands, and rural areas covering 17%, or 33,150 hectares, of the moraine that link together natural core areas. Also, such areas would include other natural corridors like river valleys just outside the moraine. The same rules would apply here as in the natural core areas, except that new aggregate extraction would be permitted.

The *countryside* area would be the rural and agricultural land covering 38%, or 74,100 hectares, of the moraine. Municipalities could approve commercial and industrial development, large recreational operations like golf courses and ski hills, as well as so-called rural residential construction.

Finally, *settlement* areas would be urban areas where municipal Official Plans already approved housing and other commercial/ industrial uses. It would cover 10%, or 19,500 hectares, of the moraine. Settlement area boundaries could not be changed without a five-year review of an Official Plan first being conducted.

Reaction was mixed. On the day of the announcement, most interest groups seemed quite pleased, but it was only days before the proposals were being picked apart. It wasn't long before the advisory panel was making amendments. Within two weeks, the residential construction provision for countryside areas dropped "estate development" – the building of large houses on one-acre-plus lots. Then, in late September, the final report was issued. The natural core area would be increased slightly, from 35% to 38%, while the natural linkage area would also increase to 24% from 17% and be set at a minimum of two kilometres in width, where no minimum had been earlier set out. The countryside and settlement areas would shrink to 30% and 8%, respectively. The changes, however, did not stop the creation of new gravel pits, but it did add one new recommendation: permitting a review every ten years of the moraine and development. As the President of the *Save the Rouge Valley System*, a group of environmentalists, pointed out, this was simply a way of weaselling out of permanent protection. As an example, he mentioned the *parkway belt* that the Davis government had established in 1975 as a greenbelt around Toronto. It wasn't many years before zoning amendments and provincial changes turned it into housing and highways.

Regardless, these revised provisions suggested that most of the moraine would be saved from development. However, to interpret their recommendations in a different way offered the possibility of significant development. In fact, there were no substantive restrictions on countryside areas at all, except for estate developments. This area was simply left to the mercies of municipalities. That being the case, 38% of the moraine would be open to development. And while natural core and linkage areas seem mostly protected, aggregate extraction was permitted. There is little more destructive than what sand and gravel pits can do to land. All over southern Ontario, there are man-made lakes that exist because pits tore holes that filled in with ground water. And other such operations were eventually turned into golf courses and housing developments because no one could reasonably argue that nature was still intact there to worry about. How long before a government allows this on the moraine where pits are eventually worked out and just sit?

It may well be that the government saw these faults and chose to further preempt censure by giving a little more. The developers' appeal to the OMB to build 8,000 new homes in north Richmond Hill was still pending. If it succeeded, it would make the entire planning exercise a joke, and would likely have seriously embarrassed both the government and then leadership contender Hodgson.

Negotiations went on privately between David Crombie, representing the government, and the developers. A trade was put forward by the former Toronto mayor. The house-builders would give up their OMB appeal and turn over their land in Richmond Hill and in Uxbridge to the province in exchange for land to develop in the proposed town of Seaton in Pickering[38]. As well, the government announced it would turn 440 hectares of the Richmond Hill land into a park.

During the announcement of this accommodation, Minister Hodgson added that the legislation to protect the moraine would include a clause guaranteeing the core and natural link areas would be protected permanently, while the rest would be reviewed after ten years. And though a hiking trail would be permitted through protected area, an interim board set up to buy land on the moraine to protect it wouldn't get provincial money to help, and the easternmost municipalities in Durham would be exempt from some of the new development rules, once again, most everyone cheered the decision. A few waited for the other shoe to drop.

Within three weeks, time enough to thoroughly evaluate the proposed legislation, the environmental movement was no longer in love. Though they still liked the deal, they pointed out the Minister would have the authority to revoke the Act in whole or in part, at any time, and they stated a desire this power be revoked. Hodgson's spokesperson said this was "standard practice". Just to add insult to injury, a few days later, bulldozers cut a path through trees in what will be the moraine's natural core as Bayview Avenue is extended north, thus destroying habitat of the threatened Jefferson salamander. The *Oak Ridges Moraine Protection Act* passed, intact, just before Christmas.

But, in March 2002, it was revealed that the terms of agreement might be met technically, but not in spirit. Though developers would be permitted 5,825 new homes in the Seaton community, the Oak Ridges Moraine would still take the brunt of development. Along with the 3,000 homes that had been approved prior to the 2001 freeze, another 4,150 units were going to be permitted on moraine land in Richmond Hill, plus another 4,800 houses in nearby Gormley. In response to a public outcry, Minister

Hodgson has said he can't understand the complaints. After all, he never promised to ban development. For many local residents and environmentalists, this no longer sounded like land protection, just a sell-out.

Of course, for doubters like me, the entire moraine saga has been about appearance over reality. Had bookies originally been giving odds on the end result, I suspect they would have favoured the government allowing the moraine to be paved over rather than them saving most of it. Even when the freeze was announced and the panel empowered to comment on development, any serious restrictions seemed unlikely. Yet when the advisory group recommended 62% moraine protection, the fact that people from the development industry made up the lion's share of its members seemed to indicate an honest effort had been made at environmental protection and proper planning. However, even then, there was a hint this was not so. Some developers began suggesting they would be seeking financial compensation from the province not just for land they could no longer develop but also for the loss of profit on houses they would not be able to build and sell. Even given the friendly relationship between the Conservative party and the development industry, it was hard to imagine the Tories would willingly make Ontario liable for billions of dollars in compensation, not to mention the risk of losing hundreds of thousands of dollars from this industry each year in political donations. The legislation and land swap conveniently seemed to solve the problems of the Tories and developers, at least in Richmond Hill. The development controls seemed sufficiently tough to keep public opinion in check, yet were clearly always going to include sufficient *loopholes* to permit massive development to continue.

In fact, this land protection legislation gave some the impression that the Harrisites were softening, returning to the days of *progressive* conservatism. But that ignores the simple reality that circumstances have changed somewhat for this party. Polls show they are falling out of favour. The VKA by-election demonstrated that they are weakening in an area – the GTA – where they had thought they were invulnerable. And they need this territory if they have any hopes of re-election. Opinion in this region has moved greatly toward saving the moraine. Be it for environmental protection or the self-serving limitation of development, people have come to oppose the building of houses that have swept over the landscape like a dust storm over the Sahara. Had the Tories not given the appearance they were willing to clamp down on their developer friends, it is very likely they would have paid for it in the GTA ridings in the next election ... or at least that is the Tories' fear. The real surprise is that they've given up on this illusion so quickly.

* * * * *

Along with being unelected and unaccountable, the OMB has also allowed its process to become so expensive that decisions are now skewed in favour of those who have money. According to *The Toronto Star*, the cost of the twelve weeks of moraine hearing that started in May 2000, would have been between $1.73 million and $2.88 million for the lawyers alone![39] Where did these numbers come from? Fifteen lawyers representing the different participants were expected to be on hand at $300-$500 per hour, or $36,000-$60,000 per day for the lot. With a four-day work week over 12 weeks, that would be up to almost $3 million. As well, several consultants would be employed. Planners and hydro-geologists hired by just one developer were estimated to cost him half-a-million dollars. As one can see by these numbers, there is no way an average person can afford to deal on a level playing field before the OMB. In fact, even municipalities often just concede defeat rather than spend tens or hundreds of thousands of dollars before this board.

7. Joseph Goebbels would be proud

I don't think it is unfair to say that the Mike Harris government has taken advertising and spin-doctoring to a whole new level. Never before has a government been so blatant in using taxpayers' dollars to pay for overt propaganda, again and again, as has this one. As well, never has a government used the *news-starved* media so often to announce, re-announce, and re-announce again the same programmes, the result making it sound like billions of dollars were being poured into services when they were often getting nothing at all.

During the 1990 election, Harris reproved the use of taxpayers' money to pay for government advertising, and promised a Conservative government would stop it. Once he became Premier, his attitude had obviously changed. Between April 1997 and mid-2001, his government put almost $200 million dollars into television, radio, and newspaper ads, as well as pamphlets mailed to homes, that could be considered little else than blatantly partisan.

. And how does one define a partisan ad? Generally, it is one that makes little or no attempt to give citizens any information they can use to access government services yet promotes the government and/or its members and/or its policies. On several occasions, Liberal leader Dalton McGuinty has sponsored a private member's bill that defines what should and should not be permitted. On the latter side, the bill said:

> *The advertising must not include the name, voice or image of a member of the Executive Council or a member of the Legislative Assembly. The advertising must not be partisan. The advertising must not have as a significant objective (the) fostering in the public a positive impression of the government, or fostering in the public a negative impression of a person or entity that is critical of the government.* (Bill 17, Taxpayer Protection Act [Government Advertising Standards], defeated on Second Reading, 2001.)

The Harris government would fail on all these points. Many of the print ads still have the Premier's face smacked on them, along with his always topical message. Some of the television and radio ads still use his voice as narrator. Virtually all hail the Tory government accomplishments and, on occasion, they're still willing to pan their critics, though it is now usually in a passive fashion.

But the Harrisites were not on this track straight away from their election. The beginning of the propaganda onslaught came with the megacity troubles. The government's advisors in the Bradgate Group became concerned that the government had let itself get bogged down in a popularity-losing proposition.[40] They felt it was time to take the fight to the people, and skip the "talking heads" of the media and the overblown rhetoric of the Liberals and NDP. An advertising campaign was devised on two tracks, political and governmental. The Conservative party would pay for one ad to tout the Harrisites' success at keeping their promises, while money would be taken from the advertising budgets of various ministries to explain to voters the alleged logic of disentanglement. The Tories spent $800,000 on their commercial, showing Harris with one foot on a hockey bench, while the government spent $2.5 million on Harris in different venues – by a fuse box, in a classroom, in a hospital. It was difficult to tell the political one apart from those supposedly governmental. These TV spots were followed up with a $300,000 government mail-out to homes in Metro Toronto explaining amalgamation.

Whether or not this particular advertising was effective is moot. The Tories felt it was, and may be backed up by the fact their popularity did not diminish appreciably during this legislative tsunami. It was the beginning of a habit that they continue to this day, except that it is now not reserved for contentious issues, but has become a regular part of government business. The party television ads are gone, for the most part, but the mail-outs continue.

Some examples:

Are we on the right track? – a pamphlet put out after the April 1998 Throne Speech bragging about the statistical "accomplishments" of the Harris government since its election.

Welfare Reform: Making Welfare Work – a 1998 pamphlet vaunting workfare, the fight against welfare fraud, the removal of disabled people from welfare, and the increases in employment with the decreases in welfare cases.

Report to Taxpayers – a spring 1999 pamphlet that talked about tax cuts, the balanced budget, and had a few people's testimonials boasting about the 'favourable business environment in Ontario'.

Safety: Protecting our Community – a pamphlet blustering about the government's actions to toughen criminal justice through boot camps, reduced paroles, added police, and a victim support phone line.

Education: Changes for the better to help your children – a fold-out "growth chart" outlining general changes to the school system.

In the fall of 2000, the Ministry of Education put out a brochure called *Learning for Life*. It was just another example of this new kind of government advertising. But a closer look might be useful to show how it was different, using McGuinty's legislative proposals. In two ways, the pamphlet is fair. 'It must not be partisan.' And there is no mention of the Progressive Conservatives, Tories, *The Common Sense Revolution*, or anything similar. As well, 'it must not foster in the public a negative impression of a person or entity that is critical of the government.' And there was none of this.

However, in two other ways, the pamphlet is very unfair. 'It must not include the name, voice or image of a member of the Executive Council or a member of the Legislative Assembly.' However, the pamphlet includes the smiling face of the Premier, and a page of him discussing what his government had done since taking power.

When our government took office in 1995, we were concerned that Ontario's students were falling behind, that our young people were not acquiring the knowledge and skills they need for personal success and active citizenship in today's global economy.

We decided that standing still in the face of rapid change would mean falling back even further, and that our publicly funded education system and our training and postsecondary (sic) programs needed bold new directions, higher standards, and a renewed commitment to excellence.

And this is the problem. As soon as the political side of the argument is put forward, it taints the rest. On the first section of the pamphlet, it says ...

Over the past five years, we've been building an agenda for quality that will prepare students for success at every stage of their educational experience. We've made a lot of changes, but a lot of changes were needed.

We've focused, increased, and protected classroom spending at the elementary and secondary levels. We've developed a new way of funding colleges and universities to encourage innovation, to improve the quality of education and to ensure that these institutions respond to the real needs of students and employers.

We've introduced a completely new curriculum from Kindergarten to Grade 12 that prepares students for success – in the workforce, in apprenticeships, in college or in university. And we're expanding the range of choices at the postsecondary (sic) level to meet growing student demand for innovative courses in new and emerging areas of the economy.

We've established province-wide standards for teaching time and class size, and we're developing standards to improve the quality of special education in Ontario's schools.

We're making our education systems accountable through regular province-wide student tests, a teacher testing program, report cards that can be easily understood, and the requirement that postsecondary (sic) institutions report annually on the success of their programs in key areas such as the percentage of students who graduate and find jobs in their areas of study.

We're helping parents and students make informed decisions about course selections and providing high school students with the information they need to select the postsecondary (sic) *program that will best prepare them for future success.*

We're working in partnership with colleges, universities and employers to ensure that our higher education system provides relevant, high-quality programs that help our young people prepare for jobs in high-demand areas, such as the high-tech and automotive sectors.

We're requiring students to study technology in every elementary grade, and we're working to bring greater learning opportunities to Ontarians across the province through the use of the Internet and other new technologies.

This is supposed to be from the Ministry of Education, yet this reads more like something out of the CSR. In fact, there is no differentiation between the government 'we' and the politician's 'we'. Once the Premier's name and his government's record are attached, it makes the whole document appear political. In fact, it is ... but it's paid for by the taxpayers.

And there is another problem. 'It must not have as a significant objective (the) fostering in the public a positive impression of the government.' I think we can see from above that this is for all intents and purposes the entire point of the exercise. But to add some specifics from the document ... in the section on "focusing resources on the classroom" ...

Ontario parents and taxpayers want to know that education spending is focused on the classroom, where it can do the most good.

As promised, the Ontario government has introduced several measures to cut the costs of administration and bureaucracy and reinvest the savings in teaching and learning, as follows:

We established a fair level of funding for public education. Before 1998, per pupil spending varied dramatically from board to board, in part because some boards could draw on a large local property tax base. Now, funding is allocated to boards based on enrolment and students' needs. No matter where they live in Ontario, parents can now be assured that there is a fair and equitable level of resources to support their child's education.

In 1998, we set province-wide standards that increased the amount of time secondary teachers actually spend teaching in the classroom. This increase brought Ontario into line with the national average. The standard is 4 hours and 10 minutes of instructional time per day. This spring, we amended the Education Act to ensure that this standard is met by all boards across the province.

From 1995 to 2000, 198 new schools were built and 150 additions or major renovations were completed. The Ontario government is putting resources into the classrooms, where they'll benefit our students the most.

Teaching in Ontario: A bright future, a rewarding career

Ontario's education reforms are leading to smaller classes and the need for more teachers. These changes, combined with the expected retirement of many thousands of teachers over the next few years, are opening up teaching opportunities for highly qualified graduates. The Ontario government has committed ongoing annual funding to support lower class sizes in elementary and secondary schools. In 2000-01, this is an investment of $263 million. As a result, school boards will need to hire nearly 3,000 more teachers. In addition, retirement will open up about 5,000 teaching positions each year over the next two years alone. This is an exciting opportunity to revitalize the teaching profession by recruiting young people with up-to-date skills into the classroom.

To meet the growing demand for new teachers, the Ontario government is working closely with Ontario's faculties of education and has increased funding for new teacher training by $45 million. A total of 6,000 additional teacher-training spaces are being created between 1999 and 2004.

Sandwiched in the middle of the page and at the bottom were two boxes, also containing further so-called information.

Spending on school board administration has declined by an estimated $150 million since 1995, while spending in the classroom has increased.

	1995	2000
Number of school boards in Ontario	*129*	*72*
Number of school board trustees	*1,992*	*589*
Senior administrators working for school boards	*777*	*512*

Information is based on current estimates.

In the 2000-2001 school year, Ontario's overall investment in

*high-quality elementary and secondary education will increase by an
estimated $300 million.*

1999 - 2000	2000 - 2001
$13.2 billion	*$13.5 billion*

I really do not think it is unfair to say these numbers and comments are
meant to 'foster ... a positive impression of the government'.

Now there will be those who do not see any real problem with this. After
all, if the government has accomplishments, why can't they do a little
bragging, especially if the boasting is fairly subtle? And why shouldn't the
Premier or Minister be allowed a little editorial licence? After all, they are
ultimately responsible for the decisions made.

The difficulty is in where to draw the line between acceptable and
unacceptable. If this brochure had said education was improving because
the Mike Harris Tories were smarter than the Liberals and New
Democrats, we would likely think this was going too far. But isn't that
exactly what was said in vaguer terms. Students 'were not acquiring the
knowledge and skills they need(ed)', so the Tories brought forward 'bold
new directions, higher standards, and a renewed commitment to
excellence'. The Ministry words were 'Over the past five years, we've
been building an agenda for quality that will prepare students for success at
every stage of their educational experience. We've made a lot of changes,
but a lot of changes were needed.' 'We've focused, increased, and
protected classroom spending ... We've developed a new way of funding
colleges and universities to encourage innovation ... We've introduced a
completely new curriculum ... ...We're expanding the range of choices at
the postsecondary (sic) level ... We've established province-wide
standards for teaching time and class size, and we're developing standards
to improve the quality of special education in Ontario's schools', etc. All-
in-all, it's pretty much saying the same thing.

And the problem with this is that it gives the party in power the vast
treasury of the province to use to promote itself. The opposition parties
have no such resource base. As a result, the government party can work to
affect its public popularity using taxpayers' money, giving it a completely
unfair advantage over its competitors. It doesn't mean you won't lose an
election, but it does mean that it isn't a level playing field, to use an over-
used cliché. If the government has the upper hand before campaigning
ever begins, how can there be an honest exercise by voters of their
democratic rights?

And this is a fundamental question I hope I have been asking throughout this book: what of democracy?

Part 5 Endnotes

1. And these numbers use averages not including junior kindergarten because there was no JK programme in 1995. With those included, the drop is much more significant.
2. I am including income tax cuts, not cuts to corporations. Though the Tories brag of their 166 tax cuts, 132 have gone to corporations.
3. This comes from Tony Clement, should he win the leadership.
4. Toronto Star. "Harris spin doctors sing same tune: It wasn't me", 16 August 2001, p. B1.
5. Toronto Star editorial. "School legislation should be scrapped", 16 June 2000, p. A26.
6. Toronto Star. "Task force on school tax credits is a farce", 10 September 2001, p. A13.
7. Schull, Michael J., Szalai, John-Paul, Schwartz, Brian and Redelmeier, Donald A. "Emergency Department Overcrowding Following Systematic Hospital Restructuring", (Journal of) Academic Emergency Medicine (Volume 8, Number 11), 2001.
8. At this time, just 200 of the 20,000 long-term care beds promised in April 1998 were open.
9. Source: Ontario Nurses Association.
10. Many of their nurses got jobs with the private contractors, but at lower wage levels and often with fewer hours.
11. Some de-listed services under Harris now include: annual eye exams (now every second year); sex-changes; facial-hair removal; and circumcisions.
12. 67.6 per 100,000 population, compared to a national average of 74.6 and New Brunswick's high of 101.9.
13. In April 2000, the Registered Nurses' Association of Ontario said 6,300 nursing positions were lost during hospital restructuring since 1995. During the present Tory leadership campaign, Witmer has reiterated her claim the NDP was to blame for most nursing cuts.
14. He made this comment in early March 1997, then apologized.
15. 50% of Ontario nursing positions are presently part-time, according to the RNAO.
16. The latest contract between the ONA and hospitals actually make nurses here the highest-paid in Canada, earning between $20-$29.51 per hour. Again, however, that doesn't mean full-time hours or reasonable shifts.
17. It also removed successor rights from OPSEU workers, presumably on the possibility that some social housing agencies might be privatized in the future.

18. Source: Canada Mortgage and Housing Corporation

19. All but one were absent or abstained.

20. Toronto Star. "Before Walkerton, it was unthinkable that Ontario drinking water was anything but safe. Did provincial cutbacks help turn this precious natural resource into a potential killer?", 8 July 2000, p. K3.

21. I have put in the proper city name, as the transcript read "Dabous".

22. Toronto Star. "Rules to cut back smog give polluters an out", 25 January 2001, p. A6.

23. Toronto Star. "Air assault", 25 August 2001, p. G25.

24. Toronto Star. "Is Drive Clean merely a feel-good program?", 26 August 2000, p. G32.

25. For 2000-2001, the LCBO had $850 million in liquor sales, in addition to $255 million in sales taxes on those sales.

26. In a recently announced policy, the LCBO will be franchising private, but affiliated, stores in communities too small for full stores.

27. In some jurisdictions that deregulated, costs were capped so ratepayers would have some confidence. However, it was claimed this distorted market price, so the Harrisites decided there would be no cap on increases in Ontario.

28. Ministry of Energy definition.

29. Toronto Star. "Consumers will get bill for the deal with British energy firm", 21 November 2001, p. A29.

30. Rae, op.cit., p. 269.

31. Results that were presented at the party's April 2001 AGM in London.

32. As well, the two-week waiting period for the second parent was to be waived.

33. Toronto Star. "Ontario to extend maternity leaves", 18 November 2000, p. A1.

34. Another change provides for employers to disagree with the union's estimate of the number of employees in the bargaining unit.

35. Source: Ontario Municipal Board.

36. Given that the Harris Tories had changed the rules, it was no longer necessary for decisions to go against someone to make an appeal to the OMB. In effect, municipalities no longer controlled their own planning decisions.

37. The NDP was humiliated by running fourth, behind the Green party candidate.

38. In the late 1960s, this area was expropriated by the government for a satellite town near the proposed new Toronto airport that was never built.

39. Toronto Star. "A dilemma: to build or not to build", 29 May 2000, B1.

40. Ibbitson, op.cit., p. 258.

Part 6

Looking into the crystal ball

1. The *Revolution* ends ...

Since World War Two, the successful election of governments in Ontario has been predicated on certain factors and, while the reality of these has sometimes been in question, it is often more important that the perception of them exists. Parties must show people they are progressive in their ideas and actions. That is, they have to show that government is willing to act for the public interest. Over the years, that defined government as being more interventionist to bring about both change people wanted, but also change people needed. Under George Drew and Leslie Frost, this meant government was to establish policies to organize flourishing growth to expand both the economic and social circumstances of people. Then, under Robarts and Davis, government was to catch up on services that a more affluent society demanded, as well as giving more protection to those who had not benefited from the better times.

At the same time, change was to be handled conservatively, with an eye to proper management. People wanted change, but needed time to adapt to it. They were perhaps grudging in their desire to pay taxes, but they expected these to be spent wisely and on programmes of which they themselves approved. They wanted these ideas, especially the economic ones, to be delineated in a clear fashion, though they did not demand extreme detail. They simply wanted to know what the government was intending, so they could approve of it through an election, then make sure that party delivered on its plan. If these progressive and conservative elements arrived, the party-in-power gained the public trust to continue with their delivery. Even if they didn't, all the time, and some progress was more by stealth than reality, voters gave their trust to the party that played the best hand.

Drew did not recognize the pattern of progressive/conservative government he was setting. That was left to Frost. He saw that people wanted government to intervene in the world insofar as it was planning for the future. Business may be the engine of growth and development, but with no context growth was all over the place – factories built beside subdivisions, jobs not created because of a lack of infrastructure, workers not adapting because they couldn't risk change without society's assistance. And it was relatively easy. People wanted change and burgeoning tax revenues permitted government to offer social and economic planning.

Robarts governed similarly, for the most part. But demands were also changing. Designs had been put in place for industry, but the work continued for people. As they prospered, they also wanted more from government. Ontario's treasury was still doing well and more reform was still easy. Yet Robarts was different than Frost. He was more the businessman and less the politician. He saw the unorganized nature of government and wanted to make it more corporate. Consolidation was to make administration more streamlined, even if the side-effect was bigger government.

Davis was less obviously progressive, right away. His days as Education minister gave him the image, but he did little to reinforce it as Premier. Then, the economy faltered and his government didn't have the same kind of leeway to offer perpetual reform. Yes, they were still taking in money, but inflation was stripping government of the ability to spend-to-reform. After the near-debacle of his first term, Davis realized that being progressive was the only road to re-election, though this type of change became more smoke-and-mirrors than full-fledged reform. Big ideas were offered in small packages, though public approval usually meant they expanded over time.

Even at that, 1981 was the last hurrah. The last term of Davis was marred by recession and a real absence of new ideas. When Frank Miller became leader, his ascendancy signalled the end, not renewal. He was too recognized as an economic driver, and his advisors convinced him to ignore progressive social policies that the party had written. It was a fundamental lack of understanding of what Ontario voters wanted. The braintrust felt his strength was economics, so focus on that. In doing so, they reinforced a public perception that the PCs were no longer a progressive party of ideas, just a conservative party of management.

Their timing was lousy, too. This tactic came when the Liberals and NDP were offering a plethora of modern, forward-thinking ideas. The difference was that the New Democrats lacked what the Tories had – economic legitimacy. Without it, the Liberals were the obvious choice.

Though it took a deal between the two opposition parties to bring David Peterson to power, a change in governing party was truly the will of the majority of people in 1985.

The Liberals were voraciously progressive. Who knows whether or not they would have been so had they not had to live up to the conditions of the accord, but they were. As well, an advancing economy was giving them the money to pursue change without concern. Peterson took them to a huge victory two years later, one which would guarantee "a Liberal dynasty".

And from this came the seeds of defeat. Majority government brought arrogant comfort. The perception that progressive reform was needed as a condition of government was lost, even though it was a time when the public was rapacious in its desire for such. Government expansion had resumed, but at the price of higher taxes. Had significant progress come with this, I suspect Ontarians would have been accepting. However, taxation without change was not.

The Liberal strategists saw a serious economic downturn coming and did not want to wait for it to call for re-election. They overestimated their popularity and underestimated the variety of issues that people held against them – Meech Lake, free trade, Patti Starr, taxes, Peterson's self-importance. So many voters turned toward the one party that demonstrated ideas, and had gained economic credibility from the days of the accord.

Bob Rae slipped into office with the worst possible conditions – massive recession driving revenues down for the first time ever, a caucus without experience and no time to learn, and a near two-thirds majority of voters who preferred a party other than the NDP becoming the government. Though Rae understood the need for being cautiously progressive, he did not take the time to plan what needed to be done. Instead, his government set out on an unprecedented spending spree, just at the time they couldn't afford it. People couldn't understand why they would go ahead and spend when it was clearly not affordable. And it was too late when Rae realized his party was being too change-oriented and not conservative enough. Most of his caucus never realized it.

The Harris Tories were anything but progressive. *Regressive* Conservative would have been more apt party moniker. They proposed undoing many of the most progressive moves by government going back as far as Davis. Yet they were perceived by the public as the *party of ideas*. They offered a cogent philosophy that contended to restore government to fiscal responsibility with re-affirmed priorities. The *progress* of change would be to re-focus it back on setting the conditions for business to thrive and for needed jobs to be created, *à la* Leslie Frost. People would be able to help themselves and government wouldn't need to be their crutch any longer.

In many ways, it was a complete subversion of the concept of progress, but it sold because of the popular mood. I think it is likely that, at any other time, the CSR would have flopped. There is no other way of putting it than to say that the prevailing public attitude in 1995 was one that was negative and vengeful. The recession had been hard, and few – save the truly wealthy – had been spared its ill-effects. People had been forced to tighten their belts, usually many times, and the prospect of this continuing made them angry. And their simmering rage focused on those they saw as not having to cut back – people on welfare got *free* money ... from them!, civil servants had whined and squealed at a 5% cut when many private sector workers had lost their jobs entirely or been forced to work far longer hours for no extra pay!, teachers only worked half-days for high pay!

For an issue to resonate with the public, they have to recognize it as an issue. Just as a farmer wanting a field of wheat, the soil must first be tilled. If he or she just went out and sprinkled the seed on the hard ground, not much would grow. The Tories recognized the attitude and focused their policies to take advantage. For they had the seed – the CSR. The ground – peoples' irritation and anxiety – was tilled by the NDP and their actions. Harris seeded the soil and ... boom! They were the agents of change, just *negative* change. They were the source for ideas, just *negative* ones. They planted the seeds of the CSR, and a rather squalid and twisted crop was harvested.

Harris and company come to power as brutal conquerors who bulldozed opposition or even those who were simply hesitant. No time could be taken to re-consider change. They had the plan and it had to be implemented quickly because even they realized they would stand no chance for re-election without some breathing period between revolutionary demolition and the next round of voting.

Yet people accepted the forced change, though most said it's too much, too fast. Why? Because many of those same people *trusted* Harris. Within weeks, he had kept promises – cutting photo radar, cutting *quotas*, cutting spending, cutting welfare benefits. While most new governments came to office, looked at the books, then said they couldn't keep their promises, Harris did and, thus, established an immediate bond with people.[1] They could trust him because he kept his word. And when the Tories would go too far, it would always be followed up by an attack on those who the public saw as deserving targets, e.g. the omnibus bill dropped their popularity, the civil service strike brought it right back. Good planning? No, just good timing.

So why were they re-elected in 1999? If Ontarians want progressive conservative government, they must have recognized that the Harris Tories were anything but progressive. Perhaps, but they were still the *party of ideas*, and the negative mood of the electorate was still at least a hangover. While the economy had been going great guns for a year or two, it hadn't resulted in tremendous advances for individuals or families. Remember, it was termed the *jobless recovery* for some time, and many of the jobs created were not full-time and did not pay well. And even when many better ones became available, they still didn't offer a lot of upward movement or pay increases. Even today, many people have seen pay hikes since 1990 that don't come close to covering the 25.2% loss to inflation. So the public was still hesitant about the Tories, but they suppressed that in hope that the "good times" would get even better.

Yet there was an alternative. The Liberals, in particular, offered a comprehensive platform chalk full of ideas for reform. Perhaps. But the *20/20 Plan* offered nothing even approaching the cogency of *The Common Sense Revolution*, and it laid out little in the way of a specific economic programme that a Liberal government would follow. It failed too greatly on offering progressive change and planned economic management. And though the Harris *Blueprint* was little better, it re-affirmed the Tories as the party of ideas, change, and management.

The Harrisites brought two substantive differences from the past. The first was that the Tories never tried to appeal to a majority of voters. Their Bradgate whiz kids had recognized that you don't need 50%+1 to win. Appealing to a simple plurality of 40-45% will pretty much get you what you want – power. The other difference was the simple mastery of the CSR. From its cogent promises and simple words came an overpowering message: *we know what we're doing and we can fix the mess! Give us a chance to prove it and you won't be disappointed.* Many promises were kept, but enough were still to be fulfilled that the image of the CSR was still there in *Blueprint* to give the Tories another term. Can that hold true again?

2. ... But what of the *Counter-Revolution*?

Many of my contemporaries are writing off the Harris Conservatives, feeling that enough people have now judged them incompetent, or just too divisive, that they're through. The truth is that, even though the Tories have faded in the polls since June 2000, they are still in an excellent position to win the next election. While they are polling in the low 30s, given the vicious and incompetent things they have done, they still have a remarkable level of support. However, that's not to say they don't have troubles.

The Walkerton tragedy damaged them permanently. It stole from them the level of trust that they had gained from keeping promises. Suddenly, the whole basis of the Harris agenda – that *government is bad* – came into question. Government is necessary. People expect it to keep their water fit to drink. As things stand now, it is unlikely they could again achieve the 45% they managed in 1999, which means any margin of victory will be tiny, at best. On the other hand, historically, 40% is the minimum necessary to win a majority in Ontario, particularly if you take your seats in rural areas, which are still over-represented. Bob Rae won with less than 38%, but that was in extreme three-way splits that were exceptional. So even if 5-10% of those who voted Conservative in 1999 move their support straight to the second party, the Tories will still stand a reasonable chance of forming a third majority. The Liberals might win some seats by large margins while losing others by small ones. They win the popular vote but lose the election. And this is not out of the question. A poll done in the light of the Premier's announced intention to retire stated that 37% of those who said they would today vote Liberal thought Harris had done a good job. Clearly, some Tory supporters of 1995 and 1999 have parked their votes with the Liberals for now. But will they keep them there?

While the focus on Harris helped the Tories immensely during their first years, perhaps it also helps them when he leaves. If the voters' trust was in him, it may be that when it was damaged by the Walkerton incident, that reflected on Harris more than his party. In other words, he may take any lack of trust with him when he goes, giving a new leader the chance to re-establish trust with the public. And halfway through their leadership campaign, the polls have already shown the Tory deficit has been cut from 20 to 12 points. Of course, if the Tories do win next time, but drop to a minority, I would expect them to be out of power nearly as fast as Frank

Miller was in 1985.

Mike Harris has announced he's retiring and a race is underway, not just for Tory leader but also to be premier. The choice of the winner will unquestionably be a major factor in Tory fortunes. However, the general caucus is another question. Though the free-for-all of the leadership contest will keep some Cabinet and backbench members in place, waiting to see if they've backed the winning horse, maybe as many as ten of Harris' caucus will not seek re-election, some because other opportunities have appeared, some because they have no future without Harris, some because they have fallen out of favour and have no political future, period. Much will depend on Harris' successor and who his friends are in caucus. (I say 'his' because I am doubtful the Tories of 1952, er, 2002, will pick a woman.) While it may allow the party a new face and time to soften the government's hard image, it is unlikely someone perceived as soft could win a leadership campaign. Tory party members are mostly those who have supported the hard-edged actions and wouldn't seem likely to support anyone who would go against them. To put it another way, moderation will have to be in muted words, not in actions, for one to be victorious.

On the up side for the government, if the Opposition parties continue to offer little of substance, the Tories will be in a good position to win again. In both 1995 and 1999, the Liberals attempted to run campaigns with platforms made up of small policies that could be criticized by the NDP as 'Blue Lite' and the Tories as weak. I am not suggesting they should come up with tyrannical commandments, but simple statements of real, from-the-gut, beliefs would go a long way. As well, they need a solidly laid-out economic statement, with numbers, to hit the Tories' strength.[2] And the NDP needs to stop apologizing for its decisions as government and actually come up with NEW ideas. It's as though the party can't get beyond June 1995 or, perhaps, September 1990. The November 2001 national convention did not create much hope of this though, as most delegates were firmly in the camp of the *status quo*.[3]

And there is always the money. The Tories have a lot of it, the other parties very little. There is no doubt that the Conservative strategy will again be to flood the airwaves and print media with advertising to promote themselves and attack the Liberals and NDP. If you've got it, you might as well use it. And they are now proposing to loosen the restrictions on what constitutes unacceptable government advertising by permitting the use of Cabinet ministers' names, faces, and voices on ads. Should it come to pass, this will permit an even greater abuse of public funds.

Also, it is only reasonable to think they will again go for the jugular of Dalton McGuinty. It was extremely effective in branding him a loser in the last election, and the Liberals have not gone very far to washing away this unpleasant tattoo. At a recent provincial council meeting in Trenton, McGuinty told the story of how a 1999 Liberal candidate was going door-to-door and came upon one answered by a young mother, with a baby in her arms and a toddler at her knee. The man explained who he was, gave her a heads-up on Liberal policies, and he eventually said his leader was Dalton McGuinty. At that moment, the toddler piped up with, "He's not up to the job". The story was meant to be amusing, though I found it somewhat pathetic. If this branding was ingrained in three-year-olds, how deep is it in the minds of 43- and 63-year-olds? A recent poll showed McGuinty with an anaemic personal approval rating of 25%, with 27% saying they would not support him. To think the Tories will not again mine this ore would be a major tactical mistake.

That having been said, however, I believe if the Liberals offer far-reaching and visionary social and economic ideas, even in a general context, and they run a reasonably competent campaign, free of major mistakes, they should win the next election. The Tories have shown they're about out of intellectual fuel, save for the neo-conservative mantras, and are ripe for the picking. However, McGuinty and his cohorts are not shoo-ins. They still need to overcome four hurdles.

First, they actually have to come out with expansive ideas, not the mushy gruel of 1995 and 1999. This means that policy development must actually translate into a substantial, but clear, platform. They cannot just pick a position between the Tories and NDP and promise to do better than them. People want to believe they're voting for politicians with vision and ideas. In 1995 they did, it was just a dark vision and negative ideas. Unfortunately, as of the Liberal policy conference in February 2002, the policies being passed are seriously lacking in vision.[4] What this will mean for a platform only time will tell.

Second, the Liberals must come up with money or spend money they don't have. Politics favours the victors, especially nowadays, as opposition parties at all levels seem to have great difficulty coming up with funding. At some point, if you don't have the cash, you're just going to have to risk it. Given the dim future for Ontario if the neo-cons get a third majority, I would suggest now is the time. The central party has recently decided to break a long-held view not to poll their membership directly for donations, as the other parties do, and this may make some difference. However, continuous losses have hurt the numbers of memberships held, so it may be too small a pool for both the party and the ridings to dip into.

Third, the Liberals still lack organization. A perfect example was party president Greg Sorbara whining about the Premier's call of a by-election in the Beaches-East York riding in August 2001. Yes, it was summer and, yes, it is unusual to call a by-election at this time. However, the incumbent, Frances Lankin had announced she was quitting in early June, for the end of July. They knew the by-election was coming, yet were still unprepared more than a month later. As well, a province-wide meeting of riding presidents and party officials on election preparedness was postponed because of the by-election call. There are so few people in the party apparatus that they seemingly can't do two things at once. I dare say this speaks volumes, given that the Liberal candidate hadn't a snowball's chance-in-hell of being elected. Michael Prue, the NDP candidate, is a popular former mayor of the former City of East York, and he was running in a riding held by the NDP since 1975. As well, the Liberal, CityTV environment personality Bob Hunter, had not been a Liberal until this time, and came with no *machine* to help him. In fact, the Liberals have often run third in the riding, as they did in 1999.[5] Regardless, the party threw in most of the resources they had on a hopeless venture. It was bad planning and affected the whole party negatively.

And fourth, the Liberals must have an effective strategy to deal with *Dalton McGuinty ... he's still not up to the job*. There is no question the Tories did great damage with this, and it seems likely that this harm will be somewhat permanent. There can be no doubt they will try it again. When Jim Flaherty announced his intention to run for the Conservative leadership, he repeated it. If the Liberals aren't able to turn the tables and again lose the battle of leadership images, they will again start behind the eight-ball. However, if the Liberals are willing to take a *team* approach, and risk going to the voters with something like "McGuinty's good, and so are the people with him", it might take some of the steam out of his unattractive *brand*. Unfortunately, the trend to this point has been to make everything *McGuinty*. These are McGuinty ideas, not Liberal ideas. This is the McGuinty party, not the Liberal party. It is learning the wrong lesson from Harris and company. If the Tories can continue to paint him as not being up to the job, that will translate into the party not being up to governing, and the Liberals may well lose again.

And then there is the NDP. Historically, the New Democrats were created from the CCF to take advantage of the massive industrialization of Ontario in the 1950s. A party dedicated to the *working man* was supposed to create a connection with the union movement and loyalty for the new, *not-*

as-socialist, party. This bonding never worked out the way it was hoped, though certainly the provincial NDP benefited more than their national counterparts ever have. However, in the last ten years or so, the party's fortunes have declined to the point where they have failed to achieve, or just barely, party status at both levels. In fact, many NDP supporters of the past now vote for Harris provincially and the Reform/Alliance federally, and New Democratic leaders don't seem to have a clue why.

Perhaps it is fair to say that federal leader Alexa McDonough unknowingly framed the NDP's paradox during the 2000 federal election. In answering a question regarding where her party would draw the line on tax hikes, she stated an annual income of $60,000 as being "wealthy". I'm sure a good percentage of active NDP supporters would agree. As she said, 88% of Canadians earn under $60,000 annually. However, in Ontario, much of the unionized sector, especially that in manufacturing, such as the auto sector, is filled with people who earn this level of salary, or more, or at least are close enough to have hopes of getting to it. They do not see themselves as rich. Most consider themselves blue-collar, working-class or low-end middle-class. Given that this is what they've been told their entire working lives, it makes sense. The reality is the NDP was never designed to represent people who made average or better wages. The CCF connection to the working man was when that person made minimal money outside a unionized environment. In many ways, the unions won their *war* against their employers (though *battles* still continue, and a new war may be in the offing) by establishing so many union shops. The CCF/NDP was founded to represent the downtrodden. Perhaps the NDP leadership needs to concede that wealthier unions just shouldn't be a major concern of theirs and concentrate on fighting for the truly poor in the service sector and of the unemployed. Of course, the problem is that unions pass along a cut of members' dues to them ... rich unions pay more. Either that or they're going to have to redefine the term *rich*, and the difficulty there is that someone who can't get more than a 20-hour week at minimum wage ($7,124 per year) might not feel much kinship with someone working 40 hours at $30 per hour ($62,400 per year). It seems it is this divergence that is presently poisoning the party.

It is my opinion that the NDP cannot reasonably hope to form a government in Ontario any time in the near future. Even if they make up their minds regarding *party of the poor* or *party of workers, rich or poor*, they are as branded as McGuinty. The Rae government was marked as incompetent and spendthrift, and lost the trust of voters. It will take new leadership and MPPs not of that government to throw off the image. Until that happens, the NDP is going to sit on the precipice of irrelevance. It is important they do not tip over. If they do, there will be no coming back.

As for the next election, the NDP leadership must decide whether it prefers the neo-conservatism of the Harrisites or what they see as the conservatism of the Liberals. After the 1999 campaign, there were New Democratic supporters who were disgusted their party had so vehemently attacked the Liberals, as they would have preferred them to another term of Harris. But this was the strategy to save the party from extermination. It assumed that NDP support can only be lost to, or come from, the Liberals. Yet many heavily unionized ridings have gone Conservative. The reality today is that support can move from left to right and back again, which means that such a strategy is pointless. Better for the NDP to set out basic policies they want to follow and flog them, over and over. In the lead-up to the 1999 election, they claimed they supported a shorter work week, as prescribed in Jeremy Rifkin's book, The End of Work[6]. Then, they failed to actually run on it. If this is something they believe, they should tell people why and make it a fundamental premise. It seems to me that the New Democrats are now so afraid of controversy that might keep them from winning an election, they don't realize they aren't going to win anyway! Better to have principles and stand up for them than hide them so you can be successful. (Liberals take note, too.)

Having a progressive and conservative nature has certainly been the key for political parties to be elected as government in Ontario. However, that is not to say it can stop you from being defeated. From Frost to Robarts, this key was passed along. It went to Davis, too, but he was forced to obscure it by a changing economy. This nature was either ignored or misunderstood by Miller ... or he couldn't make up for four years without progress. But if the days of David Peterson are a sign of anything, it is that this progressive and conservative nature must be seen in the context of the time. The demands on this government were great but, once it became a majority, it also either ignored or misunderstood what was wanted. People had a pent-up desire for reform, which was partially satisfied by the two years of the accord, but only partially. Yet the government backed away from its pace of change. At the same time, it increased taxes to pay for the new programmes, while trying to stem deficits. In other words, it was both progressive and conservative, but it came to balance the scales too far to the latter. At the same time, getting involved in federal matters and scandal tainted them, and it was clearly a combination that led to the Liberal's defeat. However, I should say that they would have been re-elected had the voters not perceived of another *progressive conservative* party waiting in the wings. I'm sure there are those who would guffaw at my suggestion that the NDP was of this nature and, perhaps, that is going too far. I would argue they were seen as such, though ... certainly not as the socialist hordes at the gate, looking to cause a *revolution*. In fact, it is most ironic that it would be the forces of conservatism that would storm the Pink Palace with their cataclysmic changes.

3. "Harrisite" rhymes with parasite

The first Tory Cabinet was one made up of people who were, for the most part, identified by voters as fairly competent private sector managers. The problem was they were lousy politicians. (The whiz kids were the political brains.) And it may have been this that made them reasonably popular with so many Ontarians. Unlike your tradition pol, they weren't interested in listening and compromising. They wanted to "do". And for a public that had been starved of reform for many years, action is what they wanted. But this inflexible nature is also what made the Tories clumsy and prone to shooting their toes off. They didn't understand using nuance and time to get what they wanted, instead of forcing things down peoples' throats. It's no wonder the distaste many dissenters have for them is so vitriolic. If the Tories want to stay in power, they need to become better politicians. They need to manage the changes they've enacted, and they need to compromise more often.

Clearly, this would seem to defy the nature of the beast. Along with their many other faults, the Harris Tories are quite narrow-minded on issues, once they've made up their minds. For example, two of the most unyielding areas for the Tories are *tax cuts create jobs* and people on welfare. These are the sort of issues where compromise would be something that people could appreciate. No matter how popular something is, voters eventually get bored with it, particularly when government harps on it. Eventually, the voters will tire of these issues, even if they agree with the Harrisites' position. At this point, the Conservatives haven't figured this out.

Dogma

In late 2001, it is apparent the economy has fallen into recession, or near-recession. The Tories' response? Advance the next scheduled tax cuts by three months.[7] I have no doubt that most members of the Harris caucus believe tax cuts create jobs, even in the face of economic proof it does not. Their dogged persistence suggests a blind obedience to this credo. The problem is ... you can't keep cutting taxes forever.

Let us assume, for a moment, everyone else is wrong and tax cuts do create jobs. The economy is bad, so government cuts taxes. Hundreds of thousands of jobs are created ... yet that doesn't stop the economy from going into recession again. In other words, the economic cycle of expansion and contraction cannot be avoided. So many people will lose their jobs again, meaning further tax cuts will simply get them new jobs. The *law of diminishing returns* applies. Eventually, tax cuts will simply create jobs that will automatically be lost in the next downturn, and nothing long-term will be gained by them. At some point, they would, in fact, fail to restore jobs, and the economy would collapse.

At the same time, there is a minimal level of services acceptable to the public, and it will take a certain amount of revenue to maintain that. In other words, taxes can only be cut so far. What happens when you hit that basement, but the economy goes into recession again? With no further tax cuts, jobs won't be created and recession may become depression. At best, the recessions will become longer and deeper and, with government cut to the bone, it will be unable to help people survive. I am not old enough to have lived during the *Dirty '30s*, but I dare say there are few people these days tough enough to withstand economic collapse.

Now let us assume that tax cuts do NOT create jobs to any appreciable level, and cutting taxes is simply undermining the revenues of the provincial government and undermining its ability to offer services the public want and need. If you're a neo-conservative, chances are that's okay, too. At some point, politicians will face one of two choices: hike taxes to pay for these services; or, allow the private sector to offer services that have been delivered by government, even though profit margins assure the services will be more expensive. Of course, the private sector can't make money offering many services and won't do so.

The difficulty appears to be that the Harrisites think you can have both with tax cuts. You undermine government and can, thus, rationalize turning over service delivery to the private sector. At the same time, cutting taxes will help create jobs and soak up all those public servants who find themselves unemployed. The problem is at a certain point you can no longer cut taxes. Government is necessary, even at a minimal level. Fire, police, nurses, teachers, and the like are needed. Government will cost some money, so there must be a minimal level of taxes. What happens when the economy goes bad one too many times and you can't cut taxes any more? Do you just abandon the public to the private sector?

There is a great fallacy amongst the right-wing in Canada that the United

States should be our model. They see it as a much superior system to ours because people are less dependent on government and are more able to look after themselves. This is usually defined as *they pay less taxes, thus they are less dependent*. However, the reality is that Americans are stuck paying for their own health care and, once that cost is included with their taxes, Canadians actually pay less for a higher level of service. In fact, Canadians making less than $60,000 have a larger disposable income than similar Americans.[8] The reason that it appears Americans pay less is because of lower tax thresholds. However, when other expenses are considered – expenses that Americans pay out-of-pocket and Canadians pay through taxes – we are better off. In fact, our poorest 35% are "absolutely better off", while most in the middle-class are somewhat better off. It is only over $75,000 when Americans begin to be significantly better off. The reality is we tax wealthier citizens at a higher rate and that skews average rates. Americans appear to be better off because they tax their rich at a far lower rate, so the average amount of take-home pay seems bigger for them. People like Mike Harris cannot, apparently, see this reality. And it should be noted that 40 million Americans have NO health insurance, while ALL Canadians have it.

Greedy, greedy ...

The other *reality* for the government is their unrelenting attitude toward people on welfare. I actually think it applies to all the poor. The Harris Tories obviously don't like the poor, though they tolerate the working ones ... just. With the minimum wage frozen, $6.85 an hour in 1995 is more like $6.00 in 2001, given 12.34% inflation. It's hard to live on this, especially when you consider that most minimum wage jobs come with part-time status and few-to-no benefits. And for those unable to find work, the situation is ghastly, no matter what the Tories may believe. For an individual collecting welfare benefits, the maximum of $540 per month works out to about $124.62 per week, or $17.80 per day. And given this has also been frozen since the 21.6% cut in 1995, it is actually more like $473.36 a month, or $15.60 per day. Imagine trying to live on that. Pardon ... *survive* on that.

So why do the Harrisites have such a dislike for the poor. The only obvious answer is that they have no empathy for them. I believe this comes from their self-image. They see themselves as self-made men and women ... successful in business, successful in politics. They came from backgrounds that were modest, yet they were able to overcome this to accomplish what they have. If you're poor, it's because you haven't worked hard enough to escape it. Harris himself said, "I can't tell you how many millionaires started out with minimum wage jobs". So why should these indolent be able to *feed at the public trough* for free? Thus, you must be put to work, even if it is the make-work offered through workfare.

The difficulty is that many of these allegedly self-made people were far less poor in their circumstances than they let on. It is a common malady of the well-off and politicians to re-make their youth in the image of something that had to be overcome. Mike Harris suffers from this. I believe it was shortly after he became premier, in the light of the Tsubouchi tuna affair, that he suggested to media reporters he could remember his days existing on bologna sandwiches in his youth. When contacted for verification, his father is said to have angrily responded that it was never that way at his house, and a long-time friend commented that eating at Deane Harris' place was like feasting at the Royal York Hotel. Ernie Eves has commented on his "working-class background". Yet his father was a plant supervisor, who could afford to see his son got a university education. While a couple of the Conservative caucus might have an argument, the vast majority are of solidly middle-class backgrounds, and many of these have benefited greatly from the advantages of being early baby-boomers.

As for feeding at the public trough, more than a few of the present Conservative caucus have filled up before being elected to the Legislature. Along with Harris, there is John Baird, Toby Barrett, Marcel Beaubien, Tony Clement, Brian Coburn, Diane Cunningham, Carl DeFaria, Garfield Dunlop, Janet Ecker, Brenda Elliott, Doug Galt, Garry Guzzo, Ernie Hardeman, John Hastings, Chris Hodgson, Cam Jackson, Helen Johns, Bert Johnson, Morley Kells, Frank Klees, Margaret Marland, Gerry Martiniuk, Bart Maves, Frank Mazzilli, Tina Molinari, Julia Munro, Bill Murdoch, Marilyn Mushinski, John O'Toole, Jerry Oullette, Bob Runciman, Joe Spina, Gary Stewart, Chris Stockwell, Joe Tascona, David Tilson, David Tsubouchi, Jim Wilson, Elizabeth Witmer, and David Young, all having received public money as trustees, political staff, municipal politicians, or as public servants. That's 41 of 56, or 73%. And that doesn't include those who had businesses that got government contracts, or Tories from the first term, which would add to the number. For people who were supposedly there to fix government, they sure were a big part of the problem. Their hypocrisy is still one.

And their noses are still well down in the trough. After their re-election, the Tories suddenly felt the need to get a pay raise. Now they had always been direct that the pay *cut* they had taken in 1996 was just until the budget was balanced. Such a promise had been in the legislation that did away with the *gold-plated pensions*. However, when raises were being proposed in 2000, it was as though these *tax-fighters* had lost their minds as to what was an acceptable boost.

However, one should begin back in 1995 when the Harrisites kept their election promise to review these *excessive* pensions. A five-member commission was established to examine the compensation of MPPs and to recommend changes. It reported on 27 November 1995, with recommendations that the, then, current pension arrangement was "overly generous" and should be reduced, since the tax-free allowances were not supported by documented expenses they should be eliminated, and that compensation of MPPs should be "measured against a benchmark reflecting private-sector norms and practices, and this benchmark should be updated regularly".

While the government made a big deal out of getting rid of the tax-free allowance of MPPs, it turned out that the reality had not been a cut but a hike. What they did was to actually convert these allowances to salary, and turned annual pay of $71,000 into $78,000, with an extra $7,000 in benefits and $3,900 in RRSP contribution. Nevertheless, the Premier continued to say he favoured a 10% *restoration* to make up for the Social Contract cut of 1993 (which had actually been 5.5%).

Once the budget was balanced, the Tories set up a task force of the speaker, the chair of the original commission, and two others, to make an independent recommendation on an MPP pay raise. In spring 2000, it suggested 32.6%, which would have jumped basic pay to $103,458. The argument was always the same: the salary must rise to attract the best and brightest, who would undoubtedly make more in the private sector. This raise would at least make being a provincial politician somewhat competitive with what business would pay. According to reports, the Harrisites were surprised and confused when the opposition parties vehemently attacked this as excessive. They had assumed, since the Liberals and NDP supported the task force's appointment, they would support its recommendation. However, with the Tories offering 2% to public service workers, perhaps they should have been a bit less nonplussed.

They left the issue on the back burner until the fall, when a government report was leaked suggesting the Tories wanted a 42.2% increase to achieve parity with federal MPs. After all, they shared the same-sized ridings. Of course, this would have meant they were paid more than MPs and the Premier would have made more than the Prime Minister, but there wasn't much quibble in the public. Everyone, including Harris supporters like the Canadian Taxpayers Federation, was stunned by the manifest greed. Yet the government did not back down right away. In fact, both Harris and House Leader Norm Sterling defended the amount initially. However, after a raucous caucus meeting, those who felt they'd get the raise at the cost of not being re-elected won the day.

Even at that, they weren't done. Sterling approached the opposition again, this time to suggest a 17% hike to be phased in over three years. They declined, and held the line suggested by McGuinty that 2% a year, as the civil service was to receive, was fair. Like children who don't get their way, the Tories sulked and said, as a result of this lack of cooperation, there would be no raise for any MPP.

Even that wasn't the end. Too many government members had become enamoured of the $110,945 annual salary they had lost out on, and they continued to push for a raise. Over the winter, another idea was floated. This one would see the Integrity Commissioner, former Ontario Supreme Court Justice Gregory Evans, decide the matter. In this way, the whole procedure could be seen to be done fairly, so a fair amount could be proposed. Of course, it didn't hurt that Evans owed his job to the Tory government. And though it was said he was to determine a fair rate of pay for MPPs, no one questioned that this meant a raise, not a cut ... not even the opposition, who seemed to have quietly accepted that a pay raise was a good thing, after all. As a result, the necessary legislation was passed on 28 June 2001.

Evans was back with a decision within two months. He concluded a significant pay hike was in order, and justified this by accepting a rather high-range Conference Board of Canada statistic that private sector salaries had risen 31.9% from 1991 to 2000[9], that "a multi-year salary freeze distorts the principle of fairness", and included a comparison of the pay of other legislatures, the federal parliament, and the City of Toronto. He recommended annual pay raises of three percent, retroactive to 1 January 2001, for each year of the term remaining. Then, after the next election, MPP pay would immediately jump 25%, with a full review of pay and benefits to be done in 2005. In other words, pay would go from 2000's $78,007 to $80,347 for 2001, $82,758 in 2002, $85,240 in 2003 and, then, if an election were held in that year, the post-election sum would be $106,550. That would be a 36.6% pay hike over the period of three years. If the government waited until 2004 to have an election, that year's salary would be $87,798, rising to $109,747 after an election, or a 40.7% increase.[10] And between the election and the 2005 review, annual increases would be at the rate of the Ontario Industrial Average Wage

Index average, not to exceed 7%. In effect, the Tories were getting the snootful they wanted, just over a longer time and they have to get re-elected to get the big boost. No one but politicians and their familiars seemed to support this. Coming on the heels of a hefty 20% federal hike in MP's pay, all it did was increase public cynicism that politicians were truly out to line their own pockets.[11]

Though I personally can't see it happening, my suggestion would be for any of the parties to promise to cut MPP pay back to a more reasonable amount in any slate of election promises. Except for politicians and their most ardent supporters, no one believes this amount of pay is fair. In fact, I would suggest that those regular Tory members who have been most fervently in favour of *The Common Sense Revolution* may be those most disgusted by this monster pay hike. A key part of the Harris agenda was to restore fiscal competence to public administration. Yet this increase to MPPs will mean that their wages will cost $2.1 million more than they did before the number of MPPs was cut from 130 to 103. How does higher cost for fewer representatives make sense? How is that value for money?

4. Whither democracy?

In <u>Promised Land</u>, author John Ibbitson says that, when Harris first took over, he addressed the deputy ministers and told them, while the government welcomed their input on policy implementation, the policies themselves were not open to debate. As well ...

> ... *He reminded (them) that they owed their first allegiance, not to their minister, but to Harris himself. This was a timely reiteration of a political reality in parliamentary democracies. Deputy ministers are not appointed by ministers, but by the cabinet secretary, who is in turn appointed by the premier. As such, the senior bureaucracy owes its first loyalty to the chief executive – one reason that ministers are sometimes the last to know what's going on in their departments. Harris wanted to remind the mandarinate that he and his political staff intended to keep firm, central control of the government's agenda. Ministers should be under no illusion that they were sovereign within their own departments.* (Ibbitson, pg. 101)

Not to disagree with Mr. Ibbitson but, in two university degrees in Political Science, I never met a professor who taught this version of 'loyalty'. In fact, I wholly disagree with the idea that deputy ministers owe their first loyalty to the leader of government. The whole point is that they have no loyalty beyond *the people*, and they do their jobs in a neutral fashion, avoiding the quicksand of political loyalty. And I don't mean this just as an avoidance of partisan allegiance. I mean that they do their jobs to the best of their ability, period. And while it is not unheard of for a leader to bypass a minister for the opinions of bureaucrats, why would one want to demand loyalty to himself before to their minister? If the deputy minister goes straight to the premier, what's the point of having a minister at all? Perhaps ministers are not to be sovereign within their own departments, but they are supposed to be trusted to run them, then answer for their performance to the leader. The sort of arrangement Harris assigned is much more common of a dictatorship than a democracy.

This desire for centralized control probably goes back to the dissolution of the PC party apparatus in 1990, when the party people all came from the ranks of volunteers. Harris and his whiz kids became accustomed to having no one to question them, no institutionalized party mechanisms to guarantee their accountability. In fact, given that they only had to answer to the, then, low expectations of party members, they were functionally accountable to no one but themselves. Once they got into power, they simply imposed a system that would remove the normal back-up supplied by ministers. The only ministers who have any real say at all are those in the Planning and Policy Committee, but even influence there is filtered through the Premier's Office. It was one of many moves that, intentionally or not, has profoundly violated the tenets of a democratic state.

There is increasing, though far from widespread, discussion of whether or not our democracy is at risk. Governments of all stripes in most western democracies seem more and more willing to restrain or deny the rights of people. This is especially so in the light of the terrorist attack on the United States on 11 September 2001. Most people seem quite willing to allow government to chisel away at rights in exchange for the promise of greater security. Yet at what point does the loss of rights indicate that democracy itself is in question?

In fact, the assault on democratic rights has been going on for some time. I do not think that people have stopped believing in democratic principles. It's much more a function of *taking it for granted* and *not seeing it as a priority*. In a criminal sense, this comes from fear. People fear they or their families will be victims of crime. If rights must be denied to repeat offenders, for example, that is a price they must pay for having committed crimes. After the terrorist attacks, Parliament passed a law giving police and justice officials the power to deny rights to those *suspected* of certain crimes. There were those who were satisfied these powers will be reviewed after five years, in hopes they will no longer be needed because the threat will have diminished.[12]

However, rights cannot be removed *temporarily* or at all. Denial of a right for five years or five seconds means it is not a *right*, just a privilege which can be revoked. Democracy is not based on privileges. It is based on fundamental laws of justice than cannot be denied, diminished, or revoked. They are absolute precedents from which all liberty grows. Deny them and you deny freedom and you have no real democracy. And that is true whether you are talking about terrorists who kill thousands or violent thugs who defile children. Rights are rights for all, as revolting as it might occasionally seem. If you deny them for terrorists and paedophiles, a government may eventually deny them for much lesser crimes or just things they perceive as crimes ... like disagreeing with government policies.

Democracy shows itself in many ways. The public having the ability to dispense with governments on a regular basis is a core precept, as is their ability to know what that government and its representatives are doing in their name, and why they are doing it. Clearly, the Harris government has not respected democracy in this sense. They have shown a remarkable disdain for the Legislature, undoubtedly due to the hurry they were in to get things done, particularly during their first term. As was seen with the omnibus Bill 26, they were willing to go to great lengths to implement their agenda. But it wasn't just their rush, the Tories also wanted to avoid debate over the issues. They began to use all the measures available to take advantage of both.

Their biggest stick was time allocation, or closure. This is when the government can use the Standing Orders of the Legislature to only permit a certain period of debate on an issue. Effectively, it means a majority government can ram through any legislation. During the three sessions of the 36th Parliament, the Harris Tories passed 41 of 118 bills under time allocation. That was 34.7% of all bills passed over the four years, 1995-1999. As I write this, of the 39 bills passed during the 37th Parliament, the Tory government has subjected 24 to time allocation motions. That's 61.5%. As a comparison, in the final term of Bill Davis and the short-lived Miller government, 292 bills were passed, of which time allocation was introduced three times. During the Peterson minority from 1985 to 1987, time allocation was used for one of 129 bills. Over the Peterson majority, there were three time allocation motions for 183 bills.[13] That's seven of 604.

While I and others criticize their seeming lack of concern for the niceties of parliamentary tradition, the Harrisites were actually just taking their hints from the previous NDP regime. Though the Conservatives took all these measures to new heights, the Rae government was actually the trailblazer for them. During their time in government, they used time allocation 21 times on 163 pieces of legislation. And the Tories were not short on their condemnation of the NDP, at the time.

One result of this guillotining of debate is that bills are not receiving the scrutiny they used to, not just by parliamentarians but by the public, as well. Under the Rae New Democrats, it took a bill an average of 183 days from First Reading to enactment. During the Harrisites' first term, that dropped to 129 days. By the end of the first year of their second term, that had become 35 days, which included an average of just three days for committee hearings.[14] There is no question that the Tories hate public hearings, and now usually limit their time as well as not making them accessible to all citizens, just those who are invited to speak. While the second term has been far less ambitious, the government is showing that time allocation is now just an accepted measure for them. Over time, denying democratic debate has simply become a function of efficiency.

And the Harrisites are not shy about filibustering their own Legislative debates. This time is now often spent by backbenchers throwing *softball* questions at ministers, both so the government can put forward its own views, repeatedly, but often to take time away from the Opposition parties, who might actually make cogent points that could be picked up by the media and passed along to voters.

The other thing that has changed in the last few years is how little time the Legislature is actually in session. Before the NDP, it was not uncommon for it to be in session a good portion of the time, though I cannot exaggerate and suggest the Ontario government sits anything close to as long as the federal one, historically. However, Bob Rae often found that being in session simply gave his opponents more of an opportunity to criticize. During his first session in 1991, the Legislature sat for 102 days, then 94 during the second in 1992. In the next two years, over the third session, it sat for 169 days. In 1995, prior to the election, the Legislature was not recalled.

The Tories, once in power, brought the Legislature back for 40 days, then 102 in 1996, 121 in 1997, then a dip to 72 in 1998, and just 7 days in 1999 before the election. After that, MPPs met 122 days over the rest of 1999 and 2000. In 2001, they were in session 81 days.

To put it another way, the NDP had the Legislature meet 365 times in 55 months, or 21.8% of the time. The Tories have had the Legislature in session 545 times in 77 months (not including the 1999 election month), or 23.3% of the time. These are hardly inspiring numbers for democratic governments. Meeting 85 days a year, less than two full days per week, hardly seems acceptable to allow the public a true opportunity to take in and understand the plethora of legislation presented for them.

There are other disturbing changes in democratic representation: legal influence peddling by politicians; and, making elections about money. It was a mere 25 years ago that Bill Davis was forced to change election financing rules to cut down on the appearance of donations in exchange for contracts, jobs, favours. Over the years, rules were tightened further, as they were for municipal politicians.[15] Even with these reforms, there is no question that election and political party financing has been a question of concern over the years since. From time to time, scandals have resulted from improper contributions and lax conformity to rules. However, no government has truly taken the problem seriously. That's not entirely true. The Harris Tories have, in fact, taken advantage to make the problems worse.

As I said earlier, money truly does distort the decisions made by politicians. If it didn't, why was the business community so chummy to Mike Harris during the days between 1990 and 1995 when the Tories were on the skids and did not appear likely to form the government any time in the near future? The answer is simple. Making small contributions to them, on the chance they would win, was an investment in *influence*. If you gave them nothing and they came to power, they would owe you nothing. Such a government would have a free hand to act on issues while taking positions that might not have favoured business. Certainly, the NDP had shown they were not their best friends (though they were not the ogres business people had feared). So, business leaders gave the Liberals some, but the Tories much more. They were, after all, promising corporate Ontario all the goodies it could imagine. That was one *gravy train* not to miss.

And the Tories instantly recognized their new friends and rewarded them with massive tax cuts and a business-friendly environment that cut regulations, needed or not. They also understood that raising limits on contributions and spending would bring them even more money. When people shake hands, the *grease* on one palm usually gets spread widely around. With money comes influence. For the Tories and for business, this is a symbiotic and mutually-productive relationship. It's also completely legal.

However, it is a terrible assault on democratic governance. When political parties cannot fight elections on a fairly even basis, the advantage will always be with the one with the most money. In 1988, John Turner scored heavily in the televised leaders' debate over the terrible risks of a free trade agreement with the United States. However, the Liberals ran out of money before they could counter the onslaught of ads from the Tories promoting it. In the end, money decided an issue of extreme national importance. In the months before the 1999 elections, the Ontario Tories spent amazing sums on advertising to smear Dalton McGuinty and attack the Liberals as spendthrifts. This was money they could not have spent during the election because it would have caused them to go over the legislated limits. And by changing the law to omit certain costs, the Tories set themselves up to spend even more than their opponents. By the time the election was over, the Liberals and NDP had spent about $6 million, but were a combined $4-plus million in debt. The Conservatives had blown their entire $8 million stash, and had spent another $2 million as well. While the totals may have been similar, the Harrisites were out of debt within months. The Liberals are still $2 million in debt and the NDP are just in the black. By the next election, if the rules remain the same, the Tories will have an even greater advantage than in 1999, because the opposition parties must spend so much time and effort to get themselves out of the hole, while the government simply soaks in the contributions for the spending spree to come.

And it's not just at the central party level where this advantage exists, it's also at the riding level. For the 1999 election, the Conservative party *gave* their unheld ridings $60,000 each to spend on their campaigns. In ridings that were held, especially by Cabinet ministers, they had a great upper hand. As an example, in my riding, Simcoe-Grey, Jim Wilson collected over $22,000 from businesses or business groups for his campaign, plus his riding association took in nearly $16,000. Thirty-eight-thousand dollars makes up just over half the legal spending his campaign was permitted. The Liberal riding association and campaign took in just $8,500 from business and unions, or just 22% of what the Tories took in. Now, there's no question they were better at collecting the money, but this is a difference that is hard to accept as fair, especially given the sources. Yes, a good portion of it comes from local businesses, who may or may not have Tory allegiances. However, even more comes in from multinational corporations and businesses directly affected by the decisions of Jim Wilson, as minister.

Between 1995 and 2000, Wilson's campaigns and riding association took in nearly $200,000 from businesses and business groups. In 2000, the provincial Simcoe-Grey Tories took in over $20,000 from businesses and business groups, many of which were waiting to see decisions regarding hydro deregulation/privatization. These included Algonquin Power Systems, the Collingwood Public Utilities Commission, Hydro One, Northland Power, Toronto Hydro, and the Municipal Electric Association. The year before, there was money from CU Power Canada, Enron Canada, and Northland Power. And when Wilson was Health minister, pharmaceutical companies and health care interests were donating him money. Even a hospital, under review by the HSRC, made a contribution. It was all within legal limits, but how can anyone think it doesn't *buy* influence? Having influence over politicians is not consistent with democracy.

But it is not just commercial interests and politicians who are showing disdain for democratic principles. The public itself seems far less concerned in what is going on, even though it intimately affects most of their everyday lives. They don't buy influence. Quite the opposite. They are showing little interest at all.

Public participation in our democratic system of government is in decline. Over time, voter turn-out is dropping. In the 1950s and '60s, it was typical to see 65-70% of eligible voters cast ballots in an Ontario election. Unfortunately, there hasn't been a turn-out of 70% since 1971, which was 73.5%. The best turn-out in the last two decades was 64.4% in 1990. In the last two contests, turn-out has been 63% and 58.3%, respectively. It is also well down in federal elections, with the 2000 election having the lowest turn-out ever. As well, fewer people are members of political parties or appear to participate in the political process. More people show apathy, or even antipathy, toward government and politics in general.

The reasons for this vary. One is our *first-past-the-post* electoral system, which sees the candidate with the most votes win a riding. It is described as such because it is essentially the same as a horse race. It doesn't matter if you win by five furlongs or a nose. Its design permits a minority of those turning out to vote to cause the election of a party with a majority of the seats. As a result, the intent of the majority of voters is stymied, and they lose the instinctive connection between their ballot and their government. All citizens of age have the right to vote, but each voter must believe that their ballot can make a difference. If, election after election, they do not see their attitudes and desires reflected in the policies of government, people become complacent, concluding their vote does not matter. As a result, they see no reason to participate in the process. Over time, apathy may actually turn into alienation from the democratic system. This means that citizens do not hold their government to a high standard, and settle for a mediocrity that guarantees even further disaffection and decline.

Our first-past-the-post election system basically comes out of the idea that whoever gets the most votes wins. It's a simple, and rather unsophisticated, method that ignores majority rule. Of course, it comes from the 18th and 19th centuries, when the majority was not permitted to rule and the elite considered the average person as too ignorant to understand anything more complicated. While many individual ridings are won by a candidate receiving a majority of the vote, many others are won by far less. In 1990, for example, one constituency was won with 30.9%. And general elections are seldom won by a party with the support of a majority of the voters. In Ontario, it hasn't happened since 1937, when there were only two parties, the Liberals and Conservatives.

The problem with plurality decisions is that they usually result in majority governments. That means that the majority will is actually stymied, as the majority votes against the party that controls the parliament. For example, these are the numbers for the last four Ontario elections, each of which resulted in a majority government.

Table 1

Year	Conservative			Liberal			NDP		
	Seats	% seats	% vote	Seats	% seats	% vote	Seats	% seats	% vote
1999	59	57.3	45.1	35	34	39.9	9	8.7	12.6
1995	82	63.1	44.8	30	23.1	31.1	17	13.1	20.6
1990	20	15.4	23.5	36	27.7	32.4	74	56.9	37.6
1987	16	12.3	24.7	95	73.1	47.3	19	14.6	25.7

Table 2

Year	Government			Opposition		
	Seats	% seats	% vote	Seats	% seats	% vote
1999	59	57.3	45.1	44	42.7	54.9
1995	82	63.1	44.8	48	36.9	55.2
1990	74	56.9	37.6	56	43.1	62.4
1987	95	73.1	47.3	35	26.9	52.7

The only reasonable conclusion is that the first-past-the-post system is fundamentally flawed. There are those who believe it is the best, given the flaws of other systems, but I think that is simply the view of those who benefit from the one we have now. After all, picking up a majority government from a plurality of the vote is quite convenient for the winners. It is one of the basic reasons the losers tend not to propose a different electoral system. They believe, one day, they will win based on this flaw. However, there is the stirring of change afoot.

Dalton McGuinty, as part of the Liberal policy-making process, has suggested keeping our present system but using a *preferential*, also called an *alternative*, ballot. This is used by the Ontario Liberals as well as the federal Alliance in leadership and riding nomination campaigns. It allows voters to rank those running in their riding according to preference. For example, I might prefer the Liberal 1, then the New Democrat 2, then the Tory 3. If none of these won a majority after the first count, the third-place person would drop off. If that was the Liberal, then my vote would go to the New Democratic candidate, even if this person was running second. Then, one of the two would be declared victor, as one or the other would now have a majority of the vote. The advantage of this is that, generally, a majority of voters will get their second choice[16], and it is almost as efficient as first-past-the-post, as all voting occurs just once.

The disadvantages are twofold. First, people do not always want to vote for everyone. If I knew the New Democrat to be a crook and the Tory to be a vociferous Harris supporter, I wouldn't want to vote for either of them. If I chose the Liberal 1, and no one else, then (s)he dropped off, I would effectively be disenfranchised (admittedly by choice). Though the results of nomination elections are secret, I have heard that a good percentage of voters, perhaps as high as 50%, do not make choices beyond Number 1. This is far too high to legitimately claim that the winner will have a majority.

The bigger difficulty with the preferential ballot is that it can exacerbate already substantial wins. A preferential ballot immediately turns voting into results. It can mean that trends of election day run even stronger than they might otherwise. In any election where there has been a substantial majority, such as 1987, 1990, and 1995, many who did not choose the winner might well have selected them number 2. Had this occurred, the new government might have gained an even greater majority, making the opposition even weaker and less in a position to hold it accountable.

The first-past-the-post system must be replaced with one that better mirrors the will of the majority. Given our parliamentary system, there are really only three possible alternatives: *proportional representation* (PR), a *run-off* system, or one that mixes systems.

The one element that makes PR very popular with those uninspired by the present electoral system is the exactness in which it permits the popular will to be translated into representation. That is, a party that gets 25% of the vote gets 25% of the seats. Given the results of the last provincial election, had a PR system been in place, the Tories would have received 46 seats, not 59, the Liberals 41, not 35, and the NDP 13, not 9.[17] One can see here the clear over-representation of the winner in the first-past-the-post system, at the expense of the defeated. PR appears to be the one system that is eminently fair through this virtually exact translation of votes into seats.

PR is much more widespread than many think. About 75 countries actually use it as a method of electing at least one chamber of government, though their rules tend to vary. Three examples would be in Israel, Italy, and Germany. Israel elects representatives to a unicameral legislature, the *Knesset*, for parties that receive at least 1.5% of the popular vote. In Italy, the system is made up of two chambers, each of which consists of about 75% first-past-the-post constituencies and 25% PR, the latter with a cut-off at 4%. In Germany, only one of the two chambers of parliament – the *Bundesrat* – is elected by PR, with a cut-off of 5%. Each requires the minimum cut-off in popular vote to keep out extremist and marginal parties, though Israel's fails to do so because the number is so low.

The difficulties with PR, however, are irrevocable. First, PR is a party-based system that does not allow for non-affiliated candidates. Each party runs a slate of names, one to assume each seat should that party receive 100% of the vote. For example, if Ontario had PR, for a party with 25% of the vote, the top 26 people on their list would be elected to the 103-seat Legislature. The only way an individual could run and get elected would be for he or she to receive almost 1% of the entire vote in the whole province, assuming no cut-off. That would be extremely expensive to manage and would undoubtedly take significant coordination. If there was a low-end cut-off of, say 5%, it would be next-to impossible.

Given that PR cannot work on an individual riding basis, a party slate means that present ridings would have to cease to exist, so when people vote, it will simply be to compile popular numbers province-wide. People would vote explicitly on party platforms and leaders, given that they would have no say as to whose names are on the parties' lists. The problem with this, if experience from PR jurisdictions can be considered, is that the parties tend to be run by the same people whose names are on the lists. As a result, the voters usually get more-or-less the same people in government and opposition election after election, sometimes for decades on end. And, of course, representation and accountability would cease to be local. No longer would people have an MPP chosen to explicitly represent their area, and be answerable to them.

PR has been used in what one might term regional constituencies, where party vote is compiled by region rather than right across the province. In this way, each major party, unless it is extremely weak in one area, would elect someone in each mega-riding. The problem with this is that ridings must be enormous, a particular geographic problem in rural areas. As well, regionalism can become a concern, even on a provincial basis.

And there are other general problems, as well. Since it is the exceptional PR election that results in majority support for one party, government is almost always by coalition. This is usually fine on some issues, but continuous support is difficult to maintain, and these coalitions tend to fall apart quite often. In the early 1980s, when I was a university student, Italy had become quite a joke, as it seemed to average a new government every year. In fact, it has had 58 governments since WWII. And while coalitions do tend to get things done in their early days, it becomes progressively harder to keep this up, as parties try to hold their coalitions together. This can mean government becomes enslaved to the *status quo*. Also, as is seen in Israel, tiny parties can have influence far beyond their support, as they often insist on extreme measures to be passed in exchange for their continued support of a coalition. While short term accords may work well, as was seen in the 1985-1987 government in Ontario, the benefits of coalitions tend to become increasingly questionable over time.

Run-off campaigns are a different matter. They are not based on an exact representation of the voters' wishes but on creating majorities on the basis of compromise. That is, in individual ridings, if a candidate fails to get 50%+1 of the vote, he or she is not considered elected, and a run-off election is held sometime later. The top two candidates from the first ballot run off against each other, and the voters choose from one or the other. In this way, the winner will always be no worse than a majority of the electorate's second choice, and will be determined by those whose votes would have been effectively disenfranchised in a first-past-the-post system.

In the 1999 Ontario election, just 63 of the 103 ridings were won by clear majorities – 41 Conservative, 21 Liberal, and only one NDP. Had a run-off system been in place, 40 ridings would have been contested in a second vote, including 18 Conservative, 14 Liberal, and 8 NDP. On the surface, this would appear to give the advantage to the party coming in first with this initial vote, given that it has the fewest on the line, as a proportion, in the second ballot. However, that it not necessarily the case. Given a second round of voting, it is likely the Tories would still have come in first, but not with a majority government.

It is quite likely the Harris candidates would have been defeated in between 8 and 11 of the 18 run-offs where they had led after the first vote. The Liberals would likely have gained between 7 and 10 of these seats, with the NDP taking one more. As well, it is quite possible the Liberals would have lost one to the NDP. This would have created an outcome of 48-51 Tories, 41-45 Liberals, and 9-11 New Democrats. How did I come up with these numbers? A few examples:

In the riding of Algoma-Manitoulin, Liberal Mike Brown won with 44.5% of the vote, NDPer Lynn Watson came second with 27.3%, Conservative Keith Currie third with 26.8%, and finally Libertarian Graham Hearn with 1.3%. With a run-off, Currie and Hearn would drop off, leaving Brown and Watson to fight it out. Logically, some Tory supporters would go NDP, in hopes of keeping the Liberals from winning the riding, some would vote Liberal because they agree with their policies more readily than the NDP's, and some would stay home. Now it's a mug's game to guess how many would make up each of these groups, however, if 25% did not vote and 10% of those remaining voted Liberal, Mike Brown would still have won the seat.

On the other hand, Tory Marcel Beaubien of Lambton-Kent-Middlesex might well have lost his seat, despite his polling 45.0% of the vote. Liberal Larry O'Neill ran second with 42.9%, New Democrat Jim Lee was third with 9.6%, and Freedom Party candidate Wayne Forbes fourth with 2.5%. Given that New Democrats were firmly against the government, it is likely most of their votes would have gone Liberal. Again, assuming 25% of them did not vote, but the rest went Liberal, even if Forbes' total went entirely to the Tory, O'Neill would have won.

In fact, under a run-off, one of the more high-profile races might well have seen Cabinet minister Dianne Cunningham lose to former NDP Cabinet minister Marion Boyd, the opposite of what did happen. Cunningham got 40.2% to Boyd's 36.5%. However, given Liberal Roger Caranci's 20.9%, it is likely much of this Liberal support would have gone to Boyd. Even if half the Liberal vote had stayed home, Boyd would have won in a run-off.

Given that the Conservatives were a government vociferously disliked by their opponents, it is unlikely they would have challenged to win many seats coming from behind. The one that might have been possible in a run-off system was in Prince Edward-Hastings where Liberal Ernie Parsons defeated incumbent Tory Gary Fox by just 56 votes. However, given the NDP's Bev Campbell received 7.2%, it is unlikely Fox could have won. However, if a good portion of the NDP supporters did not vote, felt Fox was the better candidate, or just voted for the greater name recognition of the incumbent, he would have had a second chance for victory. This might also have been helped by the plethora of fringe candidates who had 2.7%.

Regardless, there is no question that run-off campaigns can have a significant effect on the final outcome of elections. While first-past-the-post or preferential balloting establishes winners immediately, a run-off system permits people time to see and judge the strength of possible governments. It is for this reason some people don't care for it. It is possible that the result of the second election night might vary considerably from the first. A party that does surprisingly well during the initial vote might lose much of its headway in a run-off, simply because those who vote a second time change their minds. I suspect that had there been a run-off in 1990, Bob Rae's NDP would have been the Official Opposition again, not the government.

And while some suggest that run-offs suffer a similar trouble to the preferential ballot, with the possibility of high numbers of voters dropping off for the second count, this has not been the experience in France. In fact, in the 1997 National Assembly elections, turn-out was up for the second round to 71.4% from 68.3% in the first. At any rate, turn-out numbers tend to be higher for both rounds than what one finds in Canadian and Ontario elections.

I am not promoting a run-off election system because I feel it will benefit the Liberal party. One could reasonably hypothesize that, under normal conditions, it might be better to be the moderate party, placed between the other two, as the compromise position for voters would likely be to move toward the centre, rather than the other extreme. However, even if that is so, it does not mean this party will win a general election. I have already hypothesized the Tories would have won in 1999. (How long they would have remained in office as a minority is anybody's guess.) In fact, I would suggest it is still likely the Tories would have been victorious in 1995. They took majorities in only 40 of their 82 winning ridings on election night, but I have little doubt that, even if a couple of weeks had intervened, there was sufficient momentum to see they would have won most of the 42 minorities, in the end.

As well, any benefit to a moderate party assumes people vote left-to-right, right-to-left on the political spectrum. Yet that is clearly no longer the case, especially in Ontario, where long-time NDP supporters can switch to right-wing Conservatives with little more than the bat of an eye.

However, I have no doubt that run-offs in Ontario would result in fewer majority governments. So what, may you ask, is the point of a run-off system? What is the advantage if minority governments are created? Isn't this much the same as PR?

Not really. First, minorities would probably happen far less often than majorities, just more often than now. PR will mean virtually guaranteed minorities, as long as we have a multi-party system. Second, run-offs will tend to even out some of the distortions. Though the Tories get a majority in 1995, it might be considerably smaller than the 82 seats they received through first-past-the-post. And while this doesn't stop *The Common Sense Revolution*, it might mean slight moderations or, at least, there would have been fewer government members to seek re-election and, thus, fewer people with the advantages of incumbency. Perhaps this would demand more responsibility while in government.

The other thing that a run-off system might help bring back to people is a greater sense of democratic participation and representation. If it is true that *majority will* being stifled over and over again alienates many, then insisting that a majority select the winner could well re-affirm people's sense of their vote having meaning. If one believes they make a difference, then the entire electoral system gains legitimacy.

The biggest potential problem with run-offs is that there is no guarantee we will continue to have a functional three-party system. For example, if the NDP was to collapse, or just remain very weak, leaving the Tories and Liberals in a dominant position, a run-off system might assure majority government after majority government. This is quite damaging if these parties are also somewhat extreme in their views. For example, in the post-war Britain of Labour and Conservative governments, each spent enormous time, effort, and financial resources simply undoing what the other had done while in office. Not only is it counter-productive, but it is wasteful and divisive. Of course, this was a first-past-the-post system.

Another concern expressed over run-offs is the delay between the first and second ballots, as well as the extra costs associated with the succeeding vote. Some feel that the voters' intentions on "election day" can be spoiled by a second vote, as *sober second thought* can be altered or even reversed by advertising and campaigning. In fact, that's why these things must be strictly limited in the interim period. As to the extra cost, it would be reduced by only having to do second counts in a minority of ridings. However, there is no way around some extra expense. Of course, democracy is an expensive system to have.

The other possibility is a combination of systems. Many countries or constituent governments elect some members by proportional representation and others by first-past-the-post. This is most effective in a bicameral system where the membership of each legislature can be elected by a different method. Unfortunately, Ontario has only one chamber, and that's where this mixed system fails. In a unicameral system, it is difficult to elect representatives by different methods with each having the same level of legitimacy. Someone elected across the province by PR, thus representing all the people might be seen as more legitimate to act on province-wide issues than someone elected over a small area. On the other hand, this same person doesn't have the legitimacy of having been selected by people directly, and doesn't have to answer to them directly. This amorphous accountability is one of the biggest problems with PR and using it in mixed systems.

In my mind, a run-off system seems the best compromise for democracy in Ontario. If I was promoting change for Canada, I would go with a mixed system that retains first-past-the-post for the House of Commons but uses PR for a refurbished Senate. However, short of creating a Senate for Ontario, a run-off arrangement would permit a majority of the people to select the make-up of a government. This is the only electoral system that considers the will of the majority and, given that majority will has been denied in Ontario for about 60 years, it might be about time.

But it would be unfair to entirely blame our electoral system for the fading of democracy. As society is made up of better-educated citizens, with higher expectations, the era of representative democracy must begin to decline, as people believe they could do better than politicians and, as a result, lose patience for the system and, thus, its legitimacy declines. Who hasn't thought they could do a better job than those who buy off nurses to leave their profession, only to pay them to come back months later, or to offer contracts that pay people $575 per hour to *save* money?

As well, legitimacy declines as parties make promises they do not keep. In that sense, this may be the one area where the Harris government gets kudos. For a significant number, they perceive the Tories to have kept their word on most issues. Yes, they may have been clumsy or worse, but they did do what they said they were going to. In comparison to too many of their predecessors who found excuses not to, they did carry out their agenda. This may be particularly devastating when voters elect governments based on that party's apparently strong principles and are then disappointed. Over the last 30 years, however, conviction has been far less evident than pragmatism, as the parties have become more likely to simply fight over taxes and efficiency. This is another area where the Harris Tories may have scored points. There can be no question *The Common Sense Revolution* was based in principle.

The only possible system that can succeed will offer/demand mass citizen participation moving toward a more Athenian democracy-type system (minus the slaves, of course). It must be one that not only invites members of the community to partake, but makes it easier for them to do so. I personally believe that MPPs should face "town halls", or caucuses, on a regular basis, so that people can get across their concerns face-to-face. It would allow local input on a community-by-community basis, unadulterated by third parties or filtered communications. Of course, some politicians might not like facing their *employers* this way.

And that brings me to another concern. With most constituencies over 100,000 in population, and many others thousands of square kilometres in size, it is difficult for citizens to have any substantive contact with their MPP, and it is tough for MPPs to truly represent their constituents. The Tories made the ones we have bigger simply to save money, and not much at that. Would it not make more sense to have more ridings with more politicians? Would this not be more democratic? We must have much smaller ridings with many more representatives.

For those who are now groaning about the cost, I would suggest cutting the pay of MPPs to better match that of regular citizens. I am one of those who believes pay has gone so high that people are being attracted to politics to line their wallets. And for those who say politics has never made anyone rich, I disagree. But it's not even a question of becoming rich, it is a question of fairly representing one's constituents. How do you do that if you earn more than three or four times what an ordinary Ontarian does? And that's where we're headed.

What should politicians be paid? The Ontario example of letting the

Integrity Commissioner decide may seem to have removed the politics from the decision, or maybe not, but it is an innately political decision. After all, what is a fair recompense for what is, despite what many think, a normally difficult and tiring job that few leave without having a lot of critics or even enemies? But then again, it is also one of the few positions where you are asking for the trust of tens of thousands of people to make decisions that will fundamentally affect their lives, from what they pay for taxes to, in some cases, whether or not their disabled child gets a needed wheelchair to whether or not they sleep in the street. How many of us ask for that kind of responsibility, and shouldn't there be a price to pay for that trust?

If I want to ask you to trust me, I should be doing it because I want to help people, not because I want to feather my personal financial nest. It seems to me that pay raises have made politics far too enticing for those who are not so interested in helping others as in helping themselves. And as for the argument that the *best and brightest* will pass on public service if they aren't paid well? Rubbish. It seems to me that most politicians were much better when they were paid less. Of course, that's always countered with something like ... if it pays too little, only the rich will serve. Rubbish, again. People of good conscience will serve regardless of pay. I think high election spending limits do far more to keep *average* people from running for public office. This is what should be changed. Instead of campaigns with limits of $60,000-$70,000, they should be as low as $20,000-$25,000, which would allow fairer fights between parties and might even permit more individuals to run without affiliation.

And the buying and selling of influence must stop, yet it will not as long as campaigns are contingent on donated funds. Lower limits would help, as would lower contribution thresholds. If a campaign was limited to $25,000 in spending and maximum donations of $100 per person, with only individual donations allowed, it would be much more difficult to purchase a politician's loyalty. Of course, if a group of people, with a single consideration, were to donate most of the $25,000, the question of influence would still be there. Even better might be to have general tax money go to each party in each riding on the basis of just achieving a certain voting threshold. Get 5% and you get the $25,000. It would make for much fairer campaigns, in my mind.

Back to the question of what is fair pay. I believe it should be based on the average wage of citizens. Who am I to make a decision on your behalf if I earn two or three times what you do? My experience would be too removed from yours for me to understand your real needs. Of course, this is a real denial of the wealthy being elected to office. (Sorry, Paul Martin, but what has a multi-millionaire got in common with me?) However, a provincial (or federal) politician's salary should include the higher expenses of extra accommodation and travel. In effect, it might be I'm suggesting MPPs should be paid a base amount, with expenses that vary depending on how far they live away from the Legislature. If you live in Scarborough, you can take public transit and could be paid two TTC tokens a day extra. If you represent Moose Factory, there would have to be substantial expense money for air travel and a second accommodation in Toronto. However, if the base amount is based on the average, then it will give MPPs all the more incentive to work to increase the *real* wages of all Ontarians.

If you're going to have more provincial constituencies, to be consistent on the local level, then there should be more municipalities, not fewer, again going against the tide, this one of 35 years. Constant amalgamations have made local government less democratic and more expensive. The biggest reason, perhaps the only one, was to create economies of scale. That hasn't worked, and it has cost people control over their local affairs. Unfortunately, it is difficult to unscramble an egg.

The only possible way of restoring some semblance of local accountability would be to permit the creation of community councils to exist within their larger municipality. Historically, where these have been instituted, they have been small groups of volunteers, selected by the larger council, to look after such things as neighbourhood signage, clean-ups, and improvements, all on small, fixed budgets. Most of what they do is also subject to ratification or oversight by the larger municipal council. That is not what I am suggesting.

I see no reason why local councils could not be recreated within municipal boundaries, much like mini-counties or mini-regions. Each community could elect a small council to deal with local matters, with one member then going on to sit on the larger body. It would make municipalities much more like federations. I realize this is an idea without much detail, but I see no reason why people should not be able to determine whether or not they have a library or if their sidewalks are cleared of snow, if they are willing to pay the cost.

People must be able to participate. Democracy cannot function without the oversight of the voters. Given how little time most people have nowadays, there must be measures taken to give them this time. Shorter work weeks would allow time for this, not to mention returning to them some sense of having a life.

The other reconsideration must be how political parties represent people. The key to the Tories' strategy of governing, and getting elected, is that you shouldn't try to govern for everyone. You govern exclusively for those that support your policies. Mike Harris said, *I am not here to represent everyone, just those who voted Conservative.* Why try and spread your message across the entire electorate when 40-45% of them will get you a majority government? The more you try to broaden your party's appeal, the more you have to water down your message, or so the Harrisites think.

One of the hallmarks of government in Canada has been a tradition of consultation and compromise. Politics is about trade-offs over apparently limited resources. People have different priorities, and these are usually acknowledged by their representatives. When legislation is being prepared and then again when it's passed Second Reading and gone to public hearings, people and groups are consulted for their opinions. As a result of varying viewpoints, the legislation may be written or amended to consider the larger society – the majority will with an eye to minority rights.

The problem with Harris' *narrowcasting* is that it is the will of the minority, with little direct consideration of the majority. Government for the minority is not democracy but autocracy. Public hearings must have reasonable time allotments and be spread about geographically so people have the opportunity to participate. If political parties do not again try to govern for all, democracy will not survive.

5. A policy wonk's vision

In <u>Promised Land</u>, there is a section of photographs. One selection offers Dave Johnson, Jim Wilson, and John Snobelen, and identifies them as three of the government's "most important ministers". This was somewhat ironic, given that, by the Tories' second term, none of the three was particularly relevant. Johnson was defeated in the 1999 election, his riding targeted by teachers determined to demonstrate that they weren't without strength against the, then, Minister of Education. Wilson is still responsible for deregulating Ontario Hydro, but the delays and uncertainty about the process combined with his intemperate performance in Health to make him seem unreliable. After the 1999 election, he was dropped from the prestigious P&P Committee. Also, though he is still the youngest

member of Cabinet, Wilson's personal health seems to have become a
question. Snobelen, having started out in a major ministry like Wilson, has
gone to Natural Resources and seems stuck there, with no major policy
responsibilities to handle. Though he was billed as a management mind to
remake the Education system, his lack of political smarts has effectively
ended his political career. In the summer of 2001, he bought a horse farm
in the United States, apparently for the day he leaves Queen's Park. I
would suggest that will be soon.[18]

It is not unusual for ministers to change over a term-and-a-half of
government. However, it is unusual for most of the senior ministers to
vanish from the senior ranks. Ernie Eves was in Finance. Wilson was in
Health. Snobelen in Education. Johnson in Management Board.
Tsubouchi in Community and Social Services. Except for Tsubouchi
being in Management Board, the others are all gone. Why? As much as
anything else, it may be that *revolutionaries* are ill-suited to managing
change. Making change, but not looking after it. Of course, Harris still
says his government is not one of managers, and I cannot disagree. What
he has now are the lesser lights of the first string, and those from the
second string, running the affairs of the province. This cannot help but
mean things are not being looked after as well as they should be.

And it is their management of public administration where the Harris
Tories are guilty of abuses for which they actually receive little rebuke.
Perhaps because they don't believe they are *government*, that they need to
manage affairs, they have failed to carry off the revolutionary changes they
began, leaving them abandoned or half-finished. Either that, or they truly
want to undermine government so thoroughly that people will lose their
trust in it, and will willingly accept the turnover of many programmes to
the private sector. This has been acute in many areas, but none moreso
than the big ones, health and education.

There are those who believe that our public, universally-accessible health
care system cannot sustain itself because of rising costs. Technology may
be creating better machines to keep people healthier, but they are also
increasingly expensive. Doctors and nurses are the human element to
diagnosing and curing disease and illness, but the decline in their numbers
mean greater demand for their services, not just here but abroad. And as
baby-boomers age, the numbers of people needing health care services will
likely rise. This could mean such severe costs that continuing its public
nature might be impossible. Certainly, Health minister Tony Clement has
expressed concerns such as these. Personally, I believe this is a cop-out by
people who are ideologically opposed to public health care or who think

they can make a buck with a private system.

It is a position based on assumptions. First, taxes to pay for health will become so onerous that too many other worthy ventures will have to be abandoned. Well, I'm sure a Conservative would expect this answer from a *free-spending* Liberal but ... taxes can always go up. If people want a public, universally-accessible system, they will be willing to pay for it. Just because neo-conservatives believe the sky will fall if taxes rise doesn't make it so. If someone with a middle income decides to buy a new car, they know they will have to sacrifice in another area to pay for it. However, unless you're self-employed, people don't control their own wages (and even then only to a point). If government finds that people want more put into health care, it can increase income taxes to pay for it. But that assumes costs will rise beyond our ability to pay for them.

As we have seen, the Tories already exaggerate health costs, to try and pry more transfers from the federal government and to finance their tax cuts. Might it be the case that these costs will not rise astronomically? Some people see the possibility that, even though people age, they will remain healthier longer. If that is the case, some health services will have to be offered to a greater extent than in the past while it may be that others will need to be offered less. And for those that argue that the *baby-bust* generation – one that is much smaller than its parents' – will be stuck paying for these services, baby-boomers are wealthier than any generation that has ever existed. It may be that their taxes will be able to handle any increase with little trouble. If a difficulty exists now, it may simply be that the Harrisites have done an abysmal job of changing the focus of needed services. Though they have talked up a storm about the need for long-term care facilities and home care, they have been slow and miserly in financing the beds and the home services. And, quite frankly, who says taxes must go up?

And a third assumption is that, surprise, there are those who believe the private sector can deliver health services more cheaply. The obvious proof this is wrong is the United States. As I mentioned earlier, Americans pay substantially more for health care than Canadians, so much so that this added to their tax total means they pay more than we do. That being the case, why would we want a system that will make us pay more, not less?

However, there is no question that the system must be reformed to fix its problems. Given the Tories started to make changes to it then bailed out, it is presently in a precarious position. Primary care reform is necessary, as are modifications to the infrastructure of the system. Bringing this about will be dangerous for any government, as altering the *status quo* usually creates doubt amongst those who feel things are fine, and anything less than significant improvement will make critics think change is an exercise in public relations.

The government proposed group capitation, whereby doctors and nurses would work together to offer 24-hour-per-day care. The difficulty with fee-for-service had become obvious. Over the years, increasing numbers of doctors were billing for an increasing number of services, many of which were not needed, but paid the doctor. For example, if a patient came in with a cold, which as a virus cannot be treated, doctors tended to see them, then claim a fee from OHIP. The more patients a doctor could see, whether it was necessary or not, the more they were paid. The point of clawbacks was to stifle high-billers. If you cannot make any more past a certain amount, there is no point in seeing people who don't really need to be seen. The problem was that, for those who billed past the cap, they felt they were working for free. And while it is likely that most physicians did not abuse this, it is also on record that a few did so to extremes. As a result, payments to doctors have become the single largest expense for health care. Thus arose the concept of capitation.

So if every Ontarian had to choose one primary-care physician or a group, doctors could be paid a fixed amount, based on the age, sex and general health of every person under their care. The more patients looked after, the more money the doctor would make, regardless of the number of procedures or services performed. There would no longer be a built-in incentive for doctors to provide unnecessary treatment; yet they would risk losing business to other physicians if they did not meet patient expectations of care. (Toronto Star, "One good way to reduce MDs' bills", 7 July 1996, p. F2)

However, there was always one trouble with this plan. Managed care, as this is known, is what is offered in the United States under health management organizations, and there has been one difficulty that hasn't been overcome. People like having one doctor, not many. When you could see 20 different doctors in 20 different visits, the consistency that is supposed to exist in a practice is lost. If one doctor has to rely on records for treatment, a lot will be left out, or might be just plain wrong.

The only solution to this would be small group practices, with as few as four to five doctors, all with fairly regular hours. Though each doctor might benefit from reduced working hours, they also might run into having to work regular shifts. I might be wrong, but I think it will be difficult to find a significant portion of doctors willing to work midnight to eight.

The reality is that any changed system must become more flexible. Some doctors will be paid by fee-for-patient, some by salary, some still by fee-for-service (presumably specialists). They would have to face requirements on hospital privileges, with some having careers in hospitals and some that will never work there (once fully qualified). For those physicians who decide the cash is greener on the other side of the border, they should be released with regret, as long as they pay off the entire cost of their medical education. If they aren't going to practice here, it is necessary to recoup those costs to train others who will. And far more doctors must be trained, and such facilities paid for by government. Having said that, for those who take loans to get through school, they must locate in an under-serviced area for specific amounts of time to repay those loans. History has proven that incentives will not get enough doctors to move.

Does this sound coercive? Perhaps. I would like to think that some new doctors required to work in under-serviced areas will come to like those areas and remain. If not, then ordinary people living in those areas will have to accept that their doctor is going to change every few years and there is nothing that can be done to stop it. Frankly, I would rather have a new doctor every five years than no doctor at all.

As for nurses, we also need many more of these, and we need to retain their services for more years. For that to happen, working conditions must improve, and wages must be more consistent from a hospital position to one in a long-term care facility. A sliding wage that favours more highly-skilled nurses might help keep more, as long as there is more opportunity for young nurses to get the training they need to advance. The last two provincial contracts have elevated nurses wages considerably, to the point where a new, full-time hospital nurse can now earn almost $70,000 per year working a 40-hour week. That is a substantial improvement, but it is also a change whereby nurses will no longer be able to claim they are underpaid. The use of registered practical nurses should be able to wean doctors away from many more simple services, such as signing forms for insurance companies, and physicians will have to be willing to let them go, rather than jealously regarding nurses as competitors rather than colleagues.

Having said all that, it will be the job of government to stop wasting hundreds of millions of dollars for things like advertising and spend it on needed medical machinery. In 1999, it was said Ontario needed about 30 magnetic resonance imaging machines province-wide. Each would have cost $3 million, with another $1 million per year in operating costs. With what the Tories have wasted in propaganda over five years, nearly $250 million, they could have purchased and paid for all 30. There would have been no need for private MRI clinics that are beginning to spring up (in violation of the *Canada Health Act*, in my mind). This was either a government unable to plan, to set priorities, or it was one determined to undermine universal health care.

It may be that hospitals should no longer be the central institution of community health care. That does not mean it was appropriate for the Harrisites to allow hospitals and emergency wards to be shut down before there was an alternative. Beds were still being used by the elderly and chronically ill when these shut-downs occurred, even though most planned long-term care beds and fully-functioning home care were not up and running. Again, the Tories denied this reality and cut for the sake of cutting. A future government will have to open beds, see they are paid for, and make certain that alternatives are in place before funding for them stops. To do otherwise is to deny citizens their right to universal-access health care, something most of us have been paying for most of our lives.

Education is another area of great concern, given the upheavals of the past six years. The Tories have clearly attempted to undermine the present public system, be it because they wanted private education to get a foothold in the public treasury or because they just hate unionized teachers. The fact is that most of the troubles of education could have been fixed with a lot less acrimony.

If the Tories wanted to save money in education, they should have just gone ahead and offered early retirement to senior teachers at the beginning instead of trying to force them out through a cut in prep time. This would have saved hundreds of millions of dollars in wages and benefits, as teachers making $60,000 could have been replaced with ones making $30,000.

And instead of focusing so completely on a tougher curriculum to make students learn, they could have come up with a funding formula not based on the square footage of schools but on the needs of students. Is it really so terrible that a small community has a 50-year-old school that holds 150, rather than busing these kids to a larger town for a new warehouse that holds 2,000? And a more challenging curriculum and testing could have been instituted, over a longer period, with the assistance of teachers, rather than to spite them (though I personally think all the province-wide testing is just a waste of scarce resources).

Future governments should slow curriculum changes so that they are phased in with enough time for students to fully comprehend them. I have no problem with tougher standards. Frankly, since I had to mark university essays by 20-plus-year-olds who had trouble writing even one grammatically correct sentence, and my niece addressed my Christmas present to "Uncil" and her teacher said this was okay – spelling didn't matter – I was a real believer higher standards are vital. However, simply saying 'here they are' doesn't give kids time to learn.

As well, government must accept that teachers are an integral part of education, not just employees. Until one has taught, most people do not understand the concept of having time to prepare for a class, and then having to mark essays and tests. At university, the claim was always that to teach a three-hour class meant three-hours of preparation and three-hours of marking. I personally found preparation time to be somewhat shorter, but marking to be longer. However, it's not an unreasonable assessment to think each workday is 9-12 hours long, and often runs into weekends. I would think this would be similar for elementary teachers, and longer for those in secondary schools.

I personally believe that government must also seriously look into full-year schooling. The school year does not lengthen appreciably, but it does make better use of expensive facilities and resources. There are parents, teachers, and students who hate the idea and cite farming needs, air-conditioning, and bonding vacations as the reason to deny its logic. Sorry if I don't buy these. Less than 1% of people are today involved in agriculture, so very few kids are, either. And there is no reason that some time off could not be taken at harvest time. As to the cost of putting in air-conditioning, this is done in newer schools. As to older ones, it would indeed cost money, but not enough to reject the idea out of hand. As to vacations, well, there would still be holidays of two or three-weeks several times per year. Is this not enough? Honestly, kids could get so much more out of school when they haven't had two months to forget everything they've learned the year before, then have to spend a month reviewing it. And isn't educating these youngsters the point?

I know of many people who would love to have one single public school system for all, and who would be quite willing to re-open the constitution for discussion about creating such a system. I think this is a discussion that we need to have moreso because it would bring out exactly how people want their taxes spent on education. It would not just consider public and separate schooling but private education, as well. It is wrong for government to expand this funding without the approval of the public and without a plan that includes a whole systemic outlook.

I also think that university and college level education must be included in such a plan. I personally believe this is all one system, from junior kindergarten to post-graduate work. Until we look at it that way, education cannot be seen in context. Should Grade 1 curriculum consider the needs of the workforce in 25 years, or is education for the sake of learning? It is all one system and must be designed as such.

As such, I take a rather unpopular view, these days. Since elementary and secondary education is paid for completely through taxes, why isn't post-secondary? Free, one-time, tuition for post-secondary schooling should be available to all citizens. Society would benefit not just by having a more highly-educated society but, as Tories should love, a more highly-skilled workforce. And given that it would be little more expensive than the extension of public funding for private schools, it is hard to justify the present policy of jacking up tuition to the point where post-secondary education is becoming something unavailable to the poor and an increasing number of the middle-class. Quite frankly, it is just plain wrong to force students and their parents to assume such a large percentage of the cost. The only logic is that the Tories want there to be a more poorly-educated underclass available to employers as part-time labour that cannot afford to say no.

The future must also begin to consider the environment as an issue just as important as health and education. It seemed headed this way under the Peterson Liberals, only to be held back by the NDP's lack of money and, then, denied by the Tories' determination to turn the clock back to the Industrial Revolution. In fact, as the Walkerton tragedy showed quite horribly, the environment is undeniably tied to health. If we kill ourselves by polluting our environment, will we not totally destroy ourselves eventually?

Government must step in to do things only it can do. It can use the *stick* to force matters that are impossible to make happen otherwise. (I realize it is out of style to suggest government should *force* anything.) Urban sprawl is eating up land faster than we realize the consequences. Saving the Oak Ridges Moraine, if that is what really happens, is more a function of saving the water supply of Toronto than it is protecting the sanctity of nature. In that light, government needs to ban development in rural and agricultural areas to stop sprawl and protect ecology. It must set up zones around built-up areas that would limit growth inside those borders. So, even in a rural area that is a village surrounded by natural and agricultural land, development needs to be restricted to that village. In a place like Toronto, there is a great deal of land that can be redeveloped rather than expanding over that we need to feed and water ourselves.

Water, air, and land standards, and oversight, should become strictly a provincial responsibility. What's the difference if the province watches over them or municipalities or contracted companies? Easy. Business would do it to make money. Municipalities would have to pay for it through regressive property taxes. Only the province can protect the public interest while using progressive taxation to pay for it. Of course, the provinces could cede this to the federal government, which wouldn't bother me at all, though I think it is constitutionally and politically unlikely.

And no one should shrug their shoulders at the problem. Specifically on air pollution, Ontario was crowned the Number 2 polluter in North America in 2000, from 1997 statistics. We should adopt a system similar to what is done in places like Athens, that bans some cars from the downtown based on the level of smog. For smog days, we need to set up a classification system that would require industry to shut down depending on how bad it is. When it is more minor, only the worst polluters would have to close. On days when it is worse, all significant polluters would have to shut down. Coal-fired plants are unavoidably horrible polluters, and should be shut down permanently.

As for pollution on land, we need to get away from our lazy use of landfill to dispose of *waste*. We must begin to reduce, re-use, and recycle, not as a trite cliché but as a way of living. Blue boxes must begin to accept ALL recyclables, not just ones that can be easily resurrected for use. Food waste can be turned into compost. And we need to move away from materials that cannot be recycled, such as plastic bags and bottles, even if it costs more to use woven sacks and glass, not to mention doing away with unnecessary packaging. However, until government says 'no more garbage' and lays out real money for the alternatives, it won't happen. Business won't support this because they won't make as much money.

Of course, there will be many frightened by the idea something might cost more. Our fixation on taxes has become near paranoia. And while all taxes are now seen as suspect, there has been a movement over the last twenty years to shift taxation away from progressive income taxes to regressive sales taxes, property taxes, and fees. This can be clearly seen through the tax cuts of the last few years. Instead of chopping the regressive taxes, in fact they have been increased while the progressive income tax has been the focus of the cutting. Provincial downloading onto municipalities increased property taxes. Provincial user fees have been created or increased on a variety of occasions (in direct contravention of the CSR). The only possible reason to cut income tax while hiking these others is to benefit the wealthy more than everyone else. A cut to the sales tax would have been a far more efficient and effective method of stimulating the economy and it would have benefited everyone, especially the poor and middle-class. Instead, income taxes were slashed, which predominantly profited richer Ontarians, presumably in a deluded attempt at the failed theory of trickle-down economics.

The time has come for government to truly make taxation as fair as possible. While it is not possible to hike taxes for the rich beyond a modest level, given that they will simply move their wealth offshore, the only logical alternative is the Tobin tax. It is not named after former federal Liberal Cabinet minister and former Newfoundland premier Brian Tobin, but the late Nobel prize-winner James Tobin, a former economist at Yale University and economic advisor to President John Kennedy. First proposed back in the 1970s, Tobin suggested a tax of between 0.1% and 0.5% be levied on currency exchange transactions. This could even out some of the currency speculation that has damaged world economies over the years, as well as establish a significant new tax base for government. But suggestions for this have gone further. It has also been put forward that it could apply to stock market transactions in general. The tax would be so small as to be barely noticeable, but would be much easier and cheaper to collect than sales tax, and it would remove the onus from small businesses. Also, it would tax international speculators, not just citizens. I am not suggesting this as a new tax, but as a replacement for sales and property taxes and user fees. The amount to be raised could cut or eliminate these other types of taxes, making taxation much fairer. As well, it would mean many of the same speculators that earn money from people here would have to repay some of it to us. Given that securities fall under provincial jurisdiction, it should be possible for provinces to enact such a tax.

Speaking of money, I should touch on those who don't have much. Welfare has been turned into punishment. Going back to its beginnings, the idea was that government should offer minimal help to those unable to do so themselves, at any given time. This was as much about charity as it was about getting beggars out from underfoot. Unfortunately, it often meant a railway ticket out of town, making the very poor someone else's problem. Over time, this evolved into an organized system that paid the poor who were out of work, federally through what is now called

Employment Insurance for short periods or provincially through General
Welfare, or those unable to work, through various disability benefits or
Family Benefits. With the ascendancy of the Harrisites, they have done
what they can to turn the clock back as far as possible.

I have no doubt that they see welfare as something one should be
humiliated to collect. I can assure them, except for those who are simple
thieves defrauding the system, beneficiaries are very much humiliated.
And I'm also sure they believe that workfare is to drive the lazy out of the
system, not to get them relevant experience, as they claim. All work-for-
welfare does is deny these people the time they need to look for work and
to improve their education and training. If the government wanted to
actually help people 'escape the dependency', they'd make benefits
provisional on improving education and training, and they'd see to it
people got enough money to live and work. 'The best social assistance
program ever created is a real job ...' In that, the CSR was bang on. The
problem is workfare doesn't get very many people a real job.

And western economies demand ever-increasing numbers of jobs to
continue very high standards of living. Unfortunately, mechanization and
computerization are now making it less and less necessary to actually have
people to deliver goods. As I mentioned earlier, a shorter work week
would be beneficial for democratic purposes. However, it would also help
people have lives, and not simply work to live. I have heard arguments
that productivity has not increased sufficiently to justify this. I hardly
think this is true, numbers or not. The fact is that computerization has
completely upended our society. Computers have taken away the jobs of
millions. Though job levels may be higher than ten years ago, look at the
type of jobs created – low wage, part-time service jobs, for the most part,
or people laid-off by companies and forced to work for themselves for
lower wages and benefits of which they must pay 100% of the cost. It is
impossible to compare 1961 with 2001 for levels of productivity. The
work week should be shorter to give more people a job. If two people
work 60-hour weeks, would it not make more sense to take someone
unemployed and give them 40 of these hours? And for those who think
paying benefits to that extra body is a bad economic move, imagine the
difference of this person paying taxes instead of draining them. A shorter
work week would have the added bonus of giving people back more time
to spend with their families and friends.

But other reforms need to be made as a result of these economic changes.
Benefits should be pro-rated for part-time workers so that they receive the
same relative advantage as full-timers. It might also have the effect of

getting some companies to hire full-time instead of part-time, since most of the reason to go with the latter was to save benefit packages. Also, despite the Tory worry that the minimum wage cannot be increased because it would cost jobs, it could well be argued that increasing it would put more money in the hands of people who would spend it, increasing economic activity. It is clear that the minimum wage no longer pays anything close to what people need to survive. Had Helle Hulgaard been earning the minimum wage back in 1993, she might have had an argument about being better off on welfare. Not, I would suggest, today. I would think the minimum wage should match a percentage of average pay, somewhere between 50-75%, then be adjusted every two or three years depending on average pay change. In this way, it would not grow by inflation alone, while other wages stagnated. On the other hand, if people were benefiting at the upper end, why shouldn't those at the bottom?

With the exception of those on welfare, there might be no group considered more on the 'bottom' nowadays than youth. When they decided that many young people were just irresponsible malefactors, the Conservatives made a conscious decision to treat them as full-fledged criminals, even for relatively minor infractions. The only logical deduction as to their thinking on the matter is that young criminals become old criminals unless they are taught that punishment comes with sin.

The result is that these youthful offenders now spend most of their time in jail rather than in programmes to keep them in their communities. In his November 2000 report, Ontario Auditor Erik Peters pointed out that 4,000 young offenders were in community programmes of one sort or another. That compared to 25,000 in 1991. The logic of it seems dubious, especially given the $50 million per year cost ... especially dubious for a government that prides itself on saving money.

There are kids who now go to jail for things that, 20 years ago, got them a stern talking to. And though it may not be popular, the reality is that sending young people to jail turns them into criminals far more often than it scares them out of being criminals. If we want to teach troubled youth how to be more responsible, why don't we give them more responsibility? Would it not make more sense to keep them in their communities, working on projects to help their neighbours?

And communities are made up of all people who live in them, not just employers and home-owners. There has been a terrible ignorance of those who live in rental units since the 1970s. Oh, the political parties talk a good game, but few ever do anything. Even the NDP government did little but posture and say what they'd like to do, without acting on any real scale. Again, however, it was the Harris Tories who made bad matters worse. The removal of rent controls has attacked the poor if they actually have to move. Even if you don't, above-regulation increases are making it increasingly difficult for those on fixed incomes to stay where they are, often in apartments where they've lived for decades.

There is no question that the free market does not work with apartments. A future government must bring in a system of rent supplements to help people pay for rent. This would not be the shelter subsidy where the buildings must be owned by the government or be non-profit cooperative but one where the government actually gives a supplement to help people pay their rent in privately-owned buildings, as well. Given that private owners will benefit, rent controls would return in exchange. A small programme for rent-geared-to-income units presently exists, but only with landlords who volunteer to participate. At this time, few do. The ultimate problem is that there are so few apartment units now available because they are too expensive to build.

To this there are two possible answers: subsidize developers to build such units, a policy that was tried and rejected by most governments as being far too expensive; or, force them to put up apartments as part of any housing development. You want to build 200 houses, put up an apartment complex of 200 units as well. I realize that this would mean that the people buying the houses would be partially subsidizing the cost of the building, but so everyone in an existing house subsidizes the extension of services to their new homes. (Sorry, folks, but development charges do not cover the costs.) Again, however, this would mean government using its power to intercede in the private sector. So be it. It is in the public interest to do so.

One final area to touch on is labour, as in unions. There can be little doubt the Harris Tories have beat up on the public sector ones, OPSEU in particular, apparently because they see civil servants as a coddled special interest. But the reality is that most of these people deliver services to the people that they need and demand. Without them, the possibility for neglect becomes great as was seen by the lack of oversight of the Walkerton water system. The very people the Harrisites saw as unnecessary were the ones most needed.

But the Tories went even further, cutting back the ability for workers to actually unionize. If someone had ordered them they would not be permitted to form a business, I suspect they'd have screamed bloody murder. The fact is, with the decreasing strength of workers, employers are exploiting workers more than they have been in years. I personally know of incidences where owners are violating labour laws, yet employees refuse to stand up because, even though the jobs aren't great, they pay a lot more than welfare ... or nothing at all.

I personally believe we need to return to some of the reforms established by the Rae NDP, then abolished by the Harris Conservatives. It should be easier to unionize, because unions are necessary as the only real protectors of the rights of workers. A union is the collective conscience and will of those who don't have the power as individuals.

However, having said that, there is going too far. Unions have an unfortunate tendency to try and protect all workers, even the ones who are buffoons. Standing up for incompetence and malfeasance brings all union work into disrepute.

As well, the tendency for a union oligopoly is just as bad as that in business. When a steelworkers' union represents fish plant workers or an auto workers' union signs up fast food staff, something is amiss. Workers must be represented by those actually concerned directly with their interests and, if that means that you don't have the power of a massive organization behind you in contract negotiations or a strike, so be it.

Each pendulum has swung too far. It's time to get them back in sync.

6. Harris "sees the autumn leaves"

About halfway through writing the first draft of this book, Mike Harris decided to resign as Premier and Tory leader, effective as of a leadership convention (now set for 23 March 2002). Though he cited personal reasons, and there is no doubt his attempted (and now failed) reconciliation with his wife was a factor, it may be he's getting out before *The Common Sense Revolution* is exposed for the fatuous waste it has been. The second term of the Harrisites has really been a total failure, even in political terms, and it could be said he figured it was *time to git while the gittin's good*. *Blueprint* was not of the standard of the CSR and embodied none of the visionary ideas of it. Really, it comprised only of a handful of promises on which the Tories could legislate. As a result, there was no focus for the Conservative government in this term, and it has basically crawled toward nowhere, while facing the devastating tragedy of Walkerton, the mounting questions regarding Ipperwash, and the continuing debates over the quality of health and education. Harris himself could not apparently find the *fire in his belly* he had felt in his first term, and has meandered along with his government.

This resignation was not a complete surprise. As early as the year 2000, I and many of those I know predicted he would go. I suggested he would quit around his sixth anniversary in June 2001. However, once this passed, I thought he would stick around another year. Right up until the night before his resignation, he said he was staying to fight another election. Most of my fellow Liberals and I doubted this, but accepted that he had to say it to stave off a growing, if unofficial, leadership race that seemed to be distracting a number of potential candidates for his job.

Now the Conservatives face a leadership race that may, or may not, determine the continued course of the party. Harris has been the face of Canadian neo-conservatism, regardless of how really neo-con some people think he is. His government has been the instrument of neo-conservative policies that have seriously affected, and I believe negatively affected, the course of the vast majority of Ontarians' lives. His successor will have to decide if they want to continue along this path or choose a new one, presumably either to make the party even more ruthlessly right-wing or to moderate it back toward the party of Drew, Frost, Robarts, Davis and even Miller.

The first to declare his intention to run for the leadership was former Finance minister Ernie Eves, despite his denial just three weeks earlier. Two days later, Health minister Tony Clement announced his intention. This seemed to set out the ideological spectrum, as limited as it is, in the Conservative party. Eves is an old-time *patrician* conservative who believes in protecting the interests of modern-day aristocrats, like the wealthy, business, and the elite. As well, he says he has a social conscience, though not, it seems, one which necessarily supports a welfare state. He would consider minimal assistance for people, yet would still prefer private charities to cover people's needs. Though he plays the game as a populist, saying he is more comfortable on Main Street than Bay Street, the truth is really the opposite. Undoubtedly, most of his financial support comes from the latter, not the former. Eves advantage is that he has the fiscal *bona fides* to attract the Right as well as a more moderate group. With about six weeks left in the campaign, he is clearly well ahead and appears ready for coronation, though his opponents have begun to attack him for many things, particularly a lack of ideas.

Clement has been the true *Common Sense Revolution*ary, who hates the welfare state and believes it must be dismantled. But it goes further than that. As a neo-conservative, he follows the credo *government is bad* and wants to see it streamlined as much as possible so as to reduce it to a position of having minimal influence. He usually couches his statements, knowing most Ontarians do not support going this far. However, he has been known to speak before thinking. One such occasion ended in him being dubbed "Two-Tier Tony" for his promotion of a private health system to parallel the public one. Clement has the pedigree of the neo-con, and expects support from the hard core and Tory youth. Many believed he had a serious organizational advantage, given he has been running for the job since the 1970s, but that doesn't appear to be there. In fact, his apparent belief that most of the party membership are right-wing seems to have vanished, as he has moderated his message a surprising amount, to the point where he accuses Eves of being too right-wing.

Three others declared their intention to run over the next ten days, Finance minister Jim Flaherty, Environment minister Elizabeth Witmer, and Labour minister Chris Stockwell. As it turned out, it was Flaherty and Witmer who set out the ideological perspective. Flaherty, known as a right-winger, placed himself to the outside of Clement, declaring himself as the protector of *The Common Sense Revolution*. Though a member of the informal Tory "family values" caucus, which supports socially conservative causes such as religion in school and opposes abortion rights, Flaherty had initially also tried to play down these views and focus on economics. However, be it because he felt the albatross of a failing economy around his neck or he has lost his mind, he has spent much of the campaign making personal attacks on Eves, with ever-more outrageous policy suggestions like making homelessness "illegal". The media speculates that Flaherty feels this is his one-and-only chance to seek the leadership and is going all-out. However, given he is only 52 years old, this seems questionable. At any rate, while he has succeeded as setting himself out as the right-wing alternative, he has made a party led by him as almost unelectable.

Witmer was seen as a moderate, but she chose to adopt the *left-wing* and talk like a Liberal. She says the revolution is over, though she re-affirms it was necessary. This contradiction is fodder for her opponents, and Opposition members. If it was such a good idea, why should it end? She has also begun to repudiate certain Tory policies, such as attacking teachers and has said a privatized hydro should be delayed. She is likely attracting some interest from the few members who date back to the Davis days; those who are more progressive. As the only woman in the race, she might gain some through gender support. But she is also seen as cold and impersonal, and hasn't the warmth to attract delegates in any number.

And, at the risk of hate mail, I think it is safe to say the Ontario Tories of 2001/2002 are not prepared to pick a female leader.

Stockwell, who announced last, will likely get some interest in Toronto Conservative circles, but he is too much a maverick and has too many enemies to be seen as a legitimate contender[19]. Though his time as Speaker[20] gained him public respect for being impartial, it made him a pariah with many inside his own party. As well, Stockwell is a bit of a contradiction, even to himself. During his announcement, he took the position of supporting the next set of corporate tax cuts but he did say he didn't think the province can afford them. This has evolved into keeping them but opposing new ones. He also agreed with his competitors to keep the private school tax credit and would like to see more private sector involvement in health care, though he was careful to say only as a lessor or landlord, not as a service deliverer. However, his leadership campaigning has not stopped stories from circulating that he will resign to run for Toronto mayor should Mel Lastman not seek another term. This may simply be him getting an organization together for a city run. Most of the interest in him, at this point, seems to come from the media, which are attracted to him as the best speaker, and also because they are probably hoping for some juicy comments on his opponents.

When Eves announced, it came with the backing of 14 Cabinet members[21], including Education minister Janet Ecker and Municipal Affairs' minister Chris Hodgson, who had both been seen as strong potential candidates themselves, but were thought to need the same supporters as Eves. Not necessarily. Hodgson brings support from rural Ontario, more than the former Finance minister has himself. And while Ecker brings very little except potential trouble, given her difficulties in Education, she may help attract some women to the campaign. It seems likely both have great expectations for improved positions in an Ernie Eves' Cabinet.

Given Ontario's propensity to go with non-Toronto leaders, and the Tories' to go with someone "small town", none of these people may completely fit the bill. Though Eves is nominally from Parry Sound, he has spent more time in Toronto over the last twenty years and is most identified as the darling of Bay Street. In his announcement, he was profuse in his love of Toronto, not Parry Sound. Should he win the leadership and seek a by-election seat, it will likely come in Toronto.[22] Clement, Flaherty, and Stockwell are pretty much city boys. Witmer is from Kitchener, which is marginally better, but just.

Many commentators believed there could be a real race here, but that wasn't to be. Eves had the advantage of money, a good organization, and a powerful reputation. At this point, he has overwhelmed his opponents and is poised for a significant victory. In the unlikely event of a second ballot, it will likely be Eves versus Flaherty on that final vote. The latter's only hope is that the average party member is as right-wing as he is. It could also help him that the electoral college-type voting that again causes over-representation by rural ridings will mean he gains support over the more popinjay Eves. However, with the fight having become increasingly nasty, can whoever wins unite the party thereafter? As Frank Miller and Larry Grossman found, it's not always so easy.

And then there's winning the next election. Ultimately, Mike Harris was seen by many people as an ordinary Joe to whom they could relate. None of those presently running come across that way. It may be they will pick someone who fits their desires, but not those of regular voters. If that's the case, retirement could look pretty good for many in caucus.

But a leader is not the whole party. If there was one thing that the rise of Mike Harris to leader proved it was that it was the team behind him that packaged and polished him sufficiently to make him a legitimate contender for Premier. And though he was the focus of the party for two elections, it was those behind him who came up with the strategies for success.

The Tories continue to plan. Policy documents have been littering the party since 1991, yet each has helped set its direction and, in effect, that of the province. *The Common Sense Revolution* laid out a plan to cut back the influence and effect of government. *Blueprint* reinforced a continuation of the emasculation of the public sector in favour of individualism and private sector interests.

But they continue to plan. At their fall 2001 convention, a new agenda was presented, this one called *Seizing Tomorrow's Opportunities*. This one targets an Ontario of 2015, and the shape of things Tories want to see come. They see better public services while further cutting taxes. Given that pretty much every service offered by the Ontario government is now inferior in almost every way to what it was in 1995, this is a mirage or a lie. They see "greater choice" in health and education. It's pretty obvious that means they want to see Ontario opened up to private health services and private education. Assuming this is the vision of most Tories, then at some point there will have to be a clear election to determine if this is what most voters want. However, if this is simply the vision of those at the top, and they are trying to convince their fellow Conservatives to go along, there may yet be another revolution, this one inside that party, that sends the neo-cons on their way out the door.

There may be another reason that could see sitting MPPs and regular people flee their party, however. The darkest cloud now floating over the Harris government is the Ipperwash affair. On 4 September 1995, a group of Chippewa seized control of Ipperwash Provincial Park, a small park just east of Kettle Point on the shore of Lake Huron near Sarnia. For some time they had claimed that it was a burial ground for their ancestors, and they wanted it closed and the land turned over to their band. In the past, the police response to these situations had been a measured one of calm negotiation without confrontation. The country had seen what escalation brought at Oka, Quebec, five years earlier. But this was the early halcyon days of *The Common Sense Revolution*, and the idea of passivity was not on the minds of those government officials involved.

Legally, politicians are not to interfere in the activities of police. They must have a free hand to act, lest there be questions of conflict of interest and breach of trust. In the case of Ipperwash, it has never been clear if government politicians did indeed break this rule. The odour of something rotten has been hanging in the air for years, yet the Harrisites have done nothing to try and freshen it up. In fact, they seem to have been most eager not to clear it up, despite the stench.

In May 1993, some of these same natives *squatted* in the east end of Canadian Forces Base Ipperwash, next to the park. As well as this having been their former home, they also said there were native remains there. During WWII, the federal government had taken the land for the duration, and had never given it back. These Chippewa demanded its return in the name of the Stoney Point First Nation, a group which doesn't in fact exist. Tensions were at a fairly low level, though both sides purposely irritated the other. Late one night in August, someone put a bullet into a low-flying military helicopter, which caused police to close off the area in a vain search for the culprit. The annoying truce continued until 29 July 1995, when a number of natives boarded an old school bus and drove it through the door of a base hall. Instead of violence, however, it simply sped up the military's exit.

However, there were those in the police and Canadian Security Intelligence Service who felt these men might have connections to the Mohawk Warriors who had been behind much of the Oka mess and a good deal of cigarette smuggling in eastern Ontario. In course, a spy was recruited to see if it was true. He reported seeing no illegal guns nor drugs, nor anything else remotely questionable. And when the occupation of the park came, he had already told police it was coming. Of course, so had the natives.

Regardless, the stories flew. I was about seven weeks from moving out of nearby London when the occupation occurred. I heard that Mohawk Warriors were running guns from the United States across the lake at night, and were preparing for a fight to the death. I heard that drugs were coming across, and that this was all a front to bring in massive shipments, which they would slip out before giving up. I was also told that all was quiet, and these were just a group of peaceful people who wanted back what was rightfully theirs.

I'm sure the OPP heard these stories, as well, and were not certain which were true. However, shortly after the incident began, a command post was set up and their tactical unit was sent to the area. Within hours, this unit re-took the park by force, and Acting Sergeant Kenneth Deane shot an unarmed Anthony "Dudley" George to death. Had someone not died, the matter might have been questioned, then disappeared. But more than the death, the doubts that arose had to do with why the police changed their usual *modus operandi*, especially when it came out they had initially prepared to play their typical waiting game. A directive of 4 September said their goal was to "contain and negotiate a peaceful resolution".

The facts are still murky, and have only leaked out a little at a time, but they all seem to point back to the Premier's Office. One must remember the context. This was the heyday of the *revolution*, and the government wasn't about to give into "special interests", something the *weak-kneed lefties* of the NDP had seemed only too willing to do regarding the military base. Marcel Beaubien, the Tory MPP for the area, visited the command post only hours before the police moved in. It seems he passed along this view. Then, two hours before the OPP tactical unit took action, Premier Harris met with an OPP official. Later, he denied the meeting ever happened, though that position vanished in short order, and he returned to the earlier story. It stretches credulity but, initially, Harris denied they even discussed Ipperwash. Eventually, notes came forward from others who attended the same meeting saying that both Harris and Chris Hodgson, who was also there, were "hawkish" on clearing the park, and that the Premier "would like action to be taken ASAP to remove the occupiers". In the minutes of a ministerial meeting from the fatal night, it was noted that "police have been asked to remove the occupiers from the park".

Demands for an inquiry have been heard often and rejected again and again by the government. At first, it was said to be because Sergeant Deane was facing trial, then was being tried, then was appealing his conviction.[23] After that was over, the refusal was chalked up to the wrongful death suit filed against Harris and several other government officials by the George family. The fact they have offered to drop the case as soon as an inquiry is called has made no difference.

The speculative answer to this whole episode seems fairly obvious to most. The Tories wanted *law and order* and opposed playing footsie with those who defied that stance. Their officials, including the Premier, told the OPP to take back the park and arrest the trespassers, even though it was closed and the occupation was affecting no one generally. The fact that Dudley George was killed was simply an over-zealous officer making a mistake. However, that view is balanced by the notion that, had the Tories not interfered, he would not have died. Of course, Harris *et. al.* say they did not interfere, so case closed. The problem for them is that it is not closed and, should they leave office with the matter still up in the air, they will still be facing the personal lawsuits.

If Richard Nixon had admitted to the Watergate break-ins by the *plumbers*, he would have been damaged, but would have remained President. There are those who feel that had Harris admitted that his government people might have influenced the police to act, a head or two might have rolled, but the Tories would have continued as the government with minimal damage done. The fact is, in scandal, it's the cover-up that's a killer. If it comes out that the Harris Tories tried to hide having influenced the police, the penalty may be much higher than otherwise. Along with Walkerton, it could easily cost them their reputations and, ultimately, their position as government.

7. Final thoughts

There will be those who say I have disproved my own theory that Ontarians want progressive and conservative government. After all, they elected the Harris Tories, who have been anything but progressive. My argument is that, in the light of being offered a cogent philosophy chalk full of ideas, voters accepted this given the less profound alternatives. In fact, many actually found it attractive in a time of negativity. Perhaps this means that, rather than progressive government, people crave political parties with ideas, regardless of their nature. I think post-war history demonstrates that is not the case. Rather, people want society to advance

but at a pace that can be managed intelligently. This was the criticism of
the Harrisites that was common, even amongst many of their supporters –
too much, too fast.

Ontarians want a return to *progressive conservative* government, and it is a
necessity. A democratic system must be progressive, especially in good
economic times, or the voters, in search of new ideas, will eventually tend
to opt for more and more ideological parties that deny the political
mainstream. That, in turn, will lead to counter-reactions that cause
increasingly wild swings in government temperament. Out with the Left,
in with the Right. Out with the Right, in with the Extreme Left. Out with
the Extreme Left, in with the Extreme Right. These large ideological shifts
will mean societal cleavages that are hard on financial, social, and human
resources. We have already headed along this path, and we must get off it
before it's too late.

How do we do that? To some extent, we take Mike Harris' advice.
Governing is about setting priorities. But instead of choosing traditional
targets, as the Tories did with cutting taxes, for example, we need to focus
on why government exists. In Canada, we have defined it as *peace, order,
and good government.* I believe it goes further than that. Government
should seek what is in the public interest, protect its citizens, while helping
all the people to live, not just survive. While it may not be the job of
politicians to guarantee us a living, it is their job to see we live even
without a job. If food, water, and air are necessities of life, aren't shelter
and heat necessities of living? Yet government is getting away from all of
these areas. Necessary protections for people no longer seem to be a
priority of government.

I am not suggesting government should nursemaid us from womb to tomb.
I am stating that it is the job of government to protect the public interest.
That means seeing to it that water is pure, air is clean, and food is free of
contamination. It means people will have this pure water to drink, this
clean air to breath, and this contamination-free food is available for them
to eat. It means making certain people have a place to live, with heat and
light, at a price they can afford. That means government inspectors to
make certain people are protected, but it also means that government may
have to intervene in the affairs of business and individuals to see to it
people are protected.

Most of the Harris Tories and many of their supporters do not believe this
is the role of government. They believe government should do as little as
possible to affect business and individuals. To them, there is no public

interest, only self-interest. It should be left to the individual to do as they want within the law, little constrained by regulations. But democracy will fail if this is the case because it will no longer matter to me or you whether or not our neighbour has any say in how the province is run. All that matters is me. Of course, it may be that, at some time, someone else will decide I am a hindrance to their self-interest.

And democracy itself *will be* destroyed if parties continue to "sell out" to commercial interests. As long as those with money can buy the influence of politicians, they will control the agenda. No democracy can exist if representation is not truly for all people. Government must be for all. Democratic representation must be protected and expanded, even if it costs more. Steps must be taken to get more people to vote and participate in the political process.

What *The Common Sense Revolution* has been, more than anything, is a concerted attempt to weaken government to the point where it is no longer able to exert influence. To neo-conservatives, this is the whole point. They want government to be weak so the *equity of the free market* can reach its zenith. The problem with this is that the free market is anything but equitable. It is too open to influences that distort supply, demand, or pricing, and markets are often too small to ever balance these forces.

Many felt that rent controls skewed the market, because they did not allow prices to be fixed by supply and demand. Though demand increased as the population did, the fact that prices were held down by controls meant builders would not supply more apartments because they could not reasonably believe they would be able to make back their investments in a manner sufficiently timely as to be profitable. So, the Tories phased out these controls, stating explicitly that market forces would now permit builders to build. It hasn't happened. With prices rising, apartment owners have found that *not* expanding supply keeps those prices going up, thus increasing their profits. As well, many builders would prefer to construct houses or condominiums, which give them a better return on their investment.

This result is similar to what happened when the electricity market was deregulated in California. The power suppliers found that not increasing supply caused the price to rise and their profits to skyrocket. Why make the investment in expensive capital construction when you can simply take profit for your shareholders by doing nothing?

One of the jobs of government in democracies is to review the free market to make certain it works properly, either by establishing regulations to make sure citizens aren't cheated or to use its power to see to it capitalist inequities are smoothed out through direct intervention. When government surrenders to the free market, it means that politicians are not doing their jobs of representing and protecting people.

The profound effects of this *Common Sense Revolution* deference are only beginning to be felt. Certainly the most obvious example of this was in Walkerton. Staff cuts reduced the Environment ministry's ability to oversee municipal water services. But there are getting to be less obvious examples that have the potential to cause great difficulty.

Ninety-five full-time food inspectors were dropped between 1995 and 2000, leaving a grand total of eight to cover the whole province, along with 131 part-timers, many of whom lack the qualifications to do the job. Nevertheless, Auditor Erik Peters has found that slaughterhouses are not being required to fix unsanitary conditions, rusty equipment, and are allowing the transportation of meat in unrefrigerated trucks. Three to four percent of fruit and vegetables tested were well beyond the allowable limits for chemicals. More than 90% of goat's milk failed bacteria limits. As well, meat is almost never tested for antibiotic levels, something that is now considered quite important for human health. All of these potentially deadly failures are the result of too few qualified staff who just do not have the time to cover all these bases. This is why government grew in size in the first place – people are needed to protect the public interest, and only government is designed to do this.

In many ways, people of all political stripes in Ontario support the concept of *government for the people*. The neo-conservative Tories do so in a minimalist way, where government exists just to support the conditions that guarantee people will have *freedom of opportunity*. The rich will support themselves, and everyone else will receive sufficient protections that they will have the chance to become rich. Socialist New Democrats see 'government for the people' as 'government by the people' in that the views of all should be taken into account before proceeding with decisions. All people should have inherently the same identical rights and that government must actively work toward seeing this equality of rights translates into not 'equality of opportunity' but equality, period. Not that we all have to earn the same salary or live in identical homes, but that wealthy people need to put more into society, as they get more out of it and, in this way, lives are equalized.

Strangely, it may be the Liberal party that has adopted 'government for the people' to the least extent. As a group that has too often settled for simply espousing the derivative *middle*, between Tory and NDP, such principles have often been lost, though I personally believe a good portion of Liberals believe in such canons of conscience. And perhaps it says a good deal about the failure of the Liberals electorally in the past 100 years in Ontario that they have been unable to pass on their belief in such emotional and intellectual tenets to voters.

In the year 2000, the Simcoe-Grey Provincial Liberals wrote up such a statement and passed it along to their party leaders, in hopes that these views might be passed along to the voters. I relate it here because the words, though not perhaps profound, resonate a sentiment that I believe in profoundly. And though it was addressed to Liberals, I would suggest it applies to ALL people.

GOVERNMENT FOR THE PEOPLE

The members of a democratic legislature are elected to represent the general will of the people. Those that form the government are to act in the best interests of all the people, as they see those interests. However, in recent years, government seems more inclined to act in spite of the people, rather than for them. People have to deal with government. They have no choice.

In a representative democracy such as ours, the people give their individual authority to government to act on their behalf on the condition that government represent all the people equally. It is to act for 'the greatest good of the greatest number', while protecting the rights of minorities. Unfortunately, it is now more common for government to act more for special interests than those of the majority and, by diminishing the Legislature and its Members, it is increasingly unaccountable to the people, even at election time.

It is the opinion of the Simcoe-Grey Provincial Liberal Association that it is incumbent upon the Ontario Liberal Party to show the citizens of this province that we represent the general will. Our policies must be for all the people.

With the increasing gap between 'haves and have-nots', income tax must be used to support the majority, not through cuts that assist only the wealthy minority. Sales taxes, rising licence and user fees must be limited, as they unfairly affect those least able to pay them. Increasing debt financing means the entire social safety net and, thus, the entire social fabric of Ontario, is at risk.

Health care and education must be universally accessible, and public in nature. Higher education must be affordable for, and accessible to, all. People must be able to rely that government services will be there to help them should they be in need of them. Government must recognize that a healthy environment leads to healthy people. Decision-making, as a rule, should be in the hands of those elected to make the decisions, and they should be responsive to the public regarding them.

The Ontario Liberal Party must reject government for "the few". We must show our commitment to the people of Ontario by adopting policies that are equitable to all, represent the general will with minority protection, and are 'for the people'.

If there is one thing the election of the Harris Tories has shown, it is that they do not govern for the people. For the sake of democracy and progress in Ontario, that must end.

Part 6 Endnotes

1. Most new governments find they don't have as much money to spend, so can't spend to keep commitments. The Harrisites didn't want to spend, so they didn't need money. If it really was worse than they thought, all the better reason to cut!

2. According to pollsters, a rather odd reality is that voters perceive the Tories as the best minders of the economy, even when the economy slumping has occurred with the Tories as government.

3. The New Policy Initiative was set up to establish a new party from a coalition of anti-globalization and anti-poverty groups. And even though they were able to get through a motion for leadership contests to be based on one-member/one-vote, this was only with the compromise that labour is guaranteed a quarter of delegates. Even in change, the NDP can't overwhelmingly decide in what direction to go. The new party resolution was defeated 684-401.

4. That having been said, the Liberal party has announced a number of initiatives to improve democratic representation, most of which come from a party policy conference held in 2000. Unfortunately, they're not going to be big vote-getters.

5. In the by-election, it came out Hunter had written a book in the late 1980s, where the protagonist cruised young Thai prostitutes. Some suggested it was autobiographical, though Hunter denied this. I dare say this made less of a difference in the final result than the media suggested.

6. An excellent book that should be required reading. While some of Rifkin's solutions might have more practical answers, it is highly thought-provoking work.

7. Administratively, it can't be done, but it sounds good.

8. Wolfson, Michael and Murphy, Brian. "Income taxes in Canada and the United States". Perspectives on Labour and Income (Summer 2000, Vol. 12, No. 2). Ottawa: Statistics Canada.

9. Evans used the Conference Board of Canada annual survey results even though the average industrial wage increase was, according to him, 8.3% lower. He did not explain his reasoning for using one and not the other. As well, he made no attempt to consider the province's average wage overall, which was undoubtedly far lower than both.

10. There is also a bonus in the new salary system. Because the provincial contribution to MPP RRSPs is based on 5% of salary, it will rise from about $3,900 to about $5,400.

11. In fact, the Tories had, more quietly, earlier amended their pension bill so MPPs would have easier access to their money. In December

1999, they amended the *Pension Benefits Act* to permit LIRA holders to access the principal on their pension benefits should they run into financial hardship. However, they also amended the *MPPs Pension Act*, with the difference that MPPs elected before 1995 would be able to get to their principal without any hardship. In effect, once defeated or retired, these MPPs could have instant access to the money (with tax penalties).

12. One can only hope the court justices see fit to overturn this legislation as unconstitutional.

13. David Caplan in statement in the Ontario Legislature, 13 June 2001.

14. Toronto Star. "Tories act 'like hit-run drivers'", 12 July 2000, p. A7.

15. I recall a Toronto area councillor who announced his retirement after many years, having been a great friend of developers over that time. Nevertheless, several of these sponsored a re-election fundraising dinner. If memory serves me correctly, the 2,000 tickets went for $500 apiece, and all were purchased by a dozen or so development companies. In those days, any leftover funds raised for campaigning became the property of the councillor when (s)he left office. This man walked away with a *gold watch* worth about a million dollars.

16. Unfortunately, should there be a large number of candidates, I might end up with my third, fourth, or fifth choice.

17. This doesn't add to 103 because of votes for other parties and independent candidates. With a low-end cut-off of 5%, the results would have been 48 Tory, 42 Liberal, 13 NDP.

18. It is rumoured he may resign to permit Ernie Eves to run for a seat, should he become leader, though he has remained neutral in the leadership.

19. Stockwell's actions right after the 1995 election made him few friends inside the party. When Harris told him he hadn't made Cabinet, his reported response was to swear in the Premier's face, several times. When asked about the MPP reform that would cost him four-and-a-half years of pension, he said Harris should give up his own if he wanted the others to do the same.

20. He was elected to replace Al McLean, who resigned for sexually harassing his former special assistant. The taxpayers ended up paying over half-a-million dollars in settlement and legal costs. McLean got a patronage job.

21. As well as 12 other caucus members.

22. New Parry Sound-Muskoka MPP Norm Miller, son of Frank, has already said he won't be resigning. However, other rumours suggest Eves may run in John Snobelen's Mississauga riding, or that Jim Wilson might resign to run in what many believe is the safest Tory riding in Ontario.

23.   Deane was recently ordered dismissed by the OPP for discreditable conduct, though he is appealing. The OPP illegally paid his legal fees and is now being reimbursed by money collected through a levy on Ontario Provincial Police Association members.

Postscript

Did *The Common Sense Revolution* actually succeed? Did Mike Harris and his *team* actually achieve the goals they wanted? It will take time to decide this, but the short-term answer is ...

Did they cut provincial income taxes? Absolutely. However, if this is expanded slightly to did they improve the standard of living of Ontarians, the answer is, except for higher earners, no.

Did they cut government spending? Short-term, yes. Long-term, no. Even neo-con Jim Flaherty bemoans that the Ontario government now spends more than it has ever spent. However, they have altered some spending priorities which is causing great change.

Did they cut government barriers to job creation, investment and economic growth? If this is defined as cutting regulations, then yes. Did this come at the cost of a cut in rules and staff which helped protect Ontarians? The answer is also yes. Tory changes have resulted in deaths, indirectly perhaps but death just the same.

Did they cut the size of government? Yes and no. There are fewer civil servants, but control is more centralized in Queen's Park than ever. Staffing costs may have been reduced, but so have the democratic rights of Ontarians. The Tories defined this as "better for less". Not surprisingly, it's turned out 'less' is just less.

Did they balance the budget? Yes ... mostly on the backs of the poor, peoples' health, and kids' educations.

But these are the five points the Tories like to use as defining the CSR. *The Common Sense Revolution* went further than this. It is an ideology based on *government is bad* and people should be responsible for themselves. Whether this philosophy has taken root or not has yet to be seen. It has flowered and bloomed once, but that doesn't mean its roots are deep enough to hold it in place during a storm. Fortunately for Mike Harris, he's heading off to golf with a big, taxpayer-paid-for umbrella. And as he heads off for the greens, Harris is apparently puttering around with the idea of going into federal politics. If this is the case, it is even more important that people appreciate the damage he has done to progress and democracy in Ontario.

Bibliography

Avis, Walter S. *et.al.* Gage Canadian Dictionary. Toronto: Gage Publishing Limited, 1983.

Blizzard, Christina. Right Turn: How the Tories Took Ontario. Toronto: Dundurn Press, 1995.

Gagnon, Georgette and Rath, Dan. Not Without Cause: David Peterson's Fall From Grace. Toronto: HarperCollins, 1991.

Hoy, Claire. Bill Davis: A Biography. Toronto: Methuen, 1985.

Ibbitson, John. Promised Land: Inside the Mike Harris Revolution. Scarborough: Prentice Hall Canada Inc., 1997.

Jeffrey, Brooke. Hard Right Turn: The New Face of Neo-Conservatism in Canada. Toronto: HarperCollins Publishers Ltd., 1999.

Magnusson, Warren and Sancton, Andrew (eds.). City Politics in Canada. Toronto: University of Toronto Press, 1973.

Monahan, Patrick. Storming the Pink Palace. The NDP in Power: A Cautionary Tale. Toronto: Lester Publishing, 1995.

Montgomery, Byron. Annexation and Restructuring in Sarnia-Lambton: A Model for Ontario County Government? London: The University of Western Ontario, Department of Political Science, Local Government Program, 1990.

Rae, Bob. From Protest to Power: Personal Reflections on a Life in Politics. Toronto: Penguin Books Canada Limited, 1997.

Schull, Joseph. Ontario Since 1867. Toronto: McClelland and Stewart Limited, 1978.

Schull, Michael J., Szalai, John-Paul, Schwartz, Brian and Redelmeier, Donald A. "Emergency Department Overcrowding Following Systematic Hospital Restructuring", (Journal of) Academic Emergency Medicine (Volume 8, Number 11), 2001.

Various. Globe and Mail, 1975-2001.

Various. The Toronto Star, 1980-2002.

Various. The Toronto Sun, 1995-2001.

Wolfson, Michael and Murphy, Brian. "Income taxes in Canada and the United States". Perspectives on Labour and Income (Summer 2000, Vol. 12, No. 2). Ottawa: Statistics Canada.

Index

393, 395, 403
advisors 68-70, 75-76
attitude toward teachers 183
history 63-64
1980 election 66-67, 73, 329
opposition years 67-76
party leadership 62-63, 66
policy process 70-73
testimony at Walkerton Inquiry 274-284
view of regulation 285
view of Trudeau 68
Harris, Janet (Harrison) 68
Hastings, John 353
Health care 138, 196, 201, 204, 207, 210, 213, 257-266
compared to United States 351-352
dispute with federal government 242-244
history of national system 26-29
recommendations 375-379
restructuring 138, 139, 140, 155-165
view in CSR 87, 90, 91, 92-93
Health Services Restructuring Commission (HSRC) 138, 155-165, 259, 260, 263, 264
Hearn, Graham 367
Henry, George 11
Hepburn, Mitch 10-11, 128
Highway 407 296-298
Hobbes, Thomas 115
Hodgson, Chris 215-216, 269, 315, 324, 325, 327, 328, 353, 390, 393
Home Care and Placement Coordination 260
Hôpital Montfort (see Montfort Hospital)
Hosek, Chaviva 44, 45
Hospital for Sick Children 258
Hot buttons 120-125, 192, 203

Hôtel Dieu Hospital 158
Housing, public 15, 41, 44, 105, 172, 178, 179, 266-267, 268-270
recommendations 385-386
Hulgaard, Helle 73-74, 122
Hunter, Bob 347
Hydro One 299, 300, 301, 309, 310, 312, 362
Ibbitson, John 64, 163, 166, 171, 175, 182, 221, 356
Independent Electricity Market Operator (IMO) 299, 305, 307
Ipperwash affair 392-394
Irquhart, Ian 227-228, 252, 253
Jackson, Cam 166, 227, 259, 353
Jail, private 314-316
Jeffrey, Brooke 59, 182
Johns, Helen 152, 262, 353
Johnson, Bert 353
Johnson, Dave 149, 164, 186, 188, 191, 255, 374, 375
jobsOntario 105, 119, 136
Kells, Greg 218-219
Kells, Morley 353
Kennedy, Gerard 153, 218-221
Kieffer, Jim 271
King, Bill 69, 75
King, Mackenzie 11, 26
Klees, Frank 353
Koebel, Frank 272
Koebel, Stan 272
Kormos, Peter 224
Labour Relations Act 316
Lambe, Joseph 258-259
Lands for Life 193-195
Lankin, Frances 224, 225, 347
Laughren, Floyd 54, 81
Lawrence, Allan 16, 17
Leach, Al 141, 171-172, 174, 175, 179, 267
Leadership campaigns
Liberal 218-221
NDP 224-225